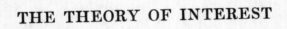

THE THEORY OF INTEREST

THE
THEORY OF INTEREST

As Determined by

IMPATIENCE

To Spend Income

and

OPPORTUNITY

To Invest It

BY

IRVING FISHER

PROFESSOR OF ECONOMICS, YALE UNIVERSITY

REPRINTS OF ECONOMIC CLASSICS

Augustus M. Kelley
New York 1961

Original edition, 1930.   Reprints, 1955 and 1961, by
kind permission of Irving N. Fisher.

TO

The Memory

OF

JOHN RAE

AND OF

EUGEN VON BÖHM-BAWERK

WHO LAID THE FOUNDATIONS

UPON WHICH

I HAVE ENDEAVORED

TO BUILD

PREFACE

THE tremendous expansion of credit during and since the World War to finance military operations as well as post-war reparations, reconstruction, and the rebuilding of industry and trade has brought the problems of capitalism and the nature and origin of interest home afresh to the minds of business men as well as to economists. This book is addressed, therefore, to financial and industrial leaders, as well as to professors and students of economics.

Inflation during and since the War caused prices to soar and real interest rates to sag in Germany and other nations far below zero, thus impoverishing millions of investors. In all countries gilt-edge securities with fixed return became highly speculative, because of the effect of monetary fluctuations on real interest rates. After the War the impatience of whole peoples to anticipate future income by borrowing to spend, coupled with the opportunity to get large returns from investments, raised interest rates and kept them high. Increased national income has made the United States a lender nation. At home, real incomes have grown amazingly because of the new scientific, industrial, and agricultural revolutions. Interest rates have declined somewhat since 1920, but are still high because the returns upon investments remain high. Impatience to spend has been exemplified by the organization of consumers' credit in the form of finance companies specially organized to accommodate and stimulate installment selling and to standardize and stabilize consumption.

This book, *The Theory of Interest*, was begun as a revision of *The Rate of Interest*, which was published in 1907, and has long since been out of print. Requests for another edition of that work have been made from time to time; but I have postponed it year by year for over two decades, because I wished to revise the presentation, and to rewrite those portions which, if I may judge from criticisms, have not been understood.

I have considered the criticisms of the former book which have come to my notice, and have, as a consequence, modified the form of presentation materially. Though, in substance, my theory of interest has been altered scarcely at all, its exposition has been so amplified and recast that it will, I anticipate, seem, to those who misunderstood my first book, more changed than it seems to me. The result has been a new book, *The Theory of Interest*, a complete rewriting of the former book, with additions of new material.

I was encouraged to write this new exposition of the theory of interest by various economists and leading business men and especially by Mr. Oswald T. Falk, one of the representatives of Great Britain at the Versailles Peace Conference, who was kind enough to say that he had gained more insight into economic theory from *The Rate of Interest* than from any other book.

Years after *The Rate of Interest* was published, I suggested the more popular term "impatience" in place of "agio" or "time preference." This catchword has been widely adopted, and, to my surprise, has led to a widespread but false impression that I had overlooked or neglected the productivity or investment opportunity side entirely. It also led many to think that, by using the new word impatience, I meant to claim a new idea. Thus I found myself credited with being the author of "the impatience theory" which I am not, and not credited with being the author of those parts lacking any catchword. It was this misunderstanding which led me, after much search, to adopt the catchword "investment opportunity" as a substitute for the inadequate term "productivity" which had come into such general use.[1]

In economics it is difficult to prove originality; for the germ of every new idea will surely be found over and over again in earlier writers. For myself, I would be satisfied to have my conclusions accepted as *true* even if their origin should be credited by the critics wholly to earlier writers. While I hope I may be credited with a certain degree of originality, every thorough student of this subject will recognize in my treatment of interest theory features of his own. My own theory is in some degree every one's theory. Every essential part of it was at least foreshadowed by John Rae in 1834.

If this combined "impatience and opportunity" theory can be said to be at all distinct from all others, it is because it explicitly analyses opportunity, and fits together impatience and opportunity and income. The income concept plays the basic rôle in the theory of interest. I venture to hope that the theory, as here presented, will be found not so much to overthrow as to co-ordinate previous theories, and to help in making the chain of explanation complete and strong.

[1] This term, investment opportunity, seems to be the nearest expression in popular language to suggest or denote the technical magnitude r employed in this book. The full expression for r is the rate of return over cost, and both cost and return are differences between two optional income streams. So far as I know, no other writer on interest has made use of income streams and their differences, or rates of return over cost per annum. The nearest approximation to this usage seems to be in the writings of Professor Herbert J. Davenport, particularly his *Economics of Entreprise*, (Macmillan, New York, 1913) pages 368, 379, 381, 394, 395, 396, 410, 411.

Chapter I is added for the purpose of giving the reader who has not read my *Nature of Capital and Income*, a brief summary of its contents.

I have, for the first time, in a book on pure economic theory, introduced mathematics into the text, instead of relegating it entirely to appendices. This is done in view of the increasing use of mathematics and the increasing numbers of students equipped to read mathematical economics and statistics.

Parts of Chapters II and XIX, with their appendices, have appeared in different form in my monograph, "Appreciation and Interest." Thanks are due to the American Economic Association for permission to use parts of this monograph unaltered. Since it appeared three decades ago, the view expressed in it (that appreciation or depreciation in the value of money should, and to some extent does, lower or raise the rate of interest) has gained considerable currency, and has been illustrated and verified by war-time experience.

Chapter XIX is made up, for the most part, of a new and intensive study of the relationships existing between prices and interest rates. These relationships are tested by new and rigorous statistical methods of analysis. While the conclusions presented as the results of these analyses are only tentative, yet they are, I think, worthy of further statistical studies into the relation of interest rates on the one hand, and prices, business activity, bank reserves, and bank loans on the other.

In the preparation of the original book I received important aid from many persons. Finance Minister Böhm-Bawerk, whose writings on interest and whose history of the subject are classic, kindly read and criticized the chapter devoted to his theory of interest. Afterward, in the third edition of his *Positive Theorie des Kapitales* and the *Exkurse* thereto, he devoted more than 100 pages to discussions and criticisms, favorable and unfavorable, of *The Rate of Interest* as it first appeared. I have taken account of his criticism in Chapter XX.

In preparing this book I have received suggestions and assistance from so many economists and others in the United States and abroad, that it is impracticable to mention them all by name. My associates, Dr. Royal Meeker, Dr. Max Sasuly, and Mr. Benjamin P. Whitaker, have contributed in helpful criticism, as well as in gathering material, preparing the manuscript for the printer, and reading the proof. I am especially indebted to my brother, Mr. Herbert W. Fisher, for his suggestions as to style and the manner of presentation, and to Professor Harry G. Brown for his criticism of my statement of the opportunity principle. Others who have helped me especially are: Prof. Lionel D. Edie, Mr. C. O. Hardy, Mr. R. G. Hawtry, Prof. Frank H. Knight, Prof. J. S. Lawrence, Prof. Arthur W. Marget, Prof. H. B. Meek, Prof. Wesley C. Mitchell, Mrs. Clara Eliot Raup, Prof. Henry Schultz, Prof. Henry R. Seager, Mr. Henry Simons, Mr. Carl Snyder, Prof. Jacob Viner.

I have also received valuable suggestions from members of my class in the economics of distribution; namely, Howard Berolzheimer, A. G. Buehler, Francis W. Hopkins, Richard A. Lester, Daniel T. Selko, Andrew Stevenson, Jr., and Ronald B. Welch.

IRVING FISHER

Yale University,
January, 1930

SUGGESTIONS TO READERS

1. The *general reader* will be chiefly interested in Parts I, II, and IV.

2. *Readers with a distaste for mathematics* will find the essential theory stated in words in Part II.

3. *Those interested in statistical analysis* should read Chapter XIX.

4. The Appendix to Chapter XIX contains the statistical tables used in the analysis presented in the text.

5. The analytical table of contents, the index, and the running page headings have been constructed with especial reference to the varying needs of different classes of readers. The book presents a complete theory of interest, and it is hoped that those who approach it from special viewpoints may, in the end, read it all.

CONTENTS

FIRST SUMMARY

CONTENTS

SECOND SUMMARY

ANALYTICAL TABLE OF CONTENTS

CHAPTER I
INCOME AND CAPITAL

CHAPTER II
MONEY INTEREST AND REAL INTEREST

CHAPTER III
SOME COMMON PITFALLS

CHAPTER IV

TIME PREFERENCE (HUMAN IMPATIENCE)

CHAPTER V

FIRST APPROXIMATION TO THE THEORY OF INTEREST

Assuming Each Person's Income Stream Foreknown and Unchangeable Except by Loans

CHAPTER VI

SECOND APPROXIMATION TO THE THEORY OF INTEREST

Assuming Income Modifiable (1) by Loans and (2) by Other Means

CHAPTER VII

THE INVESTMENT OPPORTUNITY PRINCIPLES

CHAPTER VIII

DISCUSSION OF THE SECOND APPROXIMATION

CHAPTER IX

THIRD APPROXIMATION TO THE THEORY OF INTEREST
Assuming Income Uncertain

CHAPTER X

FIRST APPROXIMATION IN GEOMETRIC TERMS

CHAPTER XI

SECOND APPROXIMATION IN GEOMETRIC TERMS

CHAPTER XII

FIRST APPROXIMATION IN TERMS OF FORMULAS

CHAPTER XIII

SECOND APPROXIMATION IN TERMS OF FORMULAS

CHAPTER XIV

THE THIRD APPROXIMATION UNADAPTED TO MATHEMATICAL FORMULATION

CHAPTER XV

THE PLACE OF INTEREST IN ECONOMICS

CHAPTER XVI

RELATION OF DISCOVERY AND INVENTION TO INTEREST RATES

CHAPTER XVII

PERSONAL AND BUSINESS LOANS

CHAPTER XVIII

SOME ILLUSTRATIVE FACTS

CHAPTER XIX

THE RELATION OF INTEREST TO MONEY AND PRICES

CHAPTER XX

OBJECTIONS CONSIDERED

CHAPTER XXI

SUMMARY

APPENDICES

LIST OF CHARTS

LIST OF TABLES IN TEXT

LIST OF TABLES IN APPENDICES

PART I. INTRODUCTION

CHAPTER I

INCOME AND CAPITAL [1]

§1. *Subjective, or Enjoyment, Income*

INCOME is a series of events.[2]

According to the modern theory of relativity the elementary reality is not matter, electricity, space, time, life or mind, but events.

[1] *The Nature of Capital and Income* (first published in 1906) was primarily intended to serve as a foundation for *The Rate of Interest* which immediately followed it. It was my expectation that the student would read the former before reading the latter.

But now, for the convenience of those who do not wish to take the time to read *The Nature of Capital and Income*, I have written this first chapter summarizing it. I have availed myself of this opportunity to redistribute the emphasis and to make those amendments in statement which further study has indicated to be desirable.

A friendly critic, Professor John B. Canning, suggests that *The Nature of Capital and Income* should have been called "The Nature of Income and Capital" and that the subject matter should have been presented in reverse order, inasmuch as income is the basis of the concept of capital value and is, in fact, the most fundamental concept in economic science.

While it might not be practicable to employ the reverse order in such a complete presentation as I aimed to make in *The Nature of Capital and Income*, I have, in this chapter, where brevity may justify some dogmatism, adopted Professor Canning's suggestions. This radical change in mode of presentation may induce some who have already read that book to review it now in the reverse order employed in this chapter. I hope also that some who have not read it may be moved, after reading this chapter, to read *The Nature of Capital and Income* in full. I have tried, in this chapter, to confine myself merely to those conclusions most essential as a preliminary for proceeding to the consideration of the origins, nature and determinants of the rate of interest.

[2] The first writer to employ the concept of events as fundamental in interest theory appears to have been John Rae, whose book, originally published in 1834, is commented on elsewhere.

[3]

THE THEORY OF INTEREST

For each individual only those events which come within the purview of his experience are of direct concern. It is these events—the psychic experiences of the individual mind—which constitute ultimate income for that individual. The outside events have significance for that individual only in so far as they are the means to these inner events of the mind. The human nervous system is, like a radio, a great receiving instrument. Our brains serve to transform into the stream of our psychic life those outside events, which happen to us and stimulate our nervous system.

But the human body is not ordinarily regarded as an owned object, and only those events in consciousness traceable to owned objects other than the human body are generally admitted to be psychic income. However, the human machine still plays a rôle in so far as, through its purposeful activities, it produces, or helps produce, other owned objects which are material sources of desirable events—food, houses, tools, and other goods, which in their turn set in motion a chain of operations whose ultimate effect is registered in our stream of consciousness. The important consideration from this point of view is that human beings are ever striving to control the stream of their psychic life by appropriating and utilizing the materials and forces of Nature.

In Man's early history he had little command over his environment. He was largely at the mercy of natural forces—wind and lightning, rain and snow, heat and cold. But today Man protects himself from these by means of those contrivances called houses, clothing, and furnaces. He diverts the lightning by means of lightning rods. He increases his food supply by means of appropriated land, farm buildings, plows, and other implements.

[4]

He then refashions the food by means of mills, grinding machinery, cook-stoves and other agencies, and by the labor of human bodies, including his own.

Neither these intermediate processes of creation and alteration nor the money transactions following them are of significance except as they are the necessary or helpful preliminaries to psychic income—human enjoyment. We must be careful lest, in fixing our eyes on such preliminaries, especially money transactions, we overlook the much more important enjoyment which it is their business to yield.

Directors and managers providing income for thousands of people sometimes think of their corporation merely as a great money-making machine. In their eyes, its one purpose is to earn money dividends for the stockholders, money interest for the bondholders, money wages and money salaries for the employees. What happens after these payments are made seems too private a matter to concern them. Yet that is the nub of the whole arrangement. It is only what we carry out of the market place into our homes and private lives which really counts. Money is of no use to us until it is spent. The ultimate wages are not paid in terms of money but in the enjoyments it buys. The dividend check becomes income in the ultimate sense only when we eat the food, wear the clothes, or ride in the automobile which are bought with the check.

§2. *Objective, or Real, Income* (*Our "Living"*)

Enjoyment income is a psychological entity and cannot be measured directly. We can approximate it indirectly, however, by going one step back of it to what is called real income. Real wages, and indeed real income in gen-

[5]

eral, consist of those final physical events in the *outer* world which give us our *inner* enjoyments.

This real income includes the shelter of a house, the music of a victrola or radio, the use of clothes, the eating of food, the reading of the newspaper and all those other innumerable events by which we make the world about us contribute to our enjoyments. Metaphorically we sometimes refer to this, our real income, as our "bread and butter."

These finals in the stream of outer events are what we call our "living," as implied in the phrases cost of living and earning a living. The final outer events and the inner events which they entail run closely parallel, or, rather, the inner events generally follow closely in time on the outer. The enjoyment of music is felt almost instantaneously as the piano or singer produces it. The enjoyment of food is experienced with the eating or soon after the eating.

These outer events, such as the use of food, or clothes, etc., are like the resultant inner events in not being very easily measured. They occur largely in the privacy of the home; they are often difficult to express in any standard units. They have no common denominator. Even the individual who experiences them cannot weigh and measure them directly. All he can do is to measure the money he paid to get them.

§3. *Cost of Living, a Measure of Real Income*

So, just as we went back of an individual's enjoyment income to his real income, we now go back of his real income, or his living, to his *cost* of living, the money measure of real income. You cannot measure in dollars either the inner event of your enjoyment while eating your dinner or the outer event of eating it, but you can find out definitely how much money that dinner cost you. In the same way, you cannot measure your enjoyment at moving picture theater, but you do know what you paid for your ticket; you cannot measure exactly what your house shelter is really worth to you, but you can tell how much you pay for your rent, or what is a fair equivalent for your rent if you happen to live in your own house. You cannot measure what it is worth to wear an evening suit, but you can find out what it costs to hire one, or a fair equivalent of its hire if, perchance, the suit belongs to you. Deducing such equivalents is an accountant's job.

The total cost of living, in the sense of money payments, is a negative item, being outgo rather than income; but it is our best practical measure of the positive items of real income for which those payments are made. For from this total valuation of positive real income may be subtracted the total valuation of the person's labor pain during the same period, if we wish to compare a laborer's income with that of a man who does no labor but lives on his income from capital (other than himself), a "rentier."

Enjoyment income, real income, and the cost of living are merely three different stages of income. All three run closely parallel to each other, although they are not exactly synchronous in time. These discrepancies, as has been intimated, are negligible as between real and enjoyment income. So also the time elapsing between the cost of living and the living is usually brief. There is a little delay between the spending of money at the box office and the seeing of the entertainment, or between paying board or rent and making use of the food or housing facilities. In many cases, the money payment follows rather than precedes the enjoyment.

§4. *Cost of an Article vs. Cost of Its Use*

The only time discrepancy worth careful noting is that which occurs when the money spent is not simply for the temporary use of some object but for the whole object, which means merely for all its possible future uses. If a house is not rented but bought, we do not count the purchase price as all spent for this year's shelter. We expect from it many more years of use. Hence out of the entire purchase price, we try to compute a fair portion of the purchase price to be charged up to this year's use. In like manner, the statisticians of cost of living should distribute by periods the cost of using a person's house furnishings, clothing, musical instruments, automobiles and other durable goods, and not charge the entire cost against the income of the year of purchase. To any given year should be charged only that year's upkeep and replacement, which measures, at least roughly, the services rendered by the goods in question during that particular year. The true real annual income from such goods is the equivalent approximately of the cost of the services given off by those goods each year.

Strictly speaking, then, in making up our income statistics, we should always calculate the value of *services*, and never the value of the objects rendering those services It is true that, in the case of short-lived objects like food, we do not ordinarily need, in practice, to go to the trouble of distinguishing their total cost from the cost of their use. A loaf of bread is worth ten cents because its use is worth ten cents. We cannot rent food; we can only buy it outright. Yet there is some discrepancy in time in

[8]

the case of foods that keep, such as flour, preserved foods and canned goods. These we may buy in one year but not use until a later year, and in such cases the money given for the food might almost be said to be invested rather than spent, like the money given for a house. A man who buys a basket of fruit and eats it within an hour is certainly spending his money for the enjoyment of eating the fruit. But, if he buys a barrel of apples in the fall to be eaten during the winter, is he spending his money or is he investing it for a deferred enjoyment? Theoretically, the barrel of apples is an investment comparable to a house or any other durable good. Practically it is classed as expenditure, although it is a border-line case.

Spending and investing differ only in degree, depending on the length of time elapsing between the expenditure and the enjoyment. To spend is to pay money for enjoyments which come very soon. To invest is to pay money for enjoyments which are deferred to a later time. We spend money for our daily bread and butter or for a seat at the theater, but we invest money in the purchase of bonds, farms, dwellings, or automobiles, or even of suits of clothes.

§5. *Measuring at the Domestic Threshold*

In practice, we can estimate with fair accuracy in all ordinary cases how much of what we pay is for this year's use. That is to say, we can find out pretty nearly our cost of living for the year. We need only reckon what is spent on personal articles and services—on everything which enters our dwellings (or enters us), food, drink, clothes, furniture, household rent, fuel and light, amusements, and so on, our "bread and butter"—exclusive of what is left over for future years, such as what we pay for securities, machinery, or real estate, or what we put into the savings bank. The domestic threshold is, in general, a pretty good line of division. The cost of almost every object which crosses it measures a portion of our real income, and few other expenditures do.

Thus, at the end of production economics, or business economics, we find home economics It is the housekeeper, the woman who spends, who takes the final steps through the cost of living toward getting the real income of the family, so that the family's enjoyment income may follow.

§6. *Money Income*

We have just been dealing with money payments for consumption goods, or money *outgo*. We may now go back one further step to money received by the individual spender, or money income. Money income includes all money *received* which is not obviously, and in the nature of the case, to be devoted to reinvestment—or, as the expression is, "earmarked" for reinvestment. In other words, all money received and readily available and intended to be used for spending is money income. It sometimes differs from real income considerably. For instance, if you more than "earn your living" of $6,000 with a salary of $10,000, you voluntarily put by the $4,000 remaining as savings. This part of your money income is saved from being turned immediately into real income. That is, instead of spending all your salary for this year's living you invest $4,000 of it to help toward the cost of living of future years. And so, the $4,000 is not only credited as income but debited as outgo. With it you buy durable objects such as land or buildings, or part rights in these, such as stocks or bonds. Your money income is in this case your salary (or it may be dividends, rent, interest, or profits) and it exceeds real income by the amount of your savings. On the other hand, you may be living beyond your (money) income. This means, expressed in terms of the concepts here used, that your real income for the year is greater than your money income.

That all one spends on his living measures real income, even when he "lives beyond his income" (beyond his *money* income), may be a hard saying to some who have never attempted to work out consistent definitions of economic concepts which will not only satisfy the requirements of economic theory but which will also bring these economic concepts into conformity with the theory and practice of accountancy. But a definition of income which satisfies both theory and practice, in both economics and accountancy, *must* reckon as income in the most basic sense all those uses, services, or living for which the cost of living is expended even though such expenditure may exceed the money income.

Thus we have a picture of three successive stages, or aspects, of a man's income:

Enjoyment or psychic income, consisting of agreeable sensations and experiences;

Real income *measured* by the cost of living;

Money income, consisting of the money received by a man for meeting his costs of living;

The last—money income—is most commonly called income; and the first—enjoyment income—is the most fundamental. But, for accounting purposes, real income, as measured by the cost of living, is the most practical.[3]

[3] Later in this chapter we shall see that these three sorts of income are all of a piece, parts of the entire economic fabric of services and

THE THEORY OF INTEREST

To recapitulate, we have seen that the enjoyment income is a psychological matter, and hence cannot be measured directly. So we look to real income instead; but even real income is a heterogeneous jumble. It includes quarts of milk, visits to the moving picture house, etc., and in that form cannot be measured easily or as a whole. Here is where the cost of living comes in. It is the practical, homogeneous [4] measure of real income. As the cost of living is expressed in terms of dollars it may, therefore, be taken as our best measure of income *in place of* enjoyment income, or real income. Between it and real income there are no important discrepancies as there are between money income and real income. Money income practically never conforms exactly to real income because either savings raise money income above real income, or deficits push money income below real income.

§7. *Capital Value*

Savings bring us to the nature of capital. Capital, in the sense of capital *value,* is simply future income discounted or, in other words, capitalized. The value of any property, or rights to wealth, is its value *as a source of income* and is found by discounting that expected income. We may, if we so choose, for logical convenience, include as property the ownership in ourselves, or we may, conformably to custom, regard human beings as in a separate category.

disservices. Which of the three comes out of our accounting depends merely on which groups of these services and disservices are included in our summation.

[4] Even this is not homogeneous as a measure of subjective enjoyment; for a dollar to the poor and a dollar to the rich are not subjectively equal. See my *A Statistical Method for Measuring "Marginal Utility" and Testing the Justice of a Progressive Income Tax.* Economic Essays contributed in honor of John Bates Clark, pp. 157-193.

INCOME AND CAPITAL

I define wealth as consisting of material objects owned by human beings (including, if you please, human beings themselves). The ownership may be divided and parcelled out among different individuals in the form of partnership rights, shares of stock, bonds, mortgages, and other forms of property rights. In whatever ways the ownership be distributed and symbolized in documents, the entire group of property rights are merely means to an end—income. Income is the alpha and omega of economics.

§8. *The Rate of Interest*

The bridge or link between income and capital is the *rate of interest.* We may define the *rate of interest as the per cent of premium* paid on money at one date in terms of money to be in hand one year later. Theoretically, of course, we may substitute for money in this statement wheat or any other sort of goods. This will be discussed in Chapter II. But practically, it is only money which is traded as between present and future. Hence, the rate of interest is sometimes called the price of money; and the market in which present and future money are traded for that price, or premium, is called the money market. If $100 today will exchange for $105 to be received one year hence, the premium on present money in terms of future money is $5 and this, as a percentage of the $100, or the rate of interest, is five per cent. That is to say, the price of today's money in terms of next year's money is five per cent above par. It should always be remembered *that interest and the rate of interest are not identical.* Interest is computed by multiplying capital value by the rate of interest.

The aim of this book is to show how the *rate* of interest is caused or determined. Some writers have chosen, for purposes of exposition, to postulate two questions involved in the theory of the rate of interest, viz., (1) why any rate of interest exists and (2) how the rate of interest is determined. This second question, however, embraces also the first, since to explain how the rate of interest is determined involves the question of whether the rate can or cannot be zero, i.e., whether a positive rate of interest must necessarily exist.

§9. *Discounting is Fundamental*

But although the rate of interest may be used either way—for computing from present to future values, or from future to present values—the latter process (discounting) is by far the more important of the two. Accountants, of course, are constantly computing in both directions; for they have to deal with both sets of problems. But the basic problem of time valuation which Nature sets us is always that of translating the future into the present, that is, the problem of ascertaining the capital value of future income. The value of capital must be computed from the value of its estimated future net income, not *vice versa*.

This statement may at first seem puzzling, for we usually think of causes and effects as running forward not backward in time. It would seem then that income must be derived from capital; and, in a sense, this is true. Income *is* derived from capital *goods*. But the *value* of the income is not derived from the *value* of the capital goods. On the contrary, the value of the capital is derived from the value of the income. Valuation is a human process in which foresight enters. Coming events cast their shadows before. Our valuations are always anticipations.

These relations are shown in the following scheme in which the arrows represent the order of sequence—(1) from capital goods to their future services, that is, income; (2) from these services to their value; and (3) from their value back to capital value:

Capital goods ⟶ Flow of services (income)

↓

Capital value ⟵ Income value

Not until we know how much income an item of capital will probably bring us can we set any valuation on that capital at all. It is true that the wheat crop depends on the land which yields it. But the value of the crop does not depend on the value of the land. On the contrary, the value of the land depends on the expected value of its crops.

The present worth of any article is what buyers are willing to give for it and sellers are ready to take for it. In order that each man may logically decide what he is willing to give or take, he must have: (1) some idea of the value of the future benefits which that article will yield, and (2) some idea of the rate of interest by which these future values may be translated into present values by discounting.

§10. *Costs, or Negative Income*

Cost of production of durable agents or capital goods has its influence included in the preceding formulation, since any cost is simply a negative item of income. Future negative items are to be discounted exactly as future positive items. It is to be remembered that at the given point of time when the value is being computed only *future* costs can enter into the valuation of any good.

[15]

Past costs have no *direct* influence on value. Only indirectly do they enter to the extent that they have determined the existing supply of goods and have thus either raised or lowered the value of the services of these goods.

In this indirect way, past costs can determine present values temporarily and until the prices of goods available are brought into conformity with the present costs of production through the operation of supply and demand. For example, the cost of producing woolen cloth declined very sharply after the close of the World War, but the price did not decline for many months because the new cloth made at less expense was not sufficient to meet the demand, hence the price remained above the new costs of production for a time. Again, the cost of making shoes advanced rapidly during the early years of the twentieth century, but the price of shoes did not advance *pari passu* with increased costs, because the supply of more cheaply made shoes was still large and for a time controlled the market price. In the same indirect way, many other influences affect the value of the services of any good, especially any alternative to those services. But none of these considerations affects the principle that the value of the good itself is the discounted value of the value (however determined) of its future services.

§11. *The Discount Principle Applied*

The principles which have been explained for obtaining the present value of a future sum apply very definitely to many commercial transactions, such as to the valuation of bank assets, which indeed exist largely in the form of discount paper, or short time loans of some other kinds.

The value of a note is always the discounted value of the future payment to which it entitles the holder.

Elaborate mathematical tables have been calculated and are used by brokers for informing their customers what price should be paid for a five per cent bond in order that the purchaser may realize 5 per cent, 4 per cent, or any other rate of interest on the prices to be paid. The price of the bond is calculated from two items, the rate of interest to be realized and the series of sums or other benefits which the bond is going to return to the investor. Aside from risk, there can never be any other factors in the calculation except these two. Of course, an investor may refuse to buy a bond at the market price because he has, as an alternative, the opportunity to buy another bond cheaper so that he can realize a higher rate on his purchase price. But that fact does not alter the principle that market prices represent discounted benefits. The only market effect of this man's refusal will be a slight tendency to lower the market price of the first bond and raise that of its rival, that is, to alter the rate of interest realized. Later we shall study more fully the effects of such alternative opportunities. Here we are concerned only to note that the price of the bond is dependent solely on two factors: (1) its benefits and (2) the interest rate by which these are discounted.

The principle is, of course, not confined to bonds. It applies in any market to all property and wealth—stocks, land (which has a discounted capital value just as truly as any other capital), buildings, machinery, or anything whatsoever. Risk aside, each has a market value dependent solely on the same two factors, the benefits,[5] or re-

---

[5] Including, of course, all benefits or services whatever from the possession of the wealth such as the option to subscribe to stock, now often

turns, expected by the investor and the market rate of interest by which those benefits are discounted.

The income which he expects may be a perpetual income (flowing uniformly or in recurring cycles) or it may be any one of innumerable other types. If we assume that five per cent is the rate of interest, any one of the following income streams will have a present value of $1000: a perpetual annuity of $50 per year; or an annuity of $50 a year for ten years, together with $1000 at the end of the period; or $100 a year for fourteen years, after which nothing at all; or $25 a year for ten years, followed by $187.50 a year for ten years, after which nothing at all.

§12. *Double Entry Bookkeeping*

We began this chapter with the enjoyment income received by a person and then travelled back, by way of real income, cost of living, and money income to capital value, which simply embodies the capitalization or anticipation of income. This was going upstream, as it were, from the enjoyer of income to its source. We may now reverse our point of view and look downstream. We then

attached to bonds, or the privilege attaching to certain bonds which permits National Banks to use the bonds for the security of National Bank notes. Some of these benefits may be very indirect and related to whole groups. A man seeking voting control as a benefit who already possesses 49 per cent may pay a specially high price for a few more shares of stock for the benefit of raising his holdings to 51 per cent. Or, a man may include in the benefits of his wealth the fun of running the business, or the social standing he thinks it gives him, or political or other power and influence, or the mere miserly sense of possession or the satisfaction in the mere process of further accumulation. However indirect, unusual, or bizarre the benefit, the principle still holds that the value of any capital good or goods is derived solely from the prospect of future benefits.

think of the income stream not so much as flowing *to* its enjoyers as flowing *from* its various sources.[6]

Capital value is income capitalized and nothing else. Income flows from, or is produced by, capital goods and human beings, so that the capital value is also the value of capital goods. The income is credited to (and outgo or cost debited to) these goods and (or including) human beings.

As every bookkeeper knows, most of the items of income (positive or negative) take the form of *money payments*. (These are not a *stock* of money, which is always capital but a *flow* of money.) Some are operations paid for—events in the productive process, such as grinding, spinning, weaving, hoisting, hauling, plowing; others are events of consumption, such as eating food, wearing clothes, hearing music, or seeing a play at the theatre; while still others are within the human mind, such as enjoyments or their opposite, labor effort or discomfort.

It might seem that in sorting and combining such a

[6] Possibly it would help to adjust our mental attitudes to this changed point of view if we could change the name of income to outcome, or output. Income suggests coming *toward us* while outcome suggests coming *from the source*. Thus the outcome from a farm is the net value of its crops; the outcome from a railway company is its dividends, etc.

Under this new procedure, we credit each item of income as outcome from its source and debit every negative item. Negative items of income are outgo. If we could change this name also, we would call it ingo, or input.

It is a mere clerical matter of bookkeeping thus to credit to its source every service rendered as so much outcome (or income) and debit it with every disservice rendered, as so much ingo (or outgo).

Having suggested these new terms, however, so that the student may mentally, or literally by lead pencil, substitute them for the old, I shall hereafter, for simplicity, adhere uniformly to the original terminology, using the term income even when we are thinking merely of its coming *from its capital source* while the recipient is forgotten.

miscellany of income items we could never avoid confusion and double counting and that the sum total would far exceed the true psychic or enjoyment income. But the fact is that almost as many negative items as positive items are included here and that, *in fact, except for enjoyment income and labor pain,* every positive item is also negative, according to its relation to the capital source. Thus when Smith pays Jones $100 (no matter where it came from), Jones receives an item of income of $100 while Smith suffers an item of outgo of the same amount; and when a coupon of $100 is cut from a bond and deposited, the bond is credited with yielding $100 and the bank account is debited with the same sum. The same principle is applicable to the final big coupon called the principal of the bond. The same item is thus entered twice, once on one side of somebody's books and the other time on the other side of somebody's books.

The bookkeeping implications of such couples of items were discovered by accountants long ago and are the basis of their double entry bookkeeping, though its economic significance has been largely overlooked. One important significance is that this double entry prevents double counting; when we take the sum total of all income items for society, including psychic as well as physical items, this double entry results in cancelling out everything except the psychic items of enjoyment and labor pain.

Every operation of production, transportation, exchange, or consumption—every process, in fact, except final enjoyment—is double faced, or two items in one. I have called such an operation an "interaction" because it is income to be credited to the capital which yields it, while it is outgo to be debited to the capital which receives it. Thus, in any complete bookkeeping, $100 worth of plowing, on the one hand, is credited jointly to the plow, the plowman, and the team, or motor, which do the plowing; that is, which yield or bestow the service. On the other hand, it is debited to the land which is plowed, that is, which receives the service.

If the plow is owned by one person and the land by another, the latter paying $100 to the former, then the service of plowing, though a self-cancelling interaction for the two persons taken together, evidently cannot be ignored by either separately. If $100 is paid for this service of plowing, the $100 item is an expense to the landowner to be subtracted from his gross income. It is no concern of his that this self-same service of plowing is counted as income by the plow-owner. So this item of $100 worth of plowing affects our accounts quite differently according to the point of view. It may be a plus item from the point of view of one person and a minus item from that of another. When, however, the two accounts are combined and the plus and minus items are added, their algebraic sum is zero. For society as a whole, therefore, no positive income results from plowing until the land has yielded its crop and the crop has been finally consumed.

Thus, simply by the mechanical, clerical processes of making bookkeepers' entries, we reach again, in the opposite order, the various stages originally described in the opening pages of this chapter. That is, the sum total of income flowing from a group of capital sources is naturally different according to which capital sources are included. There are certain cancellations within any group of capital goods which have an uncancelled fringe, and this may itself in turn disappear by cancellation if the group is enlarged by including other capital items with interactions between the new and old members. Henry Ford's mines yield a net income, the difference between certain credits and debits. If we include the railway which transports the product to the factory, certain credits to the mines from turning their product over to the railroad now disappear, being debits to the railway. If the circle be still further enlarged, say to include the Ford factories, other items likewise disappear as parts of interactions within the enlarged circle, and so on.

We must, of course, include all services as income. A dwelling renders income to the owner who dwells in it himself just as truly as when he lets it to another. In the first case, his income is shelter; in the second, his income is rent payments in money. All wealth existing at any moment is capital and yields income in some form. As a business man said to me, his pleasure yacht is capital and gives him dividends every Saturday afternoon.

§13. Simplicity Underlying Complications

In our present-day complicated economic life we are likely to be confused by the many industrial operations and money transactions. But net income still remains exactly what it was to primitive Robinson Crusoe on his island—the enjoyment from eating the berries we pick, so to speak, less the discomfort or the labor of picking them. The only difference is that today the picking is not so entirely hand-to-mouth, but is done by means of complicated apparatus and after the frequent exchange of money; that is, a long chain of middlemen, capital, and money transactions intervenes between the labor of picking at the start and the satisfaction of eating at the end.

INCOME AND CAPITAL

To continue the literal example of berry picking, we find today huckleberries picked by hired laborers on the Pocono Mountains, sorted, graded, shipped by rail and motor to New York City wholesalers, resold to retailers who sell and deliver them to the housewife in whose kitchen they are again sorted and prepared for their ultimate mission of giving enjoyment. The individual's total income when elaborately worked out, after cancelling, in pairs or couples, all such credits and debits, whether of money payments or the money value of services—in production or exchange—coincides necessarily with his enjoyment income, less the labor pain suffered in the same period, from which sort of income we started our discussion in this chapter. This coincidence occurs necessarily and automatically, by virtue of these mathematical cancellations.

It is interesting to observe that a corporation as such can have no net income. Since a corporation is a fictitious, not a real, person, each of its items without exception is doubly entered. Its stockholders may get income from it, but the corporation itself, considered as a separate person apart from these stockholders, receives none.

The *total income* of a real person is his *enjoyment income* only provided we include the credits and debits of his own body. The physical music, or vibrations which pass from his piano to his ear are, strictly speaking, only interactions to be credited to his piano and debited to his bodily ear. The music in his consciousness comes at the other, or brain, end of the auditory nerve. The piano plays to his ear, his ear to his brain, and his brain to his consciousness. His whole body mechanism is a transmitter from the outer world to his inner life, through ear, eye, and its other sense organs.

Or if the body mechanism, with its debits and credits, be omitted the total result is not his enjoyment income, subjectively considered, but the real income as above set forth. If we measure this, his real income, in money units, we find it equal to the total valuation of his cost of living less the total valuation of his own labor pain.

How to place a money valuation on a labor pain is a difficult question. This question is important in accounting theory, especially in its relation to the problems of measuring human welfare. But, fortunately for us, the difficulties of this valuation do not disturb the theory of the rate of interest, since this theory is actually concerned only with *differences* in the income stream at different times, not in a meticulous measurement of the *total*. Moreover, practically the only point in interest theory where labor pain enters is the case of a worker who suffers present labor pain in order to secure future satisfactions for himself or his family. This case is that of a laborer's savings; and all we need do here is to take the laborer's own valuation. Presumably, if the rate of interest is 5 per cent, the labor he will exert this year for the sake of $100 next year has a valuation in his mind of about $95.

But a laborer's savings are practically a negligible element in determining the rate of interest. To others than laborers the only important way labor enters is through the payment of wages and salaries, and these are money expenses incurred for the sake of future money returns. A laborer building a railway does not work for the future dividends from the railway. He is paid for immediate living by his employer in expectation of those future dividends. Thus wages are a sort of measure of labor pain to the employer of labor, whether or not they be so regarded by the laborer.[7]

If we exclude labor pain and further exclude from the laborer's bookkeeping the income items, positive and negative, flowing from his household effects—the use of furniture, clothing, food, and so on—the total income then turns out to be not his real income *but his money income*—assuming that, as is ordinarily true, all his income flows in through money payments and none in kind.

§14. *Capital Gain not Income*

The most interesting and valuable result of applying these bookkeeping principles is that thereby we automatically separate capital from income, two things which are so often confused and in so many ways. It is not uncommon for economic students to make the mistake of including capital gains as income. Capital gains, as already implied, are merely capitalization of future income. They are never present income. Therefore a true meticulous accounting, item by item, of the income, or of the services and disservices, rendered by any specified group of capital items will infallibly grind out this truth. It will never confuse capital gain in that capital group with income realized from that group. This is true whether our capital group and its income are so extended as to include enjoyment income (positive and negative) as the final net income, or whether our specific group is so restricted as to leave plowing or money payments as the uncancelled fringe.[8] We shall always find that only the income actually detached from, or given off for en-

---

[7] They may be so regarded in cases where labor is paid by the piece and the laborer is free to stop work at any point.

[8] See *The Nature of Capital and Income*, Chapters VII-X.

joyment by, that group, as in cutting coupons from a bond, will result from the summation of the accountant, who will never record as income the increase or decrease in the capital itself.

A bond price, for example, will grow with accrued interest *between* two coupon cuttings. That growth in its value is not income but increase of capital. Only when the coupon is detached does the bond render, or give off, a service, and so yield income. The income consists in the event of such off-giving, the yielding or separation, to use the language of the United States Supreme Court. If the coupon thus given off is reinvested in another bond, that event is outgo, and offsets the simultaneous income realized from the first bond. There is then *no* net income from the group but only growth of capital. If the final large payment of the principal is commonly thought of not as income (which it is if not reinvested) but as capital it is because it is usually and normally so reinvested.

Likewise, if my savings bank account gains by compound interest, there is no income but only an accretion of capital. If we adopt the fiction that the bank teller hands over that accretion at any moment to me through his window, we must also adopt the fiction that it is simultaneously handed back by me through the same window. If the first event is income, the second is outgo. If it passes both ways, or does not pass at all, there can be no net income resulting. This is good bookkeeping and sound economics. There is no escape from such mathematical conclusions. By no hocus pocus can we have our cake and eat it too. This is as impossible as perpetual motion, and fundamentally as absurd. The absurdity is especially evident when the cause of an increase or decrease in the capital value of a bond or investment is not due to any change in the expected income at all but comes through a change in the *rate of interest*. Consols and rentes fluctuate in value every day with every change in the money market. Yet the income they actually yield flows on at the same rate. Merely the capital value is found sometimes on a 3 per cent basis and sometimes on a 4 per cent basis. A rise in the market is a capital gain, but it is not income. Income may be *invested* and thus transformed into capital; or capital may be *spent* and so transformed into income. In the first case, as we have seen, capital accumulates; in the second case, capital is diminished. In the first case the man is living inside his money income; in the second case he is living beyond his money income.

If Henry Ford receives $100,000,000 in dividends but reinvests all but $50,000, then his real income is only $50,000,[9] even if his money income is $100,000,000. And if, during the year of rebuilding his factories to make his new car, he received no dividends and yet spent $40,000 in that year for living expenses and all other satisfactions, then his *real* income was this $40,000 even if his money income that year was zero.

Thus the income enjoyed in any year is radically different from the ups and downs of one's capital value in that year—whether this is caused by savings or the opposite, or by changes in the rate of interest or by so-called chance.

We may in our bookkeeping add our savings to our real income and call the sum total gain. For my part, I

[9] Except, as already stated in a previous footnote, he derives in addition to this obvious income other less tangible and more subtle income from the sense of possession, prestige, power, etc., which go with great wealth.

prefer not to call it income. For the two parts of this total—enjoyed income and accumulation of capital or capitalized future enjoyments—are unlike. The only argument for adding them together is that the recipient *could* use the savings as income and still keep his capital unchanged. Yes, he *could,* but he didn't, otherwise there would be no savings! One part is income, and the other is capital gain.

This distinction between the real income, actually enjoyed, and the accretion or accrual of capital value, that is, the capitalization of future enjoyments, is not only in general vital, but vital to the understanding of this book.[10]

We cannot understand the theory of interest so long as we play fast and loose with the concepts of capital and income. And enjoyment income, which plays the central rôle in interest theory, is never savings or increase of capital.

§15. *Capital-Income Relations*

In conclusion we may say that the chief relations between capital and income are:

(1) Capital value is income capitalized or discounted.

(2) If the rate of interest falls, the capital value (capitalized value of expected income) rises, and *vice versa.*

(3) This rise or fall in capital value is relatively great for durable goods like land, and relatively small for transitory goods like clothes.

[20] For fuller treatment of this subject the reader is referred to: *The Nature of Capital and Income; Are Savings Income,* Journal of American Economic Association, Third Series, Vol. IX, No. 1, pp. 1-27; *The Income Concept in the Light of Experience,* privately printed as English translation of article in Vol. III, of the Wieser Festschrift, *Die Wirtschaftstheorie der Gegenwart,* Vienna, 1927, 29 pp.

(4) Capital value is increased by savings, the income being decreased by the same amount that the capital is increased.

(5) These savings thus diverted from income and turned back into capital will, except for mischance, be the basis for real income later.

§16. *Application to this Book*

The problem of the rate of interest is entirely a problem of spending and investing, of deciding between various possible enjoyments constituting income, especially between relatively small but immediate enjoyments and relatively large but deferred enjoyments. There is an eternal conflict between the impulse to spend and the impulse to invest. The impulse of a man to spend is caused by his impatience to get enjoyments without delay, and his impulse to invest is caused by the opportunities to obtain by delay relatively more enjoyment either for himself or others.

For the study of interest from this point of view we need as our chief subject matter a picture of a person's income stream. We may get this most clearly by plotting day by day, month by month, or year by year, the closest statistical measure of one's real income, namely, one's cost of living.

If this income flows at a constant rate of $200 a month or $2400 a year, the picture of the income stream is as shown in Chart 1.

If the income stream flows at an increasing rate, the picture is as shown in Chart 2.

If it flows at a decreasing rate, the picture is as in Chart 3.[11]

[11] In all three examples, each month's income is represented by a rectangular column or bar. In the last two cases, the resultant row of

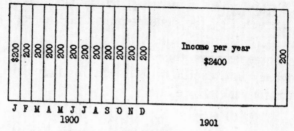

CHART 1

Income Stream Uniform.

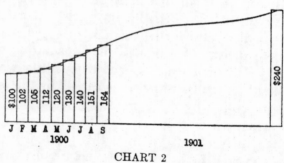

CHART 2

Income Stream Increasing.

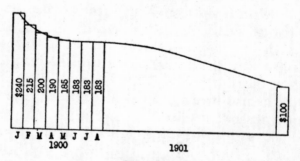

CHART 3

Income Stream Decreasing.

Of course, these particular forms are only special types; numerous other types might be given.

In interest theory the income with which we deal are not statistical records of the past but those of the expected future. What is to be one's future income stream, chosen from among several income streams available, becomes of supreme importance.

§17. *Confusions to be Avoided*

The very first effort of the beginner in this subject should be to rid his mind of all prepossessions as to the nature of income and capital. My grandchild of six recently asked the cashier of a savings bank, "Show me the money I am going to get when I grow up." The cashier gravely took him into a back room and held up a bag of coins. The vision of that bagful will doubtless persist into adult life as a picture of a savings bank account, even after he has learned in college that the total deposits of a bank far exceed the cash on hand, and that the depositor's capital is not actual cash but the right, measured in terms of cash, to the services or benefits flowing from the bank's assets, real estate, mortgages on real estate, stocks and bonds, and all the rest of its resources. Both capital and income *seem* to be simply money. We can always show a money sample, as did the cashier, and where one's capital is liquid so that it may readily be turned from one form to another via money—or rather

---

bars makes a series of flat tops or steps. But by taking days instead of months, we come nearer to a sloping curve which is a better and simpler ideal picture. Hereafter we shall use such continuous curves. But they may always be thought of as made up approximately of a series of columns or bars. For fuller discussion of such charts, see *The Nature of Capital and Income*, p. 204 ff.

credit—it is most simply and lazily pictured to the mind's eye as being itself money.

The student should also try to forget all former notions concerning the so-called supply and demand of capital as the causes of interest. Since capital is merely the translation of future expected income into present cash value, whatever supply and demand we have to deal with are rather the supply and demand of future income.

It will further help the student if he will, from the outset, divest himself of any preconception he may have acquired as to the rôle of the rate of interest in the distribution of income. This subject will be dealt with in Chapter XV; but it may be well here to point out that interest is not, as traditional doctrine would have it, a separate branch of income in addition to rent, wages and profits.

The income stream is the most fundamental fact of economic life. It is the joint product of many agencies which may be classified under many heads, such as human beings, land, and (other) capital. The hire of human beings is wages; the hire of land is land rent. What, then, is the hire of (other) capital—houses, pianos, typewriters, and so forth? Is it interest? Certainly not. Their hire is obviously house rent, piano rent, typewriter rent, and so forth, just as the man in the street calls them. Rent is the ratio of the payment to the physical object—land, houses, pianos, typewriters, and so forth—so many dollars per piano, per acre, per room. Interest, on the other hand, is the ratio of payment to the money *value* of these things—so many dollars per hundred dollars (or per cent). It is, in each case, the ratio of the net rent to the capitalized value of that rent. It applies to all the categories—to land quite as truly as to houses, pianos, typewriters. The income from land is thus both rent and interest just as truly as the income from a typewriter or a bond. We can and do capitalize land rent just as truly as we do house rent. For example, land worth "20 years purchase" yields 5 per cent interest. All this is true quite irrespective of the question of distinctions between land rent, on the one hand, and house rent, piano rent, typewriter rent, and so forth on the other.[12] It is a question of that sort of price which links one point of time with another point of time in the markets of the world. And it is a question concerning every branch of economic theory in which the time element enters. The rate of interest is the most pervasive price in the whole price structure.

As to profits, I believe the most fruitful concept is also that of the man in the street. When risk attaches to any one of the aforementioned forms of capital—human beings, land, houses, pianos, typewriters and so forth—the man in the street calls the net income profits. And profits, likewise, may be measured either (as rent) in relation to the physical units producing them, or (as interest) in relation to the values of these profits; that is, either as dollars per acre, per room, per piano and so forth; or dollars per $100 worth of land (houses, pianos, and so forth); or as dollars per share of ownership in any of these; or dollars per $100 worth of such shares. To pretend that either interest or profits is the income solely from capital goods other than land and that these two concepts are inapplicable to land—to pretend, in short, that wages, rent, interest and profits are four mutually

[12] Cf. Fetter, Frank A., *Interest Theories Old and New,* American Economic Review, March, 1914, pp. 76 and 77; Fetter, *Principles of Economics,* pp. 122-127; Davenport, H. J., *Interest Theory and Theories,* American Economic Review, Dec., 1927, pp. 636, 639.

exclusive divisions of the income stream of society is to treat different classifications of one thing as if they were themselves different things. It is as if we should speak of a certain total space as consisting partly of acres of land, partly of tons of soil, and partly of bushels of ore. Or again, it is like classifying a pack of cards into aces, clubs and red suits and pretending that these three classes are mutually exclusive.

The simple fact is that any or all income may be capitalized, including that credited to human beings, thus giving the resultant economic value of a man. William Farr, J. Shield Nicholson, Louis I. Dublin, and others have made such computations.[13] However, we so seldom capitalize wages that we have no practical need to call wages or any portion of them interest. Nor where risk is a dominant factor, as in profits, is there real need to call the income interest. For instance, hoped-for dividends, according as the hope varies, are daily and automatically capitalized in the stock market and need not themselves be called interest. Much less would it be worth while to call enterpriser's profits interest. No one ever attempted to capitalize them. But in meticulous theory, all may be capitalized and so become interest.

§18. *A Working Concept of the Rate of Interest*

While any exact and practical definition of a pure rate of interest is impossible, we may say roughly that the pure rate is the rate on loans which are practically devoid of chance. In particular, there are two chances which should thus be eliminated. One tends to raise the rate,

[13] For instance, Dr. Dublin computes the total value of the "human capital" of the United States to be 1,500 billion dollars, or about five times the value of all other capital.

namely, the chance of default. The other tends to lower it, namely, the chance to use the security as a substitute for ready cash. In short, we thus rule out, on the one hand, all risky loans, and, on the other, all bank deposits subject to withdrawal on demand, even if accorded some interest. We have left safe securities of fixed terms not likely to be transferred or transferred often before maturity. Such securities give us the nearest approach to pure interest both for short and long periods according to the time to maturity.

In this book, I shall usually confine the concept of the rate of interest to the rate in a (humanly speaking) safe loan, or other contract implying specific sums payable at one date or set of dates in consideration of repayment at another date or set of dates. The essentials in this concept are (1) definite and assured payments, and (2) definite and assured repayments, and (3) definite dates. The concept includes the concept of the rate realized on a safe security such as a bond purchased in the market. It is this that concerns us in this book. We are not primarily concerned with *total* interest, but with the *rate* of interest.

CHAPTER II

MONEY INTEREST AND REAL INTEREST

§1. *Introduction*

AT the close of the preceding chapter, the rate of interest was described as the percentage premium on present goods over future goods of the same kind. Does the kind of goods affect the premium? This important question—usually overlooked—may well engage our attention at the very outset. The number, or figure, expressing the rate of interest in terms of money does depend upon the monetary standard employed.

It is perfectly true, as is often pointed out, that when a man lends $100 this year in order to obtain $105 next year, he is really sacrificing not $100 in literal money but one hundred dollars' worth of other goods such as food, clothing, shelter, or pleasure trips, in order to obtain, next year, not $105 in literal money, but one hundred and five dollars' worth of other goods. But this fact does not remove the money factor from our problem. The money factor affects the rate of interest in many ways. The one here considered is that which occurs through a *change* in the value of the monetary standard.

If the monetary standard were always stable with reference to goods, the rate of interest, reckoned in terms of money, would be the same as if reckoned in terms of goods. When, however, money and goods change with reference to each other—in other words, when the money standard appreciates or depreciates in value in terms of goods—the numbers expressing the two rates of interest, one reckoned in terms of money and the other reckoned in terms of goods, will be quite different. Moreover, the former, or money rate, the only rate quoted in the market, will be influenced by the appreciation or depreciation.

§2. *Assuming Foresight*

The influence of such changes in the purchasing power of money on the money rate of interest will be different according to whether or not that change is *foreseen*. If it is not clearly foreseen, a change in the purchasing power of money will not, at first, greatly affect the rate of interest expressed in terms of money. Instead, if the change is in the direction of appreciation, it will injure the debtor, because to repay the principal of his debt will cost him more goods than either he or his creditor anticipated when the debt was contracted.

In so far as the appreciation is foreseen, any increased burden to the debtor in the principal may be somewhat offset by a reduction in the rate of interest. This is a fact which has seldom been recognized.[1] The assumption has been tacitly made that contracting parties are powerless to forestall gains or losses caused by an upward or downward movement of the monetary standard even when that movement is foreseen.

It is theoretically just as possible to make allowance for an expected change in the unit of value as it would be for an expected change in any other unit. If, by legislation, the unit of length were to be changed, and its change were set for a certain future date, contracts run-

---

[1] A brief outline of the history and theory of appreciation and interest is given in the Appendix to Chapter V of *The Rate of Interest*.

ning beyond that date would surely be modified accordingly. Or suppose that a yard were defined (as legend tells us it once was) as the length of the king's girdle. If the king were a child, everybody would then know that the "yard" would probably increase with the king's age, and a merchant who should agree to deliver one thousand "yards" ten years hence would make his terms correspond to his expectations.

It would be strange, if, in some similar way, an escape could not be found from the effects of changes in the monetary yardstick, provided these changes were known in advance. To offset a foreseen appreciation, therefore, it would be necessary only that the rate of interest be correspondingly lower, and to offset a foreseen depreciation, that it be correspondingly higher.[2]

Near the close of the last century, during the uncertainty as to the adoption or rejection of "free silver," a syndicate offered to buy from the United States government some $65,000,000 of bonds either on a 3 per cent basis in gold, or a 3¾ per cent basis in coin. Everyone knew that the additional ¾ per cent in the latter alternative was due to the mere *possibility* that coin might not be maintained at full gold value, but might sink to the level of the value of silver. If the alternative had been between repayment in gold and—not merely a *possible* but a *certain*—repayment in silver, the additional in-

---

[2] Since, because of ignorance and indifference, appreciations and depreciations are, as a matter of fact, never fully foreknown and their relation to interest and other business phenomena only dimly perceived, they are only partially provided against in the rate of interest itself. As I have tried to show in *Stabilizing the Dollar*, in *The Money Illusion*, and in other writings, the best remedy is to standardize, or stabilize, the dollar as we have standardized every other important unit of measure employed in business.

terest would obviously have exceeded ¾ per cent. It was stated, after the World War, that an American banking firm, when asked by a German concern for a loan in marks, offered to lend at 100 per cent per annum. The offer was rejected—fortunately for the American firm which, as it turned out, would actually have lost, and lost heavily, because the subsequent rapid depreciation of the mark far exceeded the compensatory effect of even so high an interest rate.

The exact theoretical relation between the rates of interest measured in any two diverging standards of value and the rate of foreseen appreciation or depreciation of one of these two standards relatively to the other has been developed by me with many numerical illustrations in a special monograph [3] and also in my first book on interest.[4] The two rates of interest in the two diverging standards will, in a perfect adjustment, differ from each other by an amount equal to the *rate* of divergence between the two standards.[5] Thus, in order to compensate for every one per cent of appreciation or depreciation, one point would be subtracted from, or added to, the rate of interest; that is, an interest rate of 5 per cent would become 4 per cent, or 6 per cent, respectively.

[3] *Appreciation and Interest,* Publications of the American Economic Association, Third Series, Vol. XI, No. 4, Aug., 1896, pp. 331-442.

[4] *The Rate of Interest,* Appendix to Chapter V.

[5] This is strictly true only when the rate of interest in each standard is reckoned momently, or continuously. If, as in practice, the rate is reckoned quarterly, semi-annually, or annually, this equation is slightly altered. For the mathematical demonstration of this proposition, see Appendix to Sec. 3, Chapter V, of *The Rate of Interest.* For the significance of "continuous reckoning," see *The Nature of Capital and Income,* Chapter XII; also Appendix to Sec. 12 of Chapter XIII.

THE THEORY OF INTEREST

§3. *Limitations of Theory*

We next inquire what limits, if any, are imposed on the two rates of interest in the respective standards and the rate of divergence between the two standards. From what has been said it might seem that, when the appreciation is sufficiently rapid, the rate of interest in the upward-moving standard, in order to equalize the burden, would have to be zero or even negative. For instance, if the rate of interest expressed in gold is 4 per cent, and if wheat appreciates relatively to gold at 4 per cent also, the rate of interest expressed in wheat, if perfectly adjusted, would theoretically have to sink to zero! But zero or negative interest is practically almost impossible. If it were definitely foreknown that wheat was to appreciate as fast as 4 per cent when the rate of interest in money is 4 per cent, wheat would be hoarded and so many people would want it that its present price would tend instantly to come within 4 per cent of its next year's price. This would, from that instant, prevent the rate of interest in terms of wheat from passing below the zero mark.

For instance, if interest is 4 per cent, it is impossible that wheat should be worth $1 today and $1.10 next year *foreknown today* by everybody. For, if such prices were possible, holding for a rise would give a sure return of 10 per cent (neglecting storage charges and other costs of carrying). The result of such perfect knowledge of next year's price would be that the lowest possible price of present wheat would then be the expected $1.10 discounted at 4 per cent, or about $1.06.

This very limitation on the possible rate of interest—that it cannot theoretically sink below zero—carries with it a theoretical limitation on the possible rate of (fore-known) appreciation of any good.

It is important to emphasize the fact that these limits imposed on the rates of interest and appreciation imply the possibility of hoarding wheat, or other durable commodities, including money, without loss. If money were a perishable commodity, like fruit, the limits would evidently be pushed into the region of negative quantities. One can imagine a loan expressed in strawberries or peaches, contracted in summer and payable in winter, with *negative* interest.[6] Analogously we may regard the storage and other costs of carrying wheat as permitting, to that extent, a negative rate of interest in terms of wheat. It follows that even the rate of interest in terms of money may be negative when money is in sufficient danger of being lost or stolen, as during a riot or invasion.

But as long as our monetary standard is gold or other imperishable commodity, so that there is always the opportunity to hoard some of it, no rate of interest expressed therein is likely to fall to zero, much less to fall below zero. This principle is a special case of a more general principle of opportunity which will be developed later.

§4. *Real and Money Interest*

The theoretical relation existing between interest and appreciation implies, then, that the rate of interest is always relative to the standard in which it is expressed. The fact that interest expressed in *money* is high, say 15 per cent, might conceivably indicate merely that general prices are expected to rise (i.e., money depreciate)

[6] Böhm-Bawerk, *The Positive Theory of Capital*, pp. 252 and 297; Landry, *L'Intérêt du Capital*, p. 49.

at the rate of 10 per cent, and that the rate of interest expressed in terms of *goods* is not high, but only about 5 per cent.

We thus need to distinguish between interest expressed in terms of money and interest expressed in terms of other goods. But no two forms of goods can be expected to maintain an absolutely constant price ratio toward each other. *There are, therefore, theoretically just as many rates of interest expressed in terms of goods as there are kinds of goods diverging from one another in value.*

Is there, then, no absolute standard of value in terms of which real interest should be expressed? Real income, a composite of consumption goods and services, in other words, a cost of living index in accordance with the principles set forth in Chapter I, affords a practical objective standard. By means of such an index number we may translate the nominal, or money rate of interest, into a goods rate or real rate of interest, just as we translate money wages into real wages. The cost of living plays the same rôle in both cases although the process of translating is somewhat different and more complicated in the case of interest from what it is in the case of wages, for the reason that interest involves two points of time, instead of only one; so that we must translate from money into goods not only in the present, when the money is borrowed, but also in the future, when it is repaid.

Income is the most fundamental factor in our economic lives. The derivation of the value of every durable agent or good involves the discounting or capitalizing of income as one of the steps. Consequently, a rate of interest in terms of fundamental income itself would seem to come as near as we can practically come to any basic standard in which to express a real rate of interest.

But, in actual practice, it is the rate in terms of money with which business men deal and hereafter the rate of interest, unless otherwise specified, will in this book be taken to mean this *money* rate.

The money rate and the real rate are normally identical; that is, they will, as has been said, be the same when the purchasing power of the dollar in terms of the cost of living is constant or stable. When the cost of living is not stable, the rate of interest takes the appreciation and depreciation into account to some extent, but only slightly and, in general, indirectly. That is, when prices are rising, the rate of interest tends to be high but not so high as it should be to compensate for the rise; and when prices are falling, the rate of interest tends to be low, but not so low as it should be to compensate for the fall.[7]

The principle of interest being relative to the standard used in loan contracts would be more in evidence if it were customary to make loan contracts in terms of other standards than money. The rate is actually expressed in loan contracts in terms of money and only translated into terms of goods, if at all, after the contract has been fulfilled, when it is too late to stipulate compensations for the rise or fall in monetary value. If the money rate of interest were perfectly adjusted to changes in the purchasing power of money—which means, in effect, if those changes were perfectly and universally foreseen—

---

[7] That the appreciation or depreciation of money does actually influence the rate of interest, even though feebly, is now well recognized by those who have given attention to the subject. See Professor Marshall's testimony, *Indian Currency Report*, p. 169; and Johnson, *Money and Currency*. Boston, Ginn & Company, 1905.

the relation of the rate of interest to those changes would have no practical importance but only a theoretical importance. As matters are, however, in view of almost universal lack of foresight, the relation has greater practical than theoretical importance. The business man supposes he makes his contracts in a certain rate of interest, only to wake up later and find that, in terms of real goods, the rate is quite different.

The real rate of interest in the United States from March to April, 1917, fell below minus 70 per cent! In Germany at the height of inflation, August to September, 1923, the real rate of interest fell to the absurd level of minus 99.9 per cent, which means that lenders lost all interest and nearly all their capital as well; and then suddenly prices were deflated and the real interest rate jumped to plus 100 per cent.[8]

[8] The need to show income and capital accounts in terms of *value* instead of *money units* is now coming to be recognized by progressive accountants. For a clear and complete statement of this new principle in accounting, the reader is referred to Ernest F. DeBrul. *Unintentional Falsification of Accounts.* National Association of Cost Accountants Bulletin, Vol. IX. Pp. 1035-1058. New York, National Association of Cost Accountants, 1928. The same theory is expounded by Henry W. Sweeney in his doctor's dissertation, *Stabilized Accounting,* accepted by Columbia University but not yet published. See also his article, *German Inflation Accounting,* in the Journal of Accountancy, February, 1928, pp. 104-116; Dr. Walter Mahlberg. *Bilanztechnik und Bewertung bei Schwankender Währung.* Leipzig, G. A. Gloeckner, 1923; E. Schmalenbach. *Grundlagen Dynamischer Bilanzlehre.* Leipzig, G. A. Gloeckner, 1925; Lucien Thomas. *La Tenue des Comptabilités en Période d'Instabilité Monétaire.* Paris, éditions d'experta, 1927; Lucien Thomas. *La Révision des Bilans à L'Issue de la Période d'Instabilité Monétaire.* Paris, éditions d'experta, 1928. Also compare Dr. F. Schmidt, *Die Industriekonjunktur—ein Rechenfehler!* Zeitschrift für Betriebswirtschaft, Jahrg. 1927, and *Ist Wertänderung am ruhenden Vermögen Gewinn oder Verlust?,* Zeitschrift für Betriebswirtschaft, Jahrg. 1928.

CHAPTER III

SOME COMMON PITFALLS

§1. *Introduction*

IN the last chapter we saw that the figure expressing the rate of interest depends on the standard of value in which present and future goods are expressed, and we saw how the rate of interest in one standard (such as the standard of real income) is to be derived from the rate of interest in any other standard (such as the actual monetary standard).

This translation of the rate of interest from one standard into another does not determine *the rate of interest in any standard whatever;* for it assumes that the rate in *some one* standard is already known, and merely enables us, on the basis of this known rate, to calculate the rates in other standards. The case is somewhat similar to the conversion of temperature from the Fahrenheit system into the Centigrade system. By such conversion we can calculate the Centigrade temperature, but only on condition that we already know the Fahrenheit temperature. The formula connecting the two does not enable us, in the least, to find out how hot or cold the weather is.

While the deviations of the money rate of interest from the real rate are of tremendous practical importance, they may be regarded as belonging more to the problem of money than to the problem of interest, and, in the chapters which follow, these deviations will, unless otherwise specified, be disregarded. The reader may, therefore, in this theoretical study keep to the hypothesis that the monetary unit remains unchanged in purchasing power, with the result that the money rate of interest and the real rate coincide. That is to say, the rate of interest is assumed to be at once the premium on this year's *money* in terms of next year's and the same premium on this year's *real income* in terms of next year's.

This premium, that is, the terms of exchange of this year's income and next year's, may be said to depend, in brief, on the relative supply and demand of those two portions of the income stream; and this statement may be interpreted as including almost the entire impatience and investment opportunity theory of this book. But, like many brief statements, this supply and demand statement is crude and inadequate. Crude and inadequate notions beset this subject and some of them are so common and treacherous that it seems worth while, before proceeding with further analysis, to examine these notions in order to avoid falling into their pitfalls.

To say that the rate of interest is fixed by supply and demand is merely to state, not to solve the problem.[1] Every competitive price is fixed by supply and demand. The real problem is to analyze the particular supply and demand forces operative in determining the rate of interest.

Nor are we greatly enlightened by saying that in one sense the rate of interest is the price of money. For it is

[1] In Chapters XI and XII supply and demand curves will be derived from the principles of impatience and opportunity. It will also be shown that impatience is not to be associated with demand to the exclusion of supply, nor opportunity with supply rather than demand, nor *vice versa*.

equally true, in another sense, that the purchasing power of money is the price of money. Yet the rate of interest and the purchasing power of money are two very different things.

Nor is it very illuminating to say that the rate of interest is the price paid for the use of money, especially as the money whose use is purchased is usually not money at all but credit—nor is either the money or credit literally used continuously during the loan. It disappears at the beginning and reappears at the end.

Enough has already been said to show that an increase in the quantity of money in circulation tends to raise the price level and consequently to depreciate the value of the money unit. This depreciation in turn tends to increase the rate of interest. Yet, there is a very persistent belief that an increase or decrease in the quantity of money in circulation causes a decrease or increase in the rate of interest. This fallacy seems to be based on a confused interpretation of the general observation that the rate of interest generally rises or falls with a decrease or increase in the reserve ratio of banks. While it is true that if new money first finds its way from the mint into the banks, it tends to lower the rate of interest, this effect is temporary. The maladjustment between the money in banks and in circulation is soon corrected as the demand for loans overtakes the supply. As far as the total supply of money is concerned, if this is doubled in amount and prices are thereby, in the end, doubled too, there is double the money to lend, but borrowers will require double the amount of money. At the doubled prices they will need twice the money to make the *same* purchases. The demand is doubled along with the supply and the interest rate remains as before.

THE THEORY OF INTEREST

§2. *The Exploitation Explanation of Interest*

Another very persistent idea is that to take interest is, necessarily and always, to take an unfair advantage of the debtor. This notion is something more than the obviously true idea that the rate of interest, like any other price, may be exorbitant. The contention is that there ought to be no interest at all. Throughout history this thought recurs. It seems natural that only what was borrowed should be returned. Why any addition? Interest is therefore called unnatural.

The word used by the Greeks to signify interest, or usury, was τόκος, "offspring"; and Aristotle declaimed against the taking of interest, on the ground that money, being inanimate, did not have offspring. The Mosaic law forbade interest taking between Jews, and, similarly in Rome, interest taking between Romans was prohibited. Many biblical texts show the hostile attitude of the writers, in both the Old and New Testaments, toward the practice. The Church Fathers, through the Middle Ages for over a thousand years, waged a ceaseless but fruitless war against interest taking. St. Thomas Aquinas stated that interest was an attempt to extort a price for the use of things which had already been used up, as, for instance, grain and wine. He also declared that interest constituted a *"payment for time,"* and that no such payment could be justified since time was a free gift of the Creator to which all have a natural right.

In fact, interest taking is often prohibited in primitive societies. Loans under primitive conditions are generally made for consumption rather than for productive purposes. Industry and trade being almost unknown, the demand for loans in such communities usually betokens the personal distress of the borrowers. The loan negotiations take place between two persons under isolated conditions without a regular market. The protection which a modern loan market affords against extortionate prices is absent. Thus, there is, in many cases, a sound ethical basis for the complaints against interest. But experience shows that complete prohibition of interest cannot be made effective. Interest, if not explicitly, will implicitly persist, despite all legal prohibitions. It lurks in all purchases and sales and is an inextricable part of all contracts.

Today the chief survival of the exploitation idea is among Marxian Socialists. These assert that the capitalist exploits the laborer by paying him for only part of what he produces, withholding a portion of the product of labor as interest on capital. Interest is therefore condemned as robbery. The capitalist is described as one who unjustly reaps what the laborer has sown.

Suppose that a tree twenty-five years old is worth $15, and was planted at a cost of $5 worth of labor. The laborer was paid $5 when the tree was planted. The capitalist who pays him receives the $15 twenty-five years later and thereby enjoys $10 increase of value, which is interest on his $5 investment, the cost of planting the tree. Why does not the laborer who planted the tree get this increase of $10 instead of the capitalist?

The socialist exploitation theory of interest consists virtually of two propositions: first, that the value of any product, when completed, usually exceeds the cost of production incurred during the processes of its production; and secondly, that the value of any product, when completed, "ought" to be exactly equal to that cost of production. The first of these propositions is true, but the second is false; or, at any rate, it is an ethical judgment masquerading as a scientific economic fact. Economists, strange to say, in offering answers to the socialists, have often attacked the first proposition instead of the second. The socialist is quite right in his contention that the value of the product does exceed the cost.[2] In fact, this proposition is fundamental in the whole theory of interest. There is no necessity that the value of a product must equal the costs of production. On the contrary, it never can normally be so.

In attempting to prove that the laborer should receive the whole product, the socialist stands on stronger ground than has sometimes been admitted by over-zealous defenders of the capitalist system. The socialist cannot be answered offhand simply by asserting that capital aids labor, and that the capitalist who owns a plow earns the interest payment for its use quite as truly as the laborer operating the plow earns his wages by his labor. For the socialist carries the argument back a stage earlier, and contends that the payment for the use of the plow should belong, not to the capitalist who owns it, but to the laborers who originally made it, including those who made the machinery which helped to make it. He is quite correct in his contention that the value of the uses of the plow is attributable to those who made it, and that, nevertheless, the capitalist, who now owns it, not the laborers who made it in the past, enjoys the value of these uses. The capitalist is, in a sense, always living on the product of *past* labor. An investor who gets his income from railroads, ships, or factories, all of which are products of labor, is reaping what past labor has sown.

---

[2] While this assertion is made dogmatically at this point, the proof of its soundness is contained in Chapter XX, § 7, and in the Appendix to Chapter XX.

But the investor is not, as a necessary consequence, a robber. He has bought and paid for the right, economic and moral as well as legal, to enjoy the product ascribable to the capital goods he owns. The workers' wages, under free competition, constitute payment in full for what they had produced at the time their wages were paid.

Take the case of the tree which was planted with labor worth $5, and which, 25 years later, was worth $15. The socialist virtually asks, Why should not the laborer receive $15 instead of $5 for his work? The answer is: He may receive it, provided he will wait for it 25 years. As Böhm-Bawerk says: [3]

"The perfectly just proposition that the laborer should receive the entire value of his product may be understood to mean either that the laborer should *now* receive the entire *present* value of his product, or should receive the entire future value of his product *in the future*. But Rodbertus and the Socialists expound it as if it means that the laborer should *now* receive the entire *future* value of his product."

Socialists would cease to think of interest as extortion if they would try the experiment of sending a colony of laborers into the unreclaimed lands of the West, letting them develop and irrigate those lands and build railways on them, unaided by borrowed capital. The colonists would find that interest had not disappeared by any means, but that by waiting they had themselves reaped the benefit of it. Let us say they waited five years before their lands were irrigated and their railway completed. At the end of that time they would own every cent of the earnings of both, and no capitalist could be accused of robbing them of it. But they would find that, in spite of themselves, they had now *become* capitalists, and that

[3] Böhm-Bawerk, *Capital and Interest*, p. 342.

they had become so by stinting for those five years, instead of receiving in advance, in the shape of food, clothing, and other real income, the discounted value of the railroad.

This example was almost literally realized in the case of the Mormon settlement in Utah. Those who went there originally possessed little capital, and they did not pay interest for the use of the capital of others. They created their own capital and passed from the category of laborers to that of capitalists. It will be seen, then, that capitalists are not, as such, robbers of labor, but are labor-brokers who buy work at one time and sell its products at another. Their profit or gain on the transaction, if risk be disregarded, is interest, a compensation for waiting during the time elapsing between the payment to labor and the income received by the capitalist from the sale of the product of labor.

§3. *Interest Taking Survives all Opposition*

Despite the persistence of the idea that interest is something unnatural and indefensible, despite the opposition to it by socialists and others who rebel against the existing economic system, despite all attempts to prohibit interest taking, there is not and never has been in all recorded history any time or place without the existence of interest.

Several centuries ago, as business operations increased in importance, certain exemptions and exceptions from the ineffectual prohibition of interest were secured. Pawnshops, banks, and money-lenders were licensed, and the purchase of annuities and the taking of land on mortgage for money loaned were made legitimate by subterfuge. One of the subterfuges by which the taking of interest was excused suggests the true idea of interest as an index of impatience. It was conceded that, although a loan should be professedly without interest, yet when the debtor delayed payment, he should be *fined* for his delay (*mora*), and the creditor should receive compensation in the form of *interesse*. Through this loophole it became common to make an understanding in advance by which the payment of a loan was to be delayed year after year, and with every such postponement a *fine* was to become payable.

Some of the Protestant reformers, while not denying that interest taking was wrong, admitted that it was impossible to suppress it, and proposed that it should therefore be tolerated. This toleration was in the same spirit as that in which many reformers today defend the licensing of vicious institutions, such as saloons, gambling establishments, and houses of prostitution.

Today interest taking is accepted as a matter of course except among Marxian socialists and a few others. But the persistent notion that, fundamentally, interest is unjustified has given the subject a peculiar fascination. It has been, and still is, the great economic riddle.

§4. *Naïve Productivity Explanations*

One of the most common superficialities in this field of thought is the naïve idea that interest expresses the physical productivity of land, or of nature, or of man. When the rate of interest is 5 per cent, nothing at first thought seems more plausible than that this rate obtains because capital goods will yield 5 per cent in kind. It is alleged that because fruit trees bear apples or peaches, and because a bushel of wheat sown has the power to multiply into 50 bushels, and because a herd of cattle if unmolested may double in numbers every two years interest is therefore inherent in nature. As a matter of fact, this productivity, as we shall see, is a real element in the explanation of interest; but it is not the only one nor is it as simple as it seems.

In some degree, the theory elaborated in this book is a productivity theory. I am, therefore, not attempting to refute all productivity theories indiscriminately but merely to show the inadequacy of what Böhm-Bawerk called the "naïve" productivity theory. This theory, or fallacy, is not espoused by any careful student of the interest problem, but it exists in the minds of many before they begin to analyse the problem. It confuses physical productivity [4] with value return.

Following the principles of Chapter I, we may take, as an illustration, an orchard of ten acres yielding 1000 barrels of apples a year. The physical productivity, 100 barrels per acre per year, does not of itself give any clue to what rate of return on its *value* the orchard yields. To obtain the value return on the orchard, we must reduce both physical income and capital goods (the farm) to a common standard of value. If the net annual crop of apples is worth $5000 and the orchard is worth $100,000, the ratio of the former to the latter, or 5 per cent, is a rate of value return; and if this rate is maintained without depreciation of the value of the orchard, this rate of value return is also the rate of interest. But how can we thus pass from heterogeneous quantities to homogeneous values? How can we translate the ten acres of orchard and the 1000 barrels of apples into a common standard— dollars? May not this apparently simple step beg the whole question? The important fact, and the one lost

[4] *The Nature of Capital and Income,* Chapter XI.

sight of in the naïve productivity fallacy, is that the value of the orchard is not independent of the value of its crops; and, in this dependence, lurks implicitly the rate of interest itself.

The statement that "capital produces income" is true only in the physical sense; it is not true in the value sense. That is to say, *capital value does not* produce income value. On the contrary, income value produces capital value. It is not because the orchard is worth $100,000 that the annual crop will be worth $5000, but it is because the annual crop is worth $5000 net that the orchard will be worth $100,000, if the rate of interest is 5 per cent. The $100,000 is the discounted value of the expected income of $5000 net per annum; and in the process of discounting, a rate of interest of 5 per cent is already implied. In general, it is not because a man has $100,000 worth of property that he will get $5000 a year, but it is because he will get that $5000 a year that his property is worth $100,000—if the pre-existing rate of interest remains unchanged.

In short, we are forced back to the confession that when we are dealing with the *values* of capital and income, their causal connection is the reverse of that which holds true when we are dealing with their *quantities*. The orchard is the source of the apples; but the value of the apples is the source of the value of the orchard. In the same way, a dwelling is the source of the shelter it yields; but the value of that shelter is the source of the value of the dwelling. In the same way a machine, a factory, or any other species of capital instrument is the source of the services it renders but the value of these services is the source of the value of the instrument which renders them.

[55]

This principle is complicated, but not impaired, by the fact that the cost of production of further dwellings, machines, tools, and other capital plays a part. The principle which rests on future incomes, including, of course, items of negative future income (costs) applies to any existing capital at any stage of its existence. The value of anything (as indicated in Chapter I, and more fully in *The Nature of Capital and Income*) is typified by the case of a bond whose value, as every broker knows, is calculated solely from the future services, or sums, expected and the rate of interest and the risk. The cost of producing other competing houses or other instruments so valued, in so far as that cost lies in the future, has an important influence. Past costs may also affect the value of the house by influencing through competition the value of the future services or disservices of that house, or the rate of interest, or the risk. Thus, cost plays an important rôle but not the simple one usually assumed.

Although business men are constantly employing this discounting process in the valuation of every specific item of property bought or sold, they often cherish the illusion that somehow, somewhere, there is capital which does not get its value by discounting future services but has already made value which produces interest. They persist in thinking of interest as moving forward in time instead of as discount moving backward.

The necessity of presupposing a rate of interest is reinforced by observing the effect of a *change* of the rate of productivity. If an orchard could in some sudden and *wholly unexpected* way be made to yield double its original crop per acre, only its yield in the sense of physical productivity would be doubled; its yield in the sense of the rate of interest would not necessarily be affected at all, certainly not doubled,[5] because the value of the orchard would automatically advance with an increase in its value productivity.

The rate of physical productivity is evidently not the rate of interest. The rate of physical productivity is not ordinarily even the same kind of magnitude as the rate of interest. Bushels of wheat produced per acre is an entirely different sort of ratio from the rate per cent of the net value of the yield of land relative to the value of the land. Interest is a rate per cent, an abstract number. Physical productivity is a rate of one concrete thing relatively to another concrete thing incommensurable with the first.

§5. *Two Other Pitfalls*

In this chapter I have tried at least to mention, if not completely to remove in advance, the chief pitfalls or impediments to the understanding of the interest problem. Two other pitfalls, discussed elsewhere, may be here mentioned so that the reader may be on his guard against them also.

One is the idea that interest is a *cost*. While an interest *payment*, like any other payment, is a cost or outgo to the payer, it is income to the payee. But interest itself, as it accrues, is capital gain; and is neither negative income (cost) nor positive income. The fallacious idea that it is a cost is simply the other side of the fallacious idea, discussed in Chapter I, that it is income. There are two

[5] It is true, however, as will become more apparent later, that if the *increase* in productivity is *foreseen*, the rate of interest will be temporarily raised. But after the transition period is over and the supposed doubled productivity is thereafter going on at a steady rate, the rate of interest will fall back; in fact, other things equal, it will fall below what it was before productivity was increased.

kinds of economic gain, capital gain and income gain, the former being the anticipation or discounted value of the latter. Interest is the former kind. It gradually accrues, along a discount curve as the income which it anticipates grows nearer. But it is not itself income, nor is it cost.[6]

The other pitfall is the idea that interest is a certain part of the income stream of society, the part namely which goes to capital, the other parts being rent, wages, and profits. I shall, in Chapter XV, discuss the relation of interest to the whole problem of the distribution of wealth. But it may help if the reader is again warned at this point, as he has already been warned in Chapter I, against the idea that any one part of the income stream has an exclusive relation to the rate of interest. All income is subject to discount, or capitalization, that from land as well as that from (other) capital goods. And if the whole income stream of society, including all wages, all rents and all profits were capitalized, that whole income could still be regarded as a rate per cent, i.e., interest on its own capitalization, just as truly as can the income of the bondholder or rentier.

[6] For fuller discussion see *The Rate of Interest*, pp. 38-51, and below Chapter XX, §7 and the Appendix to Chapter XX of this volume.

PART II. THE THEORY IN WORDS

CHAPTER IV

TIME PREFERENCE (HUMAN IMPATIENCE)

§1. *Preference for Present over Future Income*

IN the preceding chapter we mentioned some pitfalls in the explanation of interest. We are now ready to consider more searchingly the fundamental causes which determine the rate of interest. We shall find a place for each of the partial truths contained in the inadequate theories.

Many people think of interest as dependent directly on capital. As already suggested, it will help the reader to proceed in the following analysis if he will try to forget capital and instead think exclusively of income. Capital wealth is merely the means to the end called income, while capital value (which is the sense in which the term capital is ordinarily used by interest theorists) is merely the capitalization of expected income.

The theory of interest bears a close resemblance to the theory of prices, of which, in fact, it is a special aspect. The rate of interest expresses a price in the exchange between present and future goods. Just as, in the ordinary theory of prices, the ratio of exchange of any two articles is based, in part, on a psychological or subjective element —their comparative marginal desirability—so, in the theory of interest, the rate of interest, or the premium on the exchange between present and future goods, is based, in part, on a subjective element, a derivative of marginal desirability; namely, the marginal preference for present over future goods. This preference has been called time preference, or *human impatience*. The chief other part is an objective element, *investment opportunity*. It is the impatience factor which we shall now discuss, leaving the investment opportunity factor for discussion in later chapters.

Time preference, or impatience, plays a central rôle in the theory of interest. It is essentially what Rae calls the "effective desire for accumulation," and what Böhm-Bawerk calls the "perspective undervaluation of the future." It is the (percentage) excess of the present marginal want for [1] one more unit of *present* goods over the *present* marginal want for one more unit of *future* goods. Thus the rate of time preference, or degree of impatience, for present over future goods of like kind is readily derived from the marginal desirabilities of, or wants for, those present and future goods respectively.[2]

---

[1] Or ophelimity, utility, wantability, or the want for one more unit. See *The Nature of Capital and Income,* Chapter III; also my articles, *Is 'Utility' the Most Suitable Term for the Concept It Is Used to Denote?* American Economic Review, June, 1918, pp. 335-337; and *A Statistical Method for Measuring "Marginal Utility" and Testing the Justice of a Progressive Income Tax.* Economic Essays Contributed in Honor of John Bates Clark, pp. 157-193.

[2] To be more specific, we obtain the rate of time preference for a present dollar over a dollar one year hence by the following process:

(a) take the present want for one more present dollar; and

(b) the present want for one more dollar due one year hence; and then

(c) subtract (b) from (a); and finally

(d) measure the result (c) as a percentage of (b).

In terms of the usual illustrative figures, if a present dollar is worth 105 wantabs (want units) and a next year's dollar is now worth 100 wantabs, then the difference, 5, is 5 per cent of the latter.

For a more strictly mathematical formulation, see Appendix to Chapter XII, §1.

TIME PREFERENCE (IMPATIENCE)

§2. *Reduction to Enjoyment Income*

What are these goods which are thus contrasted? At first sight it might seem that the goods compared may be indiscriminately *wealth, property, or services*. It is true that present machines are in general preferred to future machines; present houses to future houses; land possessed today to land available next year; present food or clothing to future food or clothing; present stocks or bonds to future stocks or bonds; present music to future music, and so on. But a slight examination will show that some of these cases of preference are reducible to others.

When present capital wealth, or capital property, is preferred to future, this preference is really a preference for the income expected to flow from the first capital wealth, or capital property, as compared with the income from the second. The reason why we would choose a present fruit tree rather than a similar tree available in ten years is that the fruit yielded by the first will come earlier than the fruit yielded by the second. The reason one prefers immediate tenancy of a house to the right to occupy it in six months is that the uses of the house under the first leasehold begin six months earlier than under the second. In short, capital wealth, or capital property, available early is preferred to the capital wealth, or capital property of like kind, available at a more remote time simply and solely because the *income* from the former is available earlier than the *income* from the latter.

Thus all time preference resolves itself in the end into the preference for comparatively early *income* over comparatively remote, or deferred, *income*. Moreover, the

[63]

preference for early, or prompt, income over late, or deferred, income resolves itself into the preference for early *enjoyment* income over deferred *enjoyment* income. Any income item which consists merely of an interaction or, otherwise expressed, of a preparatory service [3] (that is, an item which, while it is income from one species of capital, is outgo in respect to another species) is wanted for the sake of the *enjoyment* income to which that interaction paves the way. The consumer prefers the service of milling flour in the present to milling flour in the future because the enjoyment of the resulting bread is available earlier in the one case than in the other. The manufacturer prefers present weaving to future weaving because the earlier the weaving takes place the sooner will he be able to sell the cloth and realize his enjoyment income.

To him, early sales are more advantageous than deferred sales, not because he desires the cloth to reach its ultimate destination sooner, but because he will the sooner be in a position to make use of the purchase price for his own personal uses—the shelter and comforts of various kinds constituting *his* income.

The manufacturer is conscious of only one step toward the ultimate goal of clothes—the money he expects to get for the cloth from the jobber to whom he sells it. But this money payment in turn discounts a further step. To the jobber this money he pays is the discounted value of the money he will receive from the wholesaler, and so on through the retailer, tailor and wearer. The result is that each is unconsciously discounting, as the ultimate link in the chain, the enjoyment to be derived by the wearer of the clothes. Of course this is not the whole

[3] See *The Nature of Capital and Income*, Chapter X.

story, but it represents the main parts relevant to the present problem.

All preference, therefore, for present over future goods resolves itself, in the last analysis, into a preference for early enjoyment income over deferred enjoyment income. This simple proposition would have received definite attention earlier in the history of economics had there been at hand a clear-cut concept of income. The stream of future enjoyment income plays the essential rôle.

But, as explained in Chapter I, for practical purposes we may well stop at the objective services of wealth, as measured by its cost—the cost of living—that is, the money values of nourishment, clothing, shelter, amusements, the gratifications of vanity, and the other miscellaneous items in our family budget. It is the money value of this income stream upon which attention now centers. Henceforth, we may think of time preference as the preference for a dollar's worth of early *real income* over a dollar's worth of deferred *real income*. It is assumed, then, that the income goods are reduced to a common money denominator, and that the prices of all items of real income—the prices of nourishment, shelter, clothing, amusements, etc.—are predetermined.

In these cases, as already noted, no appreciable time elapses between valuation and realization. We pay for a basket of fruit and eat it forthwith. But we pay for a fruit tree and wait years for the fruit. So in the prices of many other enjoyable services—nourishment, shelter, etc.—no discount element, or rate of interest, enters or, at any rate, it does not enter in the direct way in which it enters in case of interactions.[4] That is, in the present,

___

[4] It is true, of course, that, in determining economic equilibrium, every variable theoretically affects every other, and the rate of interest, as

the price of present real income contains no appreciable interest to complicate the problem because these goods are consumed so soon after purchase; and for the same reason in the future price of future real income there is no appreciable interest element. When, however, any goods *other* than enjoyable goods are considered, their values already contain a rate of interest. The price of a house is the discounted value of its future income. Hence, when we compare the values of present and future houses, *both* terms of the comparison already involve a rate of interest. Although, as will be noted more specifically later, such a complication would not necessarily beg the question, its elimination simplifies the picture.

§3. *Impatience Depends on Income*

Time preference, a concept which psychologically underlies interest, lends itself to express any situation, either preference for present as against future goods or preference for future as against present goods or for no preference. The term impatience carries with it the presumption that present goods are preferred. But I shall treat the two terms (impatience and time preference) as synonymous. Henceforth the term impatience will be the one chiefly used partly because its meaning is more self-evident, partly because it is shorter, and partly because it does carry a presumption as to the *usual* direction of the time preference. The degree of impatience varies, of course, with the individual, but when we have selected our individual, the degree of his impatience depends on his entire income stream, beginning at the present instant and stretching indefinitely into the future; that is,

one variable, must therefore be assumed to affect indirectly the price of everything else by affecting its supply and demand.

on the amount of his expected real income and the manner in which it is expected to be distributed in time. It depends in particular on the relative abundance of the early as compared with the remote income items—or what we shall call the *time shape* of the expected income stream. If income is particularly abundant in the future; that is, if the person expects an increase in his income stream, he would willingly promise to sacrifice out of that increase, when it comes, a relatively large sum for the sake of receiving a relatively small sum at once. Thus the possessor of a strawberry patch might, in winter, be willing to exchange two boxes of strawberries, due in six months, for one available today. On the other hand, if immediate income is abundant but future income scarce, the opposite relation may exist. In strawberry season, the same man might willingly give up two boxes of his then abundant crop for the right to only one box in the succeeding winter. That is, time preference may not always be a preference for present over future goods; it may, under certain conditions, be the opposite. Impatience may be and sometimes is negative!

It is, therefore, not necessary in beginning our study of interest to distinguish, as many writers do, between the principles which lead to the *existence* of interest and those which regulate the *rate* of interest. By the existence of interest these writers mean that the rate is greater than zero. It seems preferable to reverse the order of the two problems and seek first to find the principles which fix the terms on which present and future goods exchange, without restricting ourselves in advance to the thesis that, always and necessarily, present goods command a premium over future goods. If our principles permit the deviations from par to be in either direction, this will mean that the rate of interest may under certain circumstances be zero (i.e., non-existent), or even negative, so that, in such a case, future goods would command a premium over present. After these general principles have been established a special study will then be in order to discover why the rate of interest is, in actual experience, almost never zero or negative.

We noted, in Chapter II, that when gold, or any other durable commodity capable of being stored or kept without cost, is the standard of comparison, the rate of interest in terms of that standard cannot fall below zero. Does the reason why interest is, in general experience, positive rather than negative lie entirely in human nature? Or does it lie partly in the income stream? These special questions can best be answered after we have found the general principles by which the rate of interest, be it positive, negative, or zero, is determined.

4. *Interest and Price Theory*

The preference of any individual for early over deferred income depends upon his present as compared with his prospective income and corresponds to the ordinary theory of prices, which recognizes that the marginal want for any article depends upon the quantity of that article available. Both propositions are fundamental in their respective spheres.

The relationship of these problems, and others, may be schematized roughly as shown in Chart 4 which follows.

In this chart A and B represent present prices of enjoyable goods, and A' and B' prices of future enjoyable goods. A and A' refer to different years in the same place, say New York; B and B' are similar except that they relate to a different place, say London.

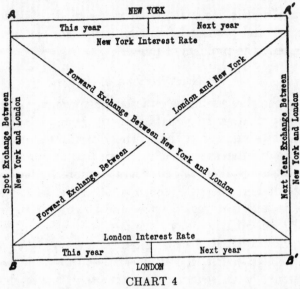

CHART 4

Interest Rates Between Different Years Comparable With Exchange Rates Between Different places.

All problems of local prices, exchange, and interest, act and react on each other in many ways. The problem of "time" foreign exchange, or forward foreign exchange, is indicated by the diagonals, and involves both interest and foreign exchange, i.e., both a time to time factor and a place to place factor combined in the same transaction. Both exchange and interest rates, as well as local prices, would be, theoretically, combined if, say, present New York wheat were quoted in terms of future London coal.

In this book, for simplicity, the problems of price determinations, in one place and at one time, are supposed to have been solved.[5] We start with the values of the

[5] For a statement of the theory of valuation in general, see Walras, *Éléments d'Économie Politique Pure*; Pareto, *Cours d'Économie Politique*; also, *Manuel d'Économie Politique*.

items in the income stream ready made. Likewise we neglect the problem of foreign exchange; we are studying only the problem of interest.

§5. *Specifications of Income*

In the above schematic picture only two periods of time are represented. In actual life there are many periods—an indefinite number of them. Theoretically there might be a rate of interest connecting every pair of possible dates. For instance, there might be a rate of interest between the present and one year hence, another between one year hence and two years hence, and so on, all these rates being quotable in today's markets. In practice no rates are actually quoted except those connecting the present (which, of course, merely means a future date *near* the present) with several more remotely future dates. A rate on a five year contract may be considered as a sort of an average of five theoretically existing rates, one for each of the five years covered.

Except when the contrary is specifically mentioned, it will henceforth be understood, for the sake of simplicity, that there is only one rate of interest, *the* rate of interest, applicable to all time intervals. This may be most conveniently pictured to mean the rate connecting today with one year hence. Even this rate of interest connecting two specific dates separated by one year depends on (or, in technical terminology, is a function of) conditions not only at these two dates but at many other dates. When it is said that the impatience of an individual depends on his future income stream, it is meant that the degree of his impatience for, say, $100 worth of this year's income over $100 worth of next year's income depends upon the entire character of his expected income stream pictured as beginning today and extending into the indefinite future, with specific increases or decreases at different periods of time.

If we wish to be still more meticulous, we may note that a person's income stream is made up of a large number of different elements, filaments, strands, or fibers, some of which represent nourishment, others shelter, others amusement, and so on—all the components of real income. In a complete enumeration of these elements, we should need to distinguish the use of each different kind of food, and the gratification of every other variety of human want. Each of these constitutes a particular thread of the income stream, extending out from the present into the indefinite future, and varying at different points of time in respect to size and probability of attainment. A person's time preference, or impatience for income, therefore, depends theoretically on the size, time shape, and probability (as looked at in the present) of this entire collection of income elements as we may picture them stretching out into the entire future.

In summary, we may say then that an individual's impatience depends on the following four characteristics of his income stream:

1. The *size* (measured in dollars) of his expected real income stream.

2. *Its expected distribution in time,* or its *time shape* —that is, whether it is constant, or increasing, or decreasing, or sometimes one and sometimes the other.

3. *Its composition*—to what extent it consists of nourishment, of shelter, of amusement, of education, and so on.

4. *Its probability,* or degree of risk or uncertainty.

We shall consider these four in order.

§6. *The Influence of Mere Size*

Our first step, then, is to show how a person's impatience depends on the *size* of his income, assuming the other three conditions to remain constant; for, evidently, it is possible that two incomes may have the same time shape, composition and risk, and yet differ in size, one being, say, twice the other in every period of time.

In general, it may be said that, other things being equal, the smaller the income, the higher the preference for present over future income; that is, the greater the impatience to acquire income as early as possible. It is true, of course, that a permanently small income implies a keen appreciation of future wants as well as of immediate wants. Poverty bears down heavily on all portions of a man's expected life. But it increases the want for immediate income *even more* than it increases the want for future income.

This influence of poverty is partly rational, because of the importance, by supplying present needs, of keeping up the continuity of life and thus maintaining the ability to cope with the future; and partly irrational, because the pressure of present needs blinds a person to the needs of the future.

As to the rational aspect, present income is absolutely indispensable, not only for present needs, but even as a pre-condition to the attainment of future income. *A man must live.* Any one who values his life would, under ordinary circumstances, prefer to rob the future for the benefit of the present—so far, at least, as to keep life going. If a person has only one loaf of bread he would not set it aside for next year even if the rate of interest were 1000 per cent; for if he did so, he would starve in the meantime. A single break in the thread of life suffices to cut off all the future. We stress the importance of the present because the present is the gateway to the future. Not only is a certain minimum of present income necessary to prevent starvation, but the nearer this minimum is approached the more precious does present income appear relative to future income.

As to the irrational aspect of the matter, the effect of poverty is often to relax foresight and self-control and to tempt us to "trust to luck" for the future, if only the all-engrossing need of present necessities can be satisfied.

We see, then, that a small income, other things being equal, tends to produce a high rate of impatience, partly from the thought that provision for the present is necessary both for the present itself and for the future as well, and partly from lack of foresight and self-control.

§7. *The Influence of Time Shape*

The concept of time shape of the income stream [6] is best treated not apart from size but as combined with size and thus will constitute a complete specification of the size at each successive period of time. Types of income of different time shapes are shown on the charts in Chapter I. Uniform income is represented in Chart 1; increasing income in Chart 2; decreasing income in Chart 3. Fluctuating income is represented in both Charts 2 and 3.

The fact that a person's income is increasing tends to make his preference for present over future income high, as compared with what it would be if his income were flowing uniformly or at a slackening rate; for an increasing income means that the present income is relatively

[6] Cf. Landry, *L'Intérêt du Capital,* Chapter X, § 149, pp. 311-315; §150, pp. 315-317.

scarce and future income relatively abundant. A man who is now enjoying an income of only $5000 a year, but who expects in ten years to be enjoying one of $10,000 a year, will today prize a dollar in hand far more than the prospect of a dollar due ten years hence. His great expectations make him impatient to realize on them in advance. He may, in fact, borrow money to eke out this year's income and promise repayments out of his supposedly more abundant income ten years later. On the other hand, a progressively dwindling income, one such that present income is relatively abundant and future income relatively scarce, tends to appease impatience—i.e., to reduce the want for present as compared with that for future income. A man who has a salary of $10,000 at present but expects to retire in a few years on half pay will not have a very high rate of preference for present over future income. He may even want to save from his present abundance in order to provide for coming needs.

These are, of course, only some of the various effects which various time shapes have on time preference. The important point is that it does make a difference to a man's time preference whether his income has one time shape or another, just as it makes a difference whether his income is, as a whole, larger or smaller.

The extent of these effects will, of course, vary greatly with different individuals. If two persons both have exactly the same sort of ascending income, one may have a rate of time preference, or degree of impatience, indicated by 10 per cent, while the other may have one of only 4 per cent. What we need to emphasize here is merely that, if for either man a descending income were substituted for an ascending income, he would experience a reduction of impatience; the first individual's might fall from 10 to 7 per cent, and the second's from, say, 4 to 3 per cent.

If, now, we consider the combined effect on time preference of both the *size* and the *time shape* of income, we shall observe that those with small incomes are much more sensitive to time shape in their feeling of impatience than are those with larger incomes. For a poor man, a *very slight* stinting of the present suffices to enhance enormously his impatience for present income; and oppositely, a *very slight* increase in his present income will suffice enormously to diminish that impatience. A rich man, on the other hand, presumably requires a relatively large variation in the comparative amounts of this year's and next year's income in order to suffer any material change in his time preference.

It will be clear to readers of Böhm-Bawerk that the dependence of time preference on the time shape of a person's income stream is practically identical with what he called the "first circumstance" making for the superiority of present over future goods:

"The first great cause of difference in value between present and future goods consists in the different circumstances of want and provision in present and future. . . . If a person is badly in want of certain goods, or of goods in general, while he has reason to hope that at a future period he will be better off, he will always value a given quantity of immediately available goods at a higher figure than the same quantity of future goods." [7]

The only important difference between this statement and that here formulated is that in this book the "provision" has the definite meaning contained in the *income* concept.

It is only for completeness that I have included in the

[7] Böhm-Bawerk, *The Positive Theory of Capital*, p. 249.

list of characteristics of income affecting interest the composition of the income. It recognizes the fact that, strictly speaking, a man's real income is not one simple homogeneous flow of money, but a mosaic or skein of threads of many heterogeneous elements of psychic experience. An income of $5000 may comprise for one individual one set of enjoyable services, and for another, an entirely different set. The inhabitants of one country may have relatively more house shelter and less food in their real incomes than those of another. Those differences will have, theoretically, an influence in one direction or the other upon the time preference. Food being a prime necessity, a decrease of the proportion of food, or nourishment, even though total income remain the same, will have an effect upon the impatience similar to the effect of the diminution of total income.

For practical purposes, however, we may ordinarily neglect the characteristic of income called composition; for ordinarily any variation in the mere composition of family budgets will very seldom be sufficient to have any appreciable effect on the rate of interest.

Hereafter, therefore, all the elements of income will be considered as lumped together in a single sum of money value. Our picture of income henceforth may be considered as a flag or pennant without regard to stripes but seen as a whole, stretching out into the future. Each man's pennant has a definite width varying with the distance from the flagstaff.

§8. *The Influence of Risk*

We come finally to the element of risk. Future income is always subject to some uncertainty, and this uncertainty must naturally have an influence on the rate of time preference, or degree of impatience, of its possessor. It is to be remembered that the degree of impatience is the percentage preference for *$1 certain* of immediate income, over *$1, also certain,* of income of one year hence, *even if all the income except that dollar be uncertain.* The influence of risk on time preference, therefore, means the influence of uncertainties in the anticipated income of an individual upon his relative valuation of present and future increments of income, both increments being *certain.*

The manner in which risk operates upon time preference will differ, among other things, according to the particular periods in the future to which the risk applies. If, as is very common, the possessor of income regards his immediately future income as fairly well assured, but fears for the safety or certainty of his income in a more remote period, he may be aroused to a high appreciation of the needs of that remote future and hence may feel forced to save out of his present relatively *certain* abundance in order to supplement his relatively *uncertain* income later on. He is likely to have a low degree of impatience for a *certain* dollar of immediate income as compared with a *certain* dollar added to a remoter uncertain income.

Such a type of income is, in fact, not uncommon. The remote future is usually less known than the immediate future, a fact which of itself means risk or uncertainty. The chance of disease, accident, disability, or death is always to be reckoned with; but under ordinary circumstances this risk is greater in the remote future than in the immediate future. As a result, uncertainty has a tendency to keep impatience down. This tendency is expressed in the phrase "to lay up for a rainy day." The greater the risk of rainy days in the future, the greater the impulse to provide for them at the expense of the present.

But sometimes the relative uncertainty is reversed, and immediate income is subject to higher risk than remote income. Such is the case in the midst of a war, in a strike, or other misfortune, believed to be temporary. Such is also the case when an individual is assured a permanent position with a salary after a certain date, but, in the meantime, must obtain a precarious subsistence. In these cases the effect of the risk element is to enhance the estimation in which immediate income is held.

Again, the risk, instead of applying especially to remote periods of time or especially to immediate periods, may apply to all periods alike. Such a general risk largely explains why salaries and wages, being relatively assured, are generally lower than the average earnings of those who take the risks incident to being their own employers. It also explains why the bondholder is content with a lower average return than the stockholder. The bondholder chooses fixed and certain income rather than a variable and uncertain one, even if the latter is, on the average, larger. In short, a risky income, if the risk applies evenly to all parts of the income stream, is equivalent to a low income. And, since a low income, as we have seen, tends to create a high impatience, risk, if distributed in time, uniformly or fairly so, tends to raise impatience.

It follows, then, that risk tends in some cases to increase and in others to decrease impatience, according to the time incidence of the risk. But there is a common principle in all these cases. Whether the result is a high or a low time preference, the primary fact is that the risk of losing the income in a particular period of time operates, in the eyes of most people, as a virtual impoverishment of the income in that period, and hence increases the estimation in which a unit of certain income in that particular period is held. If that period is a remote one, the risk to which it is subject makes for a high regard for remote income; if it is the present (immediate future), the risk makes for a high regard for immediate income; if the risk applies to all periods of time alike, it acts as a virtual decrease of income all along the line.

There are, however, exceptional individuals of the gambler type in whom caution is absent or perverted. Upon these, risk will have quite the opposite effects. Some persons who like to take great speculative chances are likely to treat the future as though it were especially well endowed, and are willing to sacrifice a large amount of their exaggerated expectations for the sake of a relatively small addition to their present income. In other words, they will have a high degree of impatience. The same individuals, if receiving an income which is risky for all periods of time alike, might, contrary to the rule, have, as a result, a low instead of a high degree of impatience.

The income to which risk applies may be, of course, either the income from articles of capital external to man or the income from man himself, considered as an income producer. In the latter case, often called earned income, the risk of losing the income is the risk of death or invalidism. This risk—the uncertainty as to human life, health and income producing power—is somewhat different from the uncertainty of income flowing from objective capital: for the cessation of life not only causes a cessation of the income produced by the dying human machine, but also a cessation of the enjoyment of all income whatsoever—or rather a transfer of the enjoyment to posterity of any income continuing after death. This is because the individual is in the double capacity of being at once a producer and a consumer.

The effect of risk, therefore, is manifold, according to the degree and range of application of risk to various periods of times. It also depends on whether or not the risk relates to the continuation of life; and if so, according to whether or not the individual's interest in the future extends beyond his own lifetime. The manner in which these various tendencies operate upon the rate of interest will be discussed in Chapter IX.

§9. *The Personal Factor*

The proposition that, in the theory of interest, the impatience of a person for income depends upon the character of his income—as to its size, time shape, and probability—does not deny that it may depend on other factors also, just as, in the theory of prices, the proposition that the marginal want for an article depends upon the quantity of that article does not deny that it may depend on other elements as well.

But the dependence of impatience on income is of chief importance; for impatience, whatever else it *depends* on, is always impatience *for* income—exactly as the dependence of the marginal want for bread on the quantity of *bread* is more important than the dependence of this marginal want for bread on the quantity of some other commodity, such as butter.[8]

We have seen, therefore, how a given man's impatience

[8] For a theoretical discussion of marginal want as a function of various factors, see my *Mathematical Investigations in the Theory of Value and Prices*. For a mathematical formulation of impatience as a function of successive installments of income, see Appendix to this chapter, §7. See also Pareto, *Manuel d'Économie Politique*, p. 546 *et seq*.

depends both upon the characteristics of his expected income stream, and on his own personal characteristics. The rate of impatience which corresponds to a specific income stream will not be the same for everybody. This has already been noted, incidentally, but requires special discussion here. One man may have an annual rate of time preference of 6 per cent, and another 10 per cent, although both have the same income. Impatience differs with different persons for the same income and with different incomes for the same person. The personal differences are caused by differences in at least six personal characteristics [9]: (1) foresight, (2) self-control, (3) habit, (4) expectation of life, (5) concern for the lives of other persons, (6) fashion.

(1) Generally speaking, the greater the foresight, the less the impatience, and *vice versa*.[10] In the case of primitive races, children, and other uninstructed groups in society, the future is seldom considered in its true proportions. This is illustrated by the story of the farmer

[9] Cf. Rae, *Sociological Theory of Capital*, p. 54; Böhm-Bawerk, *The Positive Theory of Capital*, Book V, Chapter III.

[10] To be exact, however, we should observe that lack of foresight may either increase or decrease time preference. Although most persons who lack foresight err by failing to give due weight to the importance of future needs, or, what amounts to the same thing, by estimating overconfidently the provision existing for such future needs, cases are to be found in which the opposite error is committed; that is, the individual exaggerates the needs of the future or underestimates the provision likely to be available for them. Such people stint themselves needlessly, even impairing health by insufficient food in their efforts to save for the dreaded future. Their lack of foresight in this case errs in underestimating instead of overestimating future income and so makes them too patient instead of too impatient. But in order not to complicate the text, only the former and more common error will be hereafter referred to when lack of foresight is mentioned. The reader may, in each such case, readily add the possibility of the contrary error.

who would never mend his leaky roof. When it rained he could not stop the leak, and when it did not rain there was no leak to be stopped! Among such persons, the preference for present gratification is powerful because their anticipation of the future is *weak*. In regard to foresight, Rae states: [11]

"The actual presence of the immediate object of desire in the mind, by exciting the attention, seems to rouse all the faculties, as it were, to fix their view on it, and leads them to a very lively conception of the enjoyments which it offers to their instant possession. The prospects of a future good, which future years may hold out to us, seem at such a moment dull and dubious, and are apt to be slighted, for objects on which the daylight is falling strongly, and showing us in all their freshness just within our grasp. There is no man, perhaps, to whom a good to be enjoyed to-day, would not seem of very different importance, from one exactly similar to be enjoyed twelve years hence, even though the arrival of both were equally certain."

The sagacious business man represents the other extreme; he is constantly forecasting. Many great corporations, banks, and investment trusts today maintain statistical departments largely for the purpose of gauging the future developments of business. The carefully calculated forecasts made by these and independent services tend to reduce the element of risk, and to aid intelligent speculation.

Differences in degrees of foresight and forecasting ability produce corresponding differences in the dependence of time preference on the character of income. Thus, for a given income, say $5000 a year indefinitely, the reckless might have a degree of impatience or rate of time preference of 10 per cent, when the forehanded would experience a preference of only 5 per cent. In both cases,

[11] Rae, *Sociological Theory of Capital*, p. 54.

the preference depends on the size, time shape, and risk of the income; but the particular rates corresponding to a particular income will be entirely different in the two cases. Therefore, the degree of impatience, in general, will tend to be higher in a community consisting of reckless individuals than in one consisting of the opposite type.

(2) Self-control, though distinct from foresight, is usually associated with it and has very similar effects. Foresight has to do with *thinking;* self-control, with *willing.* Though a weak will usually goes with a weak intellect, this is not necessarily so, nor always. The effect of a weak will is similar to the effect of inferior foresight. Like those workingmen who, before prohibition, could not resist the lure of the saloon on the way home Saturday night, many persons cannot deny themselves a present indulgence, even when they know what the consequences will be. Others, on the contrary, have no difficulty in stinting themselves in the face of all temptations.

(3) The third characteristic of human nature which needs to be considered is the tendency to follow grooves of habit. The influence of habit may be in either direction. Rich men's sons, accustomed to the enjoyment of a large income, are likely to put a higher valuation on present compared with future income than would persons possessing the same income but brought up under different conditions. When those habituated to luxury suffer a reverse of fortune they often find it harder to live moderately than do those of equal means who have risen instead of fallen in the economic scale; and this will be true even if foresight and self-control are inherently the same in the two cases. The former, brought up in the lap of luxury, will be more likely to be the prodigal son,

that is, the more impatient for present income. The lack of such traditions among the Negroes tends toward a high rate of impatience, while the traditions of thrift among the Scotch curb impatience.

Our thrift campaigns are designed to reduce impatience by cultivating certain habits of regular saving out of income. So also is the propaganda for life insurance with its high-pressure salesmanship. On the other hand, the corresponding salesmanship for installment buying tends, in the first instance, in the opposite direction. The individual can indulge himself in the immediate enjoyment of a radio or an auto. Yet, it must not be overlooked that, after the sale is made, there ensues a new responsibility to provide for the future payments agreed upon which may permanently improve the faculties of foresight and self-control.

(4) The fourth personal circumstance which may influence impatience for immediate real income has to do with the uncertainty of life of the recipient. We have already seen, in a somewhat different connection, that the time preference of an individual will be affected by the prospect of a long or short life, both because the termination of life brings the termination of the income from labor, and because it also terminates the person's enjoyment of all income.

It is the latter fact in which we are interested here—the manner in which the expectation of life of a person affects the dependence of impatience on his income. There will be differences among different classes, different individuals, and different ages of the same individual. The chance of death may be said to be the most important *rational* factor tending to increase impatience; anything that would tend to prolong human life would tend, at the same time, to reduce impatience. Rae goes so far as to say: [12]

"Were life to endure forever, were the capacity to enjoy in perfection all its goods, both mental and corporeal, to be prolonged with it, and were we guided solely by the dictates of reason, there could be no limit to the formation of means for future gratification, till our utmost wishes were supplied. A pleasure to be enjoyed, or a pain to be endured, fifty or a hundred years hence, would be considered deserving the same attention as if it were to befall us fifty or a hundred minutes hence, and the sacrifice of a smaller present good, for a greater future good, would be readily made, to whatever period that futurity might extend. But life, and the power to enjoy it, are the most uncertain of all things, and we are not guided altogether by reason. We know not the period when death may come upon us, but we know that it may come in a few days, and must come in a few years. Why then be providing goods that cannot be enjoyed until times, which, though not very remote, may never come to us, or until times still more remote, and which we are convinced we shall never see? If life, too, is of uncertain duration and the time that death comes between us and all our possessions unknown, the approaches of old age are at least certain, and are dulling, day by day, the relish of every pleasure."

The shortness of life thus tends powerfully to increase the degree of impatience, or rate of time preference, beyond what it would otherwise be. This is especially evident when the income streams compared are long. A lover of music will be impatient for a piano, i.e., will prefer a piano at once to a piano available next year, because, since either will outlast his own life, he will get one more year's use out of a piano available at once.

(5) But whereas the shortness and uncertainty of life tend to increase impatience, their effect is greatly mitigated by the fifth circumstance, solicitude for the welfare of one's heirs. Probably the most powerful cause tending

[12] Rae, *The Sociological Theory of Capital,* pp. 53-54.

to reduce the rate of interest is the love of one's children and the desire to provide for their good. Wherever these sentiments decay, as they did at the time of the decline and fall of the Roman Empire, and it becomes the fashion to exhaust wealth in self-indulgence and leave little or nothing to offspring, impatience and the rate of interest will tend to be high. At such times the motto, "After us the deluge," indicates the feverish desire to squander in the present, at whatever cost to the future.[13]

On the other hand, in a country like the United States, where parents regard their lives as continuing after death in the lives of their children, there exists a high appreciation of the needs of the future. This tends to produce a low degree of impatience. For persons with children, the prospect of loss of earnings through death only spurs them all the more to lay up for that rainy day in the family. For them the risk of loss of income through death is not very different from the risk of cessation of income from any ordinary investment; in such a case the risk of cessation of future income through death tends to lower their impatience for income. This act supplies the motive for life insurance. A man with a wife and children is willing to pay a high insurance premium in order that they may continue to enjoy an income after his death. This is partly responsible for the enormous extension of life insurance. At present in the United States the insurance on lives amounts to over $100,000,000,000. This represents, for the most part, an investment of the present generation for the next.

An unmarried man, on the other hand, or a man who cares only for self-indulgence and does not care for pos-

[13] See Rae, *The Sociological Theory of Capital*, p. 97.

terity, a man, in short, who wishes to "make the day and the journey alike," will not try thus to continue the income after his death. In such a case uncertainty of life is especially calculated to produce a high rate of time preference. Sailors, especially unmarried sailors, offer the classic example. They are natural spendthrifts, and when they have money use it lavishly. The risk of shipwreck is always before them, and their motto is, "A short life and a merry one." The same is even more true of the unmarried soldier. For such people the risk of cessation of life increases their impatience, since there is little future to be patient for.

Not only does regard for one's offspring lower impatience, but the increase of offspring has in part the same effect. So far as it adds to future needs rather than to immediate needs, it operates, like a descending income stream, to diminish impatience. Parents with growing families often feel the importance of providing for future years far more than parents in similar circumstances but with small families. They try harder to save and to take out life insurance; in other words, they are less impatient. Consequently, an increase of the average size of family would, other things being equal, reduce the rate of interest.

This proposition does not, of course, conflict with the converse proposition that the same prudent regard for the future which is created by the responsibilities of parenthood itself tends to diminish the number of offspring. Hence it is that the thrifty Frenchman and Dutchman have small families.

(6) The most fitful of the causes at work is probably fashion. This at the present time acts, on the one hand, to stimulate men to save and become millionaires, and

on the other hand, to stimulate millionaires to live in an ostentatious manner. Fashion is one of those potent yet illusory social forces which follow the laws of imitation so much emphasized by Tarde,[14] Le Bon,[15] Baldwin,[16] and other writers. In whatever direction the leaders of fashion first chance to move, the crowd will follow in mad pursuit until almost the whole social body will be moving in that direction. Sometimes the fashion becomes rigid, as in China, a fact emphasized by Bagehot;[17] and sometimes the effect of a too universal following is to stimulate the leaders to throw off their pursuers by taking some novel direction—which explains the constant vagaries of fashion in dress. Economic fashions may belong to either of these two groups—the fixed or the erratic. Examples of both are given by John Rae.[18] It is of vast importance to a community, in its influence both on the rate of interest and on the distribution of wealth itself, what direction fashion happens to take. For instance, should it become an established custom for millionaires to consider it "disgraceful to die rich," as Carnegie expressed it, and believe it *de rigueur* to give the bulk of their fortunes for endowing universities, libraries, hospitals, or other public institutions, the effect would be, through diffusion of benefits, to lessen the disparities in

[14] Tarde, G. *Social Laws*. English translation. New York, Macmillan and Co., 1899. Also *Les Louis de l'Imitation*. Paris, Germer Baillière et C., 1895.

[15] *The Psychology of Socialism*. English translation. London, T. Fisher Unwin, 1899. Also *The Crowd*.

[16] *Social and Ethical Interpretations in Mental Development*. New York, Macmillan and Co., 1906.

[17] Bagehot, Walter. *Physics and Politics*. New York, D. Appleton and Co., 1873, Chapter III.

[18] See *The Sociological Theory of Capital*, Appendix, Article 1, pp. 245-276.

the distribution of wealth, and also to lower the rate of interest.

§10. *The Personal Factor Summarized*

Impatience for income, therefore, depends for each individual on his income, on its size, time shape, and probability; but the particular *form* of this dependence differs according to the various characteristics of the individual. The characteristics which will tend to make his impatience great are: (1) short-sightedness, (2) a weak will, (3) the habit of spending freely, (4) emphasis upon the shortness and uncertainty of his life, (5) selfishness, or the absence of any desire to provide for his survivors, (6) slavish following of the whims of fashion. The reverse conditions will tend to lessen his impatience; namely, (1) a high degree of foresight, which enables him to give to the future such attention as it deserves; (2) a high degree of self-control, which enables him to abstain from present real income in order to increase future real income; (3) the habit of thrift; (4) emphasis upon the expectation of a long life; (5) the possession of a family and a high regard for their welfare after his death; (6) the independence to maintain a proper balance between outgo and income, regardless of Mrs. Grundy and the high-powered salesmen of devices that are useless or harmful, or which commit the purchaser beyond his income prospects.

The resultant of these various tendencies in any one individual will determine the degree of his impatience at a given time, under given conditions with a *particular income stream*. The result will differ as between individuals, and at different times for the same individual.

The same individual in the course of his life may

change from one extreme of impatience to the other. Such an alteration may be caused by a change in the person's nature (as when a spendthrift is reformed or a man, originally prudent, becomes, through intemperance, reckless and thriftless), or by variation in his income, whether in respect to size, distribution in time, or uncertainty. Everyone at some time in his life doubtless changes his degree of impatience for income. In the course of an ordinary lifetime the changes in a man's degree of impatience are probably of the following general character: as a child he will have a high degree of impatience because of his lack of foresight and self-control; when he reaches the age of young manhood he may still have a high degree of impatience, but for a different reason, namely, because he then expects a large future income. He expects to get on in the world, and he will have a high degree of impatience because of the relative abundance of the imagined future as compared with the realized present. When he gets a little further along, and has a family, the result may be a low degree of impatience, because then the needs of the future rather than its endowment will appeal to him. He will not think that he is going to be so very rich; on the contrary, he will wonder how he is going to get along with so many mouths to feed. He looks forward to the future expenses of his wife and children with the idea of providing for them—an idea which makes for a high relative regard for the future and a low relative regard for the present. Then when he gets a little older, if his children are married and have gone out into the world and are well able to take care of themselves, he may again have a high degree of impatience for income, because he expects to die, and he thinks, "Instead of piling up for the remote future, why shouldn't I enjoy myself during the few years that remain?"

§11. *Income Rather Than Capital in the Leading Rôle*

The essential fact, however, is that *for any given individual at any given time,* his impatience depends in a definite manner upon the size, time shape, and probability of his income stream.

This view, that the degree of impatience and, consequently, the rate of interest depend upon *income,* needs to be contrasted with the common view, which makes the rate of interest depend merely on the scarcity or abundance of *capital.* It is commonly believed that where capital is scarce, interest is high, and where capital is plentiful, interest is low. In a general way, there is undoubtedly some truth in this belief; and yet it contains a misinterpretation of borrowing and lending.

In the first place, we must distinguish between capital wealth and capital value. It is capital value of which most people think when they say capital. But capital value is merely capitalized income. Behind, or rather beyond, a capital of $100,000 is the stream of income which that capital represents, or rather the choice of any one among many possible streams. To fix attention on the $100,000 capital instead of on the income which is capitalized is to use the capital as a cloak to cover up the real factor in the case.

Moreover, capital value is itself dependent on a pre-existing rate of interest. As we know, the capital value of a farm will be doubled if the rate of interest is halved. In such a case there would seem to be more capital in farms than before; for the farms in a community would rise, say, from $100,000,000 to $200,000,000. But it is not the rise in capital value which produces this fall in interest. On the contrary, it is the fall in the interest rate which produces the rise in the capital. If we attempt to make the rate of interest depend on capital value, then, since capital value depends on two factors—the prospective income *and the rate of interest*—we thereby make the interest rate depend partly on income and partly on itself. The dependence on itself is of course nugatory, and we are brought back to its dependence on *income* as the only fact of real significance. It is present and future income that are traded against each other.

But, even as thus amended and explained, (that capital stands for income) the proposition that the rate of interest depends on the amount of capital is not satisfactory. For the mere amount of capital does not tell us enough about the income for which the capital stands. To know that one man has a capital worth $10,000,000 and another has a capital worth $20,000,000 shows, to be sure, that the latter man can have an income of double the value of the former; but it tells us absolutely nothing as to the time shapes of the two incomes actually selected; and the time shape of income has, as we have seen, a most profound influence on the time preference of its possessor, and time preference is a prime determiner of interest.

To illustrate this important fact, let us suppose that two communities differ in the amount of capital and the character of the income which that capital represents but, as far as possible, are similar in all other respects. One of these two communities we shall suppose has a capital of $100,000,000, invested, as in Nevada, in mines and quarries nearly exhausted, while in the other community there is $200,000,000 of capital invested in young orchards and forests, as in Florida. According to the theory that abundance of capital makes interest low, we should expect the Nevada community to have a high rate of interest compared with the Florida community. This would ordinarily be true if the two communities had income streams differing only in size with the same time shapes and probabilities. But, under our assumptions, it is evident that, unless other circumstances should interfere, the opposite would be the case; for Nevada, due to the progressive exhaustion of her mines, is faced by a decreasing future income, and in order to offset the depreciation of capital which follows from this condition,[19] she would be seeking to lend or invest part of the income of the present or immediate future, in the hope of offsetting the decreased product of the mines in the more remote future. The Florida planters, on the contrary, would be inclined to borrow against their future crops. If the two communities are supposed to be commercially connected, it would be Nevada which would lend to Florida notwithstanding the fact that the lending community was the poorer in capital of the two. From this illustration it is clear that the mere amount of capital value is not only a misleading but a very inadequate criterion of the rate of interest.[20]

Apologists for the common idea that abundance or scarcity of capital lowers or raises interest might be inclined to argue that it is not the total capital, but only the loanable capital which should be included, and that the Nevada community had more loanable capital than the Florida community. But the phrase loanable capital is merely another cloak to cover the fact that it is not the

[19] See *The Nature of Capital and Income,* Chapter XIV.

[20] One of the few defects in Rae's analysis of interest, or at any rate of his statement of it, is his emphasis on the accumulation of capital. Since this accumulation is merely in anticipation of future income, the emphasis belongs on the latter.

amount of capital, but the decision to lend or borrow it, (or the income stream which the capital stands for) which is important.

We end, therefore, by emphasizing again the importance of fixing our eyes on income and not on capital. It is only as we look through capital value at the income beyond that we reach the effective causes which operate upon the rate of interest. It has, perhaps, been the absence of a definite theory and conception of income which has so long prevented economists from seeing these relations. Borrowing and lending are in form a transfer of capital, but they are in fact a transfer of income of which that capital is merely the present value. In our theory of interest, therefore, we have to consider not primarily the *amount* of capital of a community, but the future expected income for which that capital stands.

§12. *Impatience Schedules*

Unfortunately for purposes of exposition, the relation between impatience and income cannot be expressed in a simple schedule or a simple curve, as can the relation between demand and price, or supply and price, or marginal want and quantity consumed, for the reason that income means not a single magnitude merely, but a conglomeration of magnitudes. As mathematicians would express it, to state that income impatience depends on the character of income, its size, shape, and probability is to state that this impatience is a function of all the different magnitudes which need to be specified in a complete description of that income. A geometrical representation, therefore, of the dependence of time preference on the various magnitudes which characterize income would be impossible. For a curve can be in two dimensions only and hence can represent the dependence of a magnitude on only *one* independent variable. Even a surface can only represent dependence on *two*. But for our requirement, i.e., in order to represent the dependence of a man's impatience on the infinite number of successive elements constituting his income stream, we should need not two or three dimensions simply but a space of *n* dimensions.

We may represent, however, the relation between time preference and income by a schedule like the ordinary demand schedule and supply schedule, if we make a list of income streams of all possible sizes, shapes, and probabilities, specifying for each individual income all its characteristics—its size, time shape (that is, its relative magnitude in successive time intervals), and the certainty or uncertainty of its various parts, to say nothing of its heterogeneous and varying composition. Having thus compiled a list of all possible income streams, it would only be necessary for us to assign to each of them the rate of impatience pertaining to it.

Such a schedule would be too complicated and cumbersome to be carried out in detail; but the following will roughly indicate some of the main groups of which it would consist. In this schedule I have represented, by the three horizontal lines, three different classes of income —two extreme types and one mean type—so that the corresponding rates of time preference range themselves in a descending series of numbers. The three vertical columns show three different classes of individuals, two being of extreme types, and the third of a mixed or medium type. Thus, the numbers in the table grow smaller as we proceed toward the right and as we proceed downward, the smallest numbers of all being the lower right-hand corner. This represents a man whose rate of impatience is only 1 per cent, being low both because his *income* is large, decreasing and assured, and because his *nature* is farsighted, self-controlled, accustomed to save, and desirous to provide for heirs.

TABLE 1

	TIME-PREFERENCE OF DIFFERENT INDIVIDUALS WITH DIFFERENT INCOMES Individuals who are		
	shortsighted, weak willed, accustomed to spend, without heirs	of a mixed or medium type	farsighted, self-controlled, accustomed to save, desirous to provide for heirs
Income small, increasing, precarious	20%	10%	5%
Income of a mixed or medium type	10%	5%	2%
Income large, decreasing, assured	5%	2%	1%

This schematic representation is, in the effort to be general, rather vague. We may be more specific if, instead of thinking of a man's income stream as uncertain and variable at every point, we think of it, for the moment, as certain throughout and as invariable, or frozen, at all points of time except two—the present time and one year hence.

Restricted by this highly artificial hypothesis, we can construct for the man an impatience and demand schedule and demand and supply schedules for loans and interest analogous to the ordinary utility schedule and demand or supply schedule for commodities and prices.

Thus the demand schedule might be that a certain prospective borrower is willing, for each successive one hundred dollars added to his *present* income, to give, out of *next year's* income, as follows:

For the	first	$100, $120,	his impatience rate being, therefore,	20%
" "	second	$100, $115, "	" " " "	15%
" "	third	$100, $110, "	" " " "	10%
" "	fourth	$100, $106, "	" " " "	6%
" "	fifth	$100, $105, "	" " " "	5%
" "	sixth	$100, $104, "	" " " "	4%

Such a schedule is expressed geometrically in Chapters X and XI.

Since the time preference of an individual is a derivative of his marginal want for present and his marginal want for future income, the above schedule is likewise a sort of derivative of the ordinary want schedules (utility schedules) of present and future income. But the more general schedule previously given, not restricted to two years, but recognizing uncertainty and variability of the person's income stream at all its points, is more appropriate for our present purpose.

We see then that each individual has a rate of impatience dependent on his own personal nature and on the nature of his income. If all individuals' incomes were rigid, that is, incapable of being modified, and if there were no loan or money market by which immediate and future income could be exchanged, there could be no common market rate of interest. There would be a separate rate of time preference for each individual. One man would be willing to part with $100 today for the sake of $101 next year, while another would require $200 or $1000. But nothing would happen toward equalizing these divergent rates.

But given a loan market, the individuals toward the end of the list will tend to borrow; and those toward the beginning will tend to lend. The effect of such operations is to reduce the high rates of time preference and to increase the low ones until a middle ground is reached in the common rate of interest. This process will be discussed in the following chapter.

CHAPTER V

FIRST APPROXIMATION TO THE THEORY OF INTEREST

Assuming Each Person's Income Stream Foreknown and Unchangeable Except by Loans

§1. *Hypotheses of First Approximation*

IN the last chapter we reached three conclusions:

(1) that the rate of time preference, or impatience for present over future goods, is, in the last analysis, a preference for present over future enjoyment income, or, let us say, real income;

(2) that the degree of impatience depends, for any given individual, upon the character of his real income-stream—in particular, on its size, time shape, and probability;

(3) that the nature of this dependence differs with different individuals.

The question at once arises: will not the actual degrees of impatience of different individuals necessarily be very different, and if so, what relation do these different rates have to the market rate of interest? Is the market rate of interest a sort of average of these individual degrees of impatience, or does it equalize them?

It is doubtless true that the different rates of impatience of different individuals who are not connected through a common loan market do vary widely. In a nation of hermits, in which there existed no mutual lending and borrowing, individuals would be independent of each other. But, among ourselves who have access to a common loan market, borrowing and lending do, at least, tend to bring into equality the marginal rates of impatience in different minds. Absolute equality is not reached even among those making use of such a market; but this is because of the limitations of the market and, in particular, because of the risk element. This element will be considered in the third approximation, but for simplicity of exposition is omitted in the first two approximations.

Here we shall assume a *perfectly* competitive market, one in which each individual is so small a factor as to have, singly, no perceptible influence on the rate of interest, and in which there is no limitation on the amount of lending and borrowing other than that caused by the rate of interest itself. The would-be borrower is thus supposed to be able to obtain as large or small a loan as he wishes at the market price—the rate of interest. He is not cut down to $5,000 when he is willing to borrow $100,000, merely because he cannot furnish enough collateral security or a satisfactory endorser. He can buy a loan as he can buy sugar, as much or as little as he pleases, if he will pay the price.

In the actual world, of course, no such perfect market exists. While many people in New York City can obtain as large loans as they wish, there are thousands who are unable to obtain any at all. The price of a loan is paid not in the present, as the price of sugar is paid, but in the future. What the lender gets when he makes the loan is not payment but a promise of payment, and the future being always uncertain he needs some sort of assurance that this promise will be kept. We are assuming in the first and second approximations that there will never be a lack of such assurance. This amounts almost to assuming that there is no risk in the world. The element of risk is assumed to be entirely lacking, both with respect to the certainty of the expected income streams belonging to the different individuals, and with respect to the certainty of repayment for loans. In other words, we assume that each individual in the market is free to give up any part of his income during one period of time to some other person in consideration of receiving back an addition to his own income during another period of time.

We assume further that thus to buy and sell rights to various parts of his income stream is the only method open to any individual to alter his income stream. Such trading between present and future dollars may be in the form of loans, since a loan is the sale of future money for present money, or it may be in the guise of buying and selling bonds or other securities conveying title to fixed sums of money. In any case the trading reduces itself to buying and selling titles to future income. Prior to such exchange, the income stream of each individual is assumed to be fixed in size and shape. Each capital instrument which he possesses, including himself, is assumed to be capable of only a single definite series of services contributing to his income stream. Each individual is a stipendiary with a definite income which he receives and spends according to a foreknown schedule— so much next year, so much the year after, and so forth.

Thus the assumptions of our first approximation are: (1) that each man's income stream is initially *certain* and *fixed;* (2) that he is a negligible element in a vast and perfect competitive loan market; (3) that he has free access to this market, whether as borrower or lender, to any desired extent, at the market rate; (4) that his sole method of modifying his future income stream is through such borrowing or lending (or, more exactly and generally, through trading income).

§2. *Income Prescribed*

Such assumptions are, of course, highly theoretical. They imagine a world in which incomes are produced spontaneously, as mineral water gushes from the spring. They picture these income-bearing agents as pouring forth their income streams at rates which follow a fore-known, rigid, and unchangeable schedule. There being no flexibility in the flow from any one article, there is no flexibility in the scheme of combined flow from the whole group possessed by an individual. His total real income is scheduled in advance with no possibility of modification except by borrowing or lending, buying or selling.[1]

The abstract nature of this hypothesis need not greatly trouble us for two reasons: the first, and in itself quite sufficient reason, is that most of the elements of this hypothesis will be abandoned when we reach the second approximation. It is adopted temporarily merely for simplicity of exposition. Secondly, the hypothesis might easily be made more realistic without changing its essential features. We might even alter our hypothesis of a

[1] One consequence of this assumption (to secure which the assumption was really made) is that the capitalized value of each person's income at a given rate of interest will be unchangeable. He is, so to speak, on a definite allowance, and any trading, as by borrowing, or mortgaging the future, cannot make him richer or poorer. It can only shift his income in time (with interest). The theoretical significance of this constancy will appear in the second approximation.

rigidly prescribed income stream to the hypothesis of an income stream which, while it may be *decreased* at will, cannot be increased beyond a fixed amount at each period of time. While free to decrease his income in any period, its possessor would not do so unless thereby he could secure an increase in some other period.

Not only is such an hypothesis quite thinkable, it is probably actually approximated in primitive communities. In our own day most men have opportunities (quite apart from lending to others at interest) to secure much real income in future years by temporarily sacrificing a little immediate real income as, for instance, by investing labor in building a house or machine. But we can readily suppose a situation such that this year's production and next year's production would be almost independent of each other. This situation is true of most animals and even of man in the hunting and fishing stage, and before that stage even more markedly when his only implements were his hands. And even in our own civilization, many are mere stipendiaries, virtually without any opportunity to add to future income except by lending at interest.

The essence of the hypothesis therefore on which the first approximation rests is that we are not to be bothered by the possibility of a man's thus increasing his income in one period through decreasing it in another except through the process of trading some of one year's income with another person for some of another year's income.

We may in fact for practical purposes picture the income stream of each person as thus fixed for only a few years, and assume that expectation of income beyond those years so indefinite as to have no effect on the present rate of interest. Such a community has been approximated in former years by the typical American army camp isolated in a western community in which each inhabitant, or family, had a prescribed income. A series of such hypotheses will lead us through successive approximations to an eventual picture of actuality.

§3. *Equalization of Impatience*

Under the hypothetical conditions which have been stated for the first approximation, the rates of time preference for different individuals will, by the process of borrowing and lending, become perfectly reconciled to the market rate of interest and to each other, for if, for any particular individual, the rate of preference differs from the market rate, he will, if he can, adjust the time shape of his income stream so as to bring his marginal preference rate into harmony with the interest rate. A man who, for a given income stream, has a rate of preference above the market rate will sell some of his surplus future income in return for an addition to his meager present income, i.e., he will borrow. This will have the effect of enhancing his want for one more dollar of future income and decreasing his want for one more dollar of present income. The process will continue until the rate of preference of this individual, at the margin, is equal to the rate of interest. In other words, under our hypothesis, a person whose preference rate exceeds the current rate of interest will borrow up to the point at which the two rates will become equal.

On the other hand, the man, whose temperament or whose income stream or both give him a preference rate below the market rate, will buy future income with some of his abundant present income, i.e., he will lend. The effect will be to increase his preference rate until, at the margin, it harmonizes with the rate of interest.

To put the matter in figures, let us suppose the rate of interest is 5 per cent, whereas the rate of preference of a particular individual is, to start with, 10 per cent. Then, by hypothesis, the individual is *willing* to sacrifice $1.10 of next year's income in exchange for $1 of this year's. But, in the market, he finds he is *able* to obtain $1 for this year by foregoing only $1.05 of next year's. To him this latter ratio is a cheap price. He therefore borrows, say, $100 for a year, agreeing to return $105; that is, he contracts a loan at 5 per cent, when he is willing to pay 10 per cent. This operation partly satisfies his hunger for present income by drawing on his future income, and thus reduces his time preference from 10 per cent to, say, 8 per cent. Under these circumstances he will borrow another $100, being willing to pay 8 per cent, but required to pay only 5. This operation will still further reduce his time preference, and so on through successive stages, until it is finally brought down to 5 per cent. Then, for the last or marginal $100, his rate of time preference will agree with the market rate of interest.[2]

In like manner, if another individual, entering the loan market from the opposite side, has a rate of prefer-

[2] The above-mentioned 10 per cent and 8 per cent rates of time preference are not rates actually experienced by him; they merely mean the rates of preference which he *would* have experienced had his income not been transformed to the time shape corresponding to 5 per cent. As in the general theory of prices, this marginal rate, 5 per cent, being once established, applies indifferently to all his valuations of present and future income. Every comparative estimate of present and future which he actually makes may be said to be "on the margin" of his income stream as actually determined.

ence of 2 per cent, he will become a lender instead of a borrower. He will be *willing* to lend $100 of this year's income for $102 of next year's. As he *can* lend at 5 per cent when he *would* do so at 2, he "jumps at the chance," and invests, not $100 only, but another and another. But his present income, being drawn upon by the process, is now more highly esteemed by him than before, and his future income, being supplemented, is less highly esteemed; and under the influence of successive additions to the sums lent, his rate of preference for the present will keep rising until, at the margin, it will equal the market rate of interest.

In such an ideal loan market, therefore, where every individual could freely borrow or lend, the rates of preference or impatience for present over future income for all the different individuals would become, at the margin, exactly equal to each other and to the rate of interest.

§4. *Altering Income by Loans*

To illustrate this reasoning by a chart, let us suppose the income stream to be represented as in Chart 5, and that the possessor wishes to obtain, by borrowing, a small item X′ of immediately ensuing income in return for a somewhat larger item X″ later on, X″ being the amount of X′ at interest. By such a loan he modifies his income stream from ABCD to EBD. But this change will evidently produce a change in his time preference. If the rate of time preference corresponding to the income stream represented by the unbroken line is 10 per cent, the rate of preference corresponding to the broken line will be somewhat less, say, 8 per cent. If the market rate of interest is 5 per cent, it is evident that the person will proceed to still further borrowing. By repeating the opera-

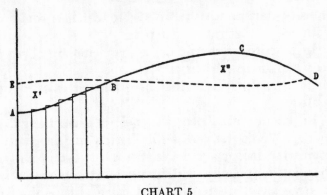

CHART 5
Effect of Borrowing Upon Present and Future Income.

tion several times he can evidently produce almost any required conformation of his income stream.

If, instead of borrowing, he wishes to lend (Chart 6) he surrenders from his present income stream the amount X' for the sake of the larger amount X" at a later time. After the operations are completed and the final conformations of the income streams are determined, the

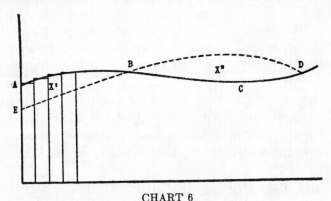

CHART 6
Effect of Lending Upon Present and Future Income.
[107]

rates of time preference are all brought into conformity with the market rate of interest.

In practice, of course, the adjustments are never perfect and, in particular, the income stream is never a smooth curve, such as it is here for convenience represented.

In practice, also, loans are effected under the guise of money. We do not confessedly borrow and lend real incomes, but money and credit. Yet money—that universal medium in practice and universal stumbling-block in theory—merely represents real income, or capitalized real income. A hundred dollars mean the power to secure income,—any income the present value of which is $100. When, therefore, a person borrows $100 today and returns $105 next year, in actual fact he secures the title to $100 worth of income—immediately future, perhaps— and parts with the title to $105 worth of income a year later. Every loan contract, or any other contract implying interest, involves, at bottom, a modification of income streams, the usual and chief modification being as to time shape.

One reason why we often forget that a money loan represents real income is that it represents so many possible varieties of real income. A fund of money is usually the capitalization not simply of one particular future program, or lay-out, of income but of a large number of optional income streams, and is not restricted, as in the first approximation, here considered, to a simple income stream and its modification by loans or their equivalent.

We may distinguish six principal types of individuals in a loan market—three borrowing types and three lending types. The first type of borrower (Chart 7) is sup-

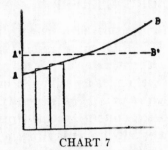

CHART 7

Effect of Borrowing Upon an Increasing Income Stream.

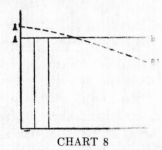

CHART 8

Effect of Borrowing Upon a Uniform Income Stream.

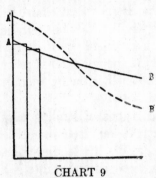

CHART 9

Effect of Borrowing Upon a Decreasing Income Stream.

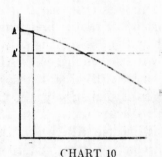

CHART 10

Effect of Lending Upon a Decreasing Income Stream.

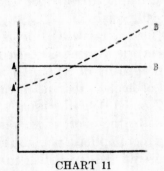

CHART 11

Effect of Lending Upon a Uniform Income Stream.

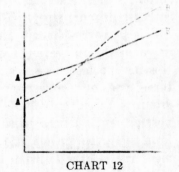

CHART 12

Effect of Lending Upon an Increasing Income Stream.

posed to be possessed of an increasing, or ascending, income stream AB, a fact which, in his mind, results in a rate of preference above the market rate. This leads him to borrow, and relatively to level up his ascending income stream toward such a position as A'B'. The second type of individual already possesses a uniform income stream AB (Chart 8), but having, a strong propensity to spend, he too experiences a rate of preference above the market rate, and will therefore modify his income stream toward the curve A'B'. The third type is shown in Chart 9 and represents even more of a spendthrift. This individual has also a rate of preference in excess of the market rate, in spite of his having a declining income stream pictured by the descending curve AB. By his borrowing, he obtains a curve A'B' of still steeper descent.

In a similar way, the three types of lenders may be graphically represented. Chart 10 represents a descending income AB, which the owner, by lending present income in return for future income, converts into a relatively uniform income A'B'; Chart 11 represents a uniform income converted, by lending, into an ascending income; and Chart 12 an ascending income converted into a still more steeply ascending income.

The borrower changes his income curve by tipping it down in the future and up in the present. The lender tips his income curve in the opposite direction. Of the three types of borrowers and of lenders, the first in each group of three (see Charts 7 and 10), is the usual and normal case. In both these cases the effort is to transform the given income into a more uniform one, the rising curve (Chart 7) being lowered and the falling curve (Chart 10) being raised toward a common horizontal position. Chart 9 and Chart 12, on the other hand, represent the extreme and unusual cases of the spendthrift and the miser.

But whatever the personal equation, it remains true that, for each individual, other things being equal, the more ascending his income curve, the higher his rate of preference; and the more descending the curve, the lower the rate of preference. If the descent of the income stream

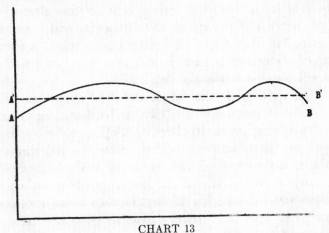

CHART 13

Effects of Alternate Borrowing and Lending Upon a Fluctuating
Income Stream.

is sufficiently rapid, the rate of preference could be made zero or even negative.[3]

These foregoing types of income streams are, of course, not the only ones which could be considered, but they are some of the more important. To them we may add the

---

[3] This is the case mentioned by Carver (*The Distribution of Wealth*, pp. 232-236), when he remarks that a man with $100 in his pocket would not think of spending it all on a dinner today, but would save at least some of it for tomorrow. Whether these conformations of the income stream resulting in zero or negative preference may ever actually be reached so that the market rate of interest itself may be zero or negative is another question.

type of fluctuating income, as represented in Chart 13, which may result in alternate borrowing and lending so as to produce a more nearly uniform income stream. Such financing over the lean parts of a year is often practiced when the income is lumped at one or two spots, such as dividend dates.

It must not be imagined that the classes of borrowers and lenders correspond respectively to the classes of poor and rich. The factors, environmental and personal, discussed in Chapter IV, will determine whether a man's rate of preference is high or low, and therefore whether he will become a spender or a saver.

When we come to the second and third approximations and have to study so-called productive loans, especially of risk-takers, or enterprisers as Professor Fetter calls them, we shall find still other influences determining whether a person shall be a borrower or lender or both. At present we are only at the first approximation where it is assumed there is no risk and no such series of opportunities to vary the income stream as lie at the basis of so-called productive loans.

§5. *Altering Income by Sale*

But borrowing and lending are not the only ways in which one's income stream may be modified. Exactly the same result may, theoretically, be accomplished simply by buying and selling property; for, since property rights are merely rights to income streams, their exchange replaces one such stream by another of equal present value but differing in time shape, composition, or uncertainty. This method of modifying one's income stream, which we shall call the method of sale, really includes the former, or method of loans, for a loan contract is, as Böhm-

Bawerk has so well said, at bottom a sale, that is, it is the exchange of the right to present or immediately ensuing income for the right to future or more remote income. A borrower is simply a seller of a note of which the lender is the buyer. A man who buys a bond, for example, may be regarded indifferently as a lender or as a buyer of property.

The concept of a loan may therefore now be dispensed with by being merged in the concept of a sale. Every sale transfers property rights; that is, it transfers the title to income of some kind. By selling some property rights and buying others it is possible to transform one's income stream at will into any desired time shape. Thus, if a man buys an orchard, he is providing himself with future income in the form of apples. If, instead, he buys apples, he is providing himself with similar but more immediate income. If he buys securities, he is providing himself with future money, convertible, when received, into apples or other real income. Inasmuch as the productive life of a mine is shorter generally than that of a railway, if his security is a share in a mine, his income stream is less lasting than if the security is stock in a railway, though at first it should be larger, relatively to the sum paid for it.

Purchasing the right to remote enjoyable income, as was explained in Chapter I, is called *investing;* while purchasing more immediate enjoyable income is *spending.* These, however, are purely relative concepts; for remote and immediate are relative terms. Buying an automobile is investing as contrasted with spending the money for food and drink, but may be called spending as contrasted with investing in real estate. And yet the antithesis between spending money and investing is important; it is the antithesis between immediate and remote income. The adjustment between the two determines the time shape of one's income stream. Spending increases immediate real income but robs the future, whereas investing provides for the future to the detriment of the present. There is often misconception in reasoning about spending and investing. For example, Henry Ford's remark has been widely reported: "No successful boy ever saved any money. They spent it as fast as they got it for things *to improve themselves.*" In this remark Mr. Ford drew no hard and fast line between spending for personal enjoyment and investment for improvement. And there is no hard and fast line. Spending merely means expending money primarily for more or less *immediate* enjoyment. Saving or investing is expending money for more or less *deferred* enjoyment. Consequently, much of what is called spending might legitimately be called investment. Even the money we spend for food, clothing and shelter is in a sense really partly invested, since our lives and capacity to work can be preserved only by means of these necessaries. Just so with a set of books, or any other durable good which increases the efficiency and hence the earning power of the purchaser; it is an example, not of spending for consumption merely, but of saving through investment. Mr. Ford cites the example of Thomas Edison as spending his early earnings as fast as he made them. But Edison did this, not for food and display, but for experimentation that resulted in time and labor saving inventions which have benefited everybody. His outlays were in a way investments.

Popular usage has devised many other terms and phrases in this field, most of which, like spending and investing, while containing meanings of importance, include also the alloy of misconception. Thus, the phrase "capital seeking investment" means that capitalists have property for which they desire, by exchange, to substitute other property, the income from which is more remote. It does not mean that there is any hard and fast line between invested and uninvested capital, much less does it mean that the inanimate capital has of itself any power to seek investment. Again, the phrase "saving capital out of income" means not spending—reserving money which would otherwise be spent for immediate enjoyable income in order to exchange it or invest it for remoter income; it does not mean the creation of new capital, though it may lead to that. Many needless controversies have centered about the phenomenon of saving chiefly because neither saving nor income was clearly defined.[4]

From what has been said it is clear that by buying and selling property an individual may change the conformation of his income stream precisely as though he were specifically lending or borrowing. Thus, suppose a man's original income stream is $1000 this year and $1500 next year, and suppose that he sells the title to this income stream, and, with the proceeds buys the title to another income stream yielding $1100 this year and $1395 next year. Although this man has not, nominally, borrowed $100 and repaid $105, he has done what amounts to the same thing; he has increased his income stream of this year by $100 and decreased that of next year by $105. The very same diagrams which were used

[4] Thus, by saving, some writers understand that capital necessarily increases, and hence the income stream is made to ascend; others, like Carver (*loc. cit.*, p. 232), apply the term broadly enough to include the case where a descending income is simply rendered less descending. The latter view harmonizes with that here presented. Saving is simply postponing enjoyable income.

before may equally well represent these operations. A man sells the income stream ABCD (Chart 5) and with the proceeds buys the stream EBD. The X′ and X″ are, as before, $100 and $105, but now appear explicitly as differences in the value of two income streams, instead of appearing as direct loans and payments.

§6. *Interest Ineradicable*

Thus interest taking cannot be prevented by prohibiting loan contracts. To forbid the particular form of sale called a loan contract would leave possible other forms of sale, and, as was shown in Chapter I, the mere act of valuation of every property right involves an implicit rate of interest. If the prohibition left individuals free to deal in bonds, it is clear that they would still virtually be borrowing and lending, but under the names of selling and purchasing; and if bonds were tabooed, they could change to preferred stock. Indeed, as long as buying and selling of any kind were permitted, the virtual effect of lending and borrowing would be retained. The possessor of a forest of young trees, not being able to mortgage their future return and being in need of an income stream of a less deferred type than that receivable from the forest itself, could simply sell his forest and with the proceeds buy, say, a farm, with a uniform flow of income, or a mine with a decreasing one. On the other hand, the possessor of a capital which is depreciating, that is, which represents an income stream great now but steadily declining, and who is eager to have an increasing income, could sell his depreciating wealth and invest the proceeds in such instruments as the forest already mentioned.

It was in such a way, as for instance by rent purchase, that the medieval prohibitions of usury were rendered nugatory. Practically, the effect of such restrictive laws is little more than to hamper and make difficult the finer adjustments of the income stream, compelling would-be borrowers to sell wealth yielding distant returns instead of mortgaging them, and would-be lenders to buy such wealth instead of lending to the present owners. It is conceivable that explicit interest might disappear under such restrictions, but implicit interest would certainly remain. The young forest sold for $10,000 would bear this price, as now, because it is the discounted value of the estimated future income; and the price of the farm, $10,000, would be determined in like manner. The rate of discount in the two cases, the $10,000 forest and the $10,000 farm, must tend to be the same, because, by buying and selling, the various parties in the community would adjust their rates of preference to a common level —an implicit rate of interest thus lurking in every contract, though never specifically mentioned therein. Interest is too omnipresent a phenomenon to be eradicated by attacking any particular form of it; nor would any one undertake to eradicate it who perceived its substance as well as its form.

§7. "Marginal" Principle Is "Maximum" Principle

The fact that, through the loan market, the marginal rate of time preference for each individual is, by borrowing or lending, made equal to the rate of interest may be stated in another way, namely, that the total present desirability of, or want for, the individual's income stream is made a maximum. For, consider again the individual who modifies his original fixed income stream by borrowing until his rate of preference is brought into unison with the market rate of interest. His degree of impatience was at first, say, 10 per cent; that is, he was willing, in order to secure an addition of $100 to his present income, to sacrifice $110 of next year's income. But he needed to sacrifice only $105; that is, he was enabled to get his loan for less than he would have been willing to pay. He was therefore a gainer to the extent of the present desirability of, or present want for, $5 of next year's income. The second $100 borrowed was equivalent, in his present estimation, to $108 of next year's income, and the same reasoning shows that, as he pays only $105, he gains to the extent of the present desirability of $3 next year; that is, he adds this present desirability to the entire present total desirability of his income stream. In like manner, each successive increment of loans adds to the present total desirability of his income, so long as he is willing to pay more than $105 of next year's income for $100 of this year's income. But, as he proceeds, his gains and his eagerness diminish until they cease altogether. At, let us say, the fifth instalment of $100, he finds himself barely willing to pay $105; the present total desirability of his income is then a maximum, and any further loan would decrease it. A sixth $100, for instance, is worth in his present estimation less than $105 due next year, say $104, and since in the loan market he would have to sacrifice $105 next year to secure it, this would mean a loss of desirability to the extent of the desirability today of $1 due in one year. Thus, by borrowing up to the point where the rate of preference for present over future income is equal to the rate of interest, five per cent, he secures the greatest total desirability, or, so-called consumer's rent.[5]

[5] We do not here need to argue as to the zero or starting point from which we measure net total desirability. The crest of a hill is the highest

Similar reasoning applies to the individual on the other side of the market, whose rate of preference is initially less than the market rate of interest. He also will bring his present net total desirability to a maximum by lending up to the point where his rate of preference corresponds to the rate of interest. At the beginning, $100 this year has to him the same present desirability as, say, $102 due one year hence, whereas in the market he may secure not $102 but $105. It is then clear that by lending $100 he gains the present desirability of $3 due one year hence. By lending each successive $100 he will add something to the total present desirability of his income, until his rate of preference for present over future income is raised to a level equal to that of the rate of interest, five per cent. Beyond that point he would lose by further lending.

§8. *Market Equilibrium*

We are now in a position to give a preliminary answer to the question, What determines the rate of interest? Thus far we have regarded the individual only, and have seen that he conforms his rate of income-impatience to the rate of interest. For him the rate of interest is a relatively fixed fact, since his own impatience and resulting action can affect it only infinitesimally. To him it is his degree of impatience which is the variable. In short, for him individually, the rate of interest is cause, and his lending and borrowing is the effect. For society as a whole, however, the order of cause and effect is reversed. This change is like the corresponding inversion of cause and effect in the theory of prices. Each individual regards the

point whether the height is measured above sea level or from the center of the earth.

market price, say, of sugar, as fixed, and adjusts his marginal utility, or desirability, to it; whereas, for the entire group of persons forming the market, the adjustment is the other way around, the price of sugar conforming to its marginal desirability to the consumer.[6] In the same way, while for the individual the rate of interest determines the degree of impatience, for society the degrees of impatience of the aggregate of individuals determine, or help to determine, the rate of interest. The rate of interest is equal to the degree of impatience upon which the whole community may *concur in order that the market of loans may be exactly cleared.*

To put the matter in figures: Suppose that at the outset the rate of interest is arbitrarily set very high, say, 20 per cent. There will be relatively few borrowers and many would-be lenders, so that the total extent to which would-be lenders are willing to reduce their income streams for the present year for the sake of a much larger future income will be, say, 100 million dollars; whereas, the extent to which would-be borrowers are willing to increase their income streams in the present at the high price of 20 per cent will be only, say, one million. Under such conditions the demand for loans is far short of the supply and the rate of interest will therefore go down. At an interest rate of 10 per cent the lenders may offer 50 millions, and the borrowers bid for 20 millions. There is still an excess of supply over demand, and interest must needs fall further. At 5 per cent we may suppose the market cleared, borrowers and lenders being willing to take or give respectively 30 millions. In like manner it can be shown that the rate would not fall below this, as in

[6] See my *Mathematical Investigations in the Theory of Value and Prices.*

that case it would result in an excess of demand over supply and cause the rate to rise again.

Thus, the rate of interest registers in the market the common marginal rate of preference for present over future income, as determined by the supply and demand of present and future income. Those who, to start with, have a high degree of impatience, strive to acquire more present income at the cost of future income, and thus tend to raise the rate of interest. These are the borrowers, the spenders, the sellers of property yielding remote income, such as bonds and stocks. On the other hand, those who, to start with, have a low rate of preference, strive to acquire more future income at the cost of present income, and so tend to lower the rate of interest. Such are the lenders, the savers, the investors.

Not only will the mechanism just described result in a rate of interest which will clear the market for loans connecting the present with next year, but, applied to exchanges between the present and the more remote future, it will make similar clearings. While some individuals may wish to exchange this year's income for next year's, others wish to exchange this year's income for that of the year after next, or for a portion of several future years' incomes. The rates of interest for these various periods are so adjusted as to clear the market *for each of the periods of time for which contracts are made.*

§9. *Four Principles*

If we retain our original assumption that every man is initially endowed with a rigidly fixed or prescribed income stream which can be freely bought and sold and thereby redistributed in time, the foregoing discussion gives us a complete theory of the causes which determine the rate of interest, or rather, the *rates* of interest, there being, theoretically, a separate rate for each time period. These rates of interest would, under these circumstances, be fully determined by the following four principles, to which all the magnitudes in the problem of interest must conform:

THE TWO IMPATIENCE PRINCIPLES

A. Empirical Principle

The rate of time preference or degree of impatience of each individual depends upon his income stream.

B. Principle of Maximum Desirability

Through the alterations in the income streams produced by loans or sales, the marginal degrees of impatience for all individuals in the market are brought into equality with each other and with the market rate of interest.

This condition B is equivalent to another, namely, that each individual exchanges present against future income, or *vice versa,* at the market rate of interest up to the point of the *maximum total desirability* of the forms of income available to him.

THE TWO MARKET PRINCIPLES

A. Principle of Clearing the Market

The market rate of interest will be such as will just clear the market, that is, will make the loans and borrowings or, more generally expressed, purchases and sales of income equal for each period of time.

FIRST APPROXIMATION

B. Principle of Repayment

All loans are repaid with interest, that is, the present value of the payments, reckoned at the time of contract, equals the present value of the repayments. More generally expressed, the plus and minus alterations or departures from a person's original income stream effected by buying and selling at two different points are such that the algebraic sum of their present values is zero.

Will these four sets of conditions determine the rate of interest? And why should there be so many conditions? Ought not one single condition to suffice?

These are really questions in mathematics. It is a fundamental principle that in order to solve an equation containing only one unknown quantity only one equation is necessary; and that to solve one containing two unknowns, two independent equations are needed; and so on, one additional equation for each additional unknown quantity introduced.

In the present problem we are trying to determine only one unknown, the rate of interest. But we can do so only by determining, at the same time, the other unknowns that are involved. To say that the rate of interest is equal to Smith's marginal rate of impatience is saying something, but not enough. It merely expresses one unknown, the rate of interest, in terms of another unknown, Smith's marginal rate; and two unknowns cannot be determined by one equation or condition. If we add that the rate of interest must also equal Jones' rate of impatience, while this statement gives us another equation it also adds another unknown and three unknowns cannot be determined by two equations; and so on. If we include Jones and everybody else in the market, we shall still be one equation short. This is equivalent to saying that the second set of conditions (Impatience Principle B) is not enough.

In a market comprising 1000 persons there will be, as our unknowns, not only the rate of interest, but 1000 rates of impatience, and the additions to or deductions from the income of these 1000 persons in each period of time. The rate of interest and these thousands of variables act and react on each other and the determination of each can be accomplished only with the determination of all the rest.

In Chapter XII this problem is stated in mathematical formulas such that the number of equations is exactly equal to the number of unknown quantities.

CHAPTER VI

SECOND APPROXIMATION TO THE THEORY OF INTEREST

Assuming Income Modifiable (1) by loans and (2) by other means

§1. *The New Hypothesis*

HITHERTO we have assumed:

(1) perfect foresight, and

(2) absence of any opportunity to alter income save by trading.

We now abandon the second of these hypotheses. Still assuming that all available income streams can be definitely foreseen, we now introduce the new hypothesis, much nearer actual life, that the income streams are not rigid, but are flexible, that is, that the owner of any item of capital-wealth or capital property, including, of course and especially, his own person, is not restricted *to a sole use* to which he may put it, but has open to his choice several possible or alternative uses, each of which will produce a separate optional income stream. He has, therefore, two kinds of choice: first, the choosing one from many optional income streams, and secondly, as under the first approximation, the choosing of the most desirable time shape of his income stream by exchanging present income against future.

The two sorts of choice are exercised concurrently in

practice and each in consideration of the other. But, for purposes of exposition, we may take one at a time. Or rather, we may suppose the double choice made and then, in order to analyze it, we go back and consider each process separately, assuming the other constant. Let the varying process be the loan, that is, let us suppose one individual to have irrevocably made his choice from among options mutually available. This done, he is limited, as in the first hypothesis, to buying and selling or borrowing and lending as a means of changing the shape of that particular income stream. In *this* process he cannot change the present value, but in making his initial choice he had the privilege of selecting that option having the maximum present value.

For example, the owner of a piece of land may use it in any one of several different ways. He may, let us say, use it to grow crops, graze animals, plant forests, extract minerals, or to support buildings. Again, the owner of a building may use it, say, for office purposes, apartments, manufacturing, salesrooms, or a warehouse. Most raw materials, too, may be used for any one of a number of purposes. Iron may be wrought into steel rails, or into machinery, implements, tools, armor for ships, or girders for buildings. And so of tools and other implements; a derrick may be used for quarrying stone, building a house, or unloading a boat. A ship may be used to carry any sort of cargo, and sent over any one of numerous different routes. Hammers, saws, nails, and other tools may be used in almost numberless ways.

Perhaps the most adaptable of all instruments of wealth is man himself. He may be simply a passive enjoyer or "transformer" [1] of the services of other wealth

---

[1] See Chapter I, or *The Nature of Capital and Income,* Chapter X.

and as such derive his satisfactions in any one or more of several different ways, sensual, esthetic, intellectual, or spiritual. Or, he may also be an active producer, and, as such, perform work in any one or more of several different ways, physical or mental. Even the skilled laborer who is most specialized and restricted has many ways to turn. And each of these varieties includes numerous subvarieties. If his work is physical, it may consist in anything from wielding a pick and shovel to the deft manipulation of the instruments employed in the jeweler's art. If his work is mental, he may be a bookkeeper, clerk, superintendent, manager, director, lawyer, physician, clergyman, editor, teacher, or scientist. Some of these options, of course, may be out of the question and, in each case, there will be only one best choice. That choice is what is now under discussion.

In consequence of such a range of choice, any given productive instrument, or any given set of productive instruments, including human beings, may produce any one of many different income streams. Men may work to produce cheap frame houses or durable stone ones; to equip a city with trolleys, elevated, or under-ground rapid transit; to secure an income stream which shall consist of the pleasures of the table, of the amusements of the theatre, of the gratification of social vanities, or of endless combinations of these groups, as well as of all others. Each individual must select one particular income stream out of a thousand possible income streams differing in size, composition, time shape, and uncertainty; but, in this chapter, the element of uncertainty is, as already stated, supposed absent, being reserved for the third approximation (Chapter IX).

As in the first approximation, a perfect market is

assumed in which each individual is so insignificant a part that he acts as if the market rate of interest were fixed and merely has to decide how much at that rate he is willing to borrow or lend.

Because of the existence of a wide range of choice, the owner of a given capital has ample opportunity to modify the income stream he derives from it by changing the uses to which that capital is put. He is seldom so committed to a definite future program but that he can consider some alternative. It is on this principle that the cotton belt of the United States, by diversifying its crops and industries, has increased its real income. The production of these Southern States has recently risen with expanding industries, diversified agriculture, water power development, and improved highways. It was largely by changing the uses to which its income, natural resources, and technological equipment had been put that the South has entered a new era.

Under the first approximation, our first glimpse of any flexibility of income was by borrowing and lending. Next we introduced the process of buying or selling and noted that this really included as a special case borrowing and lending. It might be claimed here that, just as buying and selling virtually include borrowing and lending, so the substitution of one use of a person's capital for another use may be said to include buying and selling, and therefore also to include borrowing and lending. It is evidently quite possible to say that one method of utilizing capital is to sell it. In fact, a merchant regards himself as making use of his stock in trade only in the sense of selling it.

While we could thus extend the meaning of optional uses to include buying and selling (which in turn include borrowing and lending) it will better serve the purpose of our analysis not to do so.

There are two principal reasons for this. First, borrowing and lending, the narrower method of modifying income streams, cannot be applied to society as a whole, since there is no one outside to trade with; and yet society does have opportunities radically to change the character of its income stream by changing the employment of its capital. Secondly, when borrowing and lending, or ordinary buying and selling, are employed to modify an income stream, the present value of the original income stream and the present value of the modified income stream are the same, for each $100 added to this year's income has the same present value as the $100 with interest, returned out of next year's income, so that every loan adds and subtracts equal present values. But when an income stream is modified by a change in the use of capital yielding it, the present value of the alternative, as in the case of the South, may not, and, in general, will not, be the same as the present value of the original. This fact, that the present value is not changed by buying or selling (or, in particular, by borrowing or lending) but is changed by otherwise altering the use of one's capital, marks an important distinction between the two methods of altering one's income stream. The distinction and its importance are most clearly seen by a mathematical analysis such as that shown in Chapter XI and XIII.

§2. *Optional Income Streams*

The choice among all available optional income streams will fall on that one which has the maximum desirability or wantability.

We have seen in the preceding chapter that income

streams may differ in size, time shape, composition and certainty. As among income streams of different sizes but similar in other respects, the most desirable will, of course, be the largest.

As among income streams of different composition but similar in other respects, the most desirable will be that in which, to the given individual, the marginal desirabilities of the different constituents are proportional to their several prices, in accordance with the fundamental principle of marginal desirability in the theory of prices.[2]

Finally, and principally, as among income streams differing in time shape alone, the most desirable is found in accordance with the principles which govern the rate of interest, and which are to be expounded in this book. It is, therefore, with income streams differing in time shape that we are here chiefly concerned.

In order definitely to illustrate income streams differing in time shape, let us begin by supposing only three. An individual is, let us say, possessed of a piece of land almost equally good for farming, lumbering, or mining. These terms are used merely to fix the reader's thought in concrete pictures. Logically, it would be better to designate the three optional supposititious income streams simply by the letters A, B, and C, for there is no pretense that the income streams closely resemble in more than a very general and sketchy way those of actual farming, lumbering, or mining; nor is it essential that the three products should differ in kind. Thus, the three streams might represent three different methods of producing the same product, one more roundabout or capitalistic than another. They are here given the concrete

[2] See my *Mathematical Investigations in the Theory of Value and Prices.*

names of farming, lumbering, mining, merely for convenience in distinguishing and remembering the three types, not because these types are true to these names, nor because examples concerned with land comprise opportunities any more important than those concerned with commercial or industrial examples. The only essential point is that the three series of numbers representing the income streams A, B, and C are different.

Our imaginary land owner thus has the option of securing any one of these three different income streams. While they will, in the first instance, differ in composition—one income stream consisting in the production of crops, another in the production of lumber, and the third in the production of minerals—we may, for our present purpose, assume that these are all reduced to real income measured in terms of money. That is, we here assume that the prices and values of the crops, lumber, and minerals are given and determined in accordance with the principles which determine prices.[3]

[3] It is, of course, realized that the principles of price determination involve interest just as the principles determining interest involve prices. A complete picture of economic equilibrium includes every possible variable, each acting and reacting on the others. Theoretically we cannot determine the price of bread by itself and then go on to determine, each separately, other prices, including the rate of interest. Theoretically any analysis of one part of the economic organism must include an analysis of the whole, so that a complete interest theory would have to include also price theory, wage theory and, in fact, all other economic theory.

But it is convenient to isolate a particular element by assuming the other elements to have been determined. So this book is a monograph, restricted, so far as may be, to the theory of interest, and excluding price-theory, wage theory and all other economic theory. Afterward it will be easy to dovetail together this interest theory, which assumes prices predetermined, with price theory which assumes interest predetermined, thus reaching a synthesis in which the previously assumed constants become variables. But all the principles remain valid.

THE THEORY OF INTEREST

Assuming, then, that the land owner finds predetermined prices and quantities of crops, lumber and minerals, with predetermined costs for obtaining them, he has before him simply the choice of three definite income streams, each expressible in terms of money, according as he uses his labor, land, and capital in one or the other of the following three ways:

(1) for farming purposes, which, let us say, will give him a regular and perpetual succession of crops and income equally valuable year after year, that is, with an income stream of the type AA' in Chart 14;

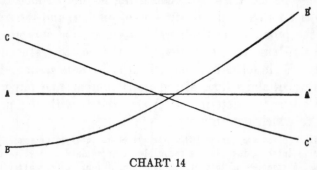

CHART 14

Three Types of Income Streams; "Farming", "Forestry", and "Mining."

(2) for forestry purposes, with very slight returns for the first few decades, and larger returns in the future, as indicated by the curve BB';

(3) for mining purposes, in which case we shall suppose that the income is greatest for the early years and thereafter gradually decreases until the mine is exhausted; illustrated by Curve CC'.

The important question now before us is: What are the principles upon which the owner of the land chooses the best one among these three income streams, A, B, and C?

SECOND APPROXIMATION

This question is fundamental and typical in the second approximation.

The rate of interest is just as relevant to this initial choice of uses for maximum present value as to the subsequent choice for shape alone, for it is used in *finding* the present value; and when the rate changes, the relative present values of differently shaped streams may change about.

We shall suppose, as heretofore, that there is a uniform rate of interest in the community and that any individual is free either to borrow or to lend at that rate and up to any amount desired. Under this hypothesis the choice among the three available options will simply fall on that one which yields the maximum present value, reckoned at the market rate of interest.

Let us assume a market rate of interest at five per cent. To reckon the three respective present values, suppose the use of the land for mining purposes will yield an income stream, let us say, as follows: $2000 the first year, $1800 the second, $1600 the third, and so on, diminishing annually by $200 to the point of the mine's exhaustion. The present value of these ten sums, discounted at five per cent, is $9110. If the land is used for farming purposes and yields a net income of $450 a year perpetually, the present value at five per cent will be $9000. If, finally, the land is used for forestry purposes, we shall suppose it yields the following sums: zero for the first two years, $300 for the third, $400 for the fourth, $500 for the fifth, and $500 thereafter forever—then the value of the land, reckoning at 5 per cent, will be $8820.

Under these conditions the choice will evidently fall on the mining use, because, for mining purposes, the land is worth $9110, which is greater than $9000, its value

[133]

for farming purposes, and than $8820, its value for
forestry purposes.

The three options may be contrasted as to distribution
in time as follows:

TABLE 2

The Three Optional Income Streams

	A For farming	B For forestry	C For mining
1st yr.	$ 450	$ 000	$2000
2nd yr.	450	000	1800
3rd yr.	450	300	1600
4th yr.	450	400	1400
5th yr.	450	500	1200
6th yr.	450	500	1000
7th yr.	450	500	800
8th yr.	450	500	600
9th yr.	450	500	400
10th yr.	450	500	200
11th yr.	450	500	000
	etc.	etc.	etc.
Present Value	$9000	$8820	$9110

The particular income stream selected will tend to
leave its impress on the time shape of the total income
stream of the individual who owns it. For, as was seen
in Chapter I, the total net, or final, income stream of any
individual during any interval of time is simply the sum
total of the items of income flowing during that interval
from all the articles of property belonging to him. Hence,
if one selects the mining use for his land, whereby the
income stream gradually decreases, its tendency will be
to produce a similarly decreasing trend in the total income
stream enjoyed by the individual. This tendency may
be counteracted, of course, by some opposing tendency,
but will have full sway if the income from all other capital
than the land remains the same in value and time shape.
It is true that the direct income from the mine is not

itself real income, but consists of services which, relatively to some other capital source, are disservices, thus constituting intermediate income or interactions. But those items are readily transformed, through a chain of credits and debits, into real, and then into enjoyment income. Thus the ore of the mine is exchanged for money, and the money spent for enjoyable services or for commodities which soon yield enjoyable services, so that the real income closely copies in time shape [4] the original intermediate income from the mine.

§3. *The Two Kinds of Choice*

The possessor of the mine, however, is not compelled thus to copy in his real income the mine's fluctuations of physical or natural income. He may counteract any fluctuations in his whole net income which may be caused, in the first instance, by the choice of income C rather than B, or A. Or, if he prefers, he may further exaggerate those fluctuations. In fact he may make the time shape of his income follow any model he likes. He may do this as described under the first approximation, by either borrowing or lending in suitable amounts and at suitable times along his income stream; or, more generally, by buying and selling income streams or parts of income streams so as to fashion the time shape of his own final net enjoyable income to suit himself.

He may, for instance, so far as time shape is concerned, achieve an even flow of income such as he could get from the farm use of his land. But he will not on that account choose this farm use in preference to the mining use; for the mining use has the larger present value, and the undesirable time shape of its income stream, under our

[4] See *The Nature of Capital and Income*, Chapters VIII, IX, XVII.

present hypothesis, can be very easily remedied. For instance, he may lend some of the proceeds of its earlier output and in later years be paid back with interest.

Of course, his loan at five per cent does not alter in the least the figure $9110, the discounted value at five per cent of all the ten items of income ($2000, $1800, $1600, $1400, $1200, $1000, $800, $600, $400, $200); it simply adds to the later of these ten figures and subtracts from the earlier ones. The present value of the additions is necessarily equal to the present value of the subtractions; for the additions are the repayments, while the subtractions are the loans, and the present value of any loan equals that of its repayment.

We may totally separate, therefore, in thought the two choices made by the land owner, namely, (1) the choice of C (mining) in preference to A and B on the ground of greater present value, and, (2) the choice of time shape. If, as just supposed for illustration, the second sort of choice is that of an even income stream, it will be at the rate of $455.50 a year perpetually. That is to say, the mine owner will lend at interest $1544.50 the first year (all but $455.50 out of his original mining income of $2000); in the second year he will lend $1344.50 (all but $455.50 out of his original $1800); and so on. When the ninth year is reached, he ceases to lend further, for the mine then yields only $400. Instead, he then ekes this out by $55.50 returned from the previous loans. Likewise, in the tenth year he ekes out the $200 from mining by $255.50 returned from loans. Thereafter he will get nothing further from mining; but his loans will have accumulated a sinking fund (of $9110) to take the place of the mine and from this fund he can annually derive a 5 per cent revenue of $455.50.

SECOND APPROXIMATION

Consequently, the net result of the double choice (mining use and even time shape) is to increase the perpetual income of $450 offered by farming to a perpetual income of $455.50. This new perpetual annuity has exactly the same time shape as that derived from the farming use, but is larger by $5.50 per annum.

Incidentally it may be observed that this mining income, thus evened out by financing into a uniform $455.50 per year, exceeds the uniform farming income of $450 in exactly the same ratio as the present value ($9110) of the mining income exceeds that ($9000) of the farming income.

The following table exhibits the operations in detail:

TABLE 3

Mining and Farming Use Compared

	Owner Receives from Mine	Of which He Lends	Leaving for Real Income	As Against Which the Farming Use Would Have Yielded
1st year	$2000	$1544.50	$455.50	$450
2nd year	1800	1344.50	455.50	450
3rd year	1600	1144.50	455.50	450
4th year	1400	944.50	455.50	450
5th year	1200	744.50	455.50	450
6th year	1000	544.50	455.50	450
7th year	800	344.50	455.50	450
8th year	600	144.50	455.50	450
9th year	400	−55.50	455.50	450
10th year	200	−255.50	455.50	450
11th year	000	−455.50	455.50	450
etc.	etc.	etc.	etc.	etc.

Or, instead of wanting a perpetual even flowing income, the land owner may prefer as his model the time shape of the forestry income. He will not, however, on that account, choose this forestry use in preference to the mining use. He will simply lend at interest from the items of mining income all of his $2000 the first year, leaving no income for that year; likewise, all of his $1800 the second; all but $310 the third; all but $413 the fourth and all but $516 the fifth, and every succeeding year until the ninth year. He will then turn around and use $116 from his loans just described to eke out his $400 and bring up his income in that year to $516. The tenth mining item, $200, will likewise be brought up to $516 after which he will depend entirely on his outside loans at five per cent, deriving therefrom exactly $516 every year.

The result will then be a series of income items exactly similar to the B, or forestry, series but each item magnified in the ratio of $9110 to $8820, the present values respectively of C and B.

The following table exhibits these operations:

TABLE 4

Mining and Forestry Use Compared

	Owner Receives from Mine	Of Which He Lends	Leaving for Real Income	As Against Which the Forestry Use Would Have Yielded
1st year	$2000	$2000	$000	$000
2nd year	1800	1800	000	000
3rd year	1600	1290	310	300
4th year	1400	987	413	400
5th year	1200	684	516	500
6th year	1000	484	516	500
7th year	800	284	516	500
8th year	600	84	516	500
9th year	400	−116	516	500
10th year	200	−316	516	500
11th year	000	−516	516	500
etc.	etc.	etc.	etc.	etc.

Since, therefore, any time shape may be transformed into any other time shape, nobody need be deterred from selecting an income because of its time shape, but everyone may choose an income exclusively on the basis of maximum present value. It will then happen that his income, as finally transformed, will be larger than it would have been if he had chosen some other use which afforded that same time shape.

All this is true under the assumption used throughout this chapter, namely, that after the most valuable option has been chosen, you can borrow and lend or buy and sell *ad libitum* and without risk. If this assumption is not true, if a person were cut off from a free loan market, the choice among optional income streams might or might not fall upon that one having the maximum present value, depending on the other circumstances involved, particularly his preferences as regards time shape.

Of course our assumption is a violent one, made in this second approximation, as in the first, in order to simplify the theory of interest. But already it must be evident that the principle involved has important practical applications. To a very considerable extent a modern business man, with access to loan markets, *can* choose from among the various options open to him on the basis of present value, and trust to loans or other financing to rectify any inconvenience in time shape.

The lines AB and A′B′ in Chart 15 picture alternative income streams, of which the descending one, AB, has the larger present value. The choice will fall on AB, and if the individual prefers the time shape of A′B′, he will then lend some of the early receipts from the income stream AB and receive back some of the latter, converting his income AB of undesirable shape into the income stream A″B″ which has the desired shape. This final income A″B″ combines the virtues of both the original alternative incomes AB and of A′B′; it possesses the superior shape of A′B′ and the superior present value of AB. As compared with A′B′ it has the same shape but a greater size.

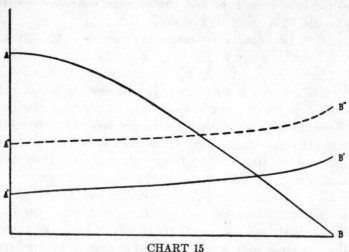

CHART 15

Enlarging Income Stream Through Double Choice.

In practice, of course, the two steps are usually made simultaneously, not successively. In fact, usually the borrowing or financing often precedes the choice of option, thus reversing the order of presentation here adopted for convenience of exposition. So it would be quite as true to say that the loan, with the choice of option it makes possible, is made to secure an increased income as it is to say that the loan is made to even up the distorted income given by the option chosen.

But were it not for the possibility here assumed of modifying the time shape of his income stream by borrowing and lending, or buying and selling, the land owner would *not* feel free to choose the one from among the optional income streams which possesed the highest present value. He might find it advantageous, or even necessary, to take one of the others, being scarcely able to live if his property offered *only* distant income. If his capital were all in the form of growing young forests, and he could not mortgage the future in some way, he would have to starve or give up some of his holdings. In actual life we find such people—people who are said to be "land poor." In fact, we are all somewhat hampered in the choice of options by difficulties and risks both in the choice of options and in the financing it requires.

But we see that, in such a fluid world of options as we are here assuming, the capitalist reaches his final income through the co-operation of two kinds of choice of incomes which, under our assumptions, may be considered and treated as entirely separate. To repeat, these two kinds of choice are: first, the choice from among many possible income streams of that particular income stream which has the highest present value, and, secondly, the choice among different possible modifications of this income stream by borrowing and lending or buying and selling. The first is a selection from among income streams of *differing market values,* and the second, a selection from among income streams of the *same* market value.

§4. *Opportunity to Invest by Change of Use of Capital*

Since this double choice results, when made, in a perfectly definite income stream, it might seem that the situation does not materially differ from the case of the rigid income stream discussed in the first approximation. But the two cases do differ materially, for under the present hypothesis (of optional income streams) the particular choice made by the individual *depends upon what the rate of interest is.* A change in that rate may shift the maximum present value to some other option, or alternative income stream, and that shift reacts on the rate of interest.

In the example cited, if the rate of interest should be 4½ per cent instead of 5 per cent, the order of choice would be changed. The present value of the land for A (farming) would be $10,000, for B (forestry), $9920, and for C (mining), $9280. The farming use, or A, would now be the best choice. Again, if the rate of interest should be 4 per cent instead of 4½ per cent, the present value of the use of the land for A, farming purposes, would be $11,250; for B, forestry purposes, $11,300; and for C, mining purposes, $9450. In this case, B, the forestry use, would be chosen.

Thus, it would pay best to employ the land for mining if the rate of interest were 5 per cent, for farming if it were 4½ per cent, and for forestry if it were 4 per cent.

The three options open to the owner of the land at these three different rates of interest may be summarized as follows:

TABLE 5

Present Values of the Three Options at Three Different Rates of Interest

Options	Present Value at		
	5%	4½%	4%
For forestry	$8,820	$ 9,920	$11,300
For farming	9,000	10,000	11,250
For mining	9,110	9,280	9,450

Thus a change in the rate of interest results in a change in the relative attractiveness of different optional income stream opportunities. A high rate of interest will encourage investment in the quickly returning incomes,

SECOND APPROXIMATION

whereas a low rate of interest will encourage investment in incomes which yield distant returns. As the business man puts it, when interest is high, he can less afford to wait for a remote return because he will "lose so much interest." An investor will, therefore, make very different choices among the various options open to him, according as interest is at one rate or another.

Consequently, the existence of various options to use one's capital introduces a new variable into the problem of interest determination. For the individual, the rate of interest will determine the choice among his optional income streams, but, for society as a whole, the order of cause and effect is reversed—the rate of interest will be influenced by the range of options open to choice. If we live in a land covered with young forests or otherwise affording plenty of opportunities for distant income but affording few opportunities for immediate income (as was the case in the pioneer days in this country) the rate of interest will, other things being equal, be very much higher than in a land full of nearly worked out mines and oil fields or otherwise affording many opportunities for immediate but few opportunities for remote income.

We are thus coming in sight of a principle, applying to interest determination, new in our study, the principle of opportunity to invest, not simply by lending but by changing the *use of one's capital*. This new principle, largely physical or technical, is just as important as the psychical principle of human impatience. It is really old in the sense that, implicitly, it has been recognized in almost all theories of interest, and explicitly in those of Rae, Landry, Walras, and Pareto. To trace this new influence on interest is the special purpose of the second approximation.

§5. *The Reasoning not "Circular"*

At first sight it may appear to those not familiar with the mathematics of simultaneous equations and variables that the reasoning is circular; the rate of interest depends on individual rates of impatience; these rates of impatience depend on the time shapes of individual income streams; and the choice of these time shapes of income streams depends, as we have just seen, on the rate of interest itself.

It is perfectly true that, in this statement, the rate of interest depends in part on a chain of factors which finally depend *in part* on the rate of interest. Yet this chain is not the vicious circle it seems, for the last step in the circle is not the inverse of the first.

To distinguish between a true and a seeming example of a circular dependence we may cite simple problems in algebra or mental arithmetic. Suppose we wish to find the height of a father who is known to be three times as tall as his child. To solve this we need to know something more about these two heights. If we are told in addition that the child's height differs from his father's by twice itself, the problem is really circular and insoluble, for the additional condition is really reducible to the first, being merely a thinly veiled inversion of it. The problem essentially states (1) that the father's height is three times the child's and (2) that the child's is one-third of the father's—an obvious circle.

But if the dependence of the father's height on the child's is essentially different from—independent of—the dependence of the child's on its father's, there is no circle. Thus supposing, as before, that the father is three times as tall as the child, let us stipulate in addition that

the child's height differs from the father's by four times
as much as the child's less two feet. This may *sound* as
circular as the first statement—the father's height is expressed in terms of the child's, and the child's is expressed
in terms of the father's; but the second stipulation is not
now reducible to the first. The heights are entirely determinate, that of the father being six feet and that of the
child, two. The mere fact that both of these magnitudes,
the father's height and the child's height, are specified
each in terms of the other does not constitute a vicious
circle. The general principle, as Cournot and other mathematical economists have often pointed out, is simply the
well known algebraic principle of simultaneous equations.
In order that the equations may determine the unknown
quantities involved, there must be as·many *independent*
equations as there are unknown quantities, although any
or all of these equations may contain all the unknowns.
(The equations are independent if no one of them can
be derived from another or the others.) Many an example
of economic confusion and wrong reasoning could be
avoided if this fundamental principle of mathematics
were more generally applied.

This mathematical principle of determinateness applies
in our present problem. Real examples of circular reasoning in the theory of interest are common enough, but the
dependence, above stated, of interest on the range of options and the dependence of the choice among them on
interest is not a case in point, for *this last determining
condition is not derivable from the others.*[5]

For our present purpose we need only present the
matter to the reader's imagination by a process of trial

[5] That this is the case under our present hypothesis is shown fully in
Chapter XIII.

and error. To find the rate of interest on which the market will finally settle, let us try successively a number of different rates. First, let us suppose a rate of 5 per cent. This rate will determine the choice between options for each individual. The land owner formerly supposed will, as we have seen, choose C, the mining use, because the present value of the income so obtained ($9110) exceeds the present values of the rival uses. Every other individual in the market, in like manner, will select that particular use for his capital which will give him the maximum present worth. With these choices made, the different individuals will then enter the market of loans or sales, desiring to modify the time shapes of their income streams to suit their particular desires.

As a result of all these choices, the total amount which all the would-be lenders are willing to lend at 5 per cent out of this year's instalment of their chosen income stream will be perfectly definite, and likewise the total amount which all the would-be borrowers are willing to take. This we saw in the preceding chapter. In other words, the demand and supply of loans for the present year, *at the given rate of interest,* 5 per cent, will both be definite quantities. Should it happen that the supply of loans exceeds the demand, it would follow that 5 per cent could not be the correct solution of the rate of interest, for it would be too high to clear the market.

In that case, let us try again; suppose a rate of 4 per cent. Following the same reasoning as before, we now find that the land owner will select the forestry opportunity for his land because the present value ($11,300) of the income from forestry—now reckoned at 4 per cent—will exceed that of the two rival income possibilities. Other capitalists will likewise select their best option from among those available to them and on the basis of these income streams—not the same as before under 5 per cent. In a word, there will now be a different supply and demand. The land owner, for instance, instead of lending, may now borrow (or sell securities) to even up his income stream. Should it then happen that the demand and supply of loans, *on the basis of 4 per cent*, are still not equal, but that, this time, the demand exceeds the supply, it would be a proof that not 4 per cent is the true solution, but some higher rate. By again changing our trial rate—part way back toward 5 per cent, we may evidently reach some intermediate point, let us say 4½ per cent, *at which rate not only will each individual choose the best use of his capital—that having the highest present worth—but also, at the same time, the demand and supply of loans engendered by all such choices will exactly clear the market, i.e., bids and offers at the given rate will be equal.* Likewise, the same clearing will be worked out for next year and for all years.[6]

The introduction, therefore, of flexibility into our income stream still leaves the rate of interest entirely determinate, even though the income streams are now, in the second approximation, not fixed or rigid but subject to choice, and even though that choice will depend on the rate of interest itself.

§6. *Summary*

For the determination of the rate of interest we must now, therefore, in the second approximation, add two new principles to the four principles already given in the first approximation described in the previous chapter.

[6] The details of such a multiform equilibrium are given in mathematical terms in Chapter XIII.

THE TWO INVESTMENT OPPORTUNITY PRINCIPLES

A. Empirical Principle

There exists, for each individual, a given specific set or list of optional income streams to choose from, differing in size and time shape (but without any uncertainty as to what will happen if any particular one is chosen).

B. Principle of Maximum Present Worth

Out of this list of options each individual will choose that particular income stream possessing the greatest present worth when calculated by means of the rate of interest as finally determined by these six conditions.

THE TWO IMPATIENCE PRINCIPLES

A. Empirical Principle

The degree of impatience, or rate of time preference, of any given individual depends upon his income stream as chosen by him and as modified by exchange.

B. Principle of Maximum Desirability

Each person, after or while first choosing the option of greatest present worth, will then modify it by exchange so as to convert it into that particular form most wanted by him.

This implies, as we have seen, that each person's degree of impatience, or rate of time preference, will at the margin, be brought to equality with the market rate of interest and, therefore, with the marginal preference rates of all the other persons.

[148]

SECOND APPROXIMATION

THE TWO MARKET PRINCIPLES

A. Principle of Clearing the Market

The rate of interest must be such as will clear the market, that is, equalize supply and demand. That is, for every time interval, the additions to some individuals' incomes caused by borrowing or selling must balance the deductions from others caused by lending or buying.

B. Principle of Repayment

The loans must be equivalent in present worth to repayments, or, more generally, the additions to any individual's income, brought about by borrowing or selling, in some time intervals must be equivalent in present worth to the deductions from his income in other time intervals brought about by lending or buying.

Thus we see that the rate of interest is determined by two principles of *investment opportunity* as well as by two principles of *impatience* and by the two self-evident *market* principles.

More briefly stated, the rate of interest is determined so as (1) to make the most of opportunities to invest, (2) to make the best adjustment for impatience and (3) to clear the market and repay debts.

In short, the theory is thus one of *investment opportunity* and *human impatience*, as well as *exchange*.

But while we have reached the two chief theoretical foundations of our subject, we are still, of course, far from the real world. The real world is vastly more complex than the imaginary world described in this chapter. In particular, we still need to take account of risk. This we shall do in the third approximation.

CHAPTER VII

THE INVESTMENT OPPORTUNITY PRINCIPLES

§1. *Eligible and Ineligible Options*

THE essential point of the preceding chapter is that the possibility of more than one use of our resources affords opportunity to invest by substituting one such use for another. Whenever there is such a choice of alternatives, as for instance by changing from the "mining" to the "farming" use of one's land, as per Table 3, there is a differential sacrifice or investment of income during the earlier years for the sake of a differential return later. The fact that such alternative uses of labor, land, and capital exist, introduces on the scene the whole subject of "productivity".

Böhm-Bawerk was profoundly right when he wrote:

"The statement of how the productivity of capital works into and together with the other two grounds of the higher valuation of present goods, I consider one of the most difficult points in the theory of interest, and, at the same time, the one which must decide the fate of that theory." [1]

I have generally avoided the term productivity of capital because it may be used ambiguously to mean physical productivity, or value return, or return over costs; and because it suggests that capital produces income value instead of the reverse; and because it attributes the

[1] *Positive Theory of Capital*, p. 277, footnote.

value of manufactured things to the cost of production, instead of to their discounted future services.

I prefer the term investment opportunity. It has some of the demerits as well as the merits belonging to any new term. It is unfamiliar and therefore requires precise definition. The concept of investment opportunity rests on that of an "option." An option is any possible income stream open to an individual by utilizing his resources, capital, labor, land, money, to produce or secure said income stream. An investment opportunity is the opportunity to shift from one such option, or optional income stream, to another.

It includes all possible opportunities to invest—those that can yield only negative returns upon the investment as well as those which are capable of yielding very large surpluses over the amount of the investment or cost.

The first (A) of the two investment opportunity principles specifies a given range of choice of optional income streams. Some of the optional income streams, however, would never be chosen, because none of their respective present values could possibly be the maximum. We have seen that the land, in our example, would be most profitably employed for farming, for mining, or for forestry, according to the rate of interest. But it would not be employed, let us say, for a quarry, no matter what might be the rate of interest.

The optional uses which are thus out of the question, whatever be the rate of interest, are called *ineligible*. The rest are the *eligible* options. We need to consider the eligible ones—any one of which might be made to have the maximum present value, given the right rate of interest to make it so.

§2. *The Method of Comparative Advantage*

The second (B) investment opportunity principle, that of maximum present value, is of great importance and has many aspects not always recognized as related to one another. Let us restate this maximum value principle in an alternative form, thus: one option will be chosen over another if its income possesses comparative advantages outweighing (in present value) its disadvantages.

To illustrate this alternative method of stating the same principle—which method might be called the method of comparative advantage—let us recur to the example of the land. We found that, when the rate of interest was 4 per cent, the owner would elect the forestry use, since this possessed the greatest present value. If we now compare, year by year, the income from the land when used for forestry purposes with the income which it might have yielded if used in one of the other ways, as for instance farming, we shall see that in some years there is an excess in favor of the forestry use, and in other years a deficiency, as shown in the table on the following page.

Here we see that, in the first four years, there are comparative disadvantages, a differential sacrifice, amounting in the four respective years to $450, $450, $150, $50. These are the disadvantages from the use of the land for forestry purposes as compared with its use for farming, but the disadvantages are offset later by advantages in return amounting to $50 each year perpetually. If prior to the first year listed above the owner has been using the land for farming purposes and was considering the advisability of changing over to forestry, he would think of the disadvantages or sacrifices of $450, $450, $150 and $50

TABLE 6

Farming and Forestry Use Compared by Method of Comparative Advantage

	Annual Value of Farming Uses	Annual Value of Forestry Uses	Difference in Favor of Forestry Use
1st year	$450	...	−$450
2nd year	450	...	−450
3rd year	450	$300	−150
4th year	450	400	−50
5th year	450	500	+50
6th year	450	500	+50
7th year	450	500	+50
8th year	450	500	+50
9th year	450	500	+50
10th year	450	500	+50
11th year	450	500	+50
Each year thereafter.......	450	500	+50

as investments or costs and the advantages of $50 each year in perpetuity as returns on these investments or costs. And he could think of the proposal to substitute the forestry use for the farming use as an *opportunity to invest* the $450, $450, $150, and $50 for the sake of securing the return of $50 each year thereafter. If, now, we take the total present value, at 4 per cent, of the deficiencies, or *investments*, of $450, $450, $150, and $50, we shall obtain $1025, whereas the present value of the returns of $50 per annum beginning in five years and continuing in perpetuity will be $1069. Thus the present value (at 4 per cent) of the gains exceeds the present value of the sacrifices or costs by the difference between $1069 and $1025. As reckoned in present estimation, the gains of income outweigh the costs or sacrifices of income. We may say, therefore, that, the rate of interest being 4 per cent, forestry is preferable to farming because of a surplus of advantages over disadvantages reckoned in present value. Thus, the opportunity to invest by

[153]

switching over from farming to forestry is, if money can be borrowed at 4 per cent, more than worth while.

But if the rate of interest were 4½ per cent, the comparison would be different. The present value of the sacrifices or costs would be $1016, and the present value of the gains or returns $932, showing a preponderance of the sacrifices or costs. That is, if the rate of interest is 4½ per cent, the cost from using the land for forestry rather than farming outweighs the returns. Therefore, when money is at 4½ per cent, the land would not be used for forestry purposes.

The general principle is, therefore, that among the various options open to the capitalist he chooses the most advantageous, or more fully expressed, the one which, compared with any other, offers advantages which in present value at the given rate of interest outweigh the disadvantages. But this is evidently merely another formulation of the original principle that the use chosen will be the one which has the maximum present value at the given rate of interest.

We may summarize the method of comparative advantage as follows: We are constantly confronted with the opportunity to choose one income stream rather than another. We inquire *what difference it makes* whether one or the other alternative is chosen. We find often it makes two kinds of differences, advantages and disadvantages. If we start with the option which has the more immediate advantages and ask whether it is or is not worth while to give up this option and adopt the other instead, we may call the proposal so to do an *opportunity to invest,* i.e., to incur certain disadvantages or, as they will hereafter be called, *costs,* for the sake of certain advantages or, as they will hereafter be called, *returns.*

[154]

And we decide whether or not this investment opportunity is worth while by weighing the costs against the returns in terms of present worth, as reckoned by the rate of interest.

§3. *The Concept of Rate of Return Over Cost*

When we compare two optional income streams, and either may be preferable to the other according as one rate of interest or another obtains, the two options would stand on a par if the right intermediate rate were used for calculating the present values of the two options. That is, this equalizing rate is such that the present values of the two options would be equal, or what amounts to the same thing, it is such that, if that rate is used for discounting, the present value of the cost of choosing one option instead of the other would be equal to the present value of the return.

This hypothetical rate of interest which if used in calculating the present worth of the two options compared would equalize them or their differences (cost and return) may be called the *rate of return over cost* and hereafter this name will generally be employed. This new magnitude (or factor) in our study plays the central rôle on the investment opportunity side of interest theory.

Let us now apply this rate of return over cost to the case of the options already used for illustration.

We have seen that, in our land example, if the rate of interest is 4 per cent, the net advantage is in favor of the forestry use, and if the rate of interest is 4½ per cent, the net advantage is in favor of the farming use. It is evident then that at some intermediate rate of interest the comparative advantages of the two uses would be exactly equal. This intermediate rate is approximately 4.2 per cent, and this equalizing rate is the rate of return over cost.

But we may reduce the comparison to its simplest form if we change the figures in the example to the following:

TABLE 7

Farming and Forestry Use Compared in Terms of Rate of Return Over Cost

	Net Value of Farming Use	Net Value of Forestry Use	Net Difference in Favor of Forestry Use
1st year	$100	$000	—$100
2nd year	100	210	+110
3rd year	100	100	000
4th year	100	100	000
Each subsequent year	100	100	000

In this case the equalizing rate, or the rate of return over cost, is evidently 10 per cent. At the cost of $100 there is a return of $110, or 10 per cent over the $100. At 10 per cent the present worth of the two will be equal; for the present worth of the return $110 due next year is, reckoning at 10 per cent, exactly $100 and the present value of the cost, $100, due immediately, is also $100.

The example just given, in which the cost ($100) is only one item and the return ($110) is also only one item received one year later, is the simplest possible example. But the same principle holds true however complicated may be the series of items constituting the costs and returns.

Perhaps the next simplest example is that in which one option shows in the present year a cost (of, say, $100) compared with the other but shows a return (of, say, $8) for *every* future year in perpetuity. Under these circumstances the equalizing rate (or the rate of return over cost) is 8 per cent.

Thus the expression "rate of return over cost" is applied to the comparative merits of two alternative income streams. I repeat that by *cost* is meant the *comparative loss* from one's income stream at first, caused by substituting one use of capital for another, and by *return* is meant the *comparative gain* which accrues usually later, by reason of this same substitution. The *cost* is literally the difference it makes today and the *return* is the *difference* it makes in the future—the first negative, the second positive.

It will be noted that this description is all inclusive. It applies to every possible cost and every possible return. The problem of the investor—and everyone is an investor in some degree and manner—is always to answer the question: "What *difference* does it make to my income stream whether I choose one way rather than another? What do I sacrifice and what do I gain?" If the cost comes first and the return comes later, he wants to know if the return exceeds the cost by enough to be worth while. The excess is his return over cost and the important magnitude is the rate per annum of this return over cost.

Usually this question, "What difference does it make?", is asked with reference to a proposed change from an old to a new layout of one's plans. Will a little more tilling of the soil bring a big or a little return, both the tilling and return in crops being translated at their market prices into money? Will a new harvesting machine at market prices make enough difference in the harvest to be worth while? Will a merger of two companies make a return in future profits sufficient to make the temporary costs involved in the merging process worth while? It will be seen, then, that the concept here used of investment opportunity is not contrary to ordinary ideas. It includes them. Every time a person considers what he calls an opportunity to invest, he weighs in his mind the differences in his expected income—the expected future additions against the more immediate subtractions. Even when the investment is not made in installments out of savings from current income, but is made in one lump sum, it must not be forgotten that this lump sum invested merely represents the sacrifice of some alternative income stream.

The rate of return over cost is not, of course, to be confused with the rate of interest which it helps to determine, any more than the rate of impatience is to be so confused.

§4. *The Principle of Return over Cost*

Now let us restate the forestry-farming-mining comparison in the land example of the preceding chapter in terms of the rate of return over cost.

If the actual market rate of interest is 4 per cent, a person using the land for farming, or thinking of so doing, would find forestry preferable. The change from farming to forestry would cost certain sacrifices of income in the first four years, as specified in Table 6, but would return certain net additions thereafter. The rate of return over cost which would be realized by choosing the forestry rather than the farming use is 4.2 per cent. He would be realizing 4.2 per cent, which is more than the market rate, 4 per cent.

If, however, the market rate of interest were 4.5 per cent, it would not pay to change from farming to forestry; for to do so would return only 4.2 per cent as compared with 4.5 per cent which he could get in the loan market.

Our farmer would prefer to invest at 4.5 per cent *by lending* in the first four years $450, $450, $150, $50 rather than sacrifice these same amounts for 4.2 per cent by giving up farming for forestry. To induce him to make a change, the *rate of return over cost must exceed the rate of interest.*[2]

Thus, by employing the concept of a rate of return over cost, we may restate the investment opportunity principle of maximum present value, or the principle of comparative advantage, as the principle of greatest return over cost. So stated the principle is:

Out of all possible options open to a person that particular one is selected, the comparison of which with any other option affords a rate of return over cost equal to or greater than the rate of interest.

§5. *Marginal Rate of Return Over Cost*

Next let us apply this statement of principle to the case in which the range of choice is not confined to a *few* definite options, but extends to an *infinite number* varying by continuous gradations. This case is really more like the facts of life than the imaginary case of a few fixed options, such as the farming, mining, or forestry uses of land. In fact, each of these three uses is in actual

[2] In case the advantages (returns) precede the disadvantages (costs), as is the case when the merits of the mining use are compared with those of the farming use, the proposition must be reversed, as follows: The earlier advantage will be chosen only in case the rate of future costs over present returns is *less* than the rate of interest. In such a case it would be more convenient, in comparing the two options, to regard them in the reverse order, that is, to consider the advantages of the farming use over the mining use, so that the disadvantages may come first, i.e., the investment precede the returns. As long as the costs always precede the returns, we need only to consider whether or not the rate of return over cost *exceeds* the rate of interest.

life not merely a single use, as was assumed for simplicity, but a whole group of optional uses. Thus, the farmer may carry farming to any degree of intensity, and the same may be said of mining or lumbering. For each particular degree of intensity he will have a different income stream. He may, for instance, find it possible at the beginning of the scale of intensity to invest an extra $100 worth of his or other labor in the present in order that one year later he may have an income of $150 more than he would otherwise have. If the rate of interest is 4 per cent per annum, he would evidently prefer this course, for while his present income is diminished by $100 he would realize an increase of $150 in his income one year later, or $50 over cost, making a rate of return over cost of 50 per cent per annum, whereas the interest is only 4 per cent. If he invests another $100 in present cultivation, this will add to his income in a year's time something less than the $150, say $130, making a rate of return of 30 per cent. And so each successive choice compared with its predecessor follows the *law of decreasing returns*. A third $100 will add, let us say, $120 or $20 more than the cost. A fourth $100 may secure a return of an additional $10 a year over and above the cost; a fifth $100 may secure a return of an additional $8; a sixth $100 may bring $6; a seventh $100, $4.

Thus far, in the scale of intensity, each option yields 4 per cent or more, while the rate of interest is 4 per cent a year. The lure of a rate of return equal to or in excess of the interest rate will induce the farmer to incur the additional cost. But the next option, let us say, is to invest an eighth $100 for an additional $3 a year. Evidently, it will not be to the farmer's advantage to take this last step; he will stop at the previous step, at which he barely gets a 4 per cent return. As we saw in the preceding section, each successive investment opportunity is chosen as long as the rate of return over cost of that option compared with the previous one is greater than the rate of interest, and that use is rejected at which the rate of return over cost becomes less than the rate of interest. The intensiveness of his farming is thus determined by the rate of interest. In our example, he will stop at the seventh $100 which barely returns the equivalent of the rate of interest. We may say, then, that he chooses that degree of intensiveness at which the rate of return over cost is barely more than the rate of interest. This envisages a series of possible income streams arranged successively in order of intensiveness of the cultivation required for each. By substituting successively one of these income streams for the preceding we incur more cost but obtain more return. The rate of the return over the cost compared with the market rate of interest is our guide as to how far to go in the series. We thus reach the *marginal* rate of return over cost.

§6. *The Illustration of Cutting a Forest*

To vary the illustration from intensive agriculture to forestry, let us apply the option selection idea to cutting a forest. Let us consider as the first option the cutting of the forest at the end of nine years, when the income stream consists of the single-item, the production of 900 cords of wood (or $900 if wood is $1 a cord).[3]

The second option is holding the forest for another

---

[3] Inasmuch as we assume that the income from the forest is all to accrue at one time—the time of cutting—instead of being distributed over a long period, the income stream becomes a single jet and might here better be called income item.

year of growth and cutting it at the end of ten years, to
receive an income item of 1000 cords (or $1000, assuming
an unchanging price of $1 a cord). The two alternatives
may be put in precisely the same tabular form as the one
previously employed for the case of forestry and farming
as follows:

TABLE 8
Optional Incomes from Forest

	10-Year Plan	9-Year Plan	Difference in Favor of 10-Year Plan
1st year	$000	$000	
2nd year	000	000	
....	...	...	
9th year	000	900	−900
10th year	1000	000	+1000

The last column shows that the ten-year plan, compared
with the nine-year plan, involves a cost of 900 in the
ninth year, but involves a return of 1000 in the tenth
year. The rate of the return (100) over the cost (900)
would thus be a little over 11 per cent. If the rate of interest in the market is 5 per cent, it would evidently pay
to wait, that is, to postpone the cutting to the tenth year.

The next option would be to cut in the eleventh year,
which, as compared with the previous or ten-year plan,
would, let us say, cost 1000 in the tenth year and return
1050 in the eleventh year—in other words, give a rate
of return over cost of 5 per cent. Evidently, then, it would
be a matter of indifference whether the forest were cut
in the tenth or eleventh year, inasmuch as the rate of
return over cost would be exactly equal to the rate of
interest.

Similar reasoning might show that the choice of the
next option, that of cutting the forest in the twelfth year,

would yield a return of say $2\frac{1}{1050}$ or 2 per cent. Inasmuch as 2 per cent is less than the rate of interest, this alternative would be rejected. Thus, equilibrium is found where the rate of return on cost equals 5 per cent, the rate of interest.

The case may be illustrated by Chart 16. Let AB represent the number of cords of wood on an acre of growing

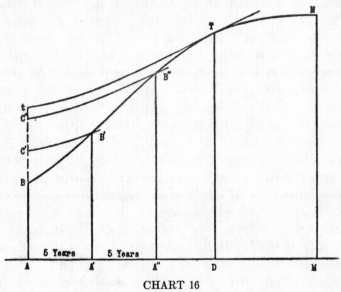

CHART 16

Selecting the Time for Cutting a Forest.

trees; let $A'\,B'$ represent the amount of wood which may be expected at the end of five years; let $A''\,B''$ represent what may be expected in ten years and so on for successive years until the forest reaches its maximum growth, MN, at the end of AM years. The percentage-slope, or rate of ascent,[4] of the curve BN at any point, therefore,

[4] *The Nature of Capital and Income,* pp. 221-222.

[163]

represents the rate of growth, at any time, of the forest. The value at present (at the point of time A) of the forest, *in terms of cords of wood*, will be represented, not by the height AB, but in a different manner, as follows: If from B' the discount curve [5] B' C' be drawn, the ordinate of which, at any time, will represent the discounted values of A' B' at that time, then AC' will represent the present value of A' B', i.e., of the amount of the wood if cut in five years. Similarly, AC'' will represent the present value of A'' B'', the wood if cut in ten years. We draw in like manner a number of discount curves until one is found, tT, which is tangent to the curve BN. At will then be the correct value of the young forest, and D will represent the time at which it should be cut. Clearly, At is quite different from AB, the amount of wood at the present time, and also from DT, the amount of wood at the time of cutting. At is the maximum present value out of all possible choices as to the time of cutting. If the forest is for some reason to be cut at once, its value will be only AB; if it is to be cut at A' its present value will be AC'; if at A'', it will be AC''; if at D, it will be At. At is the maximum, for if the forest were cut at any other point of time on either side of T the discount curve passing through that point would evidently lie below the curve tT.

At the time A, then, the wood in the forest is only AB but, assuming proper foresting, the value of the forest in terms of wood is At; the rate of growth of the forest is the percentage-slope of BN at B, but the rate of interest is the percentage-slope (the same at all points) of tT.

At the point of tangency alone, namely T, are the rate of growth and rate of interest (both in terms of wood)

[5] *The Nature of Capital and Income*, Chapter XIII.

identical, and to that extent at least there is truth in the thesis that the rate of interest is the rate of growth. This, however, is not the average rate of growth but the rate of growth at the time of cutting. This is the element of truth in the organic productivity theory of Henry George and Alexander Del Mar. These writers based their theories of interest on the productivity of those particular kinds of capital which reproduce themselves, and reached the conclusion that, in the last analysis, the rate of interest consists in the "average rate of growth of animals and plants." [6]

Evidently the theory would be substantially correct if "average" were replaced by "marginal." The example of cutting the forest illustrates the simplest theoretical case of marginal productivity as a true basis of the rate of interest.

But that this element of truth is insufficient of itself to afford a complete determination of the rate of interest is evident when we consider that the point at which the forest is to be cut itself depends, among other causes, upon the rate of interest! If the interest rate rises, the discount curves employed become steeper and the point of tangency T moves toward the left, that is, the forest will be cut earlier.

In no case, of course, is the time of cutting the time of maximum stumpage. To wait for that time would eat up too much interest. The theories of Del Mar and Henry George thus constitute a special case under the opportunity principles.

[6] Del Mar, Alexander. *Science of Money*. New York, Macmillan & Co., 1896; George, Henry. *Progress and Poverty*. New York, Sterling Publishing Co., 1879. For a general criticism of this theory see Lowry, *The Basis of Interest*, American Academy of Political and Social Science, March, 1893, pp. 53-76.

§7. *Other Similar Illustrations*

Both the preceding examples, one of intensive agriculture and the other of forest cutting, involve (1) an immediate cost and (2) a return one year later, thus reducing the marginal rate of return over cost to such simple calculations as $(105 - 100) \div 100 = 5$ per cent.

We may vary the illustration indefinitely and still preserve this elementary simplicity. A merchant has always before him an indefinite number of possible income-streams from which to choose. As in the case of the land cultivation and the forest cutting we may simplify his choice by supposing successive doses of costs of $100, each spent on more or better machinery, more or better workmen, more or better advertising, more or better supervision, and so forth, each $100 cost being immediate, and then supposing the returns to these successive doses of invested cost to come respectively one year later and to be respectively, say, $140, $130, $115, $106, $105, $104; so that the excess of return over the cost will be respectively $40, $30, $15, $6, $5, $4. Thus the rate of return over cost will be respectively 40, 30, 15, 6, 5, and 4 per cent. The enterpriser will incur the costs as long as the rate of return over these costs is greater than the market rate of interest. In this case, therefore, he will stop at 5 per cent if the market rate of interest is 5 per cent. Again we have $(\$105 - \$100) \div \$100 = 5$ per cent.

In practice, however, we seldom, if ever, have such simplicity in calculating the rate of return over cost and there are innumerable other types of contrast between the successive income streams which may be at the same time under consideration by the investor.

§8. *The Case of Perpetual Returns*

Next in simplicity is the type in which $100 of immediate cost is incurred for the sake of a perpetual annuity of $5 a year. Let us suppose the individual possesses some swamp land in a primitive condition. He has a large range of choice as to the method of utilizing this land. He wants to make the most of his opportunities. One option is to allow the land to remain a swamp. Others occur if, by clearing and draining it, it is converted into crop-yielding land, the yield varying with the thoroughness with which the clearing and draining are accomplished. Let us suppose that, under the first option, he derives a perpetual net income of $50 a year, and let us suppose that, at an immediate cost of $100 in his labor or in payment for the labor of others for clearing and draining, he can secure an addition of $25 a year. That is, as between retaining these two options, the swamp undrained and draining it partially, the latter involves a $100 decrease of immediate income and thereafter an income of $75 a year, or an increase of $25 a year. In other words, at the cost of $100 he will obtain a return of 25 per cent per annum in perpetuity.

Evidently, if the rate of interest in the market is 5 per cent, or anything less than 25 per cent, it will pay him to make such an investment, borrowing at 5 per cent if he wishes the $100 required for the improvement. Next suppose that another $100 invested in improving the swamp would yield crop returns of $90, or $15 more than before. The investment of this second $100 yields 15 per cent, and is therefore also a lucrative one, when the rate of interest is only 5 per cent. A third $100 may increase the annual crop still further, say by $10, netting a return of 10 per cent over the cost. A fourth $100 invested will cause the annual crop to be increased by $5 giving a return of 5 per cent. A fifth $100 will cause the crop to increase by $3—a return of 3 per cent. Evidently it will pay the farmer to invest in draining and improving his swamp up to the fourth $100, but not to the fifth $100. Rather than invest this fifth $100 and receive thereon an annual income of $3 a year, he would prefer to invest $100 in the savings bank and receive 5 per cent a year.

In other words, the exact degree of intensity with which he will improve and cultivate his land is determined by the current rate of interest. Should the rate of interest in the market fall from the 5 per cent just assumed to 2 per cent, it would then pay him to invest the fifth $100. For, evidently, if need be, he could borrow $100 at 2 per cent and receive from his land a return of 3 per cent. As Rae has so clearly pointed out, in communities where the rate of interest is low, swamps will be more thoroughly improved, roads better made, dwellings more durably built, and all instruments developed to a higher degree of efficiency so as to yield a lower marginal return over cost than in a community where the rate of interest is high.

§9. *The General Case*

In general, the rate of return over cost has to be derived by more complicated methods. As already indicated, the rate of return over cost is always that rate which, employed in computing the present worth of all the costs and the present worth of all the returns, will make these two equal. Or, as a mathematician would prefer to put it, the rate which, employed in computing the present worth

of the whole series of differences between the two income
streams (some differences being positive and others negative) will make the total zero.

If the rate, so computed, were taken for every possible
pair of income streams compared as to their advantages
and disadvantages, it would authentically decide in each

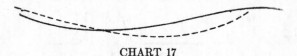

CHART 17

**Difference Between the Best and the Next Best Investment Opportunity
In the Raising of a Crop.**

case which of the pair is to be preferred. That one which
compared with the other shows a rate of return on sacrifice greater than the rate of interest would be preferred
and the other rejected. By such preferences and rejections
the individual would be led to a final *margin* of choice of
the best option. This contrasted with its nearest rival

CHART 18

**Difference Between the Best and the Next Best Investment Opportunity
in the Draining and Cultivating of Swamp Land.**

would show a marginal rate of return over cost equal to
the market rate of interest.

The problems of choosing when to cut a forest, of what
length to make a production period, how far to push any
industrial policy, to what degree of intensiveness to cultivate land, are all the same problem of choosing the
best out of innumerable possible income streams, i.e.,

problems of making the best out of one's investment opportunities.

In each problem the rival income streams present differences as to size and shape. They can best be compared

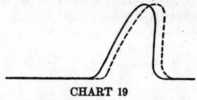

CHART 19

Difference Between the Best and the Next Best Investment Opportunity in the Cutting of a Forest.

by means of diagrams. Charts 17 to 20 show typical ways in which the income streams may conceivably be subjected to slight variation. The unbroken line in each case indicates the income stream chosen, and the dotted

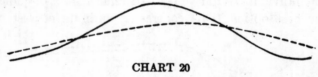

CHART 20

Alternating Investment and Return.

line the next best opportunity, rejected on behalf of the unbroken line. Chart 17 may be taken as applying to the planting of a crop; Chart 18 to the draining of a swamp; Chart 19 to the cutting of a forest; and Chart 20 to the case of alternating costs and returns.

§10. *Range of Choice Depends on Interest Rate*

Up to this point one complication in the problem of interest has been kept in the background. Although this complication does not invalidate any of the principles which have been developed, it seemed advisable not to distract attention from the essential features of the theory by introducing it prematurely. The complication referred to is, after all, more intricate than important. It consists in the fact that not only, as we have seen, does the choice between different optional income streams depend upon the rate of interest, but also that even the *range* of choice depends upon that rate. If the rate of interest is changed, a change is produced not only in the present values of the income items but in the income items themselves.

The net income from any instrument or group of instruments of wealth is the difference between the total gross income and the outgo. But many of the elements, both of income and outgo, are materially dependent upon the rate of interest. This is especially true of those items of income and outgo which are not final but merely intermediate or interactions.[7] In the case of interactions, a change in the rate of interest affects the income stream directly, because, as has been shown elsewhere,[8] the valuation of an interaction (i.e., intermediate service) involves the discount process and is therefore dependent upon the rate of interest. Thus, the iron yielded by an iron mine has its value determined in part by the discounted value of the machinery to be made of it and therefore its value will be affected by a change in the rate by which this discount is reckoned.

For present purposes, it is only necessary to emphasize the bare fact that the *range* of choice between different income streams is somewhat dependent upon the rate of interest. If the modification due to this fact were intro-

[7] See Chapter I or *The Nature of Capital and Income,* Chapters VII, VIII, IX, and X.   [8] *Ibid.,* p. 317.

duced into the tables previously given for the three different uses of land, we should find that the income streams from using the land for farming, forestry, and mining would differ according to the rate of interest.

Thus, let us suppose, as before in Chapter VI, §2, that for a rate of interest of 5 per cent the three optional income streams are:

TABLE 9

The Original Optional Income Streams of Farming, Forestry, and Mining

	Farming	Forestry	Mining
1st year	$450	$000	$2000
2nd year	450	000	1800
3rd year	450	300	1600
4th year	450	400	1400
5th year	450	500	1200
6th year	450	500	1000
7th year	450	500	800
8th year	450	500	600
9th year	450	500	400
10th year	450	500	200
Thereafter	450	500	000

In our previous discussion, when we changed the rate of interest from the 5 per cent of the foregoing table to 4 per cent, we supposed the items in the foregoing table to remain unchanged. The only change we had then to deal with was the change in their present values. Now, however, we admit the possibility of a change in the table items themselves. If the rate of interest falls to 4 per cent, the product of forest, farm, and mine will be more nearly equal to the value of the ultimate services to which they lead. The value of lumber will be more nearly equal to the value of the houses it makes, and these to the value of the shelter they give; the value of wheat from a farm will be nearer the value of the bread it will make; and the value of ore from a mine will be nearer the value of the steel it will become, and this, in turn, more nearly equal to the values of those innumerable satisfactions which come about through the use of steel. These shiftings forward of the values of the intermediate income of forest, farm and mine toward the values of the ultimate satisfactions to which they lead, combined with possible readjustments in the values of these satisfactions themselves—the values of house shelter, bread consumption, etc.—will result in a change, say, in the items in the foregoing table, where we were assuming a 5 per cent rate of interest, to the following table wherein the rate is 4 per cent.

TABLE 10

The Optional Income Streams of Farming, Forestry, and Mining, as Affected by the Rate of Interest

	Farming	Forestry	Mining
1st year	$500	$000	$2100
2nd year	500	000	1900
3rd year	500	350	1700
4th year	500	450	1500
5th year	500	600	1300
6th year	500	600	1100
7th year	500	600	850
8th year	500	600	650
9th year	500	600	450
10th year	500	600	225
Thereafter	500	600	000

If, then, the rate is 5 per cent, the land owner will make the most of his opportunities by choosing that use among the three which, computing from the figures in the *first* table, has the greatest present value; while if the rate is 4 per cent, he will choose that which, computing from the figures in the *second* table, has the greatest present value. If, then, the rate is 5 per cent, he will choose mining, since, as we saw in Chapter VI, §4, the present values, when we compute at 5 per cent, are: forestry, $8820;

farming, $9000; mining, $9110; but if the rate is 4 per cent, he will choose the highest from the present values at 4 per cent, computed from the second table. These present values now are: forestry, $13,520; farming, $12,-500; mining, $10,100.

Whatever the final outcome of all the readjustments, it is evident that the introduction of the influence of the rate of interest on the range of choice does not in any material way affect the reasoning already given in regard to the determination of the rate of interest. Since the rate of interest will itself fix the range of choice, it will still be true that, once the range of choice is fixed for a given rate of interest, the individual will choose, as before, that use which has the maximum present value. On the basis of this choice he is then led to borrow or lend in order to modify his income stream so that his degree of impatience may harmonize with the rate of interest. If, upon an assumed rate of interest, the borrowing and lending for different individuals actually cancel one another—in other words, clear the market—then the rate of interest assumed is clearly the one which solves the problem of interest; otherwise the borrowing and lending will not be in equilibrium, and some other rate of interest must be selected. By successively postulating different rates of interest, and remembering that each rate carries with it its own range of options and its own set of present values of those options, we finally obtain that rate which will clear the market.

The rate which will clear the market, while drawing into equality with itself all marginal impatience rates and all marginal rates of return on cost, is the one which solves the problem of interest under the assumed conditions.

§11. *The Investment Opportunity Principles Summarized*

The chief results of the chain of reasoning which has been followed in this chapter are that the same principle of investment opportunity may now be stated in four ways as:

The Principle of Maximum Present Value.
> Out of all options, that one is selected which has the maximum present value reckoned at the market rate of interest.

The Principle of Comparative Advantage.
> Out of all options, that one is selected the advantages of which over any other option outweighs its disadvantages, when both these advantages and disadvantages—returns and costs—are discounted at the market rate of interest.

The Principle of Return over Cost.
> Out of all options, that one is selected which, in comparison with any other, yields a rate of return over cost equal to or greater than the market rate of interest.

The Same Principle when the Options Differ by Continuous Gradations.
> Out of all options, that one is selected the differences of which from its nearest rival gives a rate of return over cost equal to the market rate of interest. Such a rate is called the *marginal* rate of return on cost.

In whichever of these aspects it is regarded, this is the principle of investment opportunity. However he reckons it, every one measures his opportunities to invest—to modify his income stream—in reference to the rate of interest by applying this principle.

We can scarcely exaggerate the importance of the concept of "rate of return over cost" and of its special variety *"marginal* rate of return over cost" as an element in our analysis of the conditions determining the rate of interest. It supplies, on the physical or technical or productivity side of the analysis, what the marginal rate of time preference supplies on the psychical side. The subject is, as has been seen, one which may be looked upon from many points of view, which may seem at first to be inconsistent yet which may be thoroughly coördinated under the foregoing generalizations.

§12. *Interrelation of Human Impatience and Investment Opportunity*

The rate of interest, then, is the resultant of three sets of principles of which the market principles are self-evident. The other two great sets of principles are the one comprising two principles of human impatience and the other comprising two principles of investment opportunity. The principles of impatience relate to subjective facts; those of investment opportunity, to objective facts. Our inner impatience urges us to hasten the coming of future income—to shift it toward the present. If incomes could be shifted at will, without shrinking in the process, they would be shifted much more than they are. But technical limitations prevent free shifting by penalizing haste and rewarding waiting. Thus Henry Ford might have continued making his Model T car. He would have thereby enjoyed a large immediate income but a gradually decreasing one. Instead, he resolved to place a better type of car on the market. To do so, he had to suspend the productive operations of his plant for a year, to scrap much of his old machinery and to provide a new installation at the cost of millions. The larger returns which he expected from the sale of the new car were only obtainable by the sacrifice of immediate income—by waiting.

Our outer opportunities urge us to postpone present income—to shift it toward the future, because it will expand in the process. Impatience is impatience to spend, while opportunity is opportunity to invest. The more we invest and postpone our gratification, the lower the investment opportunity rate becomes, but the greater the impatience rate; the more we spend and hasten our gratification, the lower the impatience rate becomes but the higher the opportunity rate.

If the pendulum swings too far toward the investment extreme and away from the spending extreme, it is brought back by the strengthening of impatience and the weakening of investment opportunity. Impatience is strengthened by growing wants, and opportunity is weakened because of the diminishing returns. If the pendulum swings too far toward the spending extreme and away from the investment extreme it is brought back by the weakening of impatience and the strengthening of opportunity for reasons opposite to those stated above.

Between these two extremes lies the equilibrium point which clears the market, and clears it at a rate of interest registering (in a perfect market) all impatience rates and all opportunity rates.

It is all a question of the *time and amount* of the series of items constituting real income. Shall we get income enjoyment now or later and how much? Shall we spend or invest?

CHAPTER VIII

DISCUSSION OF THE SECOND APPROXIMATION

§1. *Opportunity Reduced to Lowest Terms*

SINCE the second approximation contains the heart of the theory of interest, a further brief summary and discussion of the steps already taken will be helpful before proceeding to the third approximation.

Any opportunity to invest simply reduces itself to this: for a time there is more labor or less satisfaction than there would be in the absence of such opportunity, while there is expected later less labor or more satisfaction. The earlier item of labor or abstinence is less than the expected satisfaction or labor saving. This picture of temporary labor exerted, or abstinence from satisfactions which would otherwise be enjoyed, for the sake of later satisfaction or labor saving is the ultimate picture of cost and return.

When thus reduced to these lowest terms of labor and satisfaction, not only is our picture simplified, but with the simplification, we have rid it of a certain suspicion of begging the question of the interest problem. That is, as long as interactions, capital, and money were in the investment opportunity picture, interest was already implied in each of their valuations and there might remain a haunting fear that this new rate of return over cost as an interest-determining factor was simply involving us in a circle. The question might be asked: Is the rate of return a new influence? Is there really any important distinction between the rate realized on a bond, which is interest pure and simple, and the rate realized on any other investment? Are they not all simply interest, and is there anything else behind this interest besides human impatience? Is not the sum invested simply the discounted value of the return expected with due regard to the risk element, which has not yet been considered?

The answer, as should now be clear, is that the rate of return over cost really is a new element, not included in the first approximation, however mixed that element may be, in practice, with the elements considered earlier. When labor and satisfactions are concerned there is something more than exchange. The labor of planting a fruit tree is not the same thing as the discounted value of the fruit yielded by the tree, even though the value of the labor and the value of the fruit may be equal at a given time. The satisfaction from eating fruit is pleasure and the labor of planting it is pain, and these can be *directly* compared, despite the fact that in practice they are usually compared only indirectly in terms of their exchange equivalents.

Instinctively we feel the presence of this factor of rate of return over cost whenever we invest in a new enterprise. To invest in the original telephone enterprise, or in a railway under construction, seems somehow different from today buying telephone or railway securities. In the latter transactions we feel we are dealing with men—trading; in the former we feel we are dealing with Nature or our technical environment—exploiting. In fact, I came near selecting the term exploitation for a suitable catch word rather than investment opportunity to express the objective factor of a return over cost. Of course, even after the period of early exploitation is passed there are plenty of opportunities within the industry for variation in the rates of return over cost, but they are no longer so conspicuous.

Even when there is no exchange possible, as with Robinson Crusoe alone on his island, there will be dealings with Nature. Crusoe may plant trees or build a boat and balance his immediate labor against his future satisfactions without the presence of any exchange process. It would have been possible, of course, to have begun the presentation with Robinson Crusoe instead of ending with him. In that case, we should have first considered the primitive facts of labor exerted for the sake of future satisfaction, or their equivalent in berries. We could then bring in Man Friday, and proceed step by step to the complications of modern civilization. We should have seen how the primitive cost and return typified by labor and satisfaction became gradually hidden in a mass of exchanges until today we think of both in terms of money. The capitalist of today, instead of laboring for a future satisfaction, may simply abstain temporarily from a part of the satisfactions he could otherwise enjoy and, with the money which he would have spent for them, buy the labor to build a railway. The laborer is no longer the one who has to wait for the satisfactions to follow the completion of the railway. He is paid in advance and converts his pay into real wages very speedily, while the capitalist waits and receives the rewards for waiting.

In all these and the other manifold exchange relations the terms are partly set by the principles of discount in relation to impatience. But the primitive ingredients of labor and satisfaction, or their cost of living equivalents, with a time interval between, are never shuffled out of existence, however much they may be shuffled out of sight. They are ever present and exert their influence just as truly as they did with Robinson Crusoe.

In making the first of these two adjustments, the individual is not trading with other human beings, but is, as it were, trading with his environment—Nature and the Arts. That is why industry today maintains laboratories of research. These aim to improve products and service by scientific means, to develop new fields of application in by-products and materials, and to evolve new products and methods and so new investment opportunities. Trading with the environment is making the most of investment opportunity—of the future income returned per unit of present income sacrificed. Trading with mankind is making the most of impatience—of the preference for a unit of present income over a unit of future income.

When the individual sets out to trade with the environment he finds that the rate of return over cost *varies* with the extent to which he pushes this trading; he adjusts the trading so as to harmonize the marginal rate of return with the rate of interest. In his trading with other human beings, on the contrary, he finds the terms of the contract interest *fixed*, so far as any effort by him is concerned, but impatience varies with the extent to which he pushes this trading.

§2. *Investment Opportunity Essential*

Some economists, however, still seem to cling to the idea that there can be no *objective* determinant of the rate of interest. If subjective impatience, or time preference, is a true principle, they conclude that because of that fact all productivity principles must be false. But they overlook two important points. One is that, obviously and as a matter of practical fact, the technique of production does affect the rate of interest, and therefore cannot be ignored; the other, that their proposed solutions are indeterminate—i.e., they have more unknown quantities than determining conditions.

If, then, I am asked to which school I belong—subjective or objective, time preference or productivity—I answer "To both." So far as I have anything new to offer, in substance or manner of presentation, it is chiefly on the objective side.[1]

In my opinion minute differences of opinion as to the relative importance of human impatience and investment opportunity are of too little consequence to justify violent quarrels as to which of the two is the more fundamental, although I shall here and later, as occasion offers, note certain differences between them. The important point is that the two rates, that of marginal time preference and that of marginal return over cost, must be equal, granted continuity of variation, that is, variation by infinitesimal gradations. If, as Harry G. Brown,[2] in a very interesting Robinson Crusoe phantasy, assumes as a theoretical possibility, the rate of return over cost is fixed immutably at 10 per cent, the rates of impatience must conform thereto and the rate of interest can only be 10 per cent. Later in this chapter an even simpler and more easily imagined case, while at the same time more

[1] A somewhat similar treatment is that of Professor Harry G. Brown, *Economic Science and the Common Welfare*. Mathematical treatments substantially in harmony with mine are those of Walras and Pareto referred to in Appendix to Chapter XIII.

[2] H. G. Brown, *Economic Science and the Common Welfare*, pp. 137-145.

startling in its conclusions, is presented in which the technical limitations impose a fixed rate of interest and of human impatience of zero per cent. There, investment opportunity dominates.

On the other hand, we could also imagine the converse case; we could assume, as a theoretical possibility, a society of persons having an obstinate constancy in their rates of impatience, all being 10 per cent. In such a case, the marginal rate of return over cost would be adjusted thereto.

A person's rate of impatience depends on the extent to which he modifies his income stream by loans or sales. It is evident that if loans can be used to any extent desired, impatience will vary continuously with them.

The rate of return over cost, on the other hand, depends on the extent to which a person modifies his income stream by altering the way in which he utilizes his capital resources. Such alteration, while partly continuous, is partly discontinuous, as when new machinery, buildings, personnel or systems are introduced.

It was to emphasize this distinction between impatience and opportunity that I chose to begin with the case of a supposedly rigid income stream, as in the first approximation, with no opportunity to substitute any other; then to proceed to the case of three optional uses of land (distinguished for convenience as farming, mining, forestry) affording opportunity to substitute for one of them either of the others and thus disclosing in such substitution two alternative rates of return over cost; and finally to reach the supposed case of an infinite variety of income streams differing from one another by infinitesimal gradations. Only in the last named case is the rate of return over cost as variable as the rate of impatience.

It should be noted that in the first approximation, where the income stream is fixed or rigid and there is no alternative income stream, there can be no comparative cost or return and therefore no rate of return over cost. But we cannot so easily imagine a similar disappearance of impatience. It would be quite impossible to have any exchange between present and future—any rate of interest—without the existence of time preference, as it would be quite impossible to have any exchange whatever without human wants. They are an omnipresent and necessary condition of all exchange and valuation.

§3. *Options Differing in Time Shape Only*

Options differ in three chief ways corresponding to the characteristics, already noted, of the income stream, namely, (1) in composition, (2) in risk, and (3) in size and time shape. Options which differ primarily in *composition* or the kind of services rendered are illustrated by the options of using a building as a dwelling, as a shop, or as a factory. Options which differ primarily in the *probability or risk* are exemplified by the use of a ship on a hazardous voyage or in safe river transportation. Options which differ in *size and time shape* of the income stream are illustrated by the innumerable uses of land and artificial capital to produce different kinds of goods (income) of different degrees of immediateness as to the satisfactions they render.

The third group of options (which differ in the size and time shape of the income stream) is the one which especially concerns us here. First, let us suppose only one degree of flexibility, permitting variation in the time when the income items arrive but no variation in their amounts. Let us suppose, then, that the income stream from any capital is fixed in aggregate amount, but that the *times* of receiving that income are controllable at will. This species of choice occurs approximately in the case of durable goods for consumption, which neither improve nor deteriorate with time. A stock of grain, for instance, may be used at almost any time, with little difference in the efficiency of the use and little cost except for storage. The same is true of coal, cloth, iron, and other durable raw materials, as well as, to some extent, of finished products such as tools and machinery, though usually deterioration from rust, or other injury by the elements, will set in if the use is too long deferred. Another simple example is a definite sum of money in a strong box which may be spent at any time, or times, desired. Thus a strong box containing $100,000 may be so used as to yield a real income of $100,000 for one year, or $10,-000 a year for ten years, or $4,000 a year for twenty-five years.

Such options afforded by durable goods (as when to use them) are perhaps the simplest of all options. Since extreme cases are especially instructive, let us imagine a community in which the income from *all* capital is of the character just described. That is, we suppose the total *quantity* of income obtainable is absolutely fixed, but the *times* at which it can be obtained are absolutely optional. This community would then be endowed with a definite quantum of income as fixed as the quantity of money in a strong box. That is, every dollar of income sacrificed from one year's income would eke out any other income by that same amount, a dollar, no more and no less; conversely, every dollar of income enjoyed in one year would reduce indulgence elsewhere by exactly a dollar. The rate of interest would be reduced to zero.

THE THEORY OF INTEREST

§4. *The Imaginary "Hard-Tack" Illustration*

To fix our ideas, let us suppose these conditions to be realized on a desert island on which some sailors are shipwrecked and each left with a specified number of pounds of hard-tack and with no prospect of ever improving his lot. We shall suppose the use of this hard-tack to be the only real income open to these castaways, and that they have given up all hope of ever adding to it by accessions from outside or by cultivating the island which, for our hypothesis, must be barren. No change in their human nature need be assumed. We assume that they would react to the same income just as before the shipwreck. Merely their circumstances have changed. In consequence, the only possible variation of their income streams—consisting solely of the use of hard-tack—is that made possible by varying the time of its consumption. Suppose one of them has an initial stock of 100,000 pounds. He has the option of consuming his entire store during the first year, or of spreading its use over two or more years, but in any case he will eventually aggregate the same total income, measured in hard-tack, spread over the future, namely 100,000 pounds.

A little reflection will show that, in such a community, the rate of interest *in terms of hard-tack* would necessarily be zero! For, by hypothesis, the giving up of one pound of hard-tack out of present consumption can only result in an equal increase in future consumption. One pound next year can be obtained at the cost of exactly one pound this year. In other words, the *rate of return over cost* is zero. Since, as we have seen, this rate must equal the rates of preference, or impatience, and also the rate of interest, all these rates must be zero also.

[186]

DISCUSSION OF SECOND APPROXIMATION

This case is illustrated in Chart 21. One option is to consume the hard-tack at an even rate OA through the time OB. The *total income* will then be represented by the area OACB. Another option is to spread it over OB'. double the above-mentioned time, and consume it at the rate of OA', half the rate first mentioned, so that the same total income will be represented by the area OA'C'B'. The choice of the second use rather than the

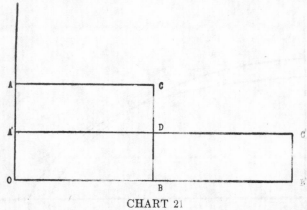

CHART 21

Zero Rate of Return, Total Income Fixed, Case

first is at the cost of that part of the earlier income represented by the rectangle AD, and gives a return exactly equal in amount represented by the rectangle DB'. If the hard-tack is not consumed at a uniform rate, the alternative income streams will not be represented by rectangles, but by the irregular and equal areas OADB and OA'DB', shown in Chart 22. The substitution of the alternative OA'DB' for OADB increases immediate income by ADA' and decreases subsequent income by the exactly equal amount BDB'.

The conclusion, that the rate of interest, under such

extreme conditions supposed in the hard-tack case, must be zero, is at first startling, but it is easy to convince ourselves of its correctness. It would be impossible for any would-be lender to obtain interest above zero on his loan for the only way in which a borrower could repay a loan would be to pay it out of his original stock of hard-tack. For assuming he had the impulse to borrow 100

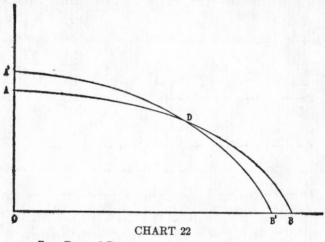

CHART 22

Zero Rate of Return, Total Income Fixed, Case 2.

pounds to consume today and pay back 105 pounds at the end of a year, he would instantly perceive that he could better consume the 100 pounds of his own hard-tack, thereby sacrificing next year not 105, but only 100 pounds out of his own stock. It is equally impossible that there should be a negative rate of interest. No one would lend 100 pounds of hard-tack today for 95 receivable a year later, when he had the option of simply storing away his 100 pounds today and taking it out, undiminished, a year later. Hence, exchanges of present for future hard-tack could not exist, except at par. There could be no premium or discount in such exchange.

Nor (to turn to the subjective side) could there be any rate of preference for present over future hard-tack. The sailors would so adjust the time shape of their respective income streams that any possible rate of preference for a present over a future allowance of hard-tack would disappear, and a pound of this year's hard-tack and a pound of next year's hard-tack would be equally balanced in present estimation. For, should a man prefer one rather than the other, he would transfer some of it from the unpreferred time to the preferred time, and this process would be continued, pound by pound, until his want for a pound of immediate hard-tack and his want for a pound of future hard-tack were brought into equilibrium. Thus, if through insufficient self-control, he prefers, however foolishly, to use up much of his store in the present and so to cut down his reserve for the future to a minimum, the very scantiness of the provision for the future will enhance his appreciation of its claims, and the very abundance of his provision for the present will diminish the urgency of his desire to indulge so freely in the present.

Provided each individual is free to apportion his share of the total stock of hard-tack between present use and future use as he pleases, and provided there is some hard-tack available for both uses, the present desire for a pound of each will necessarily be the same.

(Failure of such equilibrium of want could only occur when, as in starvation, the want for the present use was so intense as to outweigh the want for even the very last pound for future use, in which case there would be none whatever reserved for the future.)

All persons, however different in nature, would alike have a zero rate of impatience. They would differ simply in the way they distributed their income over present and future. The spendthrift and the miser would still spend and save respectively but both would value a unit of hard-tack today as the exact equivalent of one due a year hence. It is evident that some of the sailors, with a naturally keen appreciation of the future, would plan to consume their stores sparingly. Others would prefer generous rations, even with the full knowledge that starvation would thereby be brought nearer, but none of them would consume all of his stock immediately. They would, generally speaking, prefer to save out of such reckless waste at least something to satisfy the more urgent needs of the future.

In other words, a certain amount of saving (if such an operation can be called saving) would take place, without any interest at all. This conclusion coincides with conclusions expressed by Professor Carver in his *Distribution of Wealth*.[3] It shows also that the preference for present over future goods of like kind and number is not, as some writers assume, a necessary attribute of human nature, but that it depends always on the relative provisioning of the present and future.

The foregoing imaginary hard-tack case is of great help, therefore, in emphasizing the essential rôle of the rate of return over cost. This simple example, of itself, demonstrates that no theory of interest is complete which ignores the rate of return over cost. In the example we have both elements, investment opportunity and impatience, although both are at the vanishing point, that

[3] p. 232. See also Carver, T. N. *The Place of Abstinence in the Theory of Interest*, Quarterly Journal of Economics, Oct., 1893, pp. 40-61.

is, the rate of return and the rate of impatience are both zero, the former, rate of return, being fixed at zero by the technical conditions of the particular environment on the desert island, and the impatience rate being forced thereby to be zero also. In this case opportunity (or the lack of it) rules impatience.

It would be possible, of course, to make this illustration somewhat more realistic by adding to our supposed supplies of hard-tack supplies of other foods, as well as of clothing and sundry other real income. But the value of the illustration is not in any realism which can be made out of it. Rather does the fact that conditions in real life do not permit such freedom of shifting real income in time (because of change in quantity or quality) reveal some of the reasons why the rate of interest is not zero.

§5. *The Imaginary "Figs" Example*

Not only may the rate of interest conceivably be zero; it may conceivably be negative. Suppose our sailors were left not with a stock of hard-tack, but with a stock of figs which, like the hard-tack, can be used at any time as desired, but which, unlike the hard-tack, will deteriorate. The deterioration will be, let us say, at a fixed and foreknown rate of 50 per cent per annum. In this case (assuming that there is no other option available, such as preserving the figs) the rate of interest in terms of figs would be necessarily *minus* 50 per cent per annum, as may be shown by the same reasoning that established the zero rate in the hard-tack case.

More generally, this would be true if there were a world in which the only provisioning of the future consisted in carrying over initial stocks of perishable food, clothing, and so forth and if every unit so carried over into the future were predestined to melt way each year by 50 per cent.

One reason why we do not encounter such cases, with negative rates of return over cost, negative rates of interest, and negative rates of time preference is that we have other income available for the future besides what can be carried over from present stocks. Future figs will come into being from fig trees and even existing stocks of figs and other perishables may be carried over for future use by canning, cold storage, preservation and similar processes. Yet we do, even in our real world, occasionally have cases such as of spoiling strawberries, where, the rate of interest reckoned in terms of the strawberries is occasionally negative.

We see, then, that there is no absolutely necessary reason inherent in the nature of man or things why the rate of interest in terms of any commodity standard should be positive rather than negative. The fact that we seldom see an example of zero or negative interest is because of the accident that we happen to live in an environment so entirely different from that of the shipwrecked sailors.

§6. *The Imaginary "Sheep" Example*

The next example is more like that in our real world. In the real world our options are such that if present income is sacrificed for the sake of future income, the amount of future income secured thereby is greater than the present income sacrificed. That is, the income which we can extract from our environment is not, in the aggregate, a fixed quantum like a storehouse of hardtack; still less is it like a storehouse of dwindling contents. On the contrary, Nature is, to a great extent, reproductive. Growing crops and animals often make it possible to endow the future more richly than the present. Man can obtain from the forest or the farm more by waiting than by premature cutting of trees or by exhausting the soil. In other words, Nature's productivity has a strong tendency to keep up the rate of interest. Nature offers man many opportunities for future abundance at trifling present cost. So also human technique and invention tend to produce big returns over cost.

It is difficult to imagine a precise and simple case in which the rate of return over cost is fixed as in the case of the hard-tack or the figs but, instead of being zero or negative, is positive, say 10 per cent, neither more nor less. The best example is the ingenious one worked out by Professor Harry G. Brown in which fruit trees are planted at the cost of 100 units of fruit and automatically produce 110 units of fruit a year later and then die.[4] A simpler imaginary example, if we can forget certain obvious practical limitations, is that of the proverbial flock of sheep, which multiply in geometric progression affording alternately 100 units of mutton and wool today or 110 next year and ten per cent more each succeeding year. These examples symbolize a state of things in which it is always possible at the cost of 100 units out of this year's income to secure a return of 110 units next year, making a return over cost of 10 per cent. In such examples, just as in the hard-tack case with its zero per cent, or the fig case with its minus 50 per cent, the investment opportunity principles prescribe or dictate the rate of interest and the rate of time preference. These rates will in the present instance of the sheep all be 10 per cent.

[4] Brown, *Economic Science and the Common Welfare*, pp. 137-147.

We see then that, given the appropriate environment, the investment opportunity principle *may* dominate interest and force it to be zero, or minus 50 per cent, or plus 10 per cent, or any other figure. Under such conditions, the rate of impatience and the rate of interest will follow suit.

In actual life, however, any shoving of real income forward or backward in time can never be done without causing a variation in the rate of return over cost. The result is that the rate of impatience influences the rate of return quite as truly as the rate of return influences impatience.

§7. *Opportunities as to Repairs, Renewals, Betterments*

In the foregoing examples the options consisted of different employments of a particular instrument or set of instruments of capital which were assumed to retain their physical identities throughout the period of those employments. But now let us regard an instrument, or group of instruments, of capital as retaining only a sort of fictitious identity, through renewals or repairs, just as the proverbial jack-knife is said to be the same knife after its blade and then its handle have been replaced. This brings us to another large and important class of options; namely, the options of effecting, or not effecting, renewals and repairs, and the options of effecting them in any one of many different degrees. If the repairs are just sufficient for the up-keep they may be called renewals; if more than sufficient, or if involving improvement in quality, they may be called betterments. But it will be convenient to include in thought all alterations as to the form, position, or condition of an instrument or group of instruments affecting its stream of services. This will cover the whole subject of the production of reproducible goods.

This class of optional employments, when the employment involves sales from a stock, merges imperceptibly into the special case which we originally called the method of modifying an income stream by buying or selling. Thus, consider a merchant who buys and sells rugs. His stock of rugs is conveniently regarded as retaining its identity, although the particular rugs in it are continually changing. This stock yields its owner a net income equal to the difference between the gross income, consisting of the proceeds of sales, and the outgo, consisting chiefly of the cost of purchases, but including also cost of warehousing, insurance, wages of salesmen, and so on.

If the merchant buys and sells equal amounts of rugs and at a uniform rate, his stock of rugs will remain constant and its net income to be credited to that stock will theoretically, that is, under our present assumption of a riskless world, be equal to the interest upon its value. It will be standard income.[5] This income to be credited to his stock in trade is, of course, to be distinguished from that to be credited to his own efforts—his wages of superintending (neither need be called profits in a riskless world).

But the owner has many other options than that of thus maintaining a constant stock of goods. He may choose to enlarge his business as fast as he makes money from it, in which case his net realized income will be zero for a time, because all return is "plowed back" into the business. His stock will increase and eventually his income will be larger. In this option, therefore, his income stream is not contant, but ascends from zero to some

[5] See *The Nature of Capital and Income*, Chapter XIV, No. 4.

figure above the standard income which constituted the first option.

A third option is gradually to go out of business by buying less rugs than are sold, or none at all. In this case the realized income at first is very large, as it is relieved of the burden of purchases; but it declines gradually to zero.

Intermediate among these three options there are, of course, endless other options. The merchant thus has a very flexible income stream.

If the expenses and receipts for each rug bought and sold are the same, whichever option is chosen, and if the time of turnover is also the same, it will follow that all of the options possess the same present value and differ only in desirability. We should then be dealing with what we have called modifications of the income stream through buying and selling. The reason for placing optional employments of capital on a different footing from buying and selling is that the optional employments do *not* all possess the same present value. In actual fact, the rug merchant, and merchants in general, would not find that all the optional methods of proportioning sales and purchases of merchandise possessed equal present values. For one thing, if the rug merchant attempted to enlarge his business too fast he would find that his time of turnover would be lengthened, and if he reduced it too fast he would find that his selling expenses per unit of merchandise would be increased. There is, for each merchant, at any time, one particular line of business policy which is the best, namely, that which will yield him the income stream having the maximum present value. Since, therefore, the various methods of renewing one's capital usually yield income streams differing in present value, they may be properly classed as optional employments of such capital.

The propriety of such a classification becomes still more evident when, instead of mere renewals, we consider repairs and betterments, for it is clear that the income from a farm has a very different present value according as it is tilled or untilled, or tilled in different degrees of intensity, that the income from a house so neglected that a leak in the roof or a broken window pane results in injuring the interior is less valuable than the income it would yield if properly kept up, and that real estate may be underimproved or overimproved as compared with that degree of improvement which secures the best results.

In all cases the "best" results are secured when that particular series of renewals, repairs, or betterments is chosen which renders the present value of the prospective income stream the maximum. This, as we have seen, is tantamount to saying that the renewals, repairs, or betterments are carried up to the point at which the marginal rate of return over cost which they bring is equal to the rate of interest. The owner of an automobile, for instance, will replace a broken part and so prolong the life of his automobile. The first repair may cost him $10 and may save him $200. But such a twenty-fold return cannot be expected from every repair, and beyond a few such really necessary repairs, it soon becomes a question to what extent it is worth while to keep an automobile in repair. Repainting the body and regrinding the valves are both costly, and though, in such instances, the service of the automobile is increased in quantity and improved in quality, the return grows less and less as the owner strives after increased efficiency. Under our present hypothesis in which risk is disregarded, he will spend money on his automobile for repairs and renewals up to that point where the last increment of repairs will secure a return which will just cover the cost with interest. Beyond this he will not go.

In practice, of course, the choice between the various possible repairs, renewals, or betterments will involve some corresponding choice between possible employment of labor, land, and every agent of production. But I have tried here to isolate for study the services and disservices of a physical instrument subject to repairs, renewals, or betterments.

Another case of optional income streams is found in the choice between different *methods* of production, especially between different degrees of so-called capitalistic production. It is always open to the prospective house builder to build of stone, wood, or brick, to the prospective railroad builder to use steel or iron rails, to the maker of roads to use macadam, asphalt, wood, cobble, brick, or cement, or to leave the earth unchanged except for a little rolling and hardening. The choice in all cases will depend theoretically on the principles which have been already explained.

To take another example, the mere services of a house which has a durability of 100 years will be equivalent to the services of two houses, each of which has a durability of 50 years, one built today and lasting 50 years, and the other built at the expiration of that period and lasting 50 years more; yet the one house may well be better than the two. The difference between the one and the two will not be in the *services* but in the *cost* of construction. The cost of constructing the 100-year house occurs in the present; that of the two successive 50-year houses occurs half in the present and half at the end of 50 years. In order that the more durable house may have any advantage as to cost, the excess of its cost over the cost of the less durable one must be less than the present value of the cost of replacing it 50 years later.

The choice between different instruments for effecting the same purpose may, of course, depend on their relative efficiency, that is, the *rate* of flow of income, or upon their relative durability, that is, the *time* of the flow. It is true, however, as John Rae has pointed out,[6] that efficiency and durability usually go hand in hand. A house which will endure longer than another is usually more comfortable also; a tool which will cut better will usually wear out more slowly; a machine which does the fastest work will generally be the strongest and most durable.

The alternatives constantly presented to most business men are between policies which may be distinguished as temporary and permanent. The temporary policy involves the use of easily constructed instruments which soon wear out, and the permanent policy involves the construction at great cost of instruments of great durability. When one method of production requires a greater cost at first and yields a greater return afterward, it may be called, conformably to popular usage, the more capitalistic of the two. The word capitalistic refers to methods of employing capital which tend toward an ascending income stream. Although the term is not a happy one, it has a plausible justification in the fact that an ascending income stream means the accumulation of capital, or saving, and still more in the fact that only a capitalist can afford to choose a method of production which at first yields little or no income, or even costs some

---

[6] Rae, *The Sociological Theory of Capital,* p. 47.

outgo. Capital involves command over income without which no one could subsist, or at any rate subsist with comfort. The capitalist, by using his capital, even to the extent of using up some of his accumulations, can supply himself with the immediate income necessary while he is waiting for returns on his new ventures. It is as a possessor of *income* that he is enabled to subsist while waiting. He is enabled to invest in an ascending, or slowly returning, income stream only by first having at command a quickly returning income stream. We may say, therefore, that a capitalistic method is a method resulting in an ascending income stream, and it is so called because it is open chiefly to those who have command of other—often descending—income streams, such persons being necessarily capitalists, that is, possessors of much rather than little capital.

§8. *Opportunity to Change the Application of Labor*

The best example of the choice between those uses of capital instruments affording immediate and those affording remote returns is found in the case of human capital, commonly called labor. Man is the most versatile of all forms of capital, and among the wide range of choices as to the disposition of his energies is the choice between using them for immediate or for remote returns. This choice usually carries with it a choice between corresponding uses of other instruments than man, such as land or machines. But the existence of optional employments of labor, however inextricably bound up with optional employments of other instruments, deserves separate mention here both because of its importance and because it usually supplies the basis for the optional employments of other forms of capital.

DISCUSSION OF SECOND APPROXIMATION

It is almost exclusively through varying the employment of labor that the income stream of society, as a whole, is capable of changing its time shape. The individual may modify the time shape of his particular income stream through exchange, but in this case some other person must modify his income stream in the opposite manner, and the two sorts of modifications, some plus and others minus, offset each other in the total of the world's income. On the other hand, if an income is modified in time shape merely through a change in the exertions of laborers, there is no such offset, and the total social income is actually modified thereby.

The labor of a community is exerted in numerous ways, some of which bring about enjoyable income quickly, others slowly. The labor of domestic servants is of the former variety. The cook's and waitress' efforts result in the enjoyment of food within a day. Within almost as short a time, the chambermaid and the laundress promote the enjoyment of house, furniture, and clothing. The baker, the grocer, the tailor are but one step behind the cook and laundress; their efforts mature in enjoyments within a few days or weeks. And so we may pass back to labor increasingly more remote from enjoyable income, until we reach the miner whose work comes to fruition years later, or the laborer on the Panama Canal or the vehicular tunnels, whose work was in the service of coming generations.

The proportions in which these various kinds of labor may be assorted vary greatly, and it is largely through varying this assortment that the income stream of the community changes its time shape. If there are at any time relatively few persons employed as cooks, bakers, and tailors, and relatively many employed as builders, miners, canal and tunnel diggers, there will tend to be less immediately enjoyable income and correspondingly more enjoyable income in later years. Thus, by withdrawing labor from one employment and transferring it to another, it is in the power of society to determine the character of its income stream in time shape, and also in size, composition, and uncertainty. This power is exerted through the "enterpriser," to use Professor Fetter's term, according to the enterpriser's estimate of what return will come from each particular employment taken in connection with the cost involved and the ruling rate of interest.

§9. *Fluctuations in Interest Rates Self-Corrective*

Since the choice, for an individual, among different options, depends on the rate of interest in the manner described in Chapter VI, it is clear that a low rate favors the choice of the more ascending income streams, but also that the choice of such income streams reacts to raise the rate of interest. If, on the contrary, the rate is high, the opposite of both these propositions holds true; the high rate favors the choice of the less ascending income streams, but that choice reacts to lower the rate of interest.

Thus, if we apply these principles to repairs, renewals, and betterments, it is evident that the lower the rate of interest, the better can the owner of an automobile afford to keep it in repair, and the better can the owner of a railroad keep up its efficiency, and the same applies to all other instruments. But it is equally clear that the very attempt to improve the efficiency of instruments tends, in turn, to increase the rate of interest, for every repair means a reduction in present income for the sake of future—a shifting forward in time of the income stream —and this will cause a rise in the rate of interest. Thus, it follows that any fall in the rate of interest will tend to bring its own correction.

Again, it is evident that a choice of the more durable instruments, as compared with those less durable, will be favored by a low rate of interest, and a choice of short-lived instruments will be favored by a high rate of interest. If the rate of interest should fall, there would be a greater tendency to build stone houses as compared with wooden ones. The present value of the prospective services and disservices of stone houses as compared with wooden houses would be increased, for although stone houses are more expensive at the start, they endure longer, and their extra future uses, which constitute their advantage, will have a higher present value if the rate of interest is low than if it is high. We find, therefore, as John Rae has so well pointed out, that where the rate of interest is low, instruments are substantial and durable, and where the rate of interest is high they are unsubstantial and perishable.

We see, then, that the existence of numerous options has a regulative effect. Beyond the margin of choice there always lie untouched options ready to be exploited the instant the rate of interest falls. Among these, as Cassel [7] has pointed out, are waterworks of various kinds. Not only works of stupendous size but hundreds of less conspicuous improvements are subjects of possible investment as soon as the rate of interest falls low enough to make the return upon cost equal to the rate of interest. The same is true of the improving, dredging, and deepening of harbors and rivers, the use of dikes and jetties,

[7] *The Nature and Necessity of Interest*, p. 122.

the construction of irrigation works for arid lands, and Boulder Dam projects.

There is still room for much improvement in our railway systems by making them more efficient and more durable, by making the roads straighter, the roadbeds more secure, the rolling stock heavier, the bridges larger and stronger, by further electrifications, and similar improvements. In a new country where the rate of interest is high, the cheapest and most primitive form of railway is first constructed. Very often it is a narrow-gauge road with many curves, costing little to construct, though much to operate. Later, when the rate of interest falls, or the traffic so increases that the rate of return on sacrifice is greater, the broad-gauge comes into use and the curves are eliminated. This is the kind of change which has been proceeding in this country with great rapidity during recent years. There is a transition from relatively small first cost and large running expenses to precisely the opposite type of plant, in which the cost is almost all initial and the expense of operation relatively insignificant.

§10. *Wide Opportunities Stabilize Interest*

The existence of a wide variety of available income streams, then, acts as a sort of governor or balance wheel which tends to check any excessive changes in the rate of interest. Interest cannot fall or rise unduly; any such fluctuation corrects itself through the choice of appropriate income streams.

We see here a reason why interest does not suffer very violent fluctuations. It is not only true that natural processes are regular enough to prevent sudden and great changes in the income stream; it is also true that man constantly aims to prevent such changes. Man is not the slave of Nature; to some extent he is her master. He has many ways to turn. He possesses, within limits, the power to flex his income stream to suit himself. For society as a whole, the flexibility is due to the adaptability and versatility of capital—especially human capital commonly called labor; for the individual, the flexibility is greater still, since he possesses a two-fold freedom. He is not only free to choose from among innumerable different employments of capital, but he is free to choose from among different ways of exchanging with other individuals. This power to exchange is the power to trade incomes; for under whatever form an exchange takes place, at bottom what is exchanged is income and income only.

CHAPTER IX

THIRD APPROXIMATION TO THE THEORY OF INTEREST

Assuming Income Uncertain

§1. *More than One Rate of Interest*

THE great shortcoming of the first and second approximations, from the standpoint of real life, is the complete ruling out of uncertainty. This exclusion of the risk element was made in order to make the exposition simpler and to focus the reader's attention on the factors most relevant to the theory of interest. But in real life the most conspicuous characteristic of the future is in its uncertainty. Consequently, the introduction of the element of chance, or risk, will at once endow our hypothetical picture with the aspect of reality. The foundation for our study of risk in relation to interest has already been laid in Chapter IV where the relation of risk to time preference was noted.

One consequence of changing our assumption as to the certainty of future events is to compel the abandonment of the idea of a single rate of interest. Instead of a single rate of interest, representing the rate of exchange between this year and next year, we now find a great variety of so-called interest rates. These rates vary because of risk, nature of security, services in addition to the loan itself, lack of free competition among lenders or borrowers, length of time the loan has to run, and other causes

[206]

which most economists term economic friction. The very definition of loan interest as one implying no risk must now be modified so as to imply some risk that the loan may not be repaid in full according to the contract. Practically all of them are varieties of *risk*. Even in loans which theoretically are assumed to be riskless, there is always some risk. Modern corporate finance makes no pretence that risk is completely absent, but merely concerns itself with providing a more or less safe margin of protection varying with each specific case.

Furthermore, for our present purposes, contract or explicit interest is too narrow a concept. We now include not only the implicit interest realized by the investor who buys a bond, but the implicit interest realized by the investor who buys preferred stock. We may even include the rates realized on common stock, real estate, or anything else. Thus extended, the concept of interest becomes somewhat vague. And yet, if we exclude exceptional cases, there tend to emerge, at any time, several fairly definite market rates of interest according to the character of the security.

We find quoted rates on call loans, four months prime commercial paper, prime bankers' acceptances, first mortgages, second mortgages, as well as rates given by savings banks, rates allowed on active checking accounts, pawn shop rates, Morris Plan bank rates, rates realized on government bonds, railroad bonds, on other bonds, whether mortgage, debenture, or income bonds (all of which bond rates vary according to the character and credit of the issuer as well as in accordance with other circumstances), rates realized on preferred stock, and sometimes even the rates realized on common stocks. Wherever there is a sufficiently definite rate per cent per annum to be quoted as an expression of the current market, whether the quotation be in print or a verbal quotation in a broker's or banker's office, it seems proper to call it in a broad sense a rate of interest. Even when confined to such market rates, and excluding exceptional or individual rates, the rate of interest ceases to be the ideal, imaginary, single-valued magnitude hitherto assumed and takes on the myriad forms which we find in actual business transactions.

As indicated, this profuse variety is brought about chiefly by the introduction of *risks* of various sorts. The rate on call money is affected by the chance of the loan being "called" by the lender, or the sudden reduction of the total of such loans outstanding and the raising of the rate for those remaining. The rate on a loan-shark's loan is high because of the risk of non-payment by the borrower; the rate on a debenture and the rate on a second preferred stock of a moribund corporation are affected by the risk of inadequate corporate assets in event of liquidation; the rate on a government bond of a nation at war is affected by the chance of that nation's defeat; the rate of dividends on common stock is affected by the risks of the business; and so on in an infinite number of different cases.

§2. *Relations Between the Various Rates*

No very satisfactory theoretical treatment of the general relations between interest and risk has yet been worked out. But for practical purposes, a good usage is to limit the term "interest" to fairly safe loans and staple or standard market quotations and to designate by some other term, such as dividends or profits, the other less certain and less standardized rates. Another usage is to reckon as net profits or net losses the difference between these less standardized rates and a normal rate of interest so far as this can be expressed in figures. Thus a man who has invested $100,000 in common stock and is getting an income of $15,000 may think of $5,000 of this, or 5 per cent, as a fair interest on his investment and the remaining $10,000, or 10 per cent, as net profit. But we do not need here to enter into such discussions, especially in so far as they are only verbal. All that is here needed is to show briefly how risk modifies the theoretically perfect determination of the interest rate thus far made.

The rate in every loan contract is adjusted according to the degree of security given. Thus, security or guarantee may be furnished by a simple endorsement of reputable persons, in which case the degree of security will be the greater the larger the number of endorsers and the higher the credit which they possess, or it may be by the deposit of collateral securities. Thus the very name security has come to mean the properties themselves rather than their safety.

If we pass from explicit interest, or the rate of interest involved in a loan contract, to implicit interest, or the rate involved in purchases and sales of property in general, we see again that the greater the risk, the higher the basis on which a security will sell. A gilt-edge security may sell on a 3 per cent basis, when a less known or less salable security may sell only on a 6, or even on a 9 per cent basis.[1]

The period of time a loan or bond runs is also an important factor as regards risk.[2] There is a see-saw be-

[1] For a more complete treatment of the relation of risk to the interest yield of securities, see *The Nature of Capital and Income*, Chapter XVI.
[2] Even in the first and second approximations the rate of interest for different periods would not necessarily be the same.

tween the rates on short term and long term loans. That
is, if the short term rate is greatly above the long term,
it is likely to fall, or if greatly below, to rise. The long
term rates thus set a rough norm for the short term rates,
which are much more variable. When the future is regarded as safer than usual, loan contracts tend to be
longer in time than otherwise. In a stable country like
the United States, railway and government securities
are thus often drawn for half a century or more. There is
also a variability according to the degree of liquidity. A
call loan which may be recalled on a few hours' notice
has a very different relation to risk than does a mortgage,
for instance. The call rate is usually lower than time rates
because money on call is a little like money on deposit,
or ready money. It is ready, or nearly ready, for use whenever occasion demands. This readiness or convenience
takes the place of some of the interest. On the other hand,
a sudden shortage of funds in the call loan market may
send the call rates far above time rates and keep them
there until the slow working forces release "time-money"
and transfer it to the call loan market. Thus the call loan
rates are very volatile and mobile in both directions.

The element of risk will affect also the value and basis
of the collateral securities. Their availability for collateral
will increase their salability and enhance their price. On
the other hand, when, as in times of crisis, the collateral
has to be sold, it often happens that for purposes of
liquidation it is sold at a sacrifice.

§3. Limitations on Loans

The necessity of having to offer collateral will affect
not only the rate which a man has to pay, but the amount
he can borrow. It will limit therefore the extent to which

he can modify his income stream by this means. Consequently it will not be possible, as assumed in the first two approximations, for a man to modify his income stream at will; its possible modification will be limited by the fear of the borrower that he may not be able to repay and the greater fear of the lender that he may not be repaid—because the borrower's credit may not prove good. In consequence of this limitation upon his borrowing power, the borrower may not succeed in modifying his income stream sufficiently to bring his rate of preference for present over future income down to agreement with the rate or rates of interest ruling in the market; and for like reasons he may not succeed in bringing the rate of return over cost into conformity with any rate of interest.

One feature of these limitations on borrowing may here be noted. The ability and willingness to borrow depend not only on the amount of capital which the would-be borrower possesses, but also on the form in which that capital happens to exist. Some securities are readily accepted as collateral, and accepted as collateral at a high percentage of their market value, whereas others will pass with difficulty and only at a low percentage of that value. The drift, especially during the last generation, toward the corporate form of business has had a striking effect in increasing the power and readiness to borrow. Whereas formerly many businesses were conducted as partnerships and on a small scale, numerous stocks and bonds have now been substituted for the old rights of partnership and other less negotiable forms of security. Similarly the small local companies, the stock of which was held almost exclusively by one family or group of friends, have been merged into large nationally known companies, the securities of which are widely marketable. This increase in size of business units, although it tends to decrease their number, has resulted in a rapid growth of the number of securities listed on the stock exchanges. The possessors of these securities have far wider opportunities to make use of collateral, and the tendency to borrow has received a decided impulse.

Where, on the other hand, the security needed is not available in the convenient form of engraved certificates, there is often considerable difficulty in negotiating a loan. A poor man may see what he believes to be an investment opportunity to make millions by exploiting an invention of his own, and he may be right. This option would have a much higher present value than the one he actually chooses, if only he could borrow the money needed to exploit it. But, being poor and hence without adequate collateral or other guarantees, he cannot get the loan. His choice of income stream, therefore, although the maximum open to him, is quite different from what it would be if he had that collateral or guarantee. If he goes into the enterprise at all he must choose a stopping point far short of what he would choose were he a large capitalist. This means that his marginal rate of return over cost will be higher than the market rate of interest, just as his rate of impatience will be higher than the market rate of interest. The last $100 he ventures to put in may promise a yield of 25 per cent as compared with a rate of interest of 5 per cent. Yet he does not go further into debt because he cannot. Supposing a definite limit of possible debt, all he can do toward further investing must be out of his own income, obtained by abstinence. But this possibility is also limited. He cannot cut his income down to zero, or he would starve. He can however cut it "to the quick", stopping at the point where his impatience has risen to meet the rate of return over cost which in turn will tend to fall with each additional dollar invested.

The story is told of the inventor of rubber making a last desperate—and, fortunately, successful—sacrifice in his experiments in which he resorted to burning up his furniture because he could not get funds with which to buy fuel.

Many such cases exist—cases of limitation on loans— which prevent a person's degree of impatience and his rate of return over cost from reaching the level of the rate of interest. But there is another part of the picture. The poor man who cannot borrow enough to exploit his invention can often find substitutes for loans and lenders. He may associate himself with others in a joint stock company and get the required capital partly from loans, by selling bonds secured by mortgage, partly by selling debentures on a higher interest basis, partly by selling preferred stock on a still higher basis, and partly by selling common stock. That is, the risks are recognized and pooled. One result may be to bring both his estimated rate of return over cost and his rate of impatience more nearly into harmony with these various rates of interest when due account has been taken of the various risks involved.

§4. *Risk and Small Loans*

Where the borrowing takes place in pawn shops, the rate of interest is usually very high, not so much because of the inadequacy of the security as because of its inconvenient form. The pawnbroker will need to charge a high rate of interest, if it is to be called interest, partly because he needs storage room for the security he accepts, partly because he needs special clerks and experts to appraise the articles deposited, and partly because, in many cases, when not redeemed, he has to make an effort to find markets in which to sell them. He is, moreover, able to secure these high rates partly because pawnbroking is in bad odor, so that those who go into the business find a relative monopoly, and partly because of the fact that the customers usually have, either from poverty or from personal peculiarity, a relatively high preference for present over future income. While the effect of their accommodation at the pawn shop is to reduce their impatience to some extent, it will not reduce it to the general level in the community, because these persons do not have access to the loan market in which the ordinary business man deals. To them, undoubtedly, the fact that they cannot borrow except at high, or usurious, rates is often a great hardship, but it has one beneficent effect, that is, the discouraging of the improvident from getting unwisely into debt.

One of the very greatest needs has always been to sift out the relatively safe and sane from the relatively risky and reckless loans of the poor in order to encourage the one and discourage the other. When this has been more fully accomplished, the scandal of the loan shark will be largely a thing of the past. A loan which, to the short-sighted or weak willed borrower, seems to be a blessing, but which is really sure to prove a curse, ought certainly to be discouraged no matter what may be the rate of interest. The Russell Sage Foundation has studied the loan shark problem intensively and as a result has formulated a model small loans act which has been adopted by the legislatures in a large number of our States. This model act recognizes the greater risk and trouble involved in small loans for short periods, by permitting a maximum rate per month of 3½ per cent.

Only in the present generation has the age-long curse of the loan shark been met by constructive measures on a large scale. These are based on the simple principle that a man's friends and neighbors possess the necessary knowledge whereby to distinguish between a safe and unsafe extension of credit to him. The Morris Plan banks are founded on that principle. More effective are the Credit Unions founded by Edward Filene and others in America somewhat on the models of the Raiffeisen and other plans in Europe. Labor banks are rendering a similar service. These are enabling the poor to make effective use of personal character as a substitute for collateral security and are thereby greatly reducing the rate of interest on the loans of the poor. In 1928 one large bank in Wall Street instituted a similar system for loans without collateral to salaried employees. These devices and others are doing much to solve the problem of accommodating the reliable man of small means with loans at rates comparable with those ruling in the markets for the well-to-do.

§5. *Salability as a Safeguard*

When a security, because it is well known, or for any other reason, has a high degree of salability, that is, can be sold on short notice without risk of great sacrifice, its price will be higher than less favored securities, and the rate it yields will therefore be low. Salability is a safeguard against contingencies which may make quick selling advisable. In other words, in a world of chance and sudden changes, quick salability, or liquidity, is a great advantage. For this reason, the rate of interest on individual mortgages will be higher than the rate of interest on more marketable securities. It is, in general, advantageous to have stock listed on the stock exchange, for, being thus widely known, should the necessity to sell arise, such a stock will find a more ready market.

The most salable of all properties is, of course, money; and as Karl Menger pointed out, it is precisely this salability which makes it money. The *convenience* of surely being able, without any previous preparation, to dispose of it for any exchange, in other words, its *liquidity*, is itself a sufficient return upon the capital which a man seems to keep idle in money form. This liquidity of our cash balance takes the place of any rate of interest in the ordinary sense of the word. A man who keeps an average cash balance of $100, rather than put his money in a savings bank to yield him $5 a year, does so because of its liquidity. Its readiness for use at a moment's notice is, to him, worth at least $5 a year. There is a certain experienced buyer and seller of forests, in Michigan, who makes a practice of keeping a ready cash balance in banks of several million dollars in order better to be able to compete with other forest purchasers by having available spot cash to offer some forest owner who, becoming forest-poor, wishes to sell. Forests are extremely non-liquid while cash balances are extremely liquid.

§6. *General Income Risks*

Even when there is no risk (humanly speaking) in the loan itself, the rate realized on it is affected by risk in other connections. The uncertainty of life itself casts a shadow on every business transaction into which time enters. Uncertainty of human life increases the rate of preference for present over future income for many people,[3] although for those with loved dependents it may decrease impatience. Consequently the rate of interest, even on the safest loans, will, in general, be raised by the existence of such life risks. The sailor or soldier who looks forward to a short or precarious existence will be less likely to make permanent investments, or, if he should make them, is less likely to pay a high price for them. Only a low price, that is, a high rate of interest, will induce him to invest for long ahead.

When the risk relates, however, not to the individual's duration of life, but to his income stream, the effect upon the rate of interest will depend upon which portions of the income stream are most subject to risk. If the immediately ensuing income is insecure, whereas the remoter income is sure, the rate of preference for an additional *sure* dollar immediately over an additional *sure* dollar in the remoter period will, as was shown in Chapter IV, tend to be high, and consequently the effect of such a risk of immediate income upon the rate of interest will be to raise it. A *risky* immediate income acts on interest like a *small* immediate income.

But if, as is ordinarily the case, the risk applies more especially to the remoter income than to the immediate, the effect is the exact opposite, namely, to lower the rate of interest on a safe loan. The *risky* remote income acts as the equivalent of a *small* remote income. This example is, perhaps, the most usual case. If a man regards the income for the next few years as sure, but is in doubt as to its continuance into the more remote future, he will be more keenly alive to the needs of that future, and will consequently have a less keen preference for the present.

[3] See Carver, *The Distribution of Wealth*, p. 256, and Cassel, *A Theory of Social Economy*, pp. 246-247.

He will then be willing, even at a very low rate of interest, to invest, out of his present assured income, something to eke out with certainty the uncertain income of the future. The effect of risk in this case, therefore, is to lower the rate of interest on safe loans, though at the same time, as already explained, it will raise the rate of interest on unsafe loans. Consequently, in times of great social unrest and danger, making the future risky, we witness the anomalous combination of high rates where inadequate security is given coexistent with low rates on investments regarded as perfectly safe. When an investor cannot find many investments into which he may put his money without risk of losing it, he will pay a high price—i.e., accept a low rate of return—for the few which are open to him. It has been noted in times of revolution that some capitalists have preferred to forego the chance of all interest and merely to hoard their capital in money form, even paying for storage charges, a payment which amounts to a negative rate of interest. During the World War some investors in the warring countries sought safekeeping for their funds in neutral countries.

§7. *Securities Classified as to Risk*

When risk thus operates to lower the rate of interest on safe investments and to raise the rate on unsafe investments, there immediately arises a tendency to differentiate two classes of securities and two classes of investors —precarious securities and adventurous investors on the one hand, and safe securities and conservative investors on the other. Some risk is inevitable in every business, but is regarded by most people as a burden; hence the few who are able and willing to assume this burden tend to become a separate class. When enterprises came to be organized in corporate form, this classification of investors was recognized by dividing the securities into stocks and bonds, the stockholder being the person who assumes the risk and, theoretically at least, guaranteeing that the bondholder shall be free of all risk. Which person shall fall into the class of risk-takers and which not is determined by their relative coefficients of caution,[4] as well as by the relative degree of risk which an enterprise would involve for the various individuals concerned. The same enterprise may be perilous for one and comparatively safe for another because of superior knowledge on the part of the latter, and the same degree of risk may repel one individual more than another, owing to differences in temperament or, most important of all, to differences in amount of available capital.[5]

This shifting of risk from those on whom it bears heavily to those who can more easily assume it discloses another motive for borrowing and lending besides those which were discussed in a previous chapter. Borrowing or lending in corporate finance usually indicates not simply a difference in time shape as between two income streams, but also a difference of risk. The object of lending which was emphasized in earlier chapters, before the risk element was introduced into the discussion, was to alter the time shape of the income stream, the borrower desiring to increase his present income and decrease his future, and the lender desiring, on the contrary, to decrease his present income and add to his future. But the ordinary stockholder and bondholder do not differ in this way so much as they do in respect to risk. They are both

---

[4] See *The Nature of Capital and Income*, Chapter XVI, §6.
[5] *Ibid.*, Appendix to Chapter XVI, p. 409.

investors, and the positions, in which they stand as to the effect of their investment on the time shape of their income, are really very similar. But the stockholder has a risk attached to his income stream from which the bond-holder seeks to be free. It is this difference in risk which is the primary reason for the distinction between stock-holders and bondholders. The bondholder gives up his chance of a high income for the assurance, or imagined assurance, of a steady income. The stockholder gives up assurance for the chance of bigger gains.

The existence of this risk, tending as we have seen to raise the rate of interest on unsafe loans and lower that on safe loans, has, as its effect, the lowering of the price of stocks and the raising of the price of bonds from what would have been their respective prices had the risk in question been absent.

In the last few years, however, this disparity has been decreased from both ends. The public have come to believe that they have paid too dearly for the supposed safety of bonds and that stocks have been too cheap. Studies of various writers, especially Edgar Smith [6] and Kenneth Van Strum [7] have shown that in the long run stocks yield more than bonds. Economists have pointed out that the safety of bonds is largely illusory [8] since every bondholder runs the risk of a fall in the purchasing power of money and this risk does not attach to the same degree to common stock, while the risks that do attach to them may be reduced, or insured against, by diversifi-

[6] Smith, Edgar L. *Common Stocks as Long Term Investments.* New York, The Macmillan Company, 1924.

[7] Van Strum, Kenneth, *Investing In Purchasing Power.* Boston, Barron's, 1925.

[8] See *The Money Illusion.* Also *When Are Gilt-Edged Bonds Safe?* Magazine of Wall Street, Apr. 25, 1925.

cation. The principle of insurance [9] of any kind is by pooling those risks virtually to reduce them. This raises the value of the aggregate capital subject in detail to these risks.

It is in this way that investment trusts and investment counsel tend to diminish the risk to the common stock investor. This new movement has created a new demand for such stocks and raised their prices; at the same time it has tended to decrease the demand for, and to lower the price of, bonds.

Again, *speculation* in grain, for example by setting aside a certain class of persons to assume the risks of trade, has the effect of reducing these risks by putting them in the hands of those who have most knowledge, for, as we have seen, risk varies inversely with knowledge. In this way, the whole plane of business is put more nearly on a uniform basis so far as the rate of interest is concerned.

Risk is especially conspicuous in the financing of new inventions or discoveries where past experience is a poor guide. When new inventions are made, uncertainty is introduced, speculation follows, and then comes great wealth or great ruin according to the success or failure of the ventures. The history of gold and silver discoveries, of the invention of rubber, of steel, and of electrical appliances is filled with tales of wrecked fortunes, by the side of which stand the stories of the fortunes of those few who drew the lucky cards, and who are among today's multi-millionaires.

The rates of interest are always based upon expectation, however little this hope may later be justified by realization. Man makes his guess of the future and stakes

[9] See *The Nature of Capital and Income*, Chapter XVI.

his action upon it. In his guess he discounts everything he can foresee or estimate, even future inventions and their effects. In an estimate which I saw in print of the value of a copper mine, allowance was made for future inventions which might reasonably be expected. In the same way, too, the buyer of machinery allows not simply for its depreciation through physical wear, but for its obsolescence. New investments in steam railroads are to-day made with due regard to the possibility that the road may, within a few years, be run by electricity, or that it will be injured by competition of bus lines or helped by terminal connections with them.

It may easily happen that, in a country consisting of overly sanguine persons, or during a boom period when business men are overhopeful, the rate of interest will be out of line with what actual events, as later developed, would justify. It seems likely that, in ordinary communities, realization justifies the average expectation. But in an individual case this is not always true; otherwise there would be no such thing as risk. Risk is synonymous with uncertainty—lack of knowledge. Our present behavior can only be affected by the expected future,—not the future as it will turn out but the future as it appears to ``s beforehand through the veil of the unknown.

§8. *Effect of Risk on the Six Principles*

We see, then, that the element of risk introduces disturbances into those determining conditions which were expressed in previous chapters as explaining the rate of interest. To summarize these disturbances, we may now apply the risk factor to each of the six conditions which were originally stated as determining interest. We shall find that its effects are as follows:

THIRD APPROXIMATION

THE TWO PRINCIPLES AS TO INVESTMENT OPPORTUNITY

A. Empirical Principle

The condition that each individual has a given range of choice still holds true, but these choices are no longer confined to absolutely *certain* optional income streams, but now include options with risk. That is to say, each individual finds open to his choice a given set of options (and opportunities to shift options, that is, opportunities to invest) which options differ in size, time shape, composition and *risk*.

B. Principle of Maximum Present Value

When risk was left out of account, it was stated that from among a number of different options the individual would select that one which has the maximum present value—in other words, that one which, compared with its nearest neighbors, possesses a rate of return over cost equal to the rate of time preference, and therefore to the rate of interest.

When the risk element is introduced, it may still be said that the maximum present value is selected, but in translating future uncertain income into present cash value, use must now be made of the probability and caution factors.

But when we try to express this principle of maximum present value in its alternative form in terms of the marginal rate of return over cost, we must qualify this expression to: the marginal rate of *anticipated* return over cost.

Three consequences follow. First, that the rate of return over cost which will actually be realized may turn out to be widely different from that originally anticipated.

THE THEORY OF INTEREST

Second, there is in the market not simply one single anticipation; there are many, each with a different degree of risk allowed for in it. Third, the need of security may be such as to limit also the choice of options.

THE TWO PRINCIPLES AS TO IMPATIENCE

A. Empirical Principle

The rate of time preference depends upon the character of the income stream, but it must now take into account the fact that both the immediate and the future (especially the future) portions of that stream are subject to risk. There are many rates of time preference, or impatience, according to the risks involved. But they all depend on the character of the expected and possible income stream of each individual—its size, shape, composition and especially the degree of uncertainty attaching to various parts of it as well as the degree of uncertainty of life of the recipient.

B. The Principle of Maximum Desirability

It is still true, of course, that the individual decides on the option most wanted. But, in a world of uncertainty there are two features not present in a world of certainty. One (which however does not affect the formulation of the principle) is that what is now desired may prove disappointing. That is, though it seems, when chosen, the most desirable course, it may not prove the most desirable in the sense of deserving, in view of later developments, to be desired. The other new feature is that the most desired income stream is no longer necessarily synonymous with that which harmonizes the rate of preference with the rate of interest.

[224]

THIRD APPROXIMATION

Rates of time preference in any one market *tend* toward equality by the practice of borrowing and lending, and more generally, that of buying and selling, but this equality is no longer, in all cases, attainable, because of limitations on the freedom to modify the income stream at will, limitations growing out of the existence of the element of risk and consequent limitations on the borrowing power.

THE TWO MARKET PRINCIPLES

A. Principle of Clearing the Market

In the first two approximations, where the element of risk was considered absent, it was shown that the aggregate modification of the income streams of all individuals for every period of time was zero. What was borrowed equaled what was lent, or what was added by sale was equal to what was subtracted by purchase. The same principle still applies, for what one person pays, another person must receive. The only difference is that, in a world of chance, the actual payments may be quite different from those originally anticipated and agreed upon, that is, will often be defaulted, in whole or in part.

B. Principle of Repayment

In the former approximations, the total present value of the prospective modifications of one's income stream was zero, that is, the present value of the loans equaled the present value of the borrowings, or the present value of the additions and subtractions caused by buying and selling balanced each other. In our present discussion, in which future income is recognized as uncertain, this principle still holds true, but only in the sense that the present

THE THEORY OF INTEREST

market values balance at the moment when the future loans or other modifications are planned and decided upon. The fact of risk means that later there may be a wide discrepancy between the actual realization and the original expectation. In liquidation there may be default or bankruptcy. When the case is not one of a loan contract, but relates merely to the difference in income streams of two kinds of property bought and sold, the discrepancy between what was expected and what is actually realized may be still wider. Only *viewed in the present* is the estimated value of the future return still the equivalent of the estimated cost.

We thus see that, instead of the series of simple equalities which we found to hold true in the vacuum case, so to speak, where risk was absent, we have only a *tendency* toward equalities, interfered with by the limitations of the loan market, and which, therefore, result in a series of *in*equalities. Rates of interest, rates of preference, and rates of return over cost are only ideally, not really, equal.

We conclude by summarizing in the accompanying table the interest-determining conditions not simply for the third approximation but for all three of our three successive approximations (distinguished by the numerals 1, 2, 3).

In this summary tabulation the "Principles as to Investment Opportunity" are formally inserted, under the first approximation, in order to complete the correspondence with the other two approximations, but of course they merely re-express the hypothesis under which the first approximation was made. They are therefore bracketed, since only the remaining four conditions are of real significance for the first approximation.

The first and second approximations were, of course,

merely preparatory to the third, which alone corresponds to the actual world of facts. Yet the other two approximations are of even greater importance than the third from the point of view of theoretical analysis. They tell us what *would* happen under their respective hypotheses. Both these hypotheses are simpler than reality; hence they lend themselves better to formal analysis and mathematical expression.

Moreover, to know what would happen under these hypothetical conditions enables us better to understand what does happen under actual conditions, just as the knowledge that a projectile would follow a parabola if it were in a vacuum enables the student of practical gunnery better to understand the actual behavior of his bullets or shells. In fact, no scientific law is a perfect statement of what *does* happen, but only what *would* happen *if* certain conditions existed which never do actually exist.[10] Science consists of the formulation of conditional truths, not of historical facts, though by successive approximations, the conditions assumed may be made nearly to coincide with reality.[11]

The second approximation gives a clear cut theory applicable to the clear cut hypotheses on which it is based. The third approximation cannot avoid some degree of vagueness.

[10] See the writer's *Economics as a Science*, Proceedings of the American Association for Advancement of Science, Vol. LVI, 1907.
[11] See Appendix to Chapter IX, No. 1.

PART III. THE THEORY IN MATHEMATICS

CHAPTER X

FIRST APPROXIMATION IN GEOMETRIC TERMS

§1. *Introduction*

WE found in Chapter V that, if the degree of any given individual's impatience depended solely on his income stream, and if that stream could not be modified through the loan market or otherwise, his impatience could not be modified either. In such a world of hermits, each person would have his own individual rate of time preference, the various individual rates ranging from several thousand per cent per annum down to zero, or below. In such a world, since there would be no loans, there would be no market rate of interest.

But we also perceived that, as soon as our hermits are allowed to swap income streams, one man exchanging some of this year's income for some future income of another, then these myriad rates of time preference or impatience tend to come together toward a common rate, and, on the assumption that no risk attends these transactions, a uniform market rate of interest would actually be reached. In such a perfect loan market the degree of impatience of each person would become equal to that of every other person and to the rate of interest.

§2. *The Map of This Year's and Next Year's Income*

Expressing the problem with the aid of the graphic method, the determination of the rate of interest may be reduced to a simple problem of geometry, just as the problem of price may be shown by supply and demand curves.

To depict adequately the elements of the interest problem, however, a new kind of chart is required. Our first task is to see the relation of this new kind of chart to those hitherto used in this book. First, then, let us recur to Charts 1, 2, and 3, in Chapter I, which picture a person's income stream over a period of years. This sort of

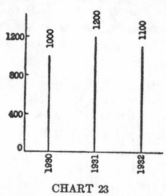

CHART 23

Annual Income Represented by Lines Instead of Bars.

chart consists of a row of vertical bars representing the real income, as measured by the cost of living in successive periods—days, months, or years. To prevent confusion, let us, for our present graphic purpose, shrink these vertical bars into mere vertical lines, without breadth. Then, each year's income may be pictured as if it were all concentrated at a point of time, say in the middle of the month or year concerned. Since the rate of interest is usually expressed in *per annum* terms, it will simplify the discussion if these lines are drawn, as in Chart 23, disregarding all time units other than years. To make our

[232]

picture still more concrete, specific figures may be attached to specific years, the person's income for 1930 being set at $1000, that for 1931 at $1200, and so on.

We are now ready to pass to the new and radically different method of representing the real income stream. In the chart just described, horizontal distance measures time, while vertical distance measures amount or size. The reader is now asked to shake off these conceptions. Moreover, throughout Chapters X and XI, he must be on his guard against their unconscious return. In the new charts there is no time scale; time is not measured at all; both axes measure amount of income. The horizontal axis represents the first year's income, the vertical, the second year's income. Thus the point P_1 in Chart 24, through its latitude and longitude, stands in a sense for both years' incomes combined. It represents what may be called a given individual's income combination, income stream, income position, or income situation for the given pair of years. On Chart 24 may be shown a complete map of all possible income combinations, or income positions, so far as two years, or periods of time, are concerned. To represent the third year, so easily shown in Chart 23 under the old method, we should need in this new method a third dimension. The chart would then cease to be a chart and become a three dimensional model.[1]

If on the map for two years, we were to draw a straight line from the origin toward the "northeast", midway between the two axes, every point on it would have its longitude and latitude equal, that is, would represent dif-

[1] The reader who wishes, after finishing this chapter, to pursue the geometric analogy into more dimensions than the two here considered may do so by reading the Appendix to this Chapter.

ferent income situations in which the incomes of two years were equal. A poor man—poor in both years—would be situated near the origin, and a rich man far from the origin. A man who has less income this year than he expects to get next year would be situated above this

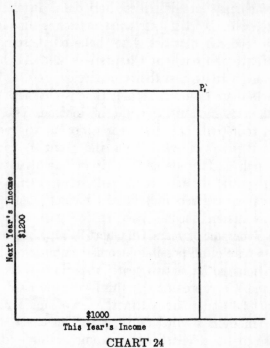

CHART 24

Income Position this Year and Next Year Represented by Point(P*1*).

midway line, his latitude (meaning next year's income) being more than his longitude (meaning this year's). If we move his position sufficiently to the left, so as to reduce his longitude (this year's income), he will be like a man stranded on a polar expedition—with rations run short, though he might be assured by radio of plentiful supplies next year. On the other hand, a man who is more abundantly provided with income this year than he expects to be next year would be situated *below* the midway line, his longitude being greater than his latitude.

In this way, within the northeast quadrant (the only one shown in the charts) we can, by fixing the point P at all possible positions, represent all possible combinations of this year's and next year's income.

§3. *The Market Line*

Assuming that the individual's incomes for all other years remain unchanged, we shall now study the effects, for this one man, of changing the income amounts of the two years pictured. These changes are assumed to be caused wholly by trading some of his income of one year for some of another man's income for the other year. Except for such trading, his income situation is supposed to be fixed. He has, let us suppose, a rigid allowance of $1000 for this year and $1200 for next year with no opportunity to change these figures except by swapping some of one year's income for some of another's.

Suppose, for instance, that at a rate of interest of 10 per cent the individual borrows $100 in 1930 in return for $110 which he is to pay back in 1931. In Chart 23, such changes would be represented by lengthening the 1930 vertical line from $1000 to $1100 and by shrinking the 1931 vertical line from $1200, not to $1100 but to $1090. In Chart 25 these changes are represented by shifting the income position from P_1, the originally fixed income position, to M_1, whose longitude is $100 more and latitude $110 less.

If, as shown in Chart 26, the individual borrows a second $100, promising to repay $110, his income position shifts again, this time from M_1' to M_1'', that is, from this-year-1100-and-next-year-1090 to this-year-1200-and-next-year-980. Borrowing a third $100 would bring him to M_1''', (this-year-1300-and-next-year-870). Every additional borrowing of $100 adds $100 to this year's income and subtracts $110 from next year's income. Chart 26 pictures these successive changes as a "staircase" of which

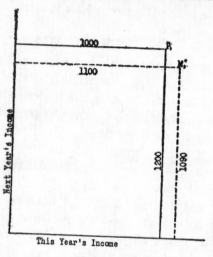

CHART 25

Effect of Borrowing Upon an Individual's Income Position.

each "tread" is $100 and each "riser" is $110. The stairs are steep. So long as there exists a rate of interest their descent is *necessarily always* faster than 45 degrees—that is, future income decreases faster than present income increases; the riser is more than 100 per cent of the tread—more by the rate of interest.[2]

[2] The steps could be drawn just as well on the under side of the line as shown by dotted lines on the chart. If the steps were to consist, not of successive $100 loans, but of successive $1 loans the steps to P_1, M_1',

If the rate of interest were zero, each $100 borrowed would require only $100 to be returned next year. The riser would equal the tread; the Market line would make an angle of 45° with the axis, and its slope would equal

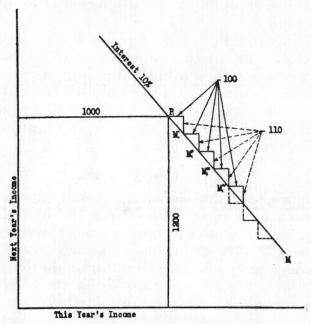

CHART 26

Successive Changes in an Individual's Income Position Produced by Successive Borrowings at the Market Rate of Interest.

unity, or, in other words, 100 per cent. Thus in this new method of charting, a given rate of interest is represented by the algebraic difference between the slope of the given Market line, and the 100 per cent slope of the 45° zero interest line.

M_1'', M_1''', etc., would be a hundred times as numerous and correspondingly smaller.

Evidently the line $P_1 M_1$ is a straight line. It may be called the Market line, Loan line, or Rate of Interest line, and, if prolonged, will contain all the positions to which this particular individual (who may be called Individual *1*) *can* shift his income position by borrowing or lending.

If, starting at P_1, he shifts *down* this straight staircase (southeast) he is a *borrower* or a *seller* of next year's income, because he is adding to this year's income and subtracting from next year's. If, instead, he shifts *up* the staircase (northwest) he is a *lender* or *buyer* of next year's income, subtracting from this year's income and adding to next.

§4. *The Willingness Line*

So far we have used the new type of chart only to show how the individual *can* move—change his income situation. The next question is: in which one of the two directions on the Market line *will* he actually move? The answer depends on his degree of impatience compared with the market rate of interest. We have seen how the market rate of interest is represented graphically by the slope, relatively to 45°, of the Market line in Chart 26. We are now ready to make a similar graphic representation of the individual's rate of time preference or impatience. This is expressed by a series of curved lines showing on what terms, at any income position (such as P_1), the individual would be *willing* to lend or borrow, say $100. What one is *willing* to do and what he *can* do are two quite different things. The Market line of Chart 26 shows what he *can* do, while the Willingness lines, now to be described, will show what he would be *willing* to do.

Individual *1*'s impatience is such that he would be

willing, if necessary, as shown in Chart 27, to borrow his
first $100 at 30 per cent, considerably above the market
rate, 10 per cent. That is, he would be willing to sacrifice
$130 out of next year's income in order to add $100 to
this year's income. To get a second $100 this year, he

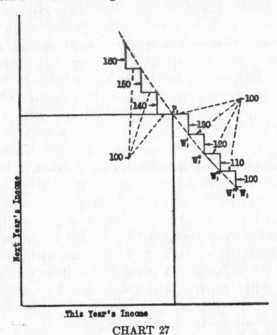

CHART 27

Varying Degrees of Impatience Represented by the Slope of the W_1 line.

would not be willing to pay quite so much, but only, say,
$120. A third $100 would be worth to him only $110; a
fourth still less, and so on. These willingness points make
a *curved* staircase, the steps being from P_1 to W_1', from
W_1' to W_1'', and so on, in which each tread is taken to be
$100, but the risers are decreasing as the borrower steps
down southeasterly, being successively 130, 120, 110. The

[239]

Willingness line, $P_1 W_1^{IV}$, is not a straight line like $P_1 M_1$ in Chart 26, but a curved line. The steepness of each step, or ratio of risers to tread, or slope of the curves shows the degree of impatience at that particular step.

The Willingness line through P_1 extends, of course, in both directions. It shows not only on what terms Individual *1* would be willing to borrow, but also on what terms he would be willing to lend. At point P_1, he is willing to lend the first $100 at 40 per cent, a second, at 50 per cent, and so on. Everyone theoretically is ready either to borrow or to lend according to the terms. Individual *1* is here represented as barely willing at P_1 either to borrow $100 at 30 per cent, or to *lend* $100 at 40 per cent. In short, he would be *willing* to substitute the combination represented by any given point on his Willingness line for the combination represented by any other point on the same line. *All* points on that line are, by hypothesis, equally desirable to Individual *1*. Each segment of the Willingness line, by the divergence of its slope from 100 per cent, shows the degree of impatience at the particular income position there represented.

Consequently, $P_1 W_1$ might be called an Impatience line quite as well as a Willingness line [3] for Individual *1*. There would be another Willingness line, or W line, for any other individual. The W lines thus differ from the Market, or M, lines which are common to everybody in the market.

§5. *The Two Lines Compared*

The M line of Chart 26 and the W line of Chart 27 are brought together in Chart 28. From P_1 we have a pair of

[3] The latter name was chosen chiefly because the initial "W," for willingness, is more convenient to use in the chart than the letter "I," especially as "I" is the initial also of interest and income.

lines, one (M_1) showing by its divergence from the 45°
slope the rate which Individual *1 can* get, as a borrower,
and the other (W_1) showing by its slope the rate at which
he is *willing* to borrow. Evidently if he is willing to pay
30 per cent for a $100 loan when he can get it at 10 per

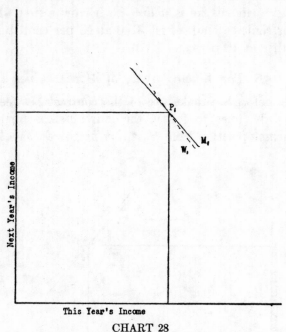

CHART 28

Intersection of M_1 Line and W_1 Line at P_1.

cent, he will borrow. Evidently also he will continue to
borrow as long as his willingness rate, i.e., his rate of
time preference or impatience, is greater than the rate of
interest, in other words as long as, at each stage, the
Willingness line is steeper than the Market line.

All that has been done so far is to describe the income
map, and to place on it a point P_1 to represent the as-

sumed fixed income situation of Individual *1*, and to draw
through this point P_1 two lines, one a straight line, the
Market line, showing the direction in which Individual *1*
can move away from P_1, and the other a curved line, the
Willingness line, showing the direction in which he is
willing to move. He is *willing* to borrow a first **$100** at
30 per cent, or lend a first **$100** at 40 per cent, but *can*
do either at 10 per cent.

§6. *The Whole Family of Market Lines*

But before we make use of the contrast between the
M and *W* lines to follow the individual as he moves
his income position from P_1 either northwest as a lender

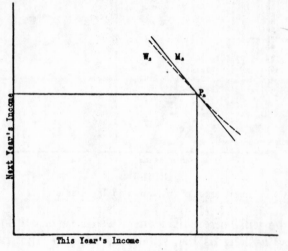

CHART 29

Intersection of M_2 Line and W_2 Line at P_2.

or southeast as a borrower, we must first complete our
pictures of the two kinds of lines. Thus far only one line
of each of the two kinds has been drawn. These are the

[242]

only lines applicable to the given income position P_1. But for every other income position in which we may place Individual *1*, the Market line would encounter a different Willingness line.

In the same way, we could picture a series of pairs of Market and Willingness lines for any other individual,

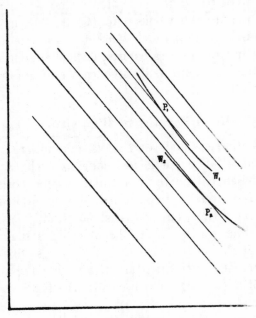

CHART 30
M Lines With Reference to W_1 and W_2 Lines.

such an Individual *2*, depicted in Chart 29. In this case, Individual *2* is represented at one position to be willing to *lend* at 2 per cent but to be able to do so at 10 per cent, the market rate; we have then the Market line P_2M_2 and the Willingness line P_2W_2. In the same way, we could draw P_3M_3 and P_3M_3, for a third individual and so on.

[243]

Under our assumption of a perfect market, all the Market lines P_1M_1, P_2M_2, P_3M_3, etc., are parallel to each other, their common divergence from a 100 per cent slope representing the one universal market rate of interest, here supposed to be 10 per cent.[4] Since the Market lines are thus parallel, they are really impersonal or independent of particular individuals, and we may consequently picture the whole map (Chart 30), as covered with straight and parallel Market lines, like the conventional picture of a rainstorm, each line being slightly steeper than 45°, and its divergence therefrom indicating a rate of interest.

§7. *Many Families of Willingness Lines*

The Willingness lines, on the other hand, are personal, or individual. The particular slope in each case is, of course, dependent on the particular income position P_1. A given Individual *1* is concerned with only one Willingness line at a time, out of his whole "family" of lines— the one line which passes through his actual income position at P_1. By comparing his Willingness line at that particular point with the Market line, we have a graphic picture of the motives which decide whether he will borrow or lend.

There always exists for him, potentially, other Willingness lines, passing not through his actual income position P_1, but through any other income position at which he could be imagined to be. These curves represent the various rates at which Individual *1* would be willing to borrow or lend if his income position were varied. Thus

[4] So large a rate as 10 per cent is used in the charts because a line with a divergence from the 100 per cent slope of less than 10 per cent cannot be clearly seen.

the number of Willingness lines for any one Individual is infinite, and every other individual will have his own family of lines.

We conceive, then, of a map for Individual *1* alone, covered with a family of such Willingness lines infinite in number, arranged so as to vary gradually from each to the next, like the lines of elevation on a geographic contour map of a mountain.[5]

While Individual *1* finds all points on any one Willingness line of *equal* desirability or "wantability," he would *rather* have his income position on lines more to the "northeast," or farther from the origin. Each Willingness line might be labelled with a number representing specifically the total desirability or "wantability" pertaining to each and all of the income positions on it. It is the locus or assemblage of these points (combinations of income for the two years) equally desirable in the estimation of Individual *1*. A greater aggregate income in the two years may be offset in respect to the resulting total desirability by a less convenient distribution between the two years and *vice versa*.[6]

But we are not yet interested in such differences of level or total desirability between the Willingness lines. We are here interested only in the *directions* of the Willingness lines at different points, representing the different

[5] Those familiar with a contour map will find the analogy a good one, since each Willingness line represents a level of desirability different from the others, the level or height being here conceived as measured in the third dimension, that is, at right angles to the page of the map.

[6] It would, of course, be possible to present the Willingness lines in terms of total desirability or wantability without supposing any hypothetical borrowing or lending; this was done in the *Rate of Interest* (Appendix to Chapter VII). The Willingness lines were there called iso-desirability lines. They might also be called lines of indifference.

degrees of impatience pertaining to different income situations. These directions, or divergences from the 45°
line, picture to us how the individual would be willing
to borrow or lend under all possible income circumstances.

§8. *A Typical Family of Willingness Lines*

While we cannot, of course, tell exactly how any human
being would act if far from the income situation in which
he is actually placed, yet we know what in a way would
be characteristic of him. Chart 31 is believed to represent

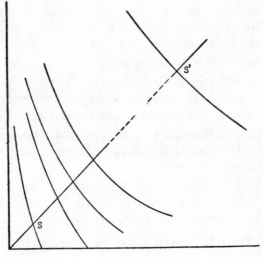

CHART 31
A Typical Family of *W* Lines.

roughly a family of Willingness lines typical of most
human beings. It is best analyzed by following the dotted
straight line *SS'* running northeast, midway between the
axes and therefore comprising points which represent, in
each case, equal incomes in both years.

[246]

IN GEOMETRIC TERMS

Four characteristic properties may be noted:

(1) At S, taken to represent a point near the minimum of subsistence—the income situation, say, of a polar explorer who is marooned and hopeless—the Willingness line is nearly vertical. In this income position of extreme need a person would scarcely be willing to lend at all, for to give up one iota of this year's income in exchange for any amount promised for next year would mean too great a privation in the present. On the contrary, in order to get an added dollar today to help keep body and soul together this year, he would be willing to give not only 10 per cent or 25 per cent but perhaps as much as 100 per cent, or 1000 per cent, or *every* dollar of next year's income even though next year is no more promising than this year.

(2) At S', taken to represent an exceedingly large income—say $1,000,000 for each of the two years—the Willingness line is nearly at right angles to the SS' line; that is, nearly at 45° to the two axes, for with such a large income the two years would seem almost on even terms. Presumably one with this income would not be willing, in order to get $1000 more income this year, to give up much over $1000 out of next year's income.

(3) As one passes between the two income situations above mentioned, from S to S', his rate of time preference will gradually decrease—from nearly infinity at S down nearly to zero at S', that is, the larger the income, other things remaining the same, the smaller the degree of impatience.

(4) Any one Willingness line grows steeper as it proceeds upward and leftward, changing from a nearly horizontal direction at its lower right end to a nearly vertical direction at the opposite end.

§9. *Time Preference May be Negative*

If these specifications are correct, some, at least, of this family of Willingness curves, especially those far distant from the origin, and low down—that is, representing small *future* and large *present* income—will have an inclination *less* steep than 45° to the horizontal axis and a slope less than 100 per cent. At such income positions the rate of time preference would be negative. It is sometimes said that it is a fundamental attribute of human nature to prefer a dinner or a dollar this year to a dinner or a dollar next year, but this statement is evidently too narrow. Unconsciously it confines our view to regions of the income map where present income is relatively small or future income relatively large. For a starving man it is notably true, that is, the Willingness lines that lie in *the left* part of the map are far steeper than 45°. Of a man expecting large future income it is also true; that is, the Willingness lines *toward the top* of the map are also very steep.

But if we turn our attention in the opposite direction—to the right, or downward, or both—we find regions on the map in which, if the foregoing description is correct, the curves flatten out and incline less than 45°; the man's income situation is such that he might even be willing to lend for nothing, or even less than nothing, simply because he would, in such a case, be so surfeited with this year's income and so short, prospectively, of next year's income that he would be thankful to get rid of some of this year's superfluity, for the sake of adding even a trifle to next year's meager real income. His situation would be like a Robinson Crusoe on a barren island, well supplied, but with foods that could serve him only this year. Such situations are rare in practice, but they are certainly imaginable and sometimes even occur. In such situations a man would be willing to save for the future without any incentive in the form of interest. But this takes us beyond our present point; for here we are concerned only with the Willingness lines, not with the Market lines.

§10. *The Personal and Impersonal Influences on Impatience*

By the aid of this map we can see, anew, and more clearly, that a man's actual degree of impatience depends on two circumstances:

(1) It depends on his "personal equation," the whole contour of his whole family of Willingness curves, representing what he would be willing to do under all sorts of income situations. The Willingness lines of a spendthrift are steeper and those of a miser less steep than the typical, or normal, man's family of curves.

(2) It depends on his particular income situation on the map which is represented by the letter P. A poor man is more impatient than a rich man of the same personal characteristics. A man with great expectations for the future but with little available for the present is more impatient than the man oppositely situated with respect to the future.

Both the family of Willingness lines and the position on the map are, of course, changing every minute. Only at one particular time does the map, with its set of curves for Individual *1*, and a particular location P_1, picture his individual circumstances. What we are doing here is to take a flash-light, as it were, of his income situation and his Willingness lines, and to analyze his behavior at the instant.

§11. *Deciding Whether to Borrow or to Lend*

Individual character and income together with the market rate of interest determine what the individual will do in any given situation. Chart 32 pictures graphically one step in the process by which an individual adjusts his degree of impatience to the market rate of interest, by borrowing or lending.

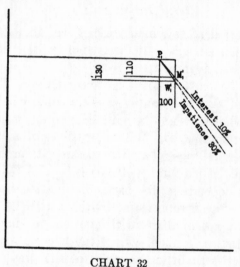

CHART 32
Adjusting Impatience to Market Rate of Interest Through Borrowing.

To summarize and repeat, with the interest rate at 10 per cent, Individual *1* may, or may not, be willing to take a $100 loan, depending upon whether or not, while his position is at P_1, his impatience is or is not greater than this 10 per cent. If, as portrayed by Chart 32, his impatience is greater—say, 30 per cent—and if he can obtain the loan at 10 per cent, he will be glad to do so. Let W_1' be the position to which he is *willing* to shift

[250]

in order to get $100 added to his present income. This position would require a sacrifice of $130 out of next year's income, which, however, he need not make for he can get his accommodation for $110 of next year's income and find himself at M_1'.

Individual *2*, on the other hand, whether because of his temperament, or because of a different time distribu-

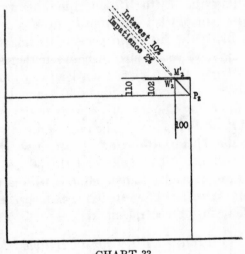

CHART 33

Adjusting Impatience to Market Rate of Interest Through Lending.

tion of his income, may behave quite differently. His position to start with, let us say, is P_2 in Chart 33. If his impatience, under these circumstances, is only 2 per cent, when the market rate is 10 per cent, he will not borrow, but will *lend*. He will continue to lend until his degree of impatience is as great as the market rate of interest, that is as long as his Willingness line, at each stage, is less steep than the Market line.

Thus, the angle at P between the M line and W line

[251]

of Individual *1*, or of any other individual, shows whether that individual is potentially a borrower or a lender. If the individual's *W* line is steeper than the *M* line, he will borrow; if it is less steep, he will lend.

Therefore, if this second individual lends $100, while the first individual borrows $100, both at 10 per cent, both will reap advantage. One will shift down a 10 per cent Market line from P_1 to M'_1, and the other will shift up the 10 per cent Market line from P_2 to M'_2.

If we had only these two persons trading this year's income for next year's income between themselves, the rate of interest agreed upon for a loan of $100 this year would not, of course, necessarily be 10 per cent, but would be determined by the respective bargaining power of Individual *1* and Individual *2*. The rate might fall anywhere between the 2 per cent, the lowest rate at which Individual *2* is willing to lend $100, and the 30 per cent, the highest rate, at which Individual *1* is willing to borrow $100. But we are less interested in such a special trade, or haggle than in the general market.

§12. *Interest Fixed for an Individual*

It is a fact long recognized by price theorists,[7] that the theoretical determination of any price in a special trade or haggle between two persons, each of whom is conscious of his influence on that one price, is more complicated than in a full-fledged competitive market in which each individual is so small a factor as to be unconscious of his influence on the market price. We here assume such a

[7] See Auspitz und Lieben. *Untersuchungen über die Theorie des Preises.* Leipzig, Dunker und Humblot, 1889, p. 405; Marshall, Alfred. *Principles of Economics.* London, Macmillan and Co., 1907, p. 332; also my *Mathematical Investigations in the Theory of Value and Prices,* p. 25.

general market, in which a single buyer, or lender, is so small a factor that he is not actuated by any consciousness of influencing the market rate of interest. Each person finds the rate fixed for him. We assume, for the purpose of the present illustration, that the rate so fixed for him by the market is 10 per cent.

§13. *How an Individual Adjusts his Income Position to the Market*

Under these assumptions it is clear that Individual *1* will borrow $100 at precisely 10 per cent, and that Individual *2* will lend $100 at precisely 10 per cent, the market rate. Their individuality will find conscious play only in determining how far they will make use of the market. Let us now see how far beyond $100 each will borrow or lend at this fixed 10 per cent rate.

To do this we need merely compare Willingness lines with the Market line. Will Individual *1*, who has shifted from P_1 to M'_1 along the 10 per cent Market line with a $100 loan, again shift from M'_1 for an additional $100 loan, along this same 10 per cent Market line? He will do so only if he is still willing to pay more than the market rate.

Whether this is true can be tested by precisely the same process as before, namely by drawing from this new income position on the Market line a new Willingness line and ascertaining whether or not it is steeper than the Market line. And so, step by step, $100 by $100, as he shifts along the Market line, we can always test whether he will shift still further. Any individual has but one Willingness line, cutting through any one income position, but when he sets out from any *P*, he is going to shift along the Market line and, at each shift, he encounters a new Willingness line.

[253]

THE THEORY OF INTEREST

On Chart 34 are represented a number of W lines which are assumed to depict Individual *1*'s varying degree of impatience at different income positions. A study of the

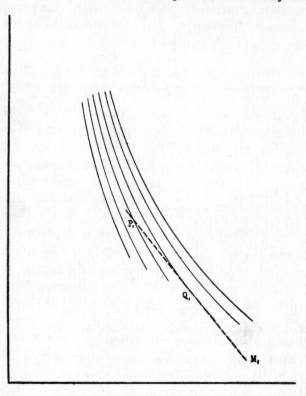

CHART 34

The Final Income Position (Q_1) of Individual *1* Fixed by Tangency of the W_1 Line to the M_1 Line at Q_1.

chart will show how Individual *1*, in income position P_1, will borrow, because his degree of impatience exceeds 10 per cent, the market rate of interest. His borrowing will continue, of course, until his degree of impatience is reduced to 10 per cent, at which point he no longer secures a net gain from borrowing. This point is located at Q_1 where the M line is tangent to Individual 1's W line through that point. There at last he reaches a position where the next $100 shift on the Market line is no longer less steep than his Willingness line but exactly as steep.

The same principles apply to Individual 2. The only differences are: first, that he shifts upward from P to his Q instead of downward—that is, he adds to next year's income at the expense of this year's income; and, secondly, that he acts in reference to a different family of Willingness lines entirely his own. Such a picture implies the utmost sensitiveness or fluidity of inducements and responses. There would be a continual readjustment of loans and borrowings, back and forth; practically every person would be either a borrower or a lender; the extent of his borrowings or loans would be very finely graduated, and constantly changing.

We have not yet pictured geometrically the whole problem of the rate of interest; but we have pictured the solution of the problem of how any one individual will adjust, under the ideal conditions assumed, his lending or borrowing to the market rate of interest. This simplified solution consists, we have seen, in finding Q at the point where the M line at a given rate of interest is tangent to one of the given family of W lines.

Having solved this *individual* problem, we now proceed to the *market* problem.

§14. *Market Equilibrium*

It may seem that little progress has yet been made toward the ultimate end of determining the rate of interest because of our initial assumption that the rate of interest is already fixed for the individual by the market formed by others. How did they fix it? Have we begged the whole question?

Only a few steps are now required to finish the whole market picture. It is true that we assumed a fixed 10 per cent rate in order to see how an individual would shift his income position to harmonize his individual degree of impatience with that, to him, fixed rate. Nevertheless, each individual, even if unconsciously, helps to make the market rate by the very act of shifting his income situation from a P position to a Q position.

This statement will be clear if we ask ourselves what would happen were we to suppose the "fixed" market rate to have been fixed too high, or too low. If we imagine the market rate to be very high, say 25 per cent, then, the bulk of individuals would try to lend and few would want to borrow. The aggregate of loans thus offered would exceed the demand and the interest rate would fall. Conversely, if the rate were too low, demand would exceed supply and the rate would rise. Since the total sums actually lent must equal, in the aggregate, those borrowed, the horizontal displacements of all the Q's in one direction must equal that of all the other Q's in the other direction. Some Q's, those of borrowers, are to the right of the corresponding P's. Others are at the left. As a group, they are neither. The average Q has the same longitude as the average P. The same is true as to latitude. In short, the geometric "center of gravity" of all the Q's must coincide with that of all the P's, in order that the loan market may be cleared.

In other words, while the market rate, as represented by the divergence of slope of the Market line, always *seems* fixed to the individual adjusting his income situation to that rate, nevertheless that rate is not really completely fixed independently of his own borrowing or lending. What the market does is to keep the Market line for different individuals parallel. There cannot be two rates in the same market at the same time—at least not in the perfect market here assumed.

But these parallel lines are always swinging a little back and forth to "clear the market." Each person's Market line may turn slightly about his P as a pivot. All Market lines turning together, that is keeping parallel, tend to reach the right inclination—that which clears the market and brings the center of gravity of the Q's into coincidence with that of the P's.

Thus, the economic problem of determining the rate of interest becomes the geometric problem of experimentally oscillating all the M lines until their common inclination brings the center of gravity of the contacts (Q's) into coincidence with the center of gravity of the P's.

We now have the complete geometric representation of the whole problem of the rate of interest under the assumptions of the first approximation—complete except that, to put the picture on a two-dimensional chart, we have had to add the restriction that "other things are equal" as to all years beyond the first and second.[8]

Thus the economic problem of determining the rate of interest is translated into the geometric problem of drawing a series of parallel straight lines through given points, P's, at such a slope as will make the center of gravity of the Q's coincide with the center of gravity of the P's. There is a one-to-one correspondence between the economic and the geometric problem, so that if the "map"

---

[8] A more complete expression, in mathematical terms, applying to any number of years, is given in Chapter XII.

is correct we have reduced the whole problem to one of geometry.

Incidentally, it may be remarked here that there is evidently nothing inherent in the geometrical construction as presented which necessitates a positive rather than a negative market rate of interest. A negative rate can theoretically emerge whenever the P's and their center of gravity are of sufficiently low latitude or great longitude, or both, so that the common slope of the Market lines tangent at the Q's with the Willingness lines, will be less than 100 per cent. That this is theoretically possible is evident from inspection, provided the Willingness lines do, as assumed, have inclinations at certain income positions less than 45°. The reasons why the rate of interest is seldom or never negative have chiefly to do with the conditions introduced under the second approximation and will be more apparent in the next chapter.

§15. *The Four Principles as Charted*

In this geometric picture we see that the four principles formerly stated in words (in Chapter V) are now interpreted geometrically on the "map" as follows:

(1) Impatience principle A (that each man's impatience or rate of time preference depends on his income stream) is represented by a family of Willingness lines for each individual.

(2) Impatience principle B (that each rate of time preference is assimilated to the market rate of interest) is represented by the tangency at each individual's point Q, thus making the slope of his W line at that point equal to the slope of the M line.

(3) Market principle A (that the market will be cleared) is represented by the fact that the aggregate

horizontal shift from P's to Q's to the right (by all borrowers combined) must equal the aggregate horizontal shift from P's to Q's to the left (by all lenders combined); and also that the two aggregate vertical shifts representing next year's repayments of loans must likewise be equal, so that the centers of gravity of the P's and the Q's coincide.

(4) Market principle B (that all loans are repaid and at one rate of interest) is represented by the fact that the Market lines are straight and parallel.

§16. *The Geometric Method*

These charts do, for the ideas they illustrate, what supply and demand curves do for the ideas illustrated by them.

Like all graphic methods, the one here applied is intended to segregate basic tendencies from the rough-and-tumble of real life, and set these tendencies going as they cannot go in real life. It condenses a year's income into an infinitesimal time; it confines our variations to two years only; it disregards the element of risk; it pictures next year's income as a certainty; it disregards the lack of security that limits the ease with which an individual can slide his series of transactions along the M line; it assumes that the market is perfect.

Again, the Willingness lines should not be drawn as continuous curves. They are actually rough and jagged, so that, for this reason alone, the nicety of adjustment which would obtain under the assumption of continuity is lost. We know also that most individuals require a considerable stimulus even to start sliding along a Market line. Besides the height of the rate of interest, there is the trouble of negotiating a loan, establishing a line of credit, and practical considerations without end. One result is that in order to reverse one's direction on the Market line, a bigger rise or fall of the interest rate would be needed than the charts as here used would suggest. It takes a push to dislodge the individual from P in either direction. The same sort of considerations cause his position Q to be determined without the nicety of precision suggested by the continuous curves.

But all these and other practical considerations do not destroy the fact that each of our four determining conditions represents a reality—a real *tendency* even when in actual practice balked or neutralized.

The relationship of the rate of time preference to income is analogous to that of marginal utility or cost to consumption or production. In order to show how the marginal desirability of sugar in the case of Individual *1* is related to his consumption of sugar, we employ a curve, which, under certain assumptions, becomes the familiar demand curve for sugar. Such a curve has come into universal use.

Why has no similar curve been used to indicate the corresponding relationship between time preference (a marginal desirability derivative) and income? There are many reasons, but perhaps chief is the difficulty of finding a suitable graphic method for variables so diverse and related to each other in so complicated a manner. The map of the Willingness, or Impatience, lines partly solves this problem. So far as two periods of time are concerned, it "puts on the map" the whole problem of interest.

§17. *Relation to Supply and Demand*

Some students familiar with demand and supply curves as applied to the loan market may feel that they can get their bearings better if the exact relation is shown between these and the "map" here used. Therefore, it seems worth while here to bridge the gap between these two sorts of representations just as, at the outset, the gap was bridged between the map and pictures of the income stream earlier in this book. We may readily and completely derive the curves of demand and supply from the map and the constructions which have been drawn on it.

The individual demand curve of Individual 1 is found as follows: Rotate the straight line PQ about P as a pivot, that is, draw a series of PQ's from P at varying slopes. On each such PQ find Q, the point of tangency with a W line. The horizontal displacement of Q to the right of P is the loan which Individual 1 is willing to take at the rate of interest represented by the slope of PQ.

Thus we have both coördinates (namely, interest rate and amount of loans demanded at that rate) given by the map. Having these coördinates, we merely need to plot them on a separate sheet in the usual way.

In the same way we may construct every other individual's demand curve. The aggregate curve of all individuals (by adding all demands at a given interest rate) gives the total demand curve in the market.

The supply curves are constructed similarly; the only difference being that for supply we use the horizontal displacement of Q to the *left* of P, instead of to the right.

Of course, at any given slope near the slope of the market rate, some individuals will have a right, and others a left, displacement, and at the market rate itself the two displacements are equal in the aggregate. This is true where the supply and demand curves intersect.

Evidently the map gives us the same relationships as

the ordinary supply and demand curves and much more. The supply and demand curves, for instance, give us only the *displacements,* or differences in income position, as between P and Q, while the map gives the whole income position of both points. And while we can reconstruct, as above, the demand and supply curve from our map, we cannot reconstruct our map from the supply and demand curves.

It may also be noted here that the supply curve is derived from the map in spite of the absence, in this first approximation, of any investment opportunity or productivity element. The significance of this fact will be more apparent in Chapter XI where under the second approximation this element is introduced.

CHAPTER XI

SECOND APPROXIMATION IN GEOMETRIC TERMS

§1. *Introduction*

Graphic illustrations of the solutions of two economic problems incident to the attainment of economic equilibrium, assuming incomes fixed, have been given in Chapter X. One was an individual problem, the other a market problem. We found their solutions respectively to be:

(1) The income situation Q_1 which Individual *1* will reach from his original income position P_1 by borrowing or lending will be found where his borrower-lender motive is balanced, i.e., where one of his Willingness lines is tangent to the Market line M; and

(2) The rate of interest, or divergency slope of the Market line from 45° will be such that the center of gravity of all Q's, as above found, will coincide with that of all the P's.

In this chapter the point P, which was assumed to be arbitrarily imposed upon the individual, is replaced by a series of optional points among which he may choose. If this group of points is shrunk into a single point, the analysis of this chapter becomes identical with that of Chapter X. In other words, Chapter X represents a special case, while this chapter represents the general problem.

In Chart 35 are represented various possible points supposed to indicate the various income situations available to Individual *1* aside from any further shifts through borrowing or lending. Instead of having no choice but a fixed position as in Chapter X, he now has the opportunity to choose any one of many income positions, but will actually confine his choice to those positions represented upon the boundary line $O_1'\ O_1^{IV}$. This may be called the *Investment Opportunity line* or briefly *the O line* for Individual *1*. Every individual, of course, has his own *O* line.

§2. *The Investment Opportunity Line*

The reason why we may exclude all points inside of this boundary line is evident. The inside points would never be chosen under any circumstances, since each inside point is excelled by some points on the boundary in respect to *both* years' incomes. Thus the point A in Chart 35 will certainly not be chosen if the individual has the opportunity to substitute any other point to the north or east of it, or between north and east.

But in no case can income be increased indefinitely. There are limits in whatever direction we try—whether this year, next year, or both. These limits make up the boundary line $O_1'\ O_1^{IV}$. Chart 35 represents Individual *1* as having the opportunity to shift his income position on this map in an eastward direction only up to the position O_1'. In other words, he can increase his income in the present year without changing his income in the next year only up to that limit O_1'. Technical limitations, including personal limitations, are assumed to forbid his pushing to the right beyond O_1'.

In the same way, starting again at A, he has the opportunity to move northward on this map—that is to increase next year's income without changing this

[264]

year's—but only up to a certain limit O_1^{IV}. Or he can move in a somewhat northeasterly direction and better himself for both years at once, but again he can do this only up to a certain limit, O_1'' or O_1'''.

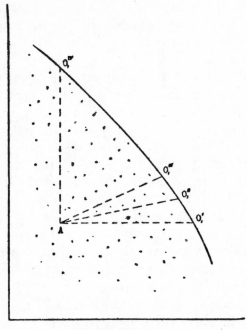

CHART 35

The Opportunity (O) Line.

The boundary line O_1' O_1^{IV}, made up of these limiting points may, of course, take various forms, but, for the present it will be assumed to be a curve concave toward the origin. It is simply a geometric picture of the technical limitations of an individual's income in the two years considered, assuming, as always, all other years' incomes to remain the same. It is the locus, or line, of options

[265]

and may be called the Option line or the Opportunity line,[1] and is designated as O_1 for Individual *1*.

§3. *The Individual's Adjustment Without Loans*

What we have seen so far is that Individual *1*, having discarded all income positions *inside* the Investment Opportunity line, has left as still eligible only the points *on* that curve.

As before, we assume that each individual is unconscious of having any influence on the market rate of interest. To fix our ideas suppose, as before, this rate to be 10 per cent. The only adjustments the individual can make are: (1) adjusting his position on the *O* line; (2) further adjusting on the *M* line. Problem (2) is analogous to that of Chapter X, so that Problem (1) is the only new one. The solution of Problem (1) will be found to point the way to the solution of the knottiest part of the interest problem, purposely omitted from the first approximation. This is the problem of investment opportunity, productivity, or technique of production in relation to the rate of interest.

The principle by which the individual may shift his position along the Investment Opportunity line is very similar to the principle already set forth in Chapter X by which he shifts along the Market line. It will be recalled that the individual shifted along the Market or

---

[1] An *option* is represented by any one point in Chart 35 not outside the area bounded by $A\ O_1'O_1{}^{IV}$. Only those points on the curve $O_1'O_1{}^{IV}$ are really eligible. The *opportunity* to move from one of these points to another implies *two* points on this line. If these two points are close together, the direction of one from the other is the slope of the tangent to the curve. Thus, the term "option" suggests a point on the curve while the term "opportunity" suggests the *direction* of the curve.

M line according to its slope when that slope is compared, at any point, with the slope of the Willingness or W lines. We saw that, if we suppose him situated at a point on the M line at which the Willingness line drawn through that point is *steeper* than the Market line, he will move away from that point *downward,* along the M line, that is, he will *borrow*; while, if situated where his W line is *less steep* than his M line he will move *upward* along the M line, that is, he will *lend*.

Similar comparisons apply to our present problem merely by substituting Opportunity line for Market line. Suppose Individual *1* to be situated, to start with, at O_1' on the Opportunity line, as shown on Chart 36. He then has the opportunity to shift to any other point on that line as formerly he could shift along the Market line. Let us, as before, proceed by small steps of $100 each. The first step is from O_1' to O_1''. The chart indicates that, by sacrificing $100 of this year's income, he *can* add $150 to next year's income, while he is *willing* to receive only $115 as indicated by his Willingness line drawn through O_1'. The $50 net return he will receive is a 50 per cent rate of return over cost. This is his investment opportunity rate. He is willing to lend $100 for a net return of $15 or 15 per cent over cost. This measures his degree of impatience or rate of time preference. Evidently, as just hinted, he will seize the opportunity to invest for a 50 per cent return when he would be willing to take 15 per cent. This choice is represented on Chart 36 by following the Opportunity line from O_1' to O_1''.

If, as a second step, another $100 *can* bring him $140 while he would be *willing* to take $120, he will seize that opportunity, too, and so move on to O_1'''. That is, he will

THE THEORY OF INTEREST

choose a 40 per cent investment opportunity when his degree of impatience is only 20 per cent. Thus, he may be pictured ascending a staircase on the Opportunity line. The successive steps, in this case, grow less steep as he proceeds. At each point he decides whether to take the next step or not by comparing its steepness with that of the *W*

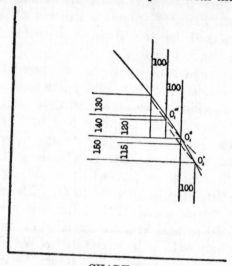

CHART 36

W Lines Showing Different Degrees of Impatience and *O* Lines Showing Different Rates of Return.

line at that point. The successive *W* lines will be more and more steep as he goes on investing successive $100's, while the Opportunity line will become less and less steep.

When the point is reached where the Opportunity line is no longer steeper than the Willingness line, he will stop investing. The Willingness line through that point will have the *same* steepness as the Opportunity line, say 30 per cent. That is, the two curves will there be tangent. This point of tangency, *R,* is shown in Chart 37.

[268]

The reasoning which has just been used is evidently exactly like that used in Chapter X, the only important difference being that then we had a *straight* line to deal with to express what the individual *can* do while here

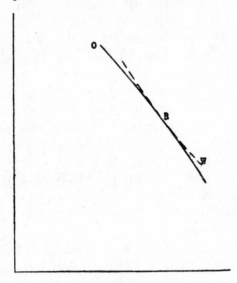

CHART 37
The Point of Tangency (*R*) of a *W* Line to the *O* Line.

we have instead a *curved* line, or at any rate, a line which need not be straight.

And the result of this reasoning so far is also similar. The stopping point is where the *can* line (in Chapter X, the Market line; here, the Opportunity line) is tangent to the Willingness line.

§4. *Individual Adjustment with Loans*

Up to this point in the second approximation we have reasoned as though the Individual did not have freedom to borrow or lend in the loan market. We purposely excluded that possibility for the moment and went ahead as if the man were shut off from the loan market completely, so that any investment must be out of his own income and not be made with borrowed money. Were this the case (as in practice it often is) Chart 37 would correctly represent the result of the individual's shift. It would be a one-way shift, entirely along the Opportunity line.

But if now we return to the hypothesis of a perfect loan market, accessible to all concerned and to any extent desired, then Chart 37 does not fully picture our problem because it fails to take account of the fact that the individual not only can shift along the Opportunity line, but can also shift along a Market line by borrowing and lending. That is, he now has *two* "can" lines, both the Market line of Chapter X and the Opportunity line of this chapter.

Chart 38 pictures the double movement of Individual *1*. Starting at O_1', he moves along the Opportunity line to P_1 where the Opportunity line becomes tangent to the M line, then along the M line to Q_1 where the M line becomes tangent to a W_1 line. That is, the fixed rate of interest will cause the individual so to shift that the marginal rate of return over cost (investment opportunity rate and the marginal rate of time preference (degree of impatience) will, each of them, be equal to the market rate of interest. Chart 38 depicts Individual *1*'s adjustment of his rate of investment opportunity and his degree of impatience to the market rate of interest. The rate of interest is, as always, represented in the slope of the M line, and the rate of return over cost is represented in the slope at P_1 of the O_1 line.

These two slopes are the same, since the two lines are there tangent.

The slopes of the M line and the O_1 line at P_1 are identical since the two lines are tangent at that point. The degree of impatience is represented by the identical

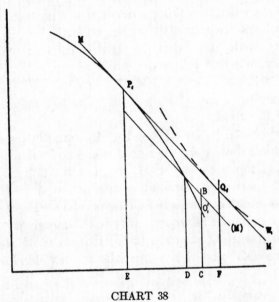

CHART 38

Point of Equilibrium Where the M Line Which is Tangent to the O Line at P is also Tangent to a Willingness Line at Q.

slopes of the M line and of the W_1 line at their point of tangency Q_1. Since the M line is a straight line, the slopes of the O_1 line and the M line at P_1 and the slopes of the M line and the W_1 line at Q_1 are all identical and the identity of the opportunity rate, the impatience rate, and the market rate is shown.

§5. *The Double Adjustment Discussed*

In such a double adjustment, P_1, the point of tangency on the Investment Opportunity line, has to be found first and Q_1, the point of tangency on a W_1 line last, for there is only one Opportunity line and only one point on it at which the slope corresponds to the rate of interest; while there are an infinite number of W lines with a point on each having that slope or direction.[2]

It is worth noting that the point P_1 thus located on the Opportunity line will be quite different from the Point R on that line shown in Chart 37 *when the individual was assumed to be cut off from loans.*[3] The two may differ in either direction.

It is also to be noted that the W_1 lines always say the last word, that is, fix the final income position at Q_1, the point of tangency of the M line to a W_1 line. All other income positions represent points reviewed in Individual *1*'s mind but rejected in favor of Q_1. The point P on any individual's Opportunity line is merely a point in transit toward Q, which is the final point of equilibrium.

If we wish to be even more realistic, our individual need

[2] The point P_1 may also be described as that income position, or option, on the Opportunity line which has the greatest present value, as has been shown in Chapter VII and as may also be shown geometrically if desired.

[3] It would not then be true that he would choose the option of highest present value. That point is not R but P_1. Thus it is not self-evident, as it might seem, that a man will always choose the income stream of highest present value in the market. He will only do so provided he has, in addition, perfect freedom to move from that situation by means of a loan market. Otherwise he might not be willing to suffer the inconvenience, say, of a very small income this year even if his expected income next year is very large. The only maximum principle preserved in all cases is not that of maximum market value but that of maximum desirability.

not be pictured as traveling along the Opportunity line at all, even on a non-stop flight to Q_1. He may, more properly, be pictured as making a more direct jump, across lots, directly from O_1' his income position on the Opportunity line to Q_1.

The reader may, starting at O_1', trace the individual by small steps of combined $100 investments and loans. Thus the first $100 step would carry him from O_1' to B. Successive investments and borrowings of equal amounts would increase the individual's next year's income while leaving his present year's income the same as before. On the chart his income position would move first from O_1' to B and then step by step in a vertical line above B. But he will not necessarily confine his borrowings to the amount of his investments. The chart represents a man whose impatience leads him to borrow for this year's consumption the amount represented by CF. His borrowings represented by the horizontal difference between O_1' and P_1 (that is the distance CE) is what is often called a productive loan, while the horizontal difference between O_1' and Q_1 (that is the distance CF) is what is called a consumption or convenience or personal loan.[4]

Properly speaking, however, no part of the *loan* is itself productive. It is the investment which is properly to be called productive. To shift along the M line adds nothing to the total present worth of the individual, for it merely substitutes $110 next year for $100 this year, or a series of such sums, and each $110 next year has the

---

[4] With another individual, on the other hand, the most desirable point might be very different. He might borrow only part of what he invests, or even not borrow at all but lend as well as invest. All depends on the particular shape and position of his O and W lines.

same present worth as $100 this year. A shift along the Opportunity line, however, does add to a man's present worth. Up to the last $100 invested, each $100 yields more than $110 next year and so possesses a greater present worth, reckoned at 10 per cent, than $100.

The sole advantage of any shift along the M line alone is to gain not more market worth, but to gain in convenience—to reach a greater total desirability. This is true in both the first approximation and the second. Every loan, merely as such, is a shift on the M line *alone*, and is in itself always a convenience loan. Strictly speaking, no loan, as such, is "productive."

It is only in so far as the loan makes a difference in the *other* shift, that along the O line, that it can claim to be called a productive loan, and it is quite true, in the case pictured, that the loan does make such a difference. That is, we call the loan productive because, without it, the investment would not be made, or would not be so great—because it would be inconvenient (or even impossible) to invest so much out of this year's income.

The essential effect of a so-called productive loan is to enable the individual (under our hypothesis of perfect fluidity and no risk) to disregard entirely what has been called the time shape of the income stream P, that is, the proportion of this to next year's income represented by P. It enables him to push P as far to the left as he wishes without threatening him with starvation, or causing him any inconvenience. He need practice no abstinence. For whatever P lacks in this year's income may be made up by loans, that is, by use of the Market line. In fact, P may be pushed even to the *left* of the vertical axis, a position of negative this year's income, which is physically impossible except as simultaneously offset by a loan so as to bring him back again to a position of real income this year.

In short the investment, or O shift, affects the *size* of income as measured in present worth of the entire income position while the loan, or M shift, affects its final shape.

The Chart 38 is evidently only one type among many and the reader who wishes to pursue the subject into special cases will find it easy to do so by varying the curves to suit himself.[5]

§6. *Market Equilibrium*

Just as in the first approximation, so in this second approximation there are two successive problems:

(1) How the individual reacts to a given rate of interest.

(2) How market equilibrium determines that rate.

The first of these two problems having now been solved, we are ready for the second, the market problem—to show how market equilibrium is established. This is precisely as in Chapter X, except that the M line, instead of rotating about a fixed point P, now rolls around the O line.

The problem, then, is simply to draw a set of straight M lines, one for each individual, each person's M line being tangent to his Opportunity line at a point P, all such M lines being parallel to each other, to find on each of them the point Q at which it is tangent to a W line of the person concerned, then to roll these straight lines around said Opportunity lines, while still keeping them

[5] Of course, the shift along the O line depends entirely on where we suppose the individual to be situated on that line in the first place. If we wish, we may suppose him to start on the opposite side of P from that hitherto pictured, in which case he does not enter into a contemplated investment but withdraws from one.

all parallel, until they so slant that the center of gravity of the Q's shall coincide with the center of gravity of the P's. This slope, thus determined, signifies the rate of interest which will clear the market.

Let us recapitulate. We have given:

(1) The Market lines, just as in the first approximation.

(2) The families of Willingness lines, one family for each individual, just as in the first approximation.

(3) The Opportunity lines, one only for each individual, that is, a series of points takes the place of the single point P_1 in the first approximation.

We also have, correspondingly, three rates:

(1) The market rate of interest represented by the slope (over and above that of 100 per cent) of each and every straight Market line.

(2) The degree of impatience, or rate of time preference, one of each person, represented by the slope of the Willingness lines and depending on his income situation, as finally determined after all adjustments have been made.

(3) The rate of return over cost, or the investment opportunity rate, one for each person, represented by the slope of the Opportunity line and depending on the position chosen on it.

The charts of this chapter interpret the second approximation exactly as the charts of Chapter X interpreted the first approximation, but with two new investment opportunity principles added to the four principles common to both Chapters X and XI and already geometrically interpreted in Chapter X. That is:

The Investment Opportunity Principle A is represented by the Opportunity line.

The Investment Opportunity Principle B is represented by the tangency of the Opportunity line with the Market line, so that the marginal rate of return over cost is equal to the rate of interest.

This last principle, combined with Impatience Principle B, means that each individual so adjusts his position (first along the Opportunity line to P and then along the Market line to Q) that the Market line PQ shall be tangent to the first at P and to the second at Q. This Q will be his income situation finally chosen. To clear the market the Q's must be so chosen that their center of gravity coincides with that of the P's.

§7. *The Nature of the Opportunity Line Discussed*

This chapter differs from Chapter X chiefly in the introduction of the concept of investment opportunity which is depicted on the charts as the Opportunity line, or O line. Just what does this line represent in the real world? Is there any distinction between investing in the opportunities offered by man's environment and lending at the market rate of interest? Is not lending, or buying a bond, just as truly investing as digging an oil well, building a factory, or making shoes? Reserving the merely verbal part of the answer, let us first go to the main question as to the possibility of definitely distinguishing the two lines.

Under the assumptions explained in Chapters V, VI, VII, and VIII, there is a clear distinction between an O line and an M line. The O line, unlike the Market lines, is not straight, is not common to all individuals, and is not a family of lines but a single line. It may be defined as the limiting line of a group of points which represent all the optional income situations available to an individual who neither borrows nor lends. Every one has opportunities to shift along his O line at a rate above or below the market rate of interest, even if it be merely in the degree of care he gives his clothes, his house, his fences, or even his food. At a certain stage it is literally true that a "stitch in time saves nine". That is, mending one's clothes yields 900 per cent. But beyond a certain point mending one's clothes, or a roof, painting a house, or tilling the soil will not repay the cost. Each activity has its marginal point and enters into the construction of every person's O line. An individual's Opportunity line is a composite of his separate potential activities—what he might do if he chose.

Of course the O line cannot be drawn without the aid of valuations which involve the market principles and so involve the rate of interest. The farmer who encounters the law of diminishing returns in agriculture buys machinery and labor and sells grain. His O line is thus somewhat dependent on the prices of machinery and, since the price of every good is a discounted valuation, it depends on the rate of interest. Only in a primitive or imaginary Robinson Crusoe land can we get a pure case of investing successive amounts of this year's income for the sake of getting a diminishing return in future years without the presence of some buying or selling as an ingredient in the make-up of the O line. It is largely because the element of the rate of interest is almost omnipresent in the valuations entering into the O line that the other and essential ingredient of technical limitations has been overlooked so generally. Even the farmer does some of that omnipresent trading, but besides this trading with other men, he is dealing with nature—the soil, the seasons, the weather, insect enemies, and all the rest. Every investment *in his farm* will have a variable decreasing return as contrasted with the (to him) constant return to be got in the loan market. Yet every investment in his farm will *somewhat* imply an interest element and will theoretically change as the interest rate changes. Thus, strictly speaking, his *O* line is not to be pictured as immovable like a rock but as subject to some slight change with every change in the slope of the *M* line. Nevertheless this fact evidently does not alter the principles by which the slope of the *M* line is determined. The *M* line still rolls around an *O* line, even if that curve changes a little as it rolls.

The *O* lines have been exemplified by the law of decreasing returns in agriculture. Such a curve is concave toward the origin and represents a law of decreasing returns in the sense that each succeeding dose of $100 invested out of this year's income will return less and less next year.

But may there not be a law of increasing return? That is, may not the curve be convex in parts instead of concave?

We may imagine the *O* line, bounding or enclosing the group of points representing the possible options, to be convex or to have any conceivable shape. It may be reentrant, jagged, discontinuous, straight in parts. It is largely for convenience that we have hitherto pictured it as concave, curved and continuous. But if it were otherwise, almost the same result would follow. The line *PQ* would still roll around it. The result would evidently be that, wherever the curve was re-entrant (convex toward the origin), the straight Market line, in rolling around the group of points, would *jump* across this chasm at the slightest provocation due to a change in the interest rate.

These re-entrant parts would be as inoperative as if they did not exist, and only the points on which the rolling took place would really count in establishing equilibrium. What is left, after dropping out such re-entrant parts as ineligible, is thus the "envelope" of the group of points representing an individual's opportunities to invest rationally and must therefore be concave toward the origin. We are justified then in assuming the curved concave Opportunity line as typical.

As to the applicability of the term investment to a shift on the M line, this is a matter of choice of words. Undoubtedly it is so applied in ordinary usage. In fact, such investments are more commonly so called than any other. I have not been able to think of a short phrase in common use which will apply exclusively to an investment the return on which varies with each successive amount invested. Perhaps "investment with diminishing returns" or "investment involving exploitation," as distinct from investment by mere sale and purchase, would come nearer to conforming both to usage and to the requirements of the case. Yet the full phrase which I have provisionally adopted, investment opportunity, seems fairly correct in its implications. We seldom speak of buying a bond as an investment *opportunity*, but investing in new industrial, mining or agricultural enterprises, such as radio production, or in oil wells, or orange groves, is spoken of as a real opportunity because the return is not a standardized market figure but subject to technical conditions as to productivity.

§8. *Investment Opportunity and Impatience*

We see then how distinct is the O line from the M line. It is still more distinct from the W line. The Willingness lines represent subjective conditions; the Opportunity line represents objective conditions. The O line of an individual is simply *one* curve, while the W line is one of many. There is some rate of time preference represented by the angle or slope of a W line on the charts, be it positive, negative, or zero, corresponding to every possible income position of an individual wherever on the chart it may be. But this is not true of the O line. There is only a limited region of options on the map, bounded by a single curve.

As already explained, if the opportunity area enclosed by the O line shrinks to a single point, there is no determinate tangent and we automatically revert to the first approximation in which there is no opportunity to choose from among options.

Thus the investment opportunity influence may, theoretically at least, vanish entirely and lead us back to the first approximation, but the impatience influence can never vanish. Practically however, investment opportunity never quite vanishes. There is always at least some flexibility in everybody's income, but in primitive society, the range of opportunity is relatively small. While the Opportunity line never entirely collapses into a mathematical point, yet, for a person in primitive society it is an almost negligible spot or ring and could exert only a negligible influence on the rate of interest, even if it were to double in diameter or were to change in form. In such a society the only important influences on the rate of interest must come largely from a change in the map, that is, in the distribution of impatience relatively to income.

But when, as in modern society, the range of investment opportunity is great, the slopes of the Opportunity lines exert a great and more controlling influence on the slope of the Market lines.

If the investment opportunity area is large so as to cause the Opportunity line to curve *slowly*, its relative fixity of slope indicates a relatively stable rate of interest. If the slope is absolutely constant and the same for all individuals, as in the case of the hard-tack island,[6] represented by a 45° straight line, or the example of Professor Harry G. Brown's imaginary fruit trees, represented by a straight line steeper than 45°, this fixed shape may, within limits, fix the rate of interest absolutely, forcing it to agree with that fixed slope whatever may be the Willingness lines representing impatience. The limits within which this would be true may readily be charted by the reader.

The most important result here is that the Opportunity line cannot be dispensed with in the theory of the rate of interest. It is something distinct from and in addition to the Impatience lines as well as to the Market lines. If those theorists who still insist on the subjective principle as the only principle of interest will try to picture its determination on this map, they will find it impossible to get any determinate direction of the Market lines without invoking the Opportunity lines. To adapt a simile of Alfred Marshall's, both blades of a pair of scissors are needed to make the scissors work.

§9. *Can Interest Disappear?*

One use of this graphic method is to help us form a more complete picture of the problem as to whether the rate of interest may ever be zero or negative.

Just as there is a prevalent idea among the economi-

[6] See Chapter VIII, §4, for discussion of these examples.

cally illiterate that all interest should be zero—should be abolished—so among the economically literate there is a prevalent idea that the rate of interest could under no imaginable conditions ever be zero or below. Let us then see, under the assumption of the second approximation, what are the conditions, if any, which will permit of a zero or negative rate of interest.

A zero rate of interest means, in our chart, that PQ has an inclination of 45°, that is, a slope of 100 per cent. Our question, therefore, is: must PQ necessarily be steeper than 45°. The slope of PQ depends entirely on the conformation of the O curve and the W curves of each person in the loan market. The less steep these curves are, the less steep will be the Market lines. We have seen that toward the southeast parts of the map the W curves are flatter than 45°, that is, a man with a relatively large income this year and a relatively small one next year would be willing, if he had to, to trade more than \$100 today to get only \$100 next year. Probably this is potentially true of everyone. It is also true that seldom if ever are actual income situations (Q's) located in this southeast region.

We turn now to the O line. For the average man in a progressive country and age, like America today, this will be steeper than in a retrograde country or in a decadent age—a country or an age in which the natural resources are becoming exhausted. But if we go sufficiently to the northwest, it will always be flatter than 45°, that is, if any investment opportunity be exploited far enough it will yield less future return than its immediate cost. This is not only true of land cultivation and extractive industries generally but of all industries. Everywhere, in the end, any law of increasing returns will give place to a law of decreasing returns. And if we keep pursuing these decreasing returns far enough there will always come a point where additional investment would be worse than useless or where the rate of return over cost is less than nothing. Even in such cases of extraordinary returns as the example of the Bell Telephone Company, to have tried to push the development faster than new construction could be built or than the public, even with every device of the advertiser, could absorb, would have been sheer waste.[7]

Thus the charts depict regions in which the O curve of each individual is less steep than 45° and regions in which his W curves are likewise less steep than 45°. But that fact does not itself prove that the resultant market rate of interest may ever actually be zero. For the flatter parts of the W curves are to the southeast, as shown in Charts 31 and 34, while the flatter parts of the O curve are to the northwest, as shown in Chart 35. If this relative position of the flatter W and O lines were peculiar only to a few individuals, negative interest might well exist. The P of such an individual might be in the northwestern part of the map and the Q in the southeastern, the Market line PQ sloping less steeply than 45° and being tangent at P to the O line and at Q to a W line. He would thus be a borrower, and there would be plenty of lenders.

But if, as is the truth, practically everybody else has

[7] Explanations of the law of diminishing returns sometimes miss this point by ignoring the time element. This element is always essential and especially in interest theory. Enlarging a factory may *in the future* lower costs and so *in time* increase the rate of return obtained or attainable, but we are here concerned with a hypothetical series of doses of costs or investments all relating to the *same* period of time such as the present year and with the return over these costs, say next year.

the same sort of map, that is, with the parts of the O and W curves which are flatter than 45° located northwest and southeast respectively; and if we should draw everybody else's PQ at the same slope as above, we would have only borrowers and no lenders at interest rates pictured by such slopes. Everyone would be glad to borrow at negative rates of interest. But a rate of interest at which there is no lending would necesarily rise. It could not clear the market. It could remain negative only if a sufficient number of people had maps on which the W lines were flatter than 45° even in the northwest and O lines flatter than 45° even in the southeast. Otherwise the center of gravity of the P's and Q's could not coincide. But there is nothing inconceivable in having such a layout overlapping the flatter-than-45° regions. In other words, if enough persons in the market were *sufficiently miserly,* or their income opportunities were *sufficiently unpromising,* or both, then the rate of interest could be zero or below.

To meet these conditions would require either a change in average human nature as to impatience under given income situations, or a change in the future prospects of production and investment opportunity, due, say, to impending exhaustion of natural resources or retrogression generally, instead of progress, in the industrial arts.

Finally, the Opportunity line can never get very much flatter than the 45° inclination, if as flat as that, so long as among our opportunities there are even the present possibilities of *preserving* food and other goods, that is postponing their uses. We can scarcely expect a time to come when we cannot do at least as well for the future as the shipwrecked sailors with their hard-tack. That is, as long as such an alternative exists as being able to postpone much of our present income by preserving the goods which yield it, the *real* rate of interest can scarcely get below zero.[8]

Our conclusion is that negative interest is theoretically possible, though in practice the necessary conditions never occur.

§10. *Does Interest Stimulate Saving?*

Just as the map helps visualize the theoretical possibility, yet practical improbability, of negative interest, so also it helps us to see clearly the answer to the much debated question whether saving is stimulated by raising the rate of interest.

If the reader will draw on the map any desired family of Willingness lines, place the individual at any desired income situation (or draw an Opportunity line to indicate all possible positions), and then incline a ruler at 45° and rotate it about that point (or roll it around that line) he will note that the points of tangency of the ruler with the several Willingness lines will themselves constitute a curve. The savings (or lendings) are evidently represented by the horizontal displacement of Q to the left of P. Opportunity and Willingness lines may easily be so constructed that, as the ruler turns clockwise interest rises and the amount saved and lent out of this year's income will first increase and then decrease.

§11. *Relation to Supply and Demand Curves*

In §17 of Chapter X it was shown how supply and demand curves can be derived from the M line and the W

---

[8] It is true that unstable money sometimes drives the *real* rate below zero unintentionally. (See Chapters II and XIX.) But the *money* rate cannot get below zero so long as the standard is, like gold, capable of being stored substantially without cost. (Chapter II.)

lines depicted in Chart 34. Supply and demand curves can equally well be derived from the M line, the O line and the W lines shown in Chart 38. A series of positions of PQ, with different slopes, gives us all the material needed, each slope giving a rate of interest and each horizontal spread between P and Q being the demand for loans (if Q is east of P) or supply of loans (if Q is west of P). The only difference is that P is not now fixed as in the first approximation, but shifts as PQ has different slopes.

It will be noted that the Opportunity line which embodies the technical or production elements in the problem has no more relation to the supply than to the demand, although this runs counter to the common notions that productivity rules one side of the market and time preference the other.

It will also be noted that the map gives us vastly more light on the analysis of interest than do the mere supply and demand curves. But even the map fails to give a complete picture because, in particular, it shows only two years. The truth seems to be that no complete visualization of this difficult problem is possible. The only complete symbolization which seems to be possible is in terms of mathematical formulas as in the next two chapters.

CHAPTER XII

FIRST APPROXIMATION IN TERMS OF FORMULAS

§1. *Case of Two Years and Three Individuals*

In this chapter, the four principles constituting the first approximation, previously expressed verbally [1] and geometrically,[2] will be expressed algebraically. Inasmuch as the equations, the solutions of which express the solution of the interest problem, are necessarily numerous and complicated, we shall first consider a simplified special case where there are to be considered only two years in which there is income and three individuals who borrow or lend. We shall then pass to the general case where there are any given number of years and any number of individuals.

In the simplified case, we assume, therefore, that each individual's degree of impatience for this year's over next year's income can be expressed as dependent solely on the amount of this year's and next year's income, the incomes of all other future years being disregarded. We also assume, for simplicity, that the income of each of the two years is concentrated at the middle of the year, making the two points just a year apart, and that borrowing and lending are so restricted as to affect only this year's and next year's income.

---

[1] In Chapter V, §9, and in Chapter IX, §9, first of the three lines, in each case.
[2] In Chapter X, §15.

Let f_1 represent the marginal rate of time preference [3] for this year's over next year's income for Individual *1* (this is the slope at Q of a Willingness line relatively to the 45° line). Let his original endowment of income for the two years [4] be respectively

$$c_1' \text{ and } c_1''.$$

(These are the longitude and latitude of P in Chapter X.) This original income stream, consisting merely of the two jets, so to speak, c_1', c_1'', is modified by borrowing this year and repaying next year. The sum borrowed this year is called x_1' (this is the horizontal shift from P to Q). To represent the final income of this year this sum x_1' is therefore to be added to the present income c_1'. Next year the debt is to be paid, and consequently the income finally arrived at for that year is c_1'' *reduced* by the sum thus paid. For the sake of uniformity, however, we shall regard both additions to and subtractions from pre-existing incomes algebraically as *additions*. Thus, the addition x_1' say $100, to the first year's income is a positive quantity, and the addition, which we shall designate by x_1'', to the second year's income, is a negative quantity — $105. The first year's income is, therefore, changed from

$$c_1' \text{ to } c_1' + x_1',$$

and the second year's from

$$c_1'' \text{ to } c_1'' + x_1''.$$

(Just as c_1' and c_1'' are the longitude and latitude of P in Chapter X, so $c_1' + x_1'$ and $c_1'' + x_1''$ are those of Q.)

[3] The relation of f, representing the rate of time preference of any individual to the *marginal desirability*, or "wantability," of this year's, and of next year's income, is given in the Appendix to this Chapter, §1.

[4] The term "year" is used for simplicity, but "month" or "day" would be equally admissible and would do less violence to facts.

By the use of this notation we avoid negative signs and so the necessity of distinguishing between the expressions for loans and repayments or for lenders and borrowers.

§2. *Impatience Principle A (Three Equations)*

The first condition determining interest, namely, Impatience Principle A, that the rate of preference for each individual depends upon his income stream, is represented for Individual *1* by the following equation:

$$f_1 = F_1 (c_1' + x_1', \; c_1'' + x_1'')$$

which expresses f_1 as dependent on, or, in mathematical language, as a function of the two income items of the two respective years, F_1 being not a symbol of a quantity but an abbreviation for "function." In case the individual lends instead of borrows, the equation represents the resulting relation between his marginal rate of preference and his income stream as modified by *lending;* the only difference is that, in this case, the particular numerical value of x' is negative and that of x'' positive. The equation is the algebraic expression for the dependence of the slope of a Willingness line on the income position of Individual *1*.

In like manner, for Individual *2*, we have the equation

$$f_2 = F_2 (c_2' + x_2', \; c_2'' + x_2''),$$

and, for the third individual,

$$f_3 = F_3 (c_3' + x_3', \; c_3'' + x_3'').$$

These three equations therefore express Impatience Principle A.

§3. *Impatience Principle B (Three Equations)*

Impatience Principle B requires that the marginal rates of time preference of the three different individuals for present over future income shall each be equal to the rate of interest, and is expressed by the following three equations: [5]

$$f_1 = i$$
$$f_2 = i$$
$$f_3 = i$$

where i denotes the rate of interest. These three equations are best written as the continuous equation:

$$i = f_1 = f_2 = f_3.$$

(These equations express the fact that at the Q's the slope of the Willingness line is the same as of the Market lines.)

§4. *Market Principle A (Two Equations)*

Market Principle A, which requires that the market be cleared, or that loans and borrowings be equal, is formulated by the following two equations:

$$x_1' + x_2' + x_3' = 0,$$
$$x_1'' + x_2'' + x_3'' = 0.$$

That is, the total of this year's borrowings is zero (lendings being regarded as negative borrowings), and the total of next year's repayments is likewise zero (payments from a person being regarded as negative payments to him).

§5. *Market Principle B (Three Equations)*

Market Principle B requires that the present value of this year's loans and the present value of next year's

[5] Strictly speaking these equalities are true only when the individual is so small a factor in the market as to have no appreciable influence on the market rate of interest. The equality of f and i implies that the total desirability, or wantability, of the individual is a maximum. (See Appendix to this chapter (Chapter XII), §2.

returns, for each individual, be equal. This condition is fulfilled in the following equations, each corresponding to one individual:

$$x_1' + \frac{x_1''}{1+i} = 0,$$

$$x_2' + \frac{x_2''}{1+i} = 0,$$

$$x_3' + \frac{x_3''}{1+i} = 0.$$

§6. *Counting Equations and Unknowns*

We now proceed to compare the number of the foregoing equations with the number of unknowns, for one of the most important advantages of an algebraic statement of any economic problem is the facility with which, by such a count, we may check up on whether the problem is solved and determinate. There are evidently 3 equations in the first set, 3 in the second, 2 in the third, and 3 in the fourth, making in all 11 equations. The unknown quantities are the marginal rates of time preference, the amounts borrowed, lent and returned, and the rate of interest as follows:

$$f_1, f_2, f_3, \text{ or 3 unknowns,}$$
$$x_1', x_2', x_3', \text{ or 3 unknowns,}$$
$$x_1'', x_2'', x_3'', \text{ or 3 unknowns,}$$

and finally,

$$i, \text{ or 1 unknown,}$$

making in all 10 unknowns.

We have, then, one more equation than necessary. But examination of the equations will show that they are not all *independent*, since any one equation in the third and fourth sets may be determined from the others of those sets. Thus, if we add together all the equations of the fourth set, we get the first equation of the third set. (namely, $x_1' + x_2' + x_3' = 0$). The addition gives

$$(x_1' + x_2' + x_3') + \frac{x_1'' + x_2'' + x_3''}{1 + i} = 0.$$

In this equation we may substitute zero for the numerator of the fraction (as is evident by consulting the second equation of the third set). Making this substitution, the above equation becomes

$$x_1' + x_2' + x_3' = 0,$$

which was to have been proved. Since we have here derived one of the five equations of the last two sets from the other four, the equations are not all independent. Any one of these five may be omitted as it could be obtained from the others. We have left then only ten equations. Since no one of these ten equations can be derived from the other nine, the ten are independent and are just sufficient to determine the ten unknown quantities, namely, the f's, x''s, x'''s and i.

§7. *Case of m Years and n Individuals*

We may now proceed to the case in which more than three individuals (let us say n individuals) and more than two years (let us say m years) are involved. We shall assume, as before, that the x's, representing loans or borrowings, are to be considered of positive value when they represent additions to income, and of negative value when they represent deductions.

§8. *Impatience Principle A* ($n(m - 1)$ *Equations*)

The equations expressing Impatience Principle A will now be in several groups, of which the first is:

$$f_1' = F_1' \left(c_1' + x_1', c_1'' + x_1'', \ldots, c_1^{(m)} + x_1^{(m)} \right),$$
$$f_2' = F_2' \left(c_2' + x_2', c_2'' + x_2'', \ldots, c_2^{(m)} + x_2^{(m)} \right),$$
$$\ldots\ldots\ldots\ldots\ldots\ldots\ldots\ldots\ldots\ldots\ldots\ldots\ldots\ldots\ldots\ldots$$
$$\ldots\ldots\ldots\ldots\ldots\ldots\ldots\ldots\ldots\ldots\ldots\ldots\ldots\ldots\ldots\ldots$$
$$f_n' = F_n' \left(c_n' + x_n', c_n'' + x_n'', \ldots, c_n^{(m)} + x_n^{(m)} \right).$$

These n equations express the rates of time preference of different individuals (f_1' of Individual *1*, f_2' of Individual *2*, ... f_n' of Individual n) for the *first* year's income compared with the next.

To express their preference for the *second* year's income compared with the next there will be another group of equations, namely:

$$f_1'' = F_1'' \left(c_1'' + x_1'', c_1''' + x_1''', \ldots, c_1^{(m)} + x_1^{(m)} \right),$$
$$f_2'' = F_2'' \left(c_2'' + x_2'', c_2''' + x_2''', \ldots, c_2^{(m)} + x_2^{(m)} \right),$$
$$\ldots\ldots\ldots\ldots\ldots\ldots\ldots\ldots\ldots\ldots\ldots\ldots\ldots\ldots\ldots\ldots$$
$$\ldots\ldots\ldots\ldots\ldots\ldots\ldots\ldots\ldots\ldots\ldots\ldots\ldots\ldots\ldots\ldots$$
$$f_n'' = F_n'' \left(c_n'' + x_n'', c_n''' + x_n''', \ldots, c_n^{(m)} + x_n^{(m)} \right).$$

For the *third* year there will be still another group, formed by inserting the superscript ''' for '', and so on up to the year $(m-1)$, for the year $(m-1)$ is the last one which has any exchange relations with the next, since that next is the last year, or year m. There will therefore be $(m-1)$ groups each of n equations, like the above group, making in all $n\,(m-1)$ equations in the entire set.

§9. *Impatience Principle B* $(n(m-1)$ *Equations*)

To express algebraically Impatience Principle B [6] we are compelled to recognize for each year a separate rate

*This principle here expressed in "marginal" terms has been alternatively stated in words in Chapter V and in geometric terms in Chapter

of interest. The rate of interest connecting the *first* year with the second will be called i', that connecting the *second* year with the third, i'', and so on to $i^{(m-1)}$. Under this principle, the rates of time preference for all the different individuals in the community for each year will be reduced to a level equal to the rate of interest. This condition, algebraically expressed, is contained in several continuous equations, of which the first is:

$$i' = f_1' = f_2' = \ldots = f_n'.$$

This expresses the fact that the rate of time preference of the first year's income compared with next is the same for all the individuals, and is equal to the rate of interest between the first year and the next. A similar continuous equation may be written with reference to the time preferences and the rate of interest as between the second year's income and the next, namely:

$$i'' = f_1'' = f_2'' = \ldots = f_n''.$$

Since the element of risk is supposed to be absent, it does not matter whether we consider these second-year rates of interest and time preference as the ones which are expected, or those which will actually obtain, for, under our assumed conditions of no risk, there is no discrepancy between expectations and realizations.

A similar set of continuous equations applies to time-exchange between each succeeding year and the next, up to that connecting year $(m - 1)$ with year m. There will therefore be $m - 1$ continuous equations of the

X as the principle of maximum desirability. The equivalence of the principle whether stated with reference to a maximum or to a marginal equality is obvious, but the mathematical reader may care to see it put in formulas as a "maximum" proposition as in the Appendix to this chapter (Chapter XII), §2.

above type. Since each such continuous equation is evidently made up of n constituent equations, there are in all $n (m-1)$ equations in the second set of equations.

§10. *Market Principle A (m Equations)*

The next set of equations, expressing Market Principle A, represents the clearing of the market. These equations are as follows:

$$x_1' + x_2' + \ldots + x_n' = 0,$$
$$x_1'' + x_2'' + \ldots + x_n'' = 0,$$
$$\cdot \quad \cdot \quad \cdot \quad \cdot \quad \cdot \quad \cdot \quad \cdot \quad \cdot$$
$$\cdot \quad \cdot \quad \cdot \quad \cdot \quad \cdot \quad \cdot \quad \cdot \quad \cdot$$
$$x_1^{(m)} + x_2^{(m)} + \ldots + x_n^{(m)} = 0.$$

There are here m equations.

§11. *Market Principle B (n Equations)*

The equations for Market Principle B express the equivalence of loans and repayments, or, more generally, the fact that for each individual the present value of the total additions (amount borrowed, or lent) to his income stream, algebraically considered, will equal zero. Thus, for Individual *1*, the addition the first or present year is x_1', the present value of which is also x_1', the addition the second year is x_1'', the present value of which is

$$\frac{x_1''}{1+i}$$

The addition the third year is x_1''', the present value of which is

$$\frac{x_1'''}{(1+i')(1+i'')}$$

This is obtained by two successive steps, namely, discounting x_1''' one year by dividing it by $1+i''$, thereby obtaining its value not in the present or first year but in the second year, and then discounting this value so obtained by dividing it in turn by $1 + i_1''$. The next item x^{IV} is converted into present value, through three such successive steps, and so on. Adding together all the present values we obtain as resulting equations for Individuals $1, 2, \ldots n:$

$$x_1' + \frac{x_1''}{1 + i'} + \cdots + \frac{x_1^{(m)}}{(1 + i')\,(1 + i'')\,\ldots\,(1 + i^{(m-1)})} = 0.$$

Similar equations will hold for each of the other individuals, namely:

$$x_2' + \frac{x_2''}{1 + i'} + \cdots + \frac{x_2^{(m)}}{(1 + i')\,(1 + i'')\,\ldots\,(1 + i^{(m-1)})} = 0.$$

. . . .

. . . .

$$x_n' + \frac{x_n''}{1 + i'} + \cdots + \frac{x_n^{(m)}}{(1 + i')\,(1 + i'')\,\ldots\,(1 + i^{(m-1)})} = 0.$$

making in all n equations.

§12. *Counting Equations and Unknowns*

We therefore have as the total number of equations the following:

$n\,(m - 1)$ equations expressing Impatience Principle A,
$n\,(m - 1)$ equations expressing Impatience Principle B,
m equations expressing Market Principle A, and
n equations expressing Market Principle B.

The sum of these gives $2\,mn + m - n$ equations in all.

We next proceed to count the unknown quantities (rates of time preference, loans, and rates of interest). First as to the f's:

For Individual 1 there are $f_1', f_1'', \ldots, f_1^{(m-1)}$, the number of which is $m - 1$, and, as there is an equal number for each of the n individuals, there will be in all $n (m - 1)$ unknown f's.

As to the x's, there will be one for each of the m years for each of the n individuals, or mn.

As to the i's, there will be one for each year up to the last year, $m - 1$. In short there will be

$$n (m - 1) \text{ unknown } f\text{'s},$$
$$mn \text{ unknown } x\text{'s},$$
$$m - 1 \text{ unknown } i\text{'s},$$

or $2 mn + m - n - 1$ unknown quantities in all. Comparing this number with the number of equations, we see that there is one more equation than the number of unknown quantities.

This is accounted for, as in the simplified case, by the fact that not all the equations are independent. This may be shown if we add together all the equations of the fourth set, and substitute in the numerators of the fractions thus obtained their value as obtained from the third set, namely, zero. We shall then evidently obtain the first equation of the third set. Consequently we may omit any one of the equations in the last two sets. There will then remain just as many equations as unknown quantities, each independent (that is non-derivable from the rest), and our solution is determinate.

In the preceding analysis, we have throughout assumed a rate of interest between two points of time a year apart. A more minute analysis would involve a greater subdivision of the income stream, and the employment of a rate of interest between each two successive time elements. This will evidently occasion no complication except to increase enormously the number of equations and unknowns.

§13. *Different Rates of Interest for Different Years*

The system of equations thus involved when n persons instead of three and m years instead of two are considered introduces very few features of the problem not already contained in the simpler set of equations for two years and three persons. The new feature of chief importance is that, instead of only one rate of interest to be determined, there are now a large number of rates. It is usually assumed, in theories of interest, that the problem is to determine "the" rate of interest, as though one rate would hold true for all time. But in the preceding equations we have $m - 1$ separate rates of interest, viz., i', i'', ..., $i^{(m-1)}$.

Under the hypothesis of a rigid allotment of future income among different time intervals, which is the hypothesis of the first approximation, there is nothing to prevent great differences in the rate of interest from year to year, even when all factors in the case are foreknown and there is every opportunity for arbitrage. By a suitable distribution of the values of c_1, c_2, ..., c_m, there may be produced any differences desired in the magnitudes of i', i'', ..., $i^{(m-1)}$. Thus if the total enjoyable income of society should be foreknown to be 10 billion dollars in the ensuing year, 1 billion in the following year, and 20 billion in the third year, and if there were no way of avoiding these enormous disparities in the social income, it is very evident that the income of the middle year would have a very high valuation compared with either of its neighbors, and therefore that the rate of interest connecting that middle year with the first year would be very low, whereas that connecting it with the third year would be very high. It might be that a member of such a community would be willing to exchange $100 of the plentiful 10 billions for the first year, for only $101 out of the scarce 1 billion of next year, but would be glad to give, out of the third year's still more plentiful 20 billions, $150 for the sake of $100 in the middle and lean year.

In actual markets we find some influence of such differences between future years (as looked at today) in the differences between short term and long term interest rates.

The reason why, in actual fact, no abrupt or large variations in the rate of interest, such as from 1 per cent to 50 per cent, is ordinarily encountered is that the supposed sudden and abrupt changes in the *income stream* seldom occur. The causes which prevent their occurrence are:

(1) The fact that history is constantly repeating itself. For instance, there is regularity in the population, so that, at any point of time, the outlook toward the next year is similar to what it was at any other point of time. The individual may grow old, but the population does not. As individuals are hurried across the stage of life, their places are constantly taken by others, so that, whatever the tendency in the individual life for the rates of preference to go up or down with age, it will not be cumulative in society. Relatively speaking, society stands still.

Again, the processes of nature recur in almost ceaseless regularity. Crops repeat themselves in a yearly cycle. Even when there are large fluctuations in crops, the variations are seldom world-wide, and a shortage in the Mississippi Valley may be compensated for by an unusually abundant crop in Russia or Asia. The resultant regularity of events is thus sufficient to maintain a fair uniformity in the income stream for society as a whole.

(2) The tendency toward uniformity is also favored in real life by the fact that the income stream is not fixed, but may be modified in other ways than by borrowing and lending as in accordance with investment opportunities. The significance of these modifications is algebraically considered in the next chapter.

CHAPTER XIII

SECOND APPROXIMATION IN TERMS OF FORMULAS

§1. *Introduction*

THE object of this chapter is to express in algebraic formulas the six principles comprising the second approximation.[1] In Chapter XII we assumed that all income streams were unalterable, except as they could be modified by borrowing and lending, or buying and selling rights to specified portions of these income streams. In the second approximation now to be put into formulas, we substitute for this hypothesis of fixity of the income streams the hypothesis of a range of choice between different income streams.

The income stream of Individual *1* no longer consists of known and fixed elements, c_1', c_1'', c_1''', etc., in successive periods but of unknown and *variable* elements which we shall designate by y_1', y_1'', y_1''', etc. (y_1' and y_1'' are the coördinates of the Opportunity line).

This elastic income stream may now be modified in two ways: by the variations in these y's, as well as by the method which we found applicable for rigid income streams, namely, the method of exchange, borrowing and lending, or buying and selling. The alterations effected by the latter means we shall designate as before by the algebraic addition of x_1', x_1'', x_1''', ..., x_1^m, for succes-

[1] These have already been expressed in words in Chapters VI and IX and geometrically in Chapter XI.

[302]

sive years. These are to be applied to the original income items (the y's), deductions being included by assigning negative numerical values. The income stream, as finally determined, will therefore be expressed by the successive items,

$$y_1' + x_1', \; y_1'' + x_1'', \; y_1''' + x_1''', \; \ldots, \; y_1^{(m)} + x_1^{(m)}.$$

§2. *Impatience Principle A.* ($n(m-1)$ *Equations*)

Impatience Principle A states that the individual rates of preference are functions of the income streams, and gives the following equations:

$$f_1' = F_1' \; (y_1' + x_1', \; y_1'' + x_1'', \; \ldots, \; y_1^{(m)} + x_1^{(m)}),$$
$$f_2' = F_2' \; (y_2' + x_2', \; y_2'' + x_2'', \; \ldots, \; y_2^{(m)} + x_2^{(m)}),$$

$$\cdots\cdots\cdots\cdots\cdots\cdots\cdots\cdots\cdots\cdots\cdots\cdots$$

$$f_n' = F_n' \; (y_n' + x_n', \; y_n'' + x_n'', \; \ldots, \; y_n^{(m)} + x_n^{(m)}).$$

But these equations express the various individuals' rates of impatience only for the first year's income compared with the next. (They are the slopes of the Willingness lines.) To express their impatience for the second year's income compared with the third, there will be another set of equations, namely:

$$f_1'' = F_1'' \; (y_1'' + x_1'', \; y_1''' + x_1''', \; \ldots\ldots, \; y_1^{(m)} + x_1^{(m)}),$$
$$f_2'' = F_2'' \; (y_2'' + x_2'', \; y_2''' + x_2''', \; \ldots\ldots, \; y_2^{(m)} + x_2^{(m)}),$$

$$\cdots\cdots\cdots\cdots\cdots\cdots\cdots\cdots\cdots\cdots\cdots\cdots$$

$$f_n'' = F_n'' \; (y_n'' + x_n'', \; y_n''' + x_n''', \; \ldots\ldots, \; y_n^{(m)} + x_n^{(m)}).$$

For the third year, as compared with its successor, there would be another similar set, with $'''$ in place of $''$, and so on to the $(m-1)$ year as compared with the last, or m year. Since each of these $(m-1)$ groups of equations contains n separate equations, there are in all $n(m-1)$ equations in the entire set expressing Impatience Principle A.

§3. *Impatience Principle B* ($n(m-1)$ *Equations*)

Impatience Principle B requires that the rates of time preference and of interest shall be equal. This relationship is represented by the same equations as given in Chapter XII, namely:

$$i' = f_1' = f_2' = \ldots\ldots = f_n',$$
$$i'' = f_1'' = f_2'' = \ldots\ldots = f_n'',$$

$$\cdots\cdots\cdots\cdots\cdots\cdots\cdots\cdots\cdots$$
$$\cdots\cdots\cdots\cdots\cdots\cdots\cdots\cdots\cdots$$

$$i^{(m-1)} = f_1^{(m-1)} = f_2^{(m-1)} = \ldots\ldots = f_n^{(m-1)}.$$

Here are $n(m-1)$ equations expressing Impatience Principle B.

§4. *Market Principle A.* (m *Equations*)

The sets of equations which express Market Principle A, the clearing of the market, are also the same as before, namely:

$$x_1' + x_2' + \ldots\ldots\ldots + x_n' = 0,$$
$$x_1'' + x_2'' + \ldots\ldots\ldots + x_n'' = 0,$$

$$\cdots\cdots\cdots\cdots\cdots\cdots\cdots\cdots$$
$$\cdots\cdots\cdots\cdots\cdots\cdots\cdots\cdots$$

$$x_1^{(m)} + x_2^{(m)} + \ldots\ldots\ldots + x_n^{(m)} = 0.$$

Here are m equations expressing Market Principle A.

§5. *Market Principle B.* (n *Equations*)

Market Principle B, the equivalence of loans and discounted repayments, is also represented algebraically as before, namely:

$$x_1' + \frac{x_1''}{(1+i')} + \frac{x_1'''}{(1+i')(1+i'')} + \cdots + \frac{x_1^{(m)}}{(1+i')(1+i'')..(1+i^{(m-1)})} = 0,$$

$$x_2' + \frac{x_2''}{(1+i')} \quad + \cdots + \quad \frac{x_2^{(m)}}{(1+i')(1+i'')\cdots(1+i^{(m-1)})} = 0,$$

$$\cdots\cdots\cdots\cdots\cdots\cdots\cdots\cdots\cdots\cdots\cdots\cdots\cdots$$

$$\cdots\cdots\cdots\cdots\cdots\cdots\cdots\cdots\cdots\cdots\cdots\cdots\cdots$$

$$x_n' + \frac{x_n''}{1+i'} \quad + \cdots + \quad \frac{x_n^{(m)}}{(1+i')(1+i'')\cdots(1+i^{(m-1)})} = 0.$$

These are n equations expressing Market Principle B.

§6. *Investment Opportunity Principle A. (n Equations)*

The equations in the four sets just reviewed differ from the equations of Chapter XII only in the first set, which contain y's in place of c's. The c's were supposed to be given or known, but the y's are new unknown quantities. Consequently, the number of unknowns is greater than the number in the first approximation, whereas the number of equations thus far expressed is the same.

The additional equations needed are supplied by the two Investment Opportunity Principles, namely, Investment Opportunity Principle A, that the range of choice is a specified list of optional income streams, and Investment Opportunity Principle B, that the choice among the optional income streams shall fall upon that one which possesses the maximum present value.

The range of choice, i.e., the complete list of optional income streams, will include many which are ineligible—those which would not be selected whatever might be the rate of interest—whether that rate be zero or one million per cent. Excluding all ineligibles the remaining options constitute the effective range of choice which in Chapter XI is pictured as the Opportunity line

If this list of options be assumed for convenience of analysis to consist of an infinite number of options varying from one to another, not by sudden jumps, but continuously, the complete list can be expressed by those possible values of y_1', y_1'', ... $y_1^{(m)}$ which will satisfy an empirical equation. There will be one such equation for each individual, thus:

$$\varphi_1(y_1', y_1'' \ldots y_1^{(m)}) = 0,$$
$$\varphi_2(y_2', y_2'', \ldots y_2^{(m)}) = 0,$$
$$\cdots\cdots\cdots\cdots\cdots\cdots\cdots\cdots$$
$$\cdots\cdots\cdots\cdots\cdots\cdots\cdots\cdots$$
$$\varphi_n(y_n', y_n'', \ldots y_n^{(m)}) = 0.$$

Here are n equations, expressing the Investment Opportunity Principle A. The form of each of these equations depends on the particular technical conditions to which the capital of the Individual concerned is subjected. It corresponds to the O line of Chapter XI except that only two years were there represented whereas here all m years are represented. Any one equation sets the limitations to which the variation of the income stream of a particular individual must conform. Each set of values of y_1', y_1'', ... $y_1^{(m)}$ which will satisfy this equation represents an optional income stream.

§7. *Opportunity Principle B.* $(n(m-1)$ *Equations)*

Out of this infinite number of options the individual has opportunity to choose any one rather than any other. That particular one will be chosen for which the present value is greater than for any other, in other words, is the maximum.

If the options differ by continuous gradations this

[306]

principle that the maximum present market value is chosen is the same [2] as the principle that r_1, the marginal rate of return over cost, shall be equal to i, the market rate of interest.

This is true for each year-to-year relation, so that we have, for Individual *1*, the following continuous equations:

$$i' = r_1' = r_2' = \ldots = r_n',$$
$$i'' = r_1'' = r_2'' = \ldots = r_n'',$$
$$\ldots\ldots\ldots\ldots\ldots\ldots\ldots\ldots$$
$$\ldots\ldots\ldots\ldots\ldots\ldots\ldots\ldots$$
$$i^{(m-1)} = r_1^{(m-1)} = r_2^{(m-1)} = \ldots = r_n^{(m-1)}.$$

Here are $n(m-1)$ equations expressing Investment Opportunity Principle B.

§8. *Counting the Equations and Unknowns*

Collecting our various counts of the numbers of equations, we have:

For Impatience Principle A, $n(m-1)$ equations
"   "   " B, $n(m-1)$ "
" Market   " A, m "
"   "   " B, n "

For Investment Opportunity Principle A, n equations
"   "   "   " B, $n(m-1)$ "

The sum total of these is $3n(m-1) + 2n + m$, or $3mn + m - n$.

To compare this number with the number of unknowns, we note that all the unknowns in the first approximation are repeated;

[2] For the mathematical statement on this equivalence see Appendix to this chapter (Chapter XIII), §3.

the number of f's being $n(m-1)$

"   "   " x's " mn

"   "   " i's " $m-1$

making a total of $2mn + m - n - 1$ carried forward from the first approximation.

In addition, the new unknowns, the y's and the r's, are introduced. There is one y for each individual for each year, the total array of y's being

$$y_1', y_1'', \ldots, y_1^{(m)},$$
$$y_2', y_2'', \ldots, y_2^{(m)},$$
$$\ldots\ldots\ldots\ldots\ldots$$
$$\ldots\ldots\ldots\ldots\ldots$$
$$y_n', y_n'', \ldots, y_n^{(m)}.$$

The number of these y's is evidently mn.

There is one r for each individual for each pair of successive years, i.e., first-and-second, second-and-third, etc., and next-to-last-and-last years, the total array of r's being

$$r_1', r_1'', \ldots, r_1^{(m-1)},$$
$$r_2', r_2'', \ldots, r_2^{(m-1)},$$
$$\ldots\ldots\ldots\ldots\ldots$$
$$\ldots\ldots\ldots\ldots\ldots$$
$$r_n', r_n'', \ldots, r_n^{(m-1)}.$$

The number of these r's is evidently $n(m-1)$.

In all, then, the number of new unknowns, additional to the number of old unknowns carried forward from the first approximation, is $mn + n(m-1)$, or $2mn - n$.

Hence we have:

number of old unknowns, $2mn + m - n - 1$,

$+$ number of new unknowns, $2mn - n$,

$=$ total number of unknowns, $4mn + m - 2n - 1$,

as compared with $3mn + m - n$ equations.

§9. *Reconciling the Numbers of Equations and Unknowns*

The reconciliation of these two discordant results is effected by two considerations. One reduces the number of equations. Just as under the first approximation, we have one less independent equation in the two sets expressing the Market Principles than the apparent number, thus making the final net number of equations

$$3mn + m - n - 1.$$

The other consideration is quite different. It subtracts from the number of unknowns. This can be done because each r, of which there are $n(m - 1)$, is a derivative from the y's. By definition r is the excess above unity of the ratio between a small increment in the y of next year to the corresponding decrement in the y of this year. The same applies to any pair of successive years. This derivative is, more explicitly expressed, a differential quotient.[3]

The reader not familiar with the notation of the differential calculus will get a clearer picture of the inherent derivability of the r's from the y's by recurring to the geometric method in Chapter XI. There y' and y'' are shown as the coördinates ("latitude" and "longitude") of the Opportunity line, while r is shown as the tangential slope of that line. It is evident that, given the Opportunity line, its tangential slope at any point is derived from it. It is not a new variable but is included in the variation of y' and y'' as the position on the curve changes.

If, now, we subtract $n(m - 1)$, the number of the r's,

[3] See Appendix to this chapter (Chapter XIII), §1.

from $4mn + m - 2n - 1$, we have, as the final net number of unknowns,

$$3mn + m - n - 1$$

which is the same as the total net number of independent equations.[4] Thus the problem is fully determinate under the assumptions made.

[4] Instead of thus banishing the r's, an alternative reconciliation is to retain them but to add for each an equation of definition of $1 + r$. Thus $1 + r_1'$ (corresponding to the slope of the Opportunity Curve) is a derivative from the y'''s and y''''s of the two successive years called this year and the next (in other words, a partial derivative) making $1 + r_1'$ dependent upon (in other words, a function of) the y's. That is,

$$r_1' = \varphi_1(y_1', y_1'', \ldots, y_1^{(m)}),$$

which function is empirical and derivable from the opportunity function φ already given.

Analogously we may express the equations of definition for $r_2', r_3' \ldots r_n'$ and likewise for the corresponding r''''s, r'''''s, etc., up to $r^{(m)}$'s making $n(m-1)$ equations of definition. In this way, retaining the r's we have $4mn + m - 2n - 1$ independent equations and the same number of unknowns.

The complication mentioned in Chapter VII, §10, that the income stream itself depends upon the rate of interest, does not affect the determinateness of the problem. It leaves the number of equations and unknowns unchanged, but merely introduces the rate of interest into the set of equations expressing the Opportunity principles. These equations now become

$$\varphi_1(y_1', y_1'', \ldots, y_1^{(m)}; i', i'', \ldots, i^{(m)}) = 0$$

etc., and their derivatives, the ψ functions, are likewise altered in form but not in number.

The mathematical reader will have perceived that I have studiously avoided the notation of the Calculus, as, unfortunately, few economic students are, as yet, familiar with that notation, and as it has seemed possible here to express the same results fairly well without its use. See, however, the Appendix to this chapter (Chapter XIII), §1-5.

§10. *Zero or Negative Rates of Interest*

We have already seen (Chapter XI, §9), that zero or negative rates of interest are theoretically possible. In terms of formulas all that is needed to make the rate of interest zero is that the forms of the F and φ functions shall be such as to produce this result. This implies that these functions shall have solution values equal to zero.

Of course it would be possible that interest, impatience, and return over cost for one particular year might be zero or negative without this being true for other years. If they were zero for all the years, we should have the interesting result that the value of a finite perpetual annuity (greater than zero per year) would be infinity. No one could buy a piece of land for instance, expected to yield a net income forever, for less than an infinite sum. A perpetual government bond from which an income forever was assured would have an infinite value. Since this is quite impracticable, we thereby reduce to an absurdity the idea that it is possible to have at one and the same time:

1. A zero rate of interest for each year forever; and
2. a perpetual annuity greater than zero per year.

But the absurdity is lessened or disappears altogether if either:

1. The zero rate of interest is confined to one year; or
2. no perpetual annuity greater than zero per year is possible.

Unusual conditions may easily reduce the rate of interest for one year to zero. As to an unproductive or barren world, like the hard-tack island, only a finite totality of income would be possible; a perpetual annuity even of one crumb of hard-tack a year would be impossible.

§11. *The Formula Method Helpful*

While this and the previous chapter are largely restatements in terms of formulas of Chapters X and XI in terms of diagrams, which, in turn were largely restatements of Chapters V and VI in terms of words, nevertheless, these formula chapters have a value of their own, just as did the geometric chapters.

In particular, the formula method has value in showing definitely the equality between the number of equations and the number of unknowns, without which no problem of determining variables is ever completely solved.

It is for this reason that these restatements are included in this book. In fact, if I were writing primarily for mathematically trained readers, I would have reversed the order, giving the first place to the formulas, following these with the charts for visualization purposes, and ending with verbal discussion. Each method contributes its distinctive help toward a complete understanding of what is, at best, a difficult problem to encompass by any method at all. I have, therefore, included in these formula chapters, as in the geometric ones, several points not well adapted to the more purely verbal presentations of Chapters V and VI.

Two corollaries follow. One is that any attempt to solve the problem of the rate of interest exclusively as one of productivity or exclusively as one of psychology is necessarily futile. The fact that there are still two schools, the productivity school and the psychological school, constantly crossing swords on this subject is a scandal in economic science and a reflection on the inadequate methods employed by these would-be destroyers of each other. Each sees half of the truth and wrongly infers that it disproves the existence of the other half. The illusion of their apparent incompatibility is solely due to the failure to *formulate* the problem literally and to count the formulas thus formulated.

The other corollary is that such a formulation reveals the necessity of positing a theoretically separate rate of interest for each separate period of time, or to put the same thing in more practical terms, to recognize the divergence between the rate for short terms and long terms. This divergence is not merely due to an imperfect market and therefore theoretically subject to annihilation by arbitrage transactions, as Böhm-Bawerk, for instance, seemed to think. They are definitely and normally distinct and due to the endless variety in the conformations of income streams. No amount of mere price arbitrage [5] could erase these differences.

Thus, there should always be, theoretically, a separate market rate of interest for each successive year. Since, in practice, no loan contracts are made in advance so that there are no market quotations for a rate of interest connecting, for example, one year in the future with two years in the future, we never encounter such separate year to year rates. We do, however, have such rates implicitly in long term loans. The rate of interest on a long term loan is virtually an average [6] of the separate rates

[5] It is true, of course, that the attempt to make an individual's income stream more even by trading one time-portion of it for another tends to even up the various rates of interest pertaining to various time periods. But this is not price arbitrage and not properly to be called arbitrage at all, being more analogous to the partial geographic equalization of freight charges in the price of wheat by international trade than to the equalization by arbitrage of wheat prices in the same market at the same time.

[6] The nature of this average has been expressed in *Appreciation and Interest*, pp. 26 to 29, and *The Rate of Interest*, pp. 369 to 373. It is

for the separate years constituting that long term. The proposition affirming the existence of separate rates for separate years amounts to this: that normally there should be a difference between the rates for short term and long term loans, sometimes one being the larger and sometimes the other, according to the whole income situation.

impossible to give a concrete example of an average of a rate of interest for a long term loan as an average of the year to year rates, because as already noted, the year to year rates have only a hypothetical existence. The nearest approach to the concrete existence of separate year to year rates is to be found in the Allied debt settlements, by which the United States agreed that Italy, France, Belgium, and other countries should repay the United States through 62 years, with specific rates of interest changing from time to time. These are equivalent to a uniform rate for the whole period according to theory. For instance, the proposed French debt settlement provided for annual payments extending over 62 years, beginning with 1926 at interest rates varying from 0 per cent for the first 5 years, 1 per cent for the next 10 years, 2 per cent for another 10 years, 2½ per cent for 8 years, 3 per cent for 7 years, and 3½ per cent for the last 22 years. The problem is to find an average rate of interest for the whole period which when applied in discounting the various payments provided for in the debt settlement, will give a present worth, as of 1925, equal to the principal of the debt fixed in that year, namely, $4,025,000,000. Clearly no form of arithmetic mean, weighted or unweighted, will give the desired rate. A rough computation indicates that the rate probably falls between 1½ per cent and 1¾ per cent. Discounting the annual payments by compound discount gives a total worth in 1925 at 1½ per cent of $4,197,990,000; at 1¾ per cent of $3,893,610,000. These results show that 1½ per cent is too low, since the present worth obtained by discounting at this rate is greater than the principal sum which was fixed at $4,025,000,000. The rate 1¾ per cent is too high because the discounted present worth is less than the principal.

Discounting the annual payments at 1.6 per cent we obtain $4,072,-630,000. We can now locate three points on a curve showing the interest rates corresponding to different present values. By projecting a parabolic curve through the three determining points, we find the ordinate of the point on the curve which has the abscissa of $4,025,000,000 is 1.64. Hence the average rate of interest for the whole period, within a very narrow margin of error, is 1.64 per cent

The contention often met with that the mathematical formulation of economic problems gives a picture of theoretical exactitude untrue to actual life is absolutely correct. But, to my mind, this is not an objection but a very definite advantage, for it brings out the principles in such sharp relief that it enables us to put our finger definitely on the points where the picture is untrue to life.

The object of any theory is not to reproduce concrete facts but to show the chief underlying principles as tendencies. There is, for instance, the very real tendency for all marginal rates of time preference and all marginal rates of return over cost to equal the market rates of interest. Yet this is only a tendency, an ideal never attained.[7]

[7] For brief comparison of Chapters XII and XIII with other mathematical formulations see Appendix to this chapter (Chapter XIII).

CHAPTER XIV

THE THIRD APPROXIMATION UNADAPTED TO MATHEMATICAL FORMULATION

§1. *Introduction*

THE second approximation fails to conform to conditions of actual life chiefly with respect to risk. While it is possible to calculate mathematically risks of a certain type like those in games of chance or in property and life insurance where the chances are capable of accurate measurement, most economic risks are not so readily measured.[1]

To attempt to formulate mathematically in any useful, complete manner the laws determining the rate of interest under the sway of chance would be like attempting to express completely the laws which determine the path of a projectile when affected by random gusts of wind. Such formulas would need to be either too general or too empirical to be of much value.

In science, the most useful formulas are those which apply to the simplest cases. For instance, in the study of projectiles, the formula of most fundamental importance is that which applies to the path of a projectile in a vacuum. Next comes the formula which applies to the path of a projectile in *still* air. Even the mathematician declines to go beyond this and to take into account the effect of wind currents, still less to write the equations

---

[1] See *The Nature of Capital and Income,* Appendix to Chapter XVI.

for the path of a boomerang or a feather. If he should do so, he would still fall short of actual conditions by assuming the wind to be constant in direction and velocity.

Scientific determination can never be perfectly exact. At best, science can only determine what *would* happen under *assumed* conditions. It can never state exactly what does or will happen under actual conditions.[2]

We have thus far stated verbally, geometrically, and algebraically the laws determining interest under the simpler conditions first, when it was assumed that the income streams of individuals were both certain and fixed in amount, but variable in time shape, and, secondly, when it was assumed that the income streams were certain, but variable in amount as well as in time shape. We have also considered verbally the interest problem under conditions of risk found in the real world.

§2. *The Six Sets of Formulas Incomplete*

All that I shall attempt here is to point out the shortcomings of the six sets of formulas in the second approximation. Impatience Principle A in the second approximation is expressed by formulas of the type:

$$f = F\left(y' + x', y'' + x'', \ldots, y^{(m)} + x^{(m)}\right)$$

indicating that a person's impatience is a function of his income stream as specifically scheduled, indefinitely in the future.

Of course, in the uncertainties of actual life no such specific scheduling is possible. The equation is true but incomplete, as f is properly not only a function of one ex-

---

[2] See my article, *Economics as a Science*, in Proceedings of the American Association for the Advancement of Science, Vol. LVI, 1907.

pected income program but of many possible such programs each with its own series of probabilities, and those probabilities are too vague even to be specifically expressed or even pictured by the person concerned. That is, the average person is merely aware that he is willing, say, to pay five per cent for a $1000 loan because he thinks his future prospects will justify it. He vaguely expects that his present $10,000 income will probably rise to $20,000 within a few years, possibly to $30,000—and possibly not rise at all. He could think of innumerable possibilities and these would imply many other variables than those above cited. Much might depend on the income of others besides himself and on the future size of his family, the state of their health, and other conditions without end. His own future income is the important matter, but that itself is dependent on all sorts of variables on which he will reckon summarily in a rule of thumb fashion.

We could, formally, rewrite for the third approximation the above equation so as to read:

$$f = F \ (\ )$$

merely refusing to attempt any enumeration of the innumerable variables inside the parentheses—among them being, perhaps, all the variables included in all the equations in the second approximation, including rates of interest as well as numberless other variables such as probabilities not there included. In so far as the latter, or new, variables enter, each of them requires a new equation in order to make the problem determinate. Such new equations would be merely empirical. Among the equations which would be needed, would be those expressing the y's and x's in terms of real income—that is, as the sum of the enjoyable services, each multiplied by its price. This would lead us into the theory of prices and the general economic equilibrium.

Impatience Principle B was expressed in the second approximation by formulas of the type:

$$i = f.$$

But now we must face not only one i but a series of i's, according as the market is the call loan market, the 60 to 90 day commercial paper market, the gilt-edge bond market, the farm mortgage market, and innumerable others, for each of which there is its own separate f and i.

These many magnitudes, including the i's, require still other empirical equations impossible to formulate satisfactorily, albeit we know in a general way that the rate on gilt-edge bonds is lower than on risky bonds, the rate on first mortgages lower than that on second mortgages, and that the long term and short term markets do influence each other. But these relations are too indefinite to be put into any equations of real usefulness, theoretical or practical.

Investment Opportunity Principle A was expressed by formulas of the type

$$\varphi \left(y', y'', \ldots, y^{(m)} \right) = 0$$

This becomes

$$\varphi \left(\ \right) = 0$$

where the blank parenthesis stands for a multitude of unknowns (and unknowables) which could be discussed *ad infinitum* and each of which, in so far as it was not already included among the variables entering into our system of equations, would require a new empirical equation of some sort in order that the problem shall be determinate. Moreover, the φ equation representing a man's ensemble of income opportunities is a composite of separate opportunities, the full and detailed expression of which would take us again into the theory of prices and general economic equilibrium.

Investment Opportunity Principle B, expressed in the second approximation by equations of the type

$$i = r,$$

would have to be replaced by as profuse a variety as replaced the $i = f$ above.

A full statement of the margins of investment opportunity would include the margins of numberless individual enterprises and adjustments in the use of every item of capital. It would again lead us into the theory of prices and general economic equilibrium. Walras and Pareto have formulated systems of equations which do this and in which the theory of interest is merely a part of a larger whole.

Market Principle A, expressed in the second approximation by equations of the type

$$x_1 + x_2 + \ldots + x_m = 0,$$

will remain true only if or in so far as performance of contracts corresponds to promises and expectations. In so far as, because of defaults, the equations fail of being precisely true, no useful mathematical relation expressing that failure seems possible.

The same is true of Market Principle B, expressed under the second approximation by formulas of the type

$$x' + \frac{x''}{1 + 1'} + \ldots + \frac{x^{(m)}}{(1 + i')(1 + i'') \ldots (1 + i^{(m-1)})} = 0$$

to say nothing of the fact that this type of equation will take many different forms in view of the variety of i's and in view of the probability factors.

[320]

THIRD APPROXIMATION

The only explicit practical inclusion of such probability factors, mathematically, is to be found in the formulas of life insurance actuaries. But these are of little
more than suggestive value in our present effort to express the determination of the rate of interest.

§3. *Conclusions*

We must, therefore, give up as a bad job any attempt
to formulate completely the influences which really determine the rate of interest. We can say that the system
of equations which has been employed *would* fully determine the rate of interest were it not for disturbing
factors; that it *does do so* in combination with those disturbing factors; and that this amounts to saying that it
expresses the fundamental tendencies underlying those
disturbing factors.

In short, the theory of interest in this book merely
covers the simple rational part of the causes actually in
operation. The other or disturbing causes are those incapable of being so simply and rationally formulated.
Some of them may be empirically studied and will be
treated in Chapter XIX. They pertain to statistics rather
than to pure economics. Rational and empirical laws in
economics are thus analogous to rational and empirical
laws of physics or astronomy. Just as we may consider
the actual behavior of the tides as a composite result of
the rational Newtonian law of attraction of the moon
and the empirical disturbances of continents, islands, in-
lets, and so forth, so we may consider the actual behavior
of the rates of interest in New York City as a composite
of the rational laws of our second approximation and the
empirical disturbances of Federal Reserve policy together
with numberless other institutional, historical, legal, and

practical factors. All of these are worthy of careful study but are not within the scope of the main problem of this book.

In some cases, as in the theory of the moon's motions, the perturbations may be worked out with a high approximation to reality by combining rationally a number of elementary influences. Such resolution of empirical problems represents the highest ideal of applied science. But until that stage is reached there remains a wide gap between rational and empirical science, and the two have to be pursued by somewhat different methods. That is the case with economic science in most of its problems today.[3]

In respect to our present problem, while there is a great field for research, the only perturbing influence of transcendent importance is that of an unstable monetary standard, and, as was seen in Chapter II, even that would make nothing more than a nominal difference in the results if it were not for the "money illusion."

But with respect to this disturbance, theory and practice are miles apart. The disturbances of unstable money often reverse the normal operation of those supposedly fundamental forces which determine the rate of interest and are the chief subject of our study in this book.

[3] See Mitchell, Wesley C., *Quantitative Analysis in Economic Theory.* American Economic Review, Vol. XV, No. 1, March 1925, pp. 1-12.

PART IV. FURTHER DISCUSSION

CHAPTER XV

THE PLACE OF INTEREST IN ECONOMICS

§1. *Interest Rates and Values of Goods*

HAVING completed the exposition of the theory of the causation and determination of the rate of interest which is most acceptable to me, it now remains to show how this theory fits into a complete system of economic theory and what results must flow from its acceptance.

Interest plays a central rôle in the theory of value and prices and in the theory of distribution. The rate of interest is fundamental and indispensable in the determination of the value (or prices) of wealth, property, and services.

As was shown in Chapter I, the price of any good is equal to the discounted value of its expected future service, including disservices as negative services. If the value of these services remains the same, a rise or fall in the rate of interest will consequently cause a fall or rise respectively in the value of all the wealth or property. The extent of this fall or rise will be the greater the further into the future the services of wealth extend. Thus, land values from which services are expected to accrue uniformly and indefinitely will be practically doubled if the rate of interest is halved, or halved if the rate of interest is doubled. The value of dwellings and other goods of definitely limited durability will fall less than half if interest rates double, and will rise to less than double if interest is halved. Fluctuations in the value of furniture will be even less extensive, clothing still less, and very perishable commodities like fruit will not be sensibly affected in price by a variation in the rate of interest. In all the foregoing cases it is, of course, assumed that the expected services remain unchanged.

§2. *Interest Rates and Values of Services*

As to the influence of the rate of interest on the price of services, we first observe that services may be either final or intermediate.[1] The value of a dinner about to be eaten involves no time of waiting and so no discount or interest. Nor does the irksomeness of labor about to be undertaken involve discount to the laborer. Both the dinner or its enjoyment and the labor are *final* items of income, the one positive and the other negative. The value of intermediate services ("interactions") is derived from the succeeding future services to which they lead. For instance, the value to a farmer of the services of his land in affording pasture for sheep will depend upon the discounted value of the services of the flock in producing wool. If he rents the land, he will calculate what he can afford to pay for it on the basis of the value of the wool which he would expect to obtain from his flock. In like manner, the value of the wool output to the woolen manufacturer is in turn influenced by the discounted value of the output of woolen cloth to which it contributes. In the next stage the value of the production of woolen cloth will depend upon the discounted value of the woolen clothing to which that cloth contributes. Finally, the value of the last named will depend upon the expected real income which the clothing will bring

[1] See Chapter I; also *The Nature of Capital and Income*, Chapter IX.

to those who wear it, in other words, upon the use or "wear" of the clothes.

Thus the final services, consisting of the use of the clothes, will have an influence on the value of all the anterior services of tailoring, manufacturing cloth, producing wool, and pasturing sheep, while each of these anterior services, when discounted, will give the value of the respective capitals which yield them, namely, the clothes, cloth, wool, sheep, and pasture land. The values, not only of all articles of wealth, but also of all intermediate services which they render, are dependent upon the values of *final enjoyable* uses. Capital values and values of final uses are linked by the rate of interest. A rise or fall in the rate of interest will be felt most by the links most distant from these final services. A change in the rate of interest will tend to affect but slightly the price of making clothing, but it will tend to affect considerably the price of pasturing sheep.

The theory of prices, so far as it can be separated into parts, includes: (1) explanation of the prices of final services on which the prices of anterior interactions depend; (2) explanation of the prices of intermediate interactions, as dependent, through the rate of interest, on the final services; (3) explanation of the prices of capital instruments as dependent, through the rate of interest, upon the prices of their final services. The first study, which seeks merely to determine the laws regulating the price of final services, is independent of the rate of interest.[2]

The second and third problems, which seek to show the dependence on final services of the intermediate ser-

[2] See my *Mathematical Investigations in the Theory of Value and Prices*. New Haven, Yale University Press, 1926.

vices and of the capital which bears them, involve the rate of interest. Under this second study will fall, as a special case, the study of the determination of economic rent, the rent both of land and of other instruments of wealth. The rent of a pasture consists of the value of the services of pasturing. This value, in accordance with the principles expounded in Chapter I, is dependent through the rate of interest upon the discounted value of the future final services to which the pasturing contributes. It is clear, then, that the rent of the land is partly dependent upon the rate of interest, and that the same dependence applies to the rent of any other instrument.

§3. *Interest Rates and Wages*

Similar considerations apply to the determination of the rate of wages. *From the standpoint of the employer,* the payment of wages to a workman supposedly represents the value of his services. These services are interactions, or intermediate services, leading ultimately to some future enjoyable service. Thus the shepherd, hired by the farmer to tend the sheep in the pasture, renders services the value of which to the farmer is estimated in precisely the same way as the value of the services of the land which the farmer hires.

Consequently, if interest varies, wages will vary. Thus, if the land is used for farming, the wages paid for planting crops will be gauged in the estimate by the farmer by discounting the value of the expected crops and will vary somewhat according to whether the discounting is at 5 per cent or at 4 per cent. In like manner the workers engaged in bridge building are presumed to be paid the discounted value of the ultimate benefits which will be yielded by the bridge. The wages of those engaged in making locomotives normally represent the discounted value of the completed locomotives, and hence, as the value of a completed locomotive is in turn the discounted value of its expected service, their wages represent the discounted value of the ultimate benefits in the series.[3] In all these cases, the rate of wages is the discounted value of some future product, and therefore tends to decrease as interest increases. But the effects in the different lines will be very unequal.

Wages of domestic servants and those engaged in putting the finishing touches on enjoyable goods will have their wages affected comparatively little by the rate of interest. On the other hand, for laborers who are engaged in work requiring much time the element of discount applied to their wages is a considerably more important factor. If a tree planter is paid $1 because this is the discounted value at 5 per cent of the $2 which the tree will be worth when matured in fifteen years, it is clear that a change in the rate of interest to 4 per cent will tend materially to increase the value of such work. Supposing the value of the matured tree still to remain at $2, the value of the services of planting it would be not one dollar but $1.15. On the other hand, for laborers engaged in a bakery or other industry in which the final satisfactions mature early, the wages are more nearly equal to the value of these products. If they produce final services worth $1, due, let us say, in one year, their wages would be 95 cents when the interest rate is 5 per cent and 96 cents if interest falls to 4 per cent.

It is clear, nevertheless, that such unequal effects com-

---

[3] This is, of course, highly theoretical; it assumes a competitive market free from legal and other restrictions.

ing from a reduction in the rate of interest, as an increase from $1 to $1.15 in one industry and from 95 cents to 96 cents in another, could not remain permanently. Labor will tend to shift from the lower paid to the higher paid occupations until equality of wages for workers of the same skill is re-established. In the end, therefore, the change in the rate of interest from 5 per cent to 4 per cent would effect a redistribution in the values of intermediate items of income and in final items of income.

Evidently then, the effect of a change in the rate of interest on the value of interactions will naturally be the more pronounced in a country where lengthy processes are usually employed than in one where the shorter ones are common. If, for instance, laborers in a given country are engaged largely in building elaborate works, such as the Panama Canal, or in digging tunnels and constructing other great engineering works, or in planting forests and otherwise investing for the sake of remote returns, a fall in the rate of interest will produce a considerable rise in wages, whereas, in a country where such lengthy processes are unknown and workmen are chiefly employed in tilling the ground and performing personal services, a change in the rate of interest will hardly affect wages or the values of other preparatory services at all.

What has been said, however, applies only to wages from the standpoint of the employer. The rate of wages is dependent upon supply as well as upon demand, that is, upon the willingness of the workman to offer his services, as well as upon the desire of the employer to secure them. From the standpoint of the laborer, wages constitute an incentive to exertion or labor. This exertion is a *final* disservice, or negative item of income, and its valuation by the laborer is *not directly affected by the rate of interest, as are other services which are not final but intermediate.* It is a great mistake to treat the subject of wages, as many authors do, exclusively from the employer's standpoint. The purpose here is not to undertake to outline a complete theory of wages, but merely to show why a complete wage theory must take cognizance of interest and must explain how the interest rate affects some wage rates and not others.

§4. *Interest and Functional Distribution*

In the theory of distribution interest must be assigned a quite different and much more important rôle than economists thus far have given to it. In classical economics the nature of interest and its place in distribution were not clearly understood. Distribution has been erroneously defined as the division of the income of society into "interest, rent, wages, and profits." Rent and interest are merely two ways of measuring the same income; rent, as the yield per acre or other physical unit, and interest as the same yield expressed as a per cent of capital value. The value of the capital is derived from the income which it yields by capitalizing it at the prevailing rate of interest. To reverse this process by multiplying the capital value by the rate of interest gives the original income, as long as the capital value remains stationary. It is not really a complex product of two factors, but, on the contrary, is the single original factor, namely, income, from which we started. As explained in previous chapters, it is this income which affords the basis for the determination of the rate of interest, and through the rate of interest, of capital value.

The final enjoyable income of society is the ultimate and basic fact from which all values are derived and toward which all economic action is bent. All of this income is derived from capital wealth, if land and man are included in that term, or if not, from capital and man, or capital, land, and man, according to the terminology adopted. This income may all be capitalized, and hence all income (excluding capital gain) may be viewed as interest upon the capital value thus found.

Viewed as above outlined *interest is not a part, but the whole, of income* (except for capital gain). It includes what is called rent and profits and even wages, for the income of the workman may be capitalized quite as truly as the income of land or machinery. Thus, instead of having interest, rent, wages, and profits as mutually exclusive portions of social income, interest may be regarded as including all four. If we prefer to exclude profits, the reason is because of the element of risk and not because profits are not discountable just as truly as rent and wages. The error of the classical economists and of their modern followers in regarding interest, rent, wages and profits as separate but coördinate incomes is partly due to the failure to perceive that, whereas all income is produced from capital wealth, capital value can emerge only from man's psychic evaluation and capitalization of that income in advance of its occurrence.

Another oversight closely associated with the last stated fallacy is that in which rent and wages are conceived as determined independently of the rate of interest, whereas we have just seen that the rate of interest enters as a vital element into the determination of both. The great defect in the theories propounded by the classical economists lay in their inability to conceive of a general equilibrium and the mutual dependence of sacrifice and enjoyment.

In discussing the theory of distribution, we shall, therefore, abandon the classical point of view entirely. The classical concepts of distribution are quite inappropriate to explain the every day facts of life and the economic structure. The phrase distribution of wealth, as understood by the ordinary man, implies the problem of the relative wealth of individuals, the problem of the rich and the poor. But the separation of the aggregate income into four abstract magnitudes, even if correctly done, has little to do with the question of how much income the different individuals in society receive.

Only on condition that society was composed of four independent and mutually exclusive groups, laborers, landlords, enterprisers, and capitalists, would the fourfold division of the classical economists be even partially adequate to explain the actual distribution of income. In fact, the four classes all overlap. The enterpriser is almost invariably a genuine capitalist and usually also performs labor; the capitalist is frequently a landlord and laborer, and even the typical laborer is today often a small capitalist and sometimes a landlord. It is true that a century ago in England the lines of social classification corresponded roughly to the abstract divisions proposed at that time by the classical economists. But this fact is of little significance except as explaining historically the origin of the classical theory of distribution.[4]

§5. *Interest and Personal Distribution*

The main problem of distribution, as I see it, is concerned with the determination and explanation of the amounts and values of capitals and incomes possessed

[4] See Cannan, Edwin, *Theories of Production and Distribution.* London, P. S. King & Son, 1903.

by different individuals in society. It is astonishing how little economists have contributed to resolving the problems of distribution so conceived. A statistical beginning was made by Professor Pareto in his presentation of interesting "curves of distribution of income." [5] For the United States, Professor W. I. King [6] and the National Bureau of Economic Research [7], and for England, Sir Josiah Stamp [8] have made and analyzed important statistical compilations on the amount and distribution of income and capital wealth by income groups and social classes. On the *theory* of distribution, especially the rôle of interest in distribution, John Rae seems to have contributed more than any other writer [9]. He showed in a vivid way that persons who had naturally what we have called in this book a low rate of impatience or preference for present over future income tended to accumulate savings, whereas those who had the opposite trait tended to spend their incomes and even their capitals.

In previous chapters it is shown that the rates of preference among different individuals are equalized by borrowing and lending or, what amounts to the same thing,

[5] Pareto, *Cours d'Économie Politique*, Vol. II, Book III.

[6] King, W. I., *The Wealth and Income of the People of the United State*, New York, The Macmillan Co., 1915.

[7] Mitchell, W. C., King, W. I., Macaulay, F. R., Knauth, O. W., *Income in the United States.* New York, National Bureau of Economic Research, Inc., 1922.

Knauth, O. W., *Distribution of Income by States in 1919.* New York, Harcourt, Brace & Co., 1922.

Leven, Maurice, and King, W. I., *Income in the Various States; Its Sources and Distribution, 1919, 1920, and 1921.* New York, National Bureau of Economic Research, Inc., 1925.

[8] Stamp, Sir Josiah, *Wealth and Taxable Capacity.* London, P. S. King & Son, Ltd., 1922. Also, *British Incomes and Property.* London, P. S. King & Son, 1916.

[9] Rae, *The Sociological Theory of Capital*, Chapter XIII.

by buying and selling. An individual whose rate of preference for present enjoyment is unduly high will contrive to modify his income stream by increasing it in the present at the expense of the future. The effects upon incomes may be traced to capital by applying the principles explained in *The Nature of Capital and Income,* Chapter XIV.

If a modification of the income stream is such as to make the rate of realized income relative to capital value exceed the standard rate of income returns, capital will be depleted to the extent of the excess, and the individual, group, or class, under consideration will grow poorer. This condition may be brought about either by borrowing immediate income and paying future income, or by selling instruments whose returns extend far into the future and buying those which yield more immediate returns. Individuals of the type of Rip Van Winkle, if in possession of land and other durable instruments, will either sell or mortgage them in order to secure the means for obtaining enjoyable services more rapidly. The effect will be upon society as a whole that those individuals who have an abnormally low estimate of the future and its needs will gradually part with the more durable instruments, and that these will tend to gravitate into the hands of those who have the opposite trait.

By this transfer an inequality in the distribution of capital is gradually effected, and this inequality once achieved tends to perpetuate itself. The poorer a man grows the more keen is his appreciation of present goods likely to become. When once the spendthrift is on the downward road, he is likely to continue in the same direction. When he has succeeded in losing all his capital except his own person, the process usually comes to an end, because civilized societies in self-protection frown upon chattel slavery and involuntary servitude. Many examples, however, of forced labor and even slavery still survive. The negro farmers of the Southern States, the Mexican peons, the peasants of Russia until recently, the forced labor and slavery in many tropical colonies, such as Java,[10] the Congo, and other African countries, are examples in point.

Reversely, when an individual has saved a considerable capital, his rate of preference for the present diminishes still further, and accumulation becomes still easier. Hence, in many countries the rich and poor come to be widely and permanently separated, the former to constitute an hereditary aristocracy of wealth and the latter, a helpless proletariat.

This progressive sifting, by which the spenders grow poorer and the savers richer, would go on even if, as assumed in our first and second approximations, there were no risk element. But it goes on far faster when as in actual life there is risk. While savings unaided by luck will ultimately enrich the saver, the process is slow as compared with the rapid enrichment which comes from the good fortune of those few who assume risks and then happen to guess right. Likewise, while millions of people lose their small properties by thriftlessness, the more rapid impoverishment comes from guessing wrong. This will often turn a rich man into a poor man within a few years and sometimes within a few days.

It should also be noted, especially when the element of uncertainty is taken into account, that borrowing may be the means of gaining great wealth quite as well as of

[10] See Day, Clive. *The Dutch in Java*. New York, The Macmillan Co., 1904, Chapter X.

losing it. The business borrower who borrows in order to invest always hopes to gain and often succeeds beyond his expectations.

The rates of return over cost in various investment opportunities play an important rôle in both. Henry Ford and others grew rich not so much because of thrift as because they took advantage of unusual investment opportunities, in which the rates of return over cost proved to be many times the market rate of interest.

Besides thrift and luck, with their opposites, there is another factor closely associated with the process of accumulation or dissipation. This is habit. It has been noted that a person's rate of preference for present over future income, given a certain income stream, will be high or low according to the past habits of the individual. If he has been accustomed to simple and inexpensive ways, he finds it fairly easy to save and ultimately to accumulate a little property. The habits of thrift being transmitted to the next generation, by imitation or by heredity or both, result in still further accumulation. The foundations of some of the world's greatest fortunes have been based upon thrift.

Reversely, if a man has been brought up in the lap of luxury, he will have a keener desire for present enjoyment than if he had been accustomed to the simple living of the poor. The children of the rich, who have been accustomed to luxurious living and who have inherited only a fraction of their parents' means, may spend beyond their means and thus start the process of the dissipation of their family fortune. In the next generation this retrograde movement is likely to gather headway and to continue until, with the gradual subdivision of the fortune and the reluctance of the successive generations to curtail their expenses, the third or fourth generation may come to actual poverty.

The accumulation and dissipation of wealth do sometimes occur in cycles. Thrift, ability, industry and good fortune enable a few individuals to rise to wealth from the ranks of the poor. A few thousand dollars accumulated under favorable circumstances may grow to several millions in the next generation or two. Then the unfavorable effects of luxury begin, and the cycle of poverty and wealth begins anew. The old adage, "From shirt sleeves to shirt sleeves in four generations," has some basis in fact. This cyclical movement is more likely to occur in countries like the United States, where, owing to the rapidly changing conditions, there is more chance either to rise or fall in the economic scale. Wherever, as in the older countries of Europe, conditions have become fixed and less subject to changes of any kind, incomes and wealth are likely to remain relatively unchanged in the same families, generation after generation. This tendency is strengthened in England, where the customs of inheritance have helped to keep large fortunes intact in the hands of the eldest son.

We are not concerned here with creating a complete theory of personal distribution and its changes. This would include the effects of many factors other than thrift. But here we are interested simply in the rôle of interest and thrift in distribution.

§6. *The Loan Market Is a Highway for Re-Distribution*

We see, then, that the existence of a market rate of interest to which the individual adjusts his rate of impatience supplies an easy highway for the movement of his fortune in one direction or the other. If an indi-

[338]

vidual has spendthrift tendencies, their indulgence is facilitated by access to a loan market; and reversely, if he desires to save, he may do so the more easily if there is a market for savings. In like manner, the business man may, by recourse to loans, either lose or gain. The inequality of the distribution of capital is thus fundamentally caused in large part by exchanging present for future income. A rate of interest is simply a market price for such exchange. If all individuals were hermits, it would be much more difficult either to accumulate or to dissipate fortunes, and the distribution of wealth would therefore be much more even.

It is true, as the socialist maintains, that inequality is due to social arrangements, but these arrangements are not, as he assumes, primarily such as take away the chance to rise in the economic scale; they are, on the contrary, arrangements which facilitate both rising and falling, according to the choices made by the individual. The improvident sink like lead to the bottom. Once there, they or their children find difficulty in rising. Accumulation is usually a slow process, and especially slow because the great numbers of the poor competing against each other reduce the values of their services to so low a point that the initial saving becomes almost impossible. While it is true that *waste begets poverty*, it is equally true that *poverty begets waste*. Whole communities and peoples, for example, the Chinese and Indians, are steeped in misery not because of any inherent extravagance, but because they are so poor they must use up all they produce, leaving no margin of savings for bettering their methods of production. Occasionally a Rockefeller, a Carnegie, or a Ford rises from near the bottom and ascends to the top. But the great masses, once they get near the bottom, are likely to remain there. Their high rates of impatience manifested through generations have brought many if not most of them to poverty. A labor leader once said to me that few labor men have any acquisitive instinct. They are a self-selected group of those impatient by nature or habit or both. They tend to spend rather than to save. The great need and opportunity for education in thrift is manifest.

This is not the place to answer the many questions which arise in such an inquiry, such as, what is the effect of change in the rate of interest in stimulating or discouraging the accumulation or dissipation of capital? [11] What is the effect on the poor of the luxurious habits of the rich? Nor are we concerned with the other factors which influence the distribution of wealth but which do not involve the rate of interest. We are at present content merely to prepare the way for their answer by indicating the nature of the problem and the relation of the theory of interest to it.

[11] See Gonner, *Interest and Savings*.

CHAPTER XVI

RELATION OF DISCOVERY AND INVENTION TO INTEREST RATES

§1. *The First Effect of Each Important Discovery and Invention Is to Increase the Rate of Interest*

THE interplay of impatience and opportunity on the rate of interest is profoundly influenced by invention and discovery. The range of man's investment opportunity widens as his knowledge extends and his utilization of the forces and materials of Nature grows. With each advance in knowledge come new opportunities to invest. The rate of return over cost rises. With the investments come distortions of the investors' income streams. These distortions are softened through loans, so far as the individual is concerned, the distortion being thus transmitted from borrower to lender and so spread over society generally. This distortion means relative abstinence from consumption during the period of producing and exploiting the new devices, followed by greater consumption later. In the meantime human impatience is increased.

In the field of transportation, for example, man originally had to depend upon his legs and arms to carry himself and his burdens. Later he invested in domesticated animals, and secured large returns on his investment, by increasing the range, speed, and efficiency of locomotion. Still later the invention of the wheel introduced the use of vehicles drawn by horses. The invention of the steam locomotive for hauling vehicles on rails enormously increased movements of goods and men, while at the same time the range and diversity of opportunities to invest were extended. Today advance in technical knowledge has multiplied investment opportunities a thousandfold in the transportation field alone. There is the possibility of street transit by surface, elevated, or subway lines. On land, men and goods are moved by steam and electric locomotives, trolleys, busses, automobiles or motorcycles. On the sea, sailing ships have been superseded by steam ships, and the old fashioned marine engine is now giving way to the steam turbine, Diesel engine and the electric motor. Man's ancient dream of flying through the air has at last been realized.

At the early stage of these space-abridging inventions society temporarily sacrifices some of its income for the sake of the greater returns to be expected later. For two generations railway construction drained off labor and caused investors to skimp. In these, as in all pioneering days, interest was high. In such periods people live on great expectations.

§2. Invention Causes Dispersion of Interest Rates

Besides tending to raise the rate of interest, invention and discovery tend to widen the gap between the interest rates on the safest securities and the rates of return over cost to those who first take advantage of the investment opportunities offered by the new devices.

Early investors make sacrifices and take great risks in the expectation of ample rewards in the shape of enhanced income. When the rewards for their sacrifices are realized these investors often reinvest their larger incomes for the sake of yet greater and more remote returns. For example, in the United States, throughout the period of national expansion from 1820 to 1880, while the growth of farming, mining and manufacture went hand in hand with canal and railroad building, social income increased sharply through investment, return, and partial reinvestment. Rising national income marks all periods of advancement in industrial arts and practices. The statistics of income recently made available by the National Bureau of Economic Research show just such rapid rise, concurrently with a period of great inventions in electricity, chemistry, automotive engineering, radio and aviation. Thus in the United States capital investment per worker rose from $560 in 1849 to $5,000 in 1919, with a greater yearly increase in capital employed than the increase in working population. Horsepower per industrial worker increased from 1914 to 1925 from 3.3 to 4.3.[1] The increased prosperity of the United States, due largely to increased utilization of inventions and scientific management, is shown by an increase of about three-eighths in national income from 1921 to 1927, with an appreciable increase in real annual wages, while salaries showed a constant rise, as expressed in purchasing power, after 1919. The total realized national income of the nation rose from $35,700,000,000 in 1913, to an estimated total of $89,000,000,000 in 1928.[2]

§3. *Invention Causes Revaluation of Capital*

Those enterprisers and risk takers who are first to enter the new investment field, opened up by an invention, or, in the slang of business, "get in on the ground floor"

[1] *Report on Recent Economic Changes,* National Bureau of Economic Research, p. 87.
[2] *Ibid.,* Chapter XII.

often obtain as a consequence a return on their original investment far greater than the rate of interest. Commodore Vanderbilt, Andrew Carnegie and Henry Ford are examples in point.

The rate of interest on loan contracts will rise as a result of those operations but only slightly. The cause of the increase which will occur is the increase in the *marginal* rate of return over cost.

In consequence of the higher interest rates, there occurs a revaluation of investment securities, and, in fact, of all capital. The value of capital, assuming that the value of the income from the capital remains the same as is true of bonds, sinks as the rate of interest rises. Bonds tend to fall while common stocks tend to rise, unless counteracting influences prove to be dominant.

This revaluation applies also to the very capital in which the new invention or discovery is embodied. If it is found that $100,000 invested in a newly discovered gold mine will result in a yield of $1,000,000 a year, that mine will no longer sell for its original cost, but for a sum far above it. It is the relation of the $1,000,000 a year to the new value of the mine, and not its relation to the original investment value or cost which will reflect the true rate of interest. Original investors in The Bell Telephone Company realized returns far beyond the normal interest on their investment, but the present investor pays a price for Bell Telephone stock commensurate with its dividends.

New devices will also cause a revaluation of the older ones which they have displaced, but in this case the new values are lower than before. The adoption of the circular saw rendered nearly valueless the mill plants equipped with the old up-and-down saw, and the band saw lowered the value of mills equipped with the circular saws. Hand looms and hand printing presses were superseded, except for special types of work, by power looms and presses. The early forms of power machines have in turn been superseded by improved machines. The automobile ruined first the carriage industry and later hurt the bicycle industry and even the perambulator industry. It is supplanting, in short hauls of freight and passengers, the railway industry, and both of these, in turn, are bound to be supplanted, in a measure, by the aviation industry, through its possibilities for producing the means of more speedy transportaton.

The reasons for these reductions in value are simple. Each new process produces a larger supply of the particular kind of service rendered. The price of this service —e.g., sawing or printing—is reduced, and consequently the capitalized value of the given amount of such service which can be expected from the older devices is reduced, and often so far reduced as to make the reproduction or even the repair of these older instruments wholly un- profitable. Thus progress constantly requires the writing off of capital value because of obsolescence.[3]

§4. *The Ultimate Effects of Invention on Interest Rate*

It is important to emphasize the *temporary* nature of the effects of invention and discovery in raising the rate of interest. The effect in raising interest lasts only so long as the rate of return over cost continues to be high and so tempts society to distort greatly its income stream in time shape. This period is the period of development

[3] The economic effects of invention, and particularly its effects upon the rate of interest, were well treated by John Rae, *The Sociological Theory of Capital*, Chapter IX, pp. 132-150; Chapter X, pp. 151-203.

and exploitation, during which society is sacrificing or investing present income, or, as it is inaccurately called, investing capital. Society, instead of confining its productive energies to the old channels and obtaining a relatively immediate return in enjoyable income, as by producing food products, clothing, etc., directs its labors to great engineering enterprises, such as constructing tunnels, railroads, highways, subways, waterworks, irrigation systems, mining and manufacturing plants. These instruments cannot begin to contribute a return in enjoyable income for many years. In contemplation, future income during this period is relatively plentiful, and in consequence of these great expectations, the rate of interest will be high.

Later, however, there will come a time when, *so far at least as the effect of that particular invention is concerned*, the income stream ceases to ascend, when most of the necessary investment has been completed, when little further exploitation is possible or advisable, and when it is only necessary to keep up the newly constructed capital at a constant level. When this period is reached, the after effect of the invention will be felt. The net effect on society will then have been to put the income stream on to a higher plateau, not to boost it uphill any more. But such a mere increase in the *size* of the income stream, while its *shape* remains constant, tends, as we have seen, not to increase, but somewhat to decrease the rate of time preference. Therefore, the *after* effect of all inventions and discoveries is not toward *increasing* but toward *decreasing* the rate of interest.

Thus, though the railway inventions led to a half century of investment in railways, during which the income stream of society rapidly increased, today the limit of steam railway investment has been nearly reached in some places, and in others the rapidity of investment has perceptibly slackened. Railroads have been an outlet for the investment of savings, and have tended to supply for them a good return. As the necessity for new railroads becomes less, this outlet diminishes, and the rates of return as well as the rates of interest in general tend to fall so far as this one influence is effective.

But while the after effect of an old invention is to reduce the rate of interest, it may, of course, be true that *new* inventions, often the result of the old, will be made rapidly enough to neutralize this tendency. It is chiefly when there is a cessation in the world's output of new inventions that the rate of interest is thus likely to fall back, but whenever invention is active the interest rate may rise continuously. It thus rises and falls according as the introduction or the exploitation of inventions is active or inactive.

The same principles apply not only to invention in the narrower mechanical sense, but also to scientific and geographical discoveries. The opening up of new mines in West Virginia, Canada, Alaska, South Africa, Australia and California caused a considerable depression in the immediate income streams of those who engaged in the exploitation of the new territory. Consequently, the rate of interest in such instances tends at first to be very high.

§5. *The Present an Age of Invention*

The present is an age of rapid invention, especially since the World War. President Hoover's Committee on Recent Economic Changes finds the "tempo" of improvement in industrial arts the most striking characteristic of our times. This increased tempo tends toward a high interest rate because of the flood of new inventions, despite the opposing influence of the old and matured inventions which have made us so much richer.

Some outstanding examples of recent inventions which greatly increase production and consumption are: the automobile; the radio; the airplane; motion pictures in all their many uses; the numerous applications of electric power in factories and on the farm; long distance telephone, which has finally solved the problem of sending messages across the Atlantic Ocean; the utilization of cellulose, formerly a waste and a nuisance, in the manufacture of building materials, paper, and rayon textiles; the use of cotton seed for oil and fertilizer; the pulverization of coal by which its fuel value is greatly increased; the liquefaction of coal which gives added supplies of much needed gasoline; the innumerable chemical and dye products made from coal.

New discoveries and inventions, by utilizing wastes from forests, fields and mines, and increasing the output of labor have greatly advanced the scale of living in America.

Furthermore, the use of a new invention spreads with lightning rapidity in this high speed and intercommunicating age, affecting the income streams with a much greater influence than formerly and, as it spreads, it leads to further inventions. This is a chief reason why today is increasingly an age of invention. Nations like Great Britain, the United States, Germany and France lead in civilization by taking the greatest advantage of this self-propagating principle of invention, and nations like China and India, so long as they give it little attention, will lag behind.

Improvements in transportation developed the world granaries of Argentina, Canada, and the Mississippi Valley. The acreage of cotton was increased to feed the New England and British mills from the Southern and Gulf States, from Egypt and India. The investments in mining stretched over continents. Chilean nitrates were brought to American farms, and fresh investments were made in works that extracted nitrogen from the air. The coal deposits of the world were made to release solar energy stored up for millions of years, and the oil wells of Oklahoma and Baku became sources of new wealth and investment to supply a motor-driven age. Investments in machines, factories, railways, highways, warehouses, sewers, and in the ramifications of urban and suburban development enlarged the opportunities for surplus funds to an almost limitless extent. Reconstruction of devastated countries after the World War gave opportunity for the investment of billions of American dollars abroad, with flotations of foreign loans in the United States, in 1927 and 1928, averaging a billion and a half each year.

§6. *Mass Production of Inventions*

Moreover today we are organizing invention and discovery as we organize everything else. Experimental laboratories have spread from universities to government bureaus and commercial concerns. Millions are now spent on research where thousands or hundreds were spent a generation ago. And inventors are thus led not only to more intensive effort but to coöperate and pool their ideas. Mr. Hoover, before he was President, took steps toward a greater organization of scientific work looking toward invention.

During 1929, the Engineering Foundation launched a

[349]

drive for five million dollars to aid scientific research. Major General George O. Squier reported in the Nation's Business for January, 1929, that in the laboratory of the American Telephone and Telegraph Company alone, $15,000,000 yearly were being devoted to the work of research which employed four thousand specialists. With respect to research General Squier added:

"We hear of expendituŕes by the millions—$200,000,000 a year by some estimates, $70,000,000 through the Government, and $130,-000,000 through commercial firms. Any comprehensive inventory of our research resources would include the bulky items of plant and equipment, and the incalculable intangibles reposed in the 300,000 physicists, chemists, engineers, mathematicians, and trained technicians. As for suggesting the substance of this tremendous adventure, we may turn to the structures erected by the General Electric Company, the United States Steel Corporation, General Motors, and the United States Rubber Company."

A survey by the National Bureau of Economic Research revealed, in its announcement of May 4, 1929, the extent to which industrial research prevailed as a new trend in manufacturing progress in the United States. Of 599 manufacturing concerns supplying information, the report stated that 52 per cent recorded the carrying on of research as a company activity. Testing laboratories were conducted by 7 per cent, leaving a minority in which no research work was being done. Some 29 per cent reported that they were supporting coöperative research conducted through trade associations, engineering societies, universities or endowed fellowships. Especially in cement manufacture, leather tanning, and gas and electric utilities, coöperative research was highly developed.

Statistical research has added its quota to investment

opportunities. There had been business depression in 1920-1921. Herbert Hoover's engineering committee on Elimination of Waste in Industry reported some of the causes of that depression. The committee had found throughout industry a faulty control of material and design, as well as of production and costs. For example, the loss from idleness in shoemaking occasioned by waiting for work and material amounted to about 35 per cent of the time. It was found that standardization of the thickness of certain walls might mean a saving of some six hundred dollars in the cost of the average house. There were six thousand brands of paper, of which half were more or less inactive, and the duplication of brands tied up money in unnecessary stock. A shoe factory with capacity of twenty-four hundred pairs a day had shortage of needed racks, reducing output to nineteen hundred pairs daily. Most plants were found with no cost systems, or with incomplete knowledge of general costs, and for this reason most of them lost money. A multitude of shops lacked modern personnel relations with their employees; the workers had no unbiased means of approach to employers, while employers lacked the means of treating with their own men. Few plants had effective employment records; the turnover of labor was high and expensive. Sales policies were defective. There were cancellations of purchases on long-term contracts ranging up to 14 per cent, and returns of goods up to 11 per cent in so-called normal years. Lack of scientific management and of scientific forms of organization found production restricted by both employers and men. Maintenance of high prices, collusion in bidding, and unfair practices contributed to limit output, as well as did the practice of "ca' canny" by workers and the restrictive rules of the unions. It was found that eighteen hundred million dollars a year might be saved in preventing illness and deaths among American workers, and eight hundred and fifty million dollars more in preventing industrial accidents.

With the publication of this report, and of the succeeding Hoover report on unemployment and business cycles, American industrial management awoke to the possibilities of economic savings and higher organization, and American investment management found its opportunities correspondingly enhanced. Loans were supplied by the banks in measured volume, according to the needs of industry. The vast American market, blessed with free trade between forty-eight state jurisdictions, was thoroughly surveyed, and the wonders of technique and research were systematically evoked in the large scale as well as in the smaller but rapidly merging industries.

§7. *Effects on Investment*

Because of these inventions, introducing economies which revolutionized industry, common stocks on the American exchanges have advanced in 1928 and 1929, so that the dividend yields of dividend paying stocks were lower than the interest yields of high grade bonds. As an example of the eagerness of the investing public to finance newly-evolving industries, the Daniel Guggenheim Fund for the Promotion of Aeronautics announced that it was no longer necessary to grant equipment loans to air-transport companies, because, it stated, the "investment public is now ready to supply the capital for enterprises of this kind." By the close of the third decade of the twentieth century America had already shot ahead of Europe in commercial aviation, and was operating more than eighteen thousand miles of airways, of which eight thousand miles were lighted for night travel. The New York Trust Company in its reports took note that airplane production for 1928 was about five times that of 1927, and that demand for almost every type of aviation market was rapidly expanding.

Among investors there was knowledge that many of the inventions and discoveries made by the agencies of research would quickly find practical use. With the certainty that epoch-making inventions and methods of higher organization were being applied in the arts, opportunities to invest were multiplied, and thousands of new investors increased the transactions of the stock exchanges.

This varied and exciting chapter in modern industrial expansion is summed up by the Hoover Committee on Recent Economic Changes in its review (p. 844):

"By no means all the increase in efficiency took the form of a net gain in current livelihood. To use the technique founded on science, men had to build machines, factories, railways, roads, warehouses and sewers. In developing new resources, they had to dig mines; to break the prairies and fence the farms; to make homes in strange habitats. And this work of re-equipping themselves for making consumers' goods was never done. Every discovery put to use on a commercial scale meant a new equipment job, often of great extent. But after all this work on the means of production was done, there remained an even larger flow of the things men eat and wear, house and amuse themselves with.

"The net gain in ability to provide for their desires brought men the possibility of raising their standard of consumption, of reducing their hours of work, of giving their children more education, of increasing their numbers. They took a slice of each of these goods, rather than all of one. They worked somewhat less hard as the decades went by; they raised their standards of consumption appreciably; they established compulsory education and reduced illiteracy; they added to the population. . . ."

THE THEORY OF INTEREST

§8. *Importance of Invention*

It has not been the purpose of this chapter to investigate the general effect of inventions, but merely their effect on the rate of interest and rates of return.

Before leaving the subject, however, it should at least be stated that invention is a chief basis for progress in civilization and for increase in the income of mankind. The inventions of fire, the alphabet, and the means of utilizing power—first of animals, then of wind and water, then of steam and electricity—and their manifold applications, especially to transportation and communication, have made it possible for the earth to support its increasing population, and deferred the Malthusian pressure upon the means of subsistence; they have made possible the stable existence of great political units such as the United States; and they have given opportunity for the presentation, diffusion, and increase of knowledge in all its forms of art, literature, and science. And thus it happens that invention is self-perpetuating. For not only has science sprung from inventions such as the printing press, the telegraph, and specific scientific instruments for observation, like microscopes and telescopes, or for measurements, like chronographs, balances, and micrometers, but modern science is now in turn yielding new inventions. Helmholtz's researches in sound led to the telephone; Maxwell's and Hertz's researches on ethereal waves led to wireless telegraphy and the radio.

The conditions for the most rapid multiplication of inventions are: (1) mental efficiency, dependent on heredity, hygienic habits, and the education (both general and technical) of human faculties, and for this the Greek motto "a sane mind in a sane body" is in point;

(2) the ease of diffusion of knowledge; (3) the size of the population within which the diffusion occurs—the larger the population the greater being the number of inventive geniuses, the greater their incentive, and the wider their sphere of influence; (4) the encouragement of invention especially through the early discovery and approval of genius, and, to some extent through patent protection. Inventors are at once the rarest and most precious flower of the industrial world. Too often they are crushed by the obstacles of poverty, prejudice, or ridicule. While this is less so today than in the days of Roger Bacon or Galileo, it still requires far too much time for the Bells, Edisons, Fords, or De Forests to get their start. The decades in which these rare brains are doing their wonderful work are at most few, and it is worth many billions of dollars for their countrymen to set them to work early. As Huxley says, it should be the business of any educational system to seek out the genius and train him for the service of his fellows, for whether he will or not, the inventor cannot keep the benefits of his invention to himself. In fact, it is seldom that he can get even a small share of the benefits. The citizens of the world at large are the beneficiaries, and being themselves not sufficiently clever to invent, they should at least be sufficiently alive to their own interests to subsidize or employ the one man in a million who can.

CHAPTER XVII

PERSONAL AND BUSINESS LOANS

§1. *Personal Loans*

In this chapter, I shall try to show that the theory of interest elaborated in this book applies to every species of loan contracts.

From the standpoint of the borrower, loan contracts may be classified as follows:

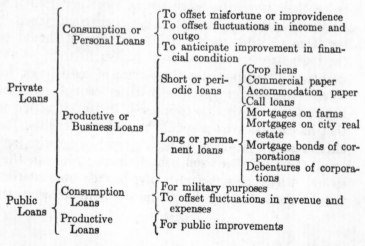

Personal loans are loans of individuals for personal purposes rather than those arising out of business relations. Of these, the first class comprises loans contracted because of misfortune or improvidence. These constitute today a very small fraction of total indebtedness. It was against interest on such loans that the biblical, classical, and medieval prohibitions and regulations were directed, and it is chiefly against interest on such loans that today, in enlightened communities, regulations affecting the rate of interest still survive. It is such loans that supply a large part of the business of pawn shops and of "loan sharks," the patrons of which are too often victims of misfortune or of improvidence.

The theory of interest which has been propounded in this book applies to this species of loan. Sickness or death in one's family, or losses from fire, theft, flood, shipwreck, or other unexpected causes, make temporary inroads upon one's income. It is to tide over such stringencies in income that a personal loan is contracted. It ekes out the inadequate income of the present by sacrificing something from the more adequate income expected in the future. Similar principles apply to the spendthrift, who, though not a victim of accidental misfortune, brings misfortune upon himself. He borrows in order to supplement an income inadequate to meet his present requirements, while he trusts to future resources for repayment. It is evident, therefore, that the loans just described are made by the borrower for the sake of correcting an income stream the time shape of which is unsatisfactory.

The second class of personal loans comprises those growing out of such fluctuations in income as are not due to misfortune or improvidence. Some persons receive their money income in very irregular and unequal installments, while their money outgo may likewise have an irregular time schedule. Unless the two series happen to synchronize, the individual will be alternately "short" and "flush." Thus, if he receives his largest dividends in January, but has to meet his largest expenses, let us say taxes, in September, he is likely to borrow at tax time for the ensuing four months, in anticipation of the January dividends. That is, he borrows at a time when his real income would otherwise be low, and repays at a time when it would otherwise be high. The effect is to level up the fluctuations of his income. He could, of course, proceed in the opposite way, lending in January when "flush" and being repaid in the fall in time to help him when "short" because of tax payments.

In brief, either he borrows, when short, because his degree of impatience, in view of the flush time coming, is higher than the rate of interest, or he lends when flush because his degree of impatience, in view of the lean time coming, is lower than the rate of interest.

The third class of personal loans comprises those which grow out of large expected additions to income or income earning power. Heirs to a fortune sometimes borrow in anticipation of bequests coming to them, the prospect of which excites their impatience. A considerable volume of such loans are made perhaps most often in Great Britain. The borrower under these circumstances borrows so that he can enjoy in the present some of the income which otherwise he would have to wait for. The same motives actuate young men preparing for the earning period of life and explain the loans which are often contracted by them for defraying the expenses of education. It was for such persons that Benjamin Franklin left his peculiar bequests to the cities of Philadelphia and Boston in 1790. To each he bequeathed £1000 to be lent out in small sums at 5 per cent to young married "artificers". The sums repaid, including interest, were to be added to the fund and again lent. Modern building and loan associations are organized to accommodate young couples and others wishing to enjoy good homes in anticipation of their power to pay for them in full. Installment buying, now so widely used to finance the buying of dwellings, furniture, automobiles, radios and other long-lasting instruments, cater to the same desires. They all appeal to young people with small immediate incomes but great expectations for the future.

It is evident that all the foregoing cases, comprising personal loans, are taken care of from the viewpoint of the borrower in the theory of interest; they are all expressions of impatience for greater income expected in the future.

§2. *Business Loans*

Business loans are commonly called productive loans, in contrast with personal or consumption loans. Business loans constitute by far the most important class of present indebtedness. Mr. George K. Holmes, formerly of the U. S. Census, at one time estimated that at least nine tenths of the indebtedness in the United States then existing was incurred for the acquirement of the more durable kinds of property, leaving not more than one tenth, and probably much less, as a consumption debt. The overwhelming preponderance of business loans has led some economists to account for interest on personal loans as a reflection of the rate of return lenders can secure by lending for production.

From another point of view it might seem that the theory which has been given in this book, based as it is on the enjoyable income stream of an individual, can apply only to consumption loans.

It is also said, with some appearance of truth, that

consumption loans are explained on principles quite other than are production loans. In personal loans the two principles of impatience are dominant, while in business loans the two principles of investment opportunity are dominant. But in either case both sets of principles play their parts. And, since the degree of impatience and the rate of return over cost both tend toward equality with the market rate of interest, each influencing the other in that direction, we reach the same result to whichever one of the two—impatience or investment opportunity—we give our main attention. Lest the rôle of impatience in business loans be overlooked, let us first fix our eyes on that.

While business loans differ from consumption loans in respect to investment opportunity principles, they do not really differ in respect to the impatience principles. Both are used to tide over lean times in anticipation of prosperity, and they are said to be contracted in order to rectify the distortion of the income stream which would otherwise result from business operations.

The truth is—and it should never be lost sight of— that the business man conducts his business with an eye always to ultimately enjoyable income whether for himself, his family or for others. In a sense it is his home that runs his business rather than his business that runs his home.

§3. *Short Term Loans*

Two classes of business loans may be distinguished, namely, short loans growing out of periodic income variations, and long loans for relatively permanent investment. The short or periodic loans are those which grow out of the change in the seasons and the ebb and flow of business. These loans are obtained usually but once a year at a specified time. The ultimate cause is the cyclical change in the position of the earth in reference to the sun. This gives rise to the cycle of the seasons, the effects of which are felt not only in agriculture, but in manufacturing, transportation, trade, and banking. The alternate congestion and thinning of the freight business, the alternate stocking and depletion of raw material in factories, the seasonal fluctuations of trade activity, both wholesale and retail, the transfer of bank deposits between New York and the West for moving crops, or for other uses, all testify to the seasonal rhythm which is constantly felt in the great network of business operations. Without some compensating apparatus, such as that for borrowing and lending, these seasonal fluctuations in production, trade, and finance would transmit themselves to the final enjoyable income streams of individuals, and those incomes instead of constituting an even flow would accrue by fits and starts, a summer of lavish enjoyment, for instance, being followed by a winter on short rations.

To show how borrowing and lending compensate for these fluctuations, we may consider first what is perhaps the most primitive type of the short term loan, namely, that contracted by poor farmers in anticipation of crops. In the South among the negroes this takes the form of what is called a crop lien, the cultivator borrowing money enough to enable him to live until crop time and pledging repayment from the crop. Here, evidently, the purpose of the loan is to eke out the meager income of actual enjoyments. The loan, in other words, is for subsistence. This case, therefore, clearly involves the impatience principles.

These same principles apply also to loans contracted in the commercial world at large. A short time commercial loan is contracted for the purpose of buying goods, with the expectation of repayment after their sale. A common form is what is called commercial paper. A ready-made-clothing house may buy overcoats in summer in order to sell them in the fall. If these operations were conducted on a strictly cash basis, the tendency would be for the income of the clothier to suffer great fluctuations. He could realize but little during the summer, on account of the enormous expense of stocking in for fall trade, whereas in the fall he could obtain large returns and live on a more elaborate scale. This would mean the alternation of famine and feast in his family. One way to avoid such a result would be to keep on hand a large supply of cash as a buffer between the money income and personal expenditure. In this case the fluctuations in his income would not affect his personal enjoyment, but would cause an ebb and flow in his volume of cash. But a more effective and less wasteful method for the merchant to take the kinks out of his stream of real income is by negotiating commercial paper. The clothier, instead of suffering the large cash expense of stocking up in summer, will make out a note to the manufacturer of overcoats. After the fall trade, this note is paid, having fulfilled its function of leveling the income stream of the clothier.

Sometimes business men contract short term loans, not for some specific transaction such as the purchase of stock in trade, but for general business purposes, as, for instance, improvement or enlargement. In this case, the extraordinary expense involved may be met by a species of loan called accommodation paper. Evidently its function is precisely the same, namely, to rectify the time shape of the income stream.

In Wall Street and other speculative centers a type of loan known as the call loan is common, subject to redemption at the pleasure of the lender or the borrower, and used by the speculator for the purchase of securities. The speculator borrows when he wishes to buy and repays when he has sold, and by adroitly arranging and placing his loans he prevents the sudden draining or flushing of his income stream which these purchases and sales would otherwise involve, if they were to be made at all.

In all the cases which have been described, the loan grows out of a purchase or group of purchases, and since the tendency of every purchase is to decrease one's income, and of every sale to increase it, it is clear that loans contracted for a purchase and extinguished by a sale may be said to have as their function the obliteration of these decreases and increases of the income stream. We see then that these commercial loans fit into the impatience part of the theory of interest which has been propounded.

§4. *Long Term Loans*

The second class of business loans is that of long term loans or permanent investments. In this class are placed mortgages, whether on farms or on urban real estate. As shown by the 1890 Census, almost two-thirds of farm mortgages are contracted to buy land, and the remainder principally for improving it, or for the purchase of farm machinery and animals, or for the purchase of other durable wealth and property. The Department of Agriculture found that 87 per cent of the mortgages of 94

North Carolina farms in 1922 was contracted to buy land, and almost 10 per cent more to make real estate improvements. These purchases or improvements, involving as they do large expenditures, would be difficult or impossible without loans. If the attempt were made to enter into them without recourse to a loan market, they would cause large, though temporary, depressions in the income streams of the farmers. The farmer who attempted to buy his farm without a loan might not be able to do so at all or at best might have to cut down his current living expenses to a minimum.

Mortgages on city lots are usually for the purpose of improving such properties by erecting buildings upon them. The expense involved would, if taken out of income, reduce the income of the owner temporarily. He naturally prefers to compensate for such extraordinary inroads by a mortgage loan which defers this expense to the future when he expects that his receipts will be larger.

We come next to the loans of business corporations and firms, such, for instance, as railroad bonds and debentures, the securities of street railroads, telegraph, and telephone companies, steel mills, textile factories, and other "industrials." These loans are usually issued for new construction, replacement, and for improvement of plant and equipment. The borrowers in this case are, in the last analysis, the stockholders. They may be said to contract the loan in order not to have the expenses of the improvement taken out of their dividends. Sometimes, of course, where the earnings are large enough they are actually applied, in part or wholly, to the making of improvements. Ordinarily, however, such a reduction in the stockholder's income stream is avoided by the device of inviting bondholders to bear the outgoes connected with the improvement, in consideration of receiving a part of the increased income which it is hoped will later follow from these improvements.

§5. *Business vs. Personal Loans*

Business loans therefore serve to reshape the income streams to conform to the time preferences of their owners just as truly as do personal loans. All financing may be considered as contrived to keep income flowing smoothly to serve human impatience.

The important difference between business loans and personal loans is not as to impatience but as to investment opportunity. In personal loans the opportunity principle plays a minor rôle or none at all. The personal borrower borrows not to invest but to remedy or prevent a present dearth of income because of illness or the desire to anticipate future income, the amount of which has little or nothing to do with the loan. The business borrower, on the other hand, borrows to remedy or prevent a dearth of present income because he wishes to invest and increase his future incomes. Each is impelled by impatience to fill a hole in his present income, but the one hole was cut by involuntary illness or voluntary spending, the other by voluntary investment.

Let us examine this difference more in detail. Let us suppose two borrowers, one a personal borrower, because of some misfortune such as an illness, and the other a business borrower, because of an investment. Let us suppose that, otherwise, they are alike in all respects affecting our present problem. Each has a prospective income of $10,000 this year and $12,500 next year, after allowing for the effects of the misfortune in one case *and for that of the investment in the other,* but before any loan is made.

Each will, let us say, borrow $1,000 this year and repay this with 5 per cent interest next year, making a total repayment of $1,050. Each, therefore, will have a finally adjusted income this year of $10,000 + $1,000 or $11,000 and next year of $12,500 — $1,050 or $11,450. The effect of the loan is thus identical on the income streams in the two cases. The difference is that the unfortunate, if deprived of his loan, could not escape from his lower income stream this year of $10,000 despite his higher income next year, whereas the business man, if deprived of his loan, could, if he chose, give up easily the investment altogether. That is, the merchant has another option which the unfortunate lacks. He has two options and therefore the opportunity to replace one by the other.

If the merchant did not have this extra option, the two cases would be so similar that not even a stickler for the distinction between a consumption loan and a production loan would assert any essential difference. For, suppose the merchant had already been committed sometime previously to the investment, not, perhaps, realizing that he would be unable to pay for it without borrowing or skimping. When the time arrives when he must of necessity pay in his money, he finds that a loan is badly needed to avoid pinching himself in income. He will now think of the loan not as enabling him to invest, for that has to be done anyway, but as enabling him to buy his bread and butter. In short, his loan, like the unfortunate's, is now a consumption loan! It is because ordinarily the merchant is *not* thus constrained to make the investment that the loan is connected in his mind with the investment rather than with his private necessities. Yet, in either case, it serves to relieve his needs. In a sense all loans are impatience loans, but in the production case he has another method of relief—not to invest at all. The essential contrast, then, between him and the unfortunate is simply that he has a possible course open to him which the latter does not have.

This is not to deny that the loan (and the investment which it makes possible) is also to be considered for the purpose of increasing his income. It is both. As stated already, had he wished, he might have refrained, ordinarily, altogether from making the investment. He would, then, let us suppose, have had an income of $11,000 a year both this year and next. He was attracted by the opportunity to invest $1,000 because while this would reduce this year's income by that amount—to $10,000—it would increase next year's by $1,500—to $12,500. The whole set of operations go together. If we separate them in thought, the true sequence is: of the two optional income streams ($11,000, $11,000, on the one hand, and $10,000, $12,500 on the other) the merchant selects the latter because it had the greater present value (or, what amounts to the same thing, because the rate, 50 per cent, of the return of $1,500 on the sacrifice of $1,000 is greater than the rate of interest, 5 per cent). That being done he then borrows because, although he will have the same present value, he will get a more desirable time shape. This description takes account of the whole series of operations, and corresponds to the principles propounded in Chapter VI. It is the extra option which gives rise to the contention that the loan produces a profit not possible or easy without it, and that it is, therefore, productive. And this is true in the sense that the loan carries with it the extra option. The loan is productive in so far as without it this extra option which is productive would not be chosen.

We have just seen that the loan phenomena can be resolved into two separate steps. Yet since it may often happen, as shown in Chapter VI, that the first step (choice of options) would not be taken unless the second step (loan) were already in contemplation, or even fully contracted, it is true that in a sense the choice of the loan includes the choice between the options. In this sense, and in this sense alone, is the loan productive. It is productive in that it gives to the merchant a productive investment opportunity. But it is better, or at any rate admissible, to say that it is this investment opportunity which is productive rather than the loan which makes it possible.

In practical life, however, the investment and the loan are not usually thought of as separate operations. Rather are they thought of as parts of the same operations. The investment, especially if a large one, would not, and often could not, be made unless the resultant distortion of the income stream is at once and by pre-arrangement, remedied by a loan. The loan is in fact often contracted for before any committal to the investment, and were it not employed, or something like it, the distortion of the income stream needed to make the investment possible would often reduce it to zero or below.

The point here is that if we do try to separate the rôles of the loan and the investment we cannot say that the loan by itself, without the investment, yields a business profit, but we can say that the investment by itself does. Adopting the latter mode of thought, we are free to think of a business loan as having, by itself, just the same function as any other loan—to even up the income stream in accordance with the principles of impatience.

§6. *Purpose of Borrowing to Increase Present Income*

We have now seen that the theory of interest which has been propounded is adequate to explain the motives which lead to borrowing in the actual business world.

The personal loan comes near to exemplifying our first approximation where there is a supposedly fixed income stream, while the business loan exemplifies the second or the full fledged third approximation where there are alternatives. Of course, even the unfortunate who needs a loan may have alternative ways to turn. No income stream in actual life is absolutely rigid. But the various opportunities open to the typical personal borrower are not very important or striking as compared with those open to a business man seeking a loan to finance some great enterprise.

The foregoing classification of loans is made from the standpoint of the borrower. From the standpoint of the lender, loans do not need to be so minutely classified.

§7. *Public Loans*

Public Loans need not be treated in detail since they have all the characteristics which belong to private loans for consumption and production. The public loan for consumption is exemplified in the war loans and the loans to anticipate future revenues. A government receives its income chiefly in taxes, and in some cases only once a year, whereas its outgo occurs day by day and month by month. It thus happens that a government is alternately accumulating a large surplus and suffering a large deficit. The inconvenient effects of this have often been commented upon, especially in this country, where the Treasury for half a century was relatively independent of such institutions of credit between the governments and certain central banks as have long existed in England, and exist now in this country. The government may correct the irregularities in its income stream by borrowing for current expenses in anticipation of taxes. The United States Government often sells short term Treasury certificates when government receipts are low, and redeems these certificates when funds come in from taxes or other sources. The opposite process may be employed. The Government may lend at interest by depositing surplus funds in banks to draw interest until needed for disbursements, or, what amounts to receiving interest, it may, by buying its own bonds or redeeming them for a sinking fund, save interest which would otherwise have to be paid. But this last operation is normally employed only when the funds are not needed later for disbursements.

The public productive, or business loan, is exemplified in loans for the purpose of constructing railroads, or other improvements which are intended to be business undertakings, such as the erection of government buildings, the improvement of roads, bridges, and harbors, the construction of municipal waterworks or schoolhouses. In all such cases it is usual to finance the enterprise by issuing bonds. The reason is that these improvements constitute an extraordinary cost, similar to the expense of a war, which if undertaken without the issue of bonds would cause a temporary and inconvenient depression in the income streams of the taxpayers. They, as a whole, could not afford any such first heavy drain, even with the prospect of substantial benefits to follow. They therefore prefer to avoid such a fluctuating income stream, and to secure instead a more uniform one. This uniformity is secured by the loan, which so far as they are concerned, spreads the expenditures over part or all of the period during which the public improvement is expected to last. We see, therefore, that this class of loans also exemplifies the theory of the relation of borrowing and lending to the time shape of an income stream. The motives which have been described as operating in the case of private loans operate in the same way with public loans. Borrowing by a public corporation shifts to the purchasers of bonds in first instance the burden of war expenditure or the cost of improvements. The taxpayers repay the bondholders when the bonds are finally paid. The effect is the same in public borrowing as in private borrowing, the shape of the income stream of the public borrower is changed in the same manner. There is present also a rate of return over cost, though one difficult to put in figures because public benefits are not usually reduced to money values.

CHAPTER XVIII

SOME ILLUSTRATIVE FACTS

§1. *Introduction*

THIS chapter consists of a brief study of the chief influences affecting the rate of interest. It is impossible to present a verification of any theory of interest. The facts are too meager, too conflicting, and too intermixed to admit of clear analysis and precise interpretation. In all places and at all times the economic causes tending to make interest high are combined with others tending to make it low. The fact, therefore, that interest is high or low, rising or falling, in conformity with the postulates of a particular theory, does not prove that the theory is the only true explanation. The best that we can expect is to show that the facts as we find them are not inconsistent with the theory maintained.

The causes making for high or low interest rates tend to counteract themselves. For instance, the economic causes, which before the World War tended to make interest high in the United States, also tended to bring in loans from other countries, especially from Great Britain, where the rate of interest was then low. The introduction of the loans prevented interest from being as high as it otherwise would have been. High interest in one community tends to increase the borrowings of that community, provided there exists another community in which the rate of interest is lower. If borrowing from abroad is not practicable, other methods of adding to present at the expense of future income may be found. If such processes go far enough they will result in a dissipation of capital, or in a slower accumulation of capital.

Contrariwise, the causes which work toward lending may result, if lending is impracticable, in some other ways of postponing consumption, and may show themselves in a more rapid accumulation or in a less rapid dissipation of capital.

The same economic causes which tend to make interest high will tend also to encourage the production of the less substantial and durable instruments, whereas those causes which tend to make interest low will favor the production of instruments of the more durable and substantial types.

In general, *high interest, borrowing, dissipation of capital, and perishability of instruments go together.* Any cause which produces any one of the four will, in general, tend also to produce the other three. Likewise *low interest, lending, accumulation, and durability of instruments, generally go together.*

The theory enunciated is that the rate of interest depends on impatience and investment opportunity. As any cause increases or decreases our impatience for immediate income, it tends to increase or decrease the rate of interest. Any cause which increases our opportunity to secure returns on investments in excess of the existing rate of return tends to increase the rate of interest; and conversely when, for any cause, opportunities to invest promise only returns less than the existing return on investment the interest rate tends to decline.

In Chapter IV were enumerated the causes which in

the nature of man tend to make interest high or low. It was there stated that foresight, self-control, and regard for posterity tend to reduce impatience for income and so tend to make interest low. We may expect to find therefore in a community possessing these qualities some or all of the four interrelated phenomena already mentioned —low interest, lending to other communities, accumulation of capital and construction of substantial capital instruments. In a community lacking these qualities we may expect to find some or all of the four opposite conditions.

§2. *Examples of Influence of Personal Characteristics*

The nations and peoples which have been most noted in the past for foresight, self-control, and regard for posterity are probably the Dutch, Scotch, English, French, Germans and Jews, and the interest rate has been relatively lower in general in the communities dominated by these peoples than in communities dominated by less thrifty peoples. They have been money lenders; they have had the habit of thrift and accumulation, and their instruments of wealth have been in general substantial. The durability of their instruments of wealth is especially seen in their buildings, both public and private, and in their ways of transportation—roads, tramways, and railroads.

John Rae observed of Holland:

"Hitherto the Dutch, of all European nations, seem to have been inclined to carry instruments to the most slowly returning orders. The durability given to all the instruments constructed by them, the care with which they are finished, and the attention paid to preserving and repairing them, have been often noticed by travelers. In the days when their industry and frugality were most remarkable,

[374]

interest was very low, government borrowing at 2 per cent, and private people at 3."[1]

On the other hand, among communities and people noted for lack of foresight and for negligence with respect to the future are India, Java,[2] the negro communities both North and South,[3] the peasant communities of Russia,[4] and the North and South American Indians, both before and after they had been subjugated by the white man. In all of these communities we find that interest is high, that there is a tendency to run into debt and to dissipate rather than accumulate capital, and that their dwellings and other instruments are of very flimsy and perishable character.

It may well be that there are other causes at work

---

[1] *The Sociological Theory of Capital*, pp. 128-129.

[2] My colleague, Professor Clive Day, finds that interest rates in Java have advanced rather than declined since the early years of the twentieth century. He cites as the best source for recent conditions the Great Investigation (*Onderzoek naar der mindere Welvaart de inlandsche Bevolking op Java en Madoera.* Batavia, 1912, IX bl Dl II. 1, page 66). The report states that on small loans under 5 florins unsecured, the annual rate runs to several hundred per cent. On secured loans, say of 25 florins more or less, the rate varies from 36% to 60%. These rates are notably higher than his estimate of 40% quoted in *The Rate of Interest*, p. 292.

[3] Professor J. S. Lawrence, of Princeton University, informs me that needy negroes often pay at the end of the week, $7.00 for $5.00 borrowed at the beginning of the week, or more than 40% per week.

[4] See Bloch, Ivan, *The Future of War.* Translated by R. C. Long. New York, Doubleday and McClure Co., 1899, p. 205. It appears that the peasant would sell a promise to labor a short time in the future at one third the current wages! See also Lanin (pseud.), *Russian Finance*, Fortnightly Review, Vol. LV, February, 1891, pp. 188, 190, 196, for typical and extreme cases. Inostranietz, *L'Usure en Russie*, Journal des Économistes, Vol. XVI, Ser. 5, 1893, pp. 233-243, states that the rates paid by poor peasants to well-to-do peasants are frequently 5 per cent per week.

to produce these results. We are here merely noting the fact that lack of foresight is one factor present. John Rae's characterization of the Indians both of North and South America as highly improvident and lacking in foresighted thrift is based on personal observation and the testimony of missionaries and travelers.[5] The negroes of Africa are perhaps even less provident than the American Indians.

In many if not all of the cases which have been cited there are, of course, other elements which would tend to explain the facts besides mere mental characteristics. Thus, the high rate of interest among the negroes and the Russian peasants is undoubtedly due in part to their poverty, though their poverty is in turn due in varying degree to their mental characteristics. Where there is too little appreciation of the needs of the future, capital tends to disappear; and the pressure of poverty tends to enhance still further the demands of the present and to press down its victims from bad to worse.

Not only do we find examples of high rates of preference for present over future goods among the prodigally rich, but often we find low rates of preference for present over future goods among the thrifty poor. Examples are especially frequent among the Scotch, the French peasants, and the Jews, whose propensity to accumulate and to lend money even in the face of misfortune and social ostracism is well known.

The factor which has been designated as "regard for posterity" deserves special attention. Perhaps the most conspicuous example of extreme disregard for posterity is found in Rome during the time of its decline and fall. Rae stresses the decay of family affection, the growth of extravagant expenditure, and the high interest rates.[7] High interest rates in Rome were evidently the result of reckless disregard of the future. Before Rome had seriously depleted her capital wealth, at about the end of the republic, the interest rate was as low as 4 to 6 per cent.[8]

§3. *Examples of Influence of Poverty*

The characteristics of foresight, self-control, and regard for posterity are partly inherent and partly induced by conditions of the environment. Among the cases which have been given are conspicuous examples of both, although it is difficult here, as always, to disentangle the influence of heredity from that of environment. We are accustomed, for instance, to ascribe to the Jews a natural racial tendency to accumulate, though this characteristic is certainly re-enforced by, if not largely due to, the extraordinary influence of Jewish tradition. Of the Scotch it would be difficult to say how much of their thrift is due to nature and how much to training handed down from father to son. The American negro is regarded as by nature a happy-go-lucky creature, but studies of negro life in Africa indicate that under favorable conditions the negro is self-denying, while recent experience with industrial schools has demonstrated the fact that forethought and saving can be readily fostered by training. Reckless wastefulness has been created in large part among the negroes by tyranny and slavery.

The influence of conditions upon accumulation may be seen everywhere, even in the most advanced industrial

[7] *The Sociological Theory of Capital*, pp. 64, 95-99, 129. Rae's authority for Roman interest rates is Boucher, *Histoire de l'Usure*, p. 25.

[8] Seligman, Edwin R. A., *Principles of Economics*. London, Longmans, Green and Co., 1907, p. 404.

countries. When postal savings banks were first introduced in England, it was objected that the English poor
for whom they were intended were so spendthrift that
they would never make use of them. But Gladstone in-
sisted that habits were an arbitrary matter, and that the
fashion of spending would be displaced by the fashion of
saving as soon as opportunity and incentive were afforded
and the principle of imitation had had time to operate.
The experience with English postal savings banks justified his prediction.[9]

Rae remarks upon the flimsiness of the Chinese buildings and implements and explains this by saying that
the people "think not so much of future years as of the
present time." [10] But the high interest rates of China are
probably not due, as Rae seemed to think, to any native
lack of industry, frugality, or parsimony on the part of
the Chinese people, as is evidenced by the large accumulations of capital made by Chinese living abroad where
they are freed from the exactions of arbitrary governors
and from the tyranny of the clan-family system. Presumably the wastefulness and high interest so evident in
China are most largely due to the action of poverty and
uncertainty.

For, as has been emphasized in previous chapters, the
rate of preference for present over future goods is not a
question of mere personal characteristics, but depends
also upon the character of one's income stream; on its
size, shape, composition, and certainty. In respect to *size,*
our theory maintains that the larger the income, *other
things such as habits, foresight and self-control being
equal,* the lower the rate of preference for present over

[9] Brown, *The Development of Thrift.*
[10] *The Sociological Theory of Capital,* pp. 88-89 and 92.

future goods. If this is true, we should expect to find poverty and riches associated respectively with a high and a low rate of interest, or with borrowing and lending, or with spending and saving, or with perishable and durable instruments. That this characterization is in general correct is not likely to be denied.

It is true of course that the *amount* loaned to the poor is small because each individual loan is necessarily small, but the *number* of these loans is very great, and the desire of the poor to borrow, when such desire exists, is very intense. The many conspicuous exceptions to these rules are explainable on other grounds. It not infrequently happens that the poor, instead of being borrowers, are lenders, but in this case either they have unusual foresight, self-control, regard for their children, and other qualities tending in the same direction, or else their income stream has such a time shape as to encourage lending rather than borrowing. Reverse conditions apply likewise to the case of many wealthy men who are borrowers not lenders. In general, a rich man borrows not from lack of self-control and foresight, but because of exceptional opportunities to invest advantageously, including opportunities to protect and extend investments already made.

As a rule, however, the poor are more eager borrowers than the rich, and are often obliged to patronize pawn shops and other agencies in which the rate of interest is inordinately high. The dwellings and other instruments of the poor are generally of a very unsubstantial character. Their clothes are selected of necessity more for cheapness than durability. Such uneconomical expenditures are often even unavoidable, and reflect a very high estimate on present as compared with future goods. The deeper the poverty, the higher the rate which the borrowers are compelled to accept. Even pawnbroking is not available for the extremely poor, but is patronized rather by the moderately poor. Those who are extremely poor cannot give the kind of security which the pawnbroker requires. On this account they become the victims of even higher rates of interest, pledging their stoves, tables, beds, and other household furniture for the loans they contract. These loans are repayable in installments such that the rate of interest is seldom lower than 100 per cent per annum.[11]

Turning from social classes to countries, it is noteworthy that in the countries in which there are large incomes we find low interest, a tendency to lend as well as to borrow, to accumulate as well as to spend, and to form durable rather than perishable instruments. In countries where incomes are low the opposite conditions prevail. Thus, incomes are large and interest rates are relatively low in the United States, Holland, France, Germany, and England, whereas the reverse conditions hold in Ireland, China, India, Java, the Philippines and other less developed countries. In Ireland, for instance, especially in the early part of the nineteenth century, the rate of interest was high. The cotter was always in debt, and his hut and other instruments were of the most unsubstantial variety.[12] Again in the Philippines the rate

[11] For details as to thirteen typical loans of this character, see U. S. Bureau of Labor Bulletin, No. 64, May, 1906, pp. 622-633. Thus "loan 1," 143 per cent, "loan 3," 224 per cent, "loan 7," 156 per cent. For later facts see Ryan, *Usury and Usury Laws;* also the publications of the Russell Sage Foundation on Small Loans, especially Raby, *The Regulation of Pawnbroking.*

[12] Longfield, Mountifort. *The Tenure of Land in Ireland* in Probyn's *Systems of Land Tenure in Various Countries.* London, Cassell, Petter, Galpin & Co., 1881, p. 16.

of interest on good security is often 2, 4, and even 10 per cent a month. The Chinese money lender frequently takes advantage of the Filipino's poverty.[13] Many of these cases may be wholly or partly explained by other causes such as have been mentioned in the last section.

§4. *Examples of Influence of Composition of Income*

As to the influence of the *composition* of income, it is even more difficult to obtain any statistical confirmation of importance. Variations in the amount of that real income which takes the form of food has an effect on the rate of interest similar to the effect of variations in the total income itself. Scarcity of food tends therefore to cause high interest, and abundance of food, low interest. During the siege of Paris the rate of interest was high, although other causes than the scarcity of bread were doubtless largely accountable for the fact. While no statistics of interest rates appear to be in existence for such periods, the testimony of eyewitnesses agree that in Belgium when starvation threatened during the World War the rates of interest were extremely high. Likewise during the blockade of Germany when the food shortage was acute, abnormally high interest rates are reported.

§5. *Examples of Influence of Risk*

As to the influence of uncertainty or *risk*, we encounter similar difficulties in getting positive inductive evidence. But evidence that in general risk tends to raise the commercial rate of interest but to lower pure interest is abundant. The first part of this proposition is a matter

[13] From a letter to the author from Professor E. W. Kemmerer; see also his article in *The Business Monthly*, Pittsburgh, April, 1907, p. 2.

THE THEORY OF INTEREST

of such common observation that no special collection of facts is necessary. Every lender or borrower knows that the rate of interest varies directly with risk. A bird in the hand is worth two in the bush.

The principle applies not only to the explicit interest in loan contracts, but to the implicit interest which goes with the possession of all capital. Where there is uncertainty whether income saved for the future will ever be of service, but the certainty that it can be of service if used immediately, the possessor needs the possibility of a very high future return in order to induce him to save. It is noteworthy that in time of war there is a ruthless destruction of crops and a tendency among the possessors of consumable wealth to enjoy it while they may. The same conditions are characteristic of communities which are in a perpetual state of political insecurity.[14] "The rate of interest is everywhere proportional to the safety of investment. For this reason we find in Korea that a loan ordinarily brings from 2 to 5 per cent per month. Good security is generally forthcoming, and one may well ask why it is so precarious to lend. The answer is not creditable to Korean justice. . . . In a land where bribery is almost second nature, and private rights are of small account unless backed up by some sort of influence, the best apparent security may prove a broken reed when the creditor comes to lean upon it."[15]

There remains the second part of the proposition in regard to risk, namely, that, while risk tends to increase the rate of interest on risky loans, it tends at the same

[14] On the uncertainties of Indian life, see Rae, *The Sociological Theory of Capital*, pp. 69 and 70.

[15] Hurlbert, H. B. *The Passing of Korea*. New York, Doubleday, Page and Co., 1906, p. 283.

time to decrease that on safe loans. This proposition is not familiar to most persons. It has usually caused surprise that during a time of political stress and danger the rates of interest on perfectly safe loans were found to be so small. Many such instances may be cited. At certain periods during the Civil War when the greatest uncertainty prevailed loans with good security were contracted at nominal rates, and bank deposits tended to accumulate for lack of sufficient outlet in secure investments. The same conditions existed in Europe during the World War. Times in which public confidence is shaken are characterized not only by high rates on unsafe loans, but by efforts on the part of timid investors to find a safe place for their savings, even if they have to sacrifice some or all of the interest upon them. They will even hoard savings in stockings and safe deposit vaults. We may even occasionally find cases in which the desire to obtain a safe method of keeping capital is so keen and so difficult to satisfy that the rate of interest is negative. The investor is then thankful enough to receive the assurance that his capital, by being intrusted to another, will not be diminished, to say nothing of being increased.

§6. *Examples of Influence of Time Shape*

We still need to exemplify the most essential part of the theory, namely, that the rate of interest depends through the rate of impatience upon the *time shape* of the income stream. The time shape may be due either to natural or artificial causes, or to choice because of a high or low rate of return on investment. If the theory is correct, we should find, other things being equal, that when in any community the income streams of its inhabitants are increasing, the rate of interest will be high, that when they are decreasing, the rate of interest will be low, and that when they alternate from one condition to the other, the rate of interest will alternate also in accordance with the period of the loan.

The most striking examples of increasing income streams are found in new countries. It may be said that before the World War the United States almost always belonged to this category. Were it possible to express by exact statistics or diagrams the size of American incomes, they would undoubtedly show a steady increase since colonial days. Statistics almost equivalent to these desiderata are available (though not very accurate) in the form of the United States Census figures of per capita wealth, as well as in statistics of production and consumption of staple commodities and of exports and imports. These, combined with common observation and the statements of historians, lead to the conclusion that American incomes have been on the increase for two hundred years. It is also true that during this period of rising incomes the rate of interest has been high. The simplest interpretation of these facts is that Americans, being constantly under the influence of great expectations from the exploitation of great natural resources, have been always ready to promise a relatively large part of their abundant prospective future income for a relatively small addition to their present, just as he who expects soon to come into a fortune wishes to anticipate its realization by contracting a loan.

Not only has the rate of interest been high in America as compared with other countries during this period of ascending incomes, but some of the other conditions having the same significance as a high rate of interest have also been in evidence. Thus, the country has been conspicuously a borrowing country, in debt to other countries. The proceeds of such loans from Europe have shown themselves in increased imports into the United States and diminished exports, creating a so-called unfavorable balance of trade. These phenomena have usually been expressed as a demand for capital, but, while it is quite true that the exploitation of our natural resources required the construction of railways and other forms of capital, this fact is better and more fully expressed in terms of income. We wanted, not the railways and machinery themselves, but the future enjoyable products to which this apparatus led. The labor of constructing these instruments necessarily tended to diminish the immediate enjoyable income of the country, but added to that of the expected future. It was to even up this disparity of immediate and remote income that loans were contracted. It does not matter whether the loans from the foreigner were received in the form of machinery and other instruments of production, or in the form of the comforts of life to support us while we ourselves constructed the instruments. In either case the essential fact is the transformation of the income stream rather than the need of capital, which is merely one of the means thereto.

Not only have we witnessed the phenomena of high rates of interest and of borrowing during this period of American development, but it is also true that the character of the instruments created was for the most part of the unsubstantial and quickly returning kinds. Our highways, as John Rae pointed out, were little more than the natural surface of the earth after the removal of trees and rocks; our railways were lightly ballasted, sometimes even narrow gauge, and crooked to avoid the necessity of excavations and tunnels; our earliest buildings were rude and unsubstantial. Everything was done, not in a permanent manner with reference to the remote future, but in order to save a large first cost.

During the last generation these conditions have been changed. The rates of interest in America are, in general, lower than formerly, and lower than in other countries, in many of which interest rates have risen.[16] We have ceased to be a borrowing nation. We bought back many of our securities from abroad, and after the World War began to buy foreign securities. This was accomplished through the excess of exports of our abundant products over imports. We are now lending billions to Europe. Europe has become a borrower, the chief reason being that in her recovery from the War her income stream is rising. During that recovery from the impaired income wrought by the War, Europe in some places offers bigger returns over costs than America. That fact, combined with Europe's poverty, makes for high interest.

The interest rate has fallen in the United States since 1920. This agrees with, or at least is consistent with, the theory that raising the level of national income tends, other things equal, to lower the rate of interest.

Again, the character of the instruments which have been now for some time in process of construction in the United States is of the most substantial kind. Steel rails have long since taken the place of iron rails; railways have been straightened by expensive tunnels, by bridges, and by excavations; dwellings and other buildings have been made more substantial; first macadamized and later cement roads have rapidly supplanted the old dirt roads; and in every direction there has been an evi-

[16] See Appendix to Chapter XIX, § 1.

dent tendency to invest a large first cost in order to reduce future running expenses.

§7. *Rising Income Means High Interest Rates*

Thus, in America and in Europe, we see exemplified on a very large scale the truth of the theory that a rising income stream raises and a falling income stream depresses the rate of interest, or that these conformations of the income stream work out their effects in other equivalent forms.

A similar causation may be seen in particular localities in the United States, especially where changes have been rapid, as in mining communities. In California in the two decades between 1850 and 1870 following the discovery of gold, the income stream of that state was increasing at a prodigious rate, while the state was isolated from the world, railroad connection with the East not having been completed until 1869. During this period of isolation and ascending income, ". . . opportunities for investment were innumerable. Hence the rates of interest were abnormally high. The current rates in the 'early days' were quoted at 1½ to 2 per cent a month. . . . The thrifty Michael Reese is said to have half repented of a generous gift to the University of California with the exclamation, 'Ah, but I lose the interest,' a very natural regret when interest was 24 per cent per annum." [17] After railway connection in 1869, Eastern loans began to flow in. The decade, 1870-1880, was one of transition during which the rates stimulated borrowing from the outside, which brought about lower interest

[17] Plehn, Carl C. *Notes Concerning the Rates of Interest in California.* Quarterly Publications of the American Statistical Association, September, 1899, pp. 351-352.

rates even though income streams continue to increase. The rate of interest consequently dropped from 11 per cent to 6 per cent.[18]

The same phenomena of enormous interest rates were also exemplified in Colorado and the Klondike. There were many instances in both these places during the transition period from poverty to affluence, when loans were contracted at over 50 per cent per annum, and the borrowers regarded themselves as lucky to get rates so low. It was also conspicuously true that the first buildings and apparatus constructed in these regions were very unsubstantial. Rude board cabins were put up in a day. Thus, high interest, borrowing, and unsubstantial capital were the phenomena which attended these communities when undergoing their rapid expansion.

In Nevada in the seventies, when the mines were increasing their product and the income of the inhabitants was tending upwards, the rate of interest was high and the people in debt. The bonded state debt itself amounted to $500,000 and drew 15 per cent interest.[19] In the next decade all these conditions were reversed. The mines were on the decline,[20] the rate of interest fell, and the state and territorial debts were largely paid off.[21] The fall of the rate of interest in this case could not have been due to the introduction of loans from outside, except so far as old debts were refunded at lower rates; fresh loans were seldom made, as the state had ceased to be a good place for new investments. At about the beginning of this century, new Nevada mines in the gold-field region

[18] Plehn, p. 353.
[19] See *Message of the Governor of the State of Nevada,* 1879.
[20] *Mines and Quarries,* 1902. Special Report U. S. Census, p. 255.
[21] See later *Messages of the Governor of the State of Nevada.*

were opened. Loans were again entering the state, and the same cycle of history, as above described, was repeated.

Lumbering communities often go through a somewhat similar cycle. The virgin forests when first attacked tend to increase rapidly the income streams of those who exploit them; then comes a period of decrease. Thus in Michigan two or three decades ago the lumber companies found a profitable investment, and borrowed in order to exploit the Michigan forests. After the exploitation was complete and the forests had been (often unwisely) exhausted, those regions ceased to be a desirable place for investment, and their owners came into the position, not of receiving, but of seeking investments.

After the trunk lines of railway were completed, connecting the Mississippi Valley with the East, there arose a great demand for loans to exploit the rich farming lands in that section of the country. The rate of interest frequently was 10 and 12 per cent and even higher. During much of this time the Northwestern Mutual Life Insurance Company up to 1880 made an average rate on all its mortgage loans, $10,000,000 in amount, of nearly 10 per cent. Another striking proof of the demand for loans in the Middle West is shown in the experience of the New York and Connecticut life insurance companies. New York up to 1880 had a law prohibiting the life insurance companies in that state from loaning on real estate outside of New York. Connecticut had no restriction in this regard, and her companies loaned extensively in the West. The result is seen in the rates of interest realized on mortgage loans of companies in the two states. Taking the period 1860-1880 as a whole, the Connecticut companies realized 1.2 per cent more than did the New

York companies. Since 1880 the Middle West has developed less feverishly, and loans on farming lands have been made at lower rates.

Australia furnishes another example of a country which, through improvement in the means of transportation and consequent great investment opportunities, created a great demand for loans. The rate during the fifties on safe securities was rather low. This rate increased until during the seventies, 7, 8, and 9 per cent were usual. After 1880 the rates declined.[22]

England may perhaps be cited as exemplifying the same phenomena which we have seen in the case of Nevada, though in a less degree. Thus as Nevada has exhausted its mines of precious metals, so England is on the road toward exhaustion of its coal and iron supplies. As coal and iron lie at the base of England's commercial power their exhaustion must carry with it the reduction of the income stream from English domestic industries. This fact has been noted with considerable alarm by some English economists, especially Jevons. But it does not necessarily indicate that the economic power of Englishmen will be greatly or even at all lessened. Its significance shows itself in the tendency of England to become an investing country. It is the part of those who have property in mines or other investments yielding terminable income not to use all of the product as income, but to reinvest some of the earlier income in order to maintain the capital. This the Englishmen have done and are doing, and, being unable to make enough satisfactory investments at home, they have placed their loans all over the world.

[22] Zartman, Lester W. *The Investments of Life Insurance Companies.* New York, Henry Holt and Co., 1906, p. 103.

The income stream produced for them by their native island is destined, perhaps, to decline, certainly not greatly to increase except during the next few years or decades of recovery from the World War. By saving from this declining income and investing in Canada, the United States, South America, Australia, South Africa, and other regions where the natural resources are being exploited and incomes are on the increase instead of on the wane, Englishmen may still maintain their capital intact or even increase it. The figures given by Giffen show that the national income increased for several decades, but that the rate of increase slackened for the decade 1875-1885 compared with 1865-1875. Whereas in the earlier decades there was a general increase in all directions, in the later decade there were many items of decrease,[23] the most notable being of mines and ironworks.[24] Among the greatest increases was that of foreign investments.[25]

§8. *Effect of Catastrophes on Interest*

The time shape of an income stream is determined, however, in part by other causes than natural resources. Among these causes, misfortune holds a high place in causing temporary depressions in the income stream, that is, in giving to it a time shape which is at first descending and afterwards ascending. The effect of such temporary depression is to produce a high valuation of immediate income during the depression period, as compared with the valuation of the income expected after the depression is over. It is a matter of common observation in private life that loans often find their source in personal

[23] Giffen, *Growth of Capital,* p. 44.
[24] *Ibid.,* p. 35.   [25] *Ibid.,* pp. 40-42.

misfortune. Investigations of pawnbrokers and small loan conditions among the poor [26] show that the chief causes for borrowing are a death or birth in the family, or a protracted illness, the expense of which even when amounting to only $10 or $20 would, without the loan, make serious inroads on the daily necessities.

We may see the operation of the same principle on a larger scale in the examples of the San Francisco earthquake, the earthquake which wrecked Yokohama and Tokyo, the plague which destroyed whole communities in Russia, and the famines of China. Had it not been for the succor rendered by more fortunate communities and countries, the income stream of some of the stricken communities and provinces in Russia and China would have sunk so low that scarcely any would have been able to survive. In addition to the aid of tens of millions of dollars in gifts, large loans were made which enabled the afflicted communities to build themselves anew. Whether these loans were used to produce sustenance, which is direct income, or to offset the cost of rebuilding and replacing destroyed capital goods, which is outgo, the effect was the same; they were for the purpose of tiding over a temporary decline, or loss, in the income stream. The permanent effect of these catastrophes on the rate of interest was slight because of the opportunity to borrow heavily from outside. Had these opportunities not existed, the depression in the income stream could not have been mitigated, and the rate of interest would inevitably have risen to a level comparable with that which prevailed in primitive times or during a gold rush.

In much the same way the income stream of a nation is affected by war. The effects in this case, however, are

[26] See U. S. Bureau of Labor Bulletin, No. 64, May, 1906, pp. 622 ff.

more complex, owing, first, to the element of uncertainty which war introduces until peace is declared, and secondly, to the fact that wars are likely to be more protracted than most other misfortunes. The effect, according to previous explanations, should be that at the beginning of the war the rates of interest on risky loans would be high. This would be especially true of the short term loans which do not outlast war. On the other hand, the rate of interest on safe loans should be lowered for short term loans, and raised for long term loans. Under the conditions of a war in its early stages, a short term loan relates to a descent in the income curve. It is repayable at a time when income is expected to be less than when the loan is contracted. The descent in the income curve, or the element of uncertainty, tends, as has been seen, to lower the rate of interest on safe loans. On the other hand, for long term loans intended to outlast the war, the rate of interest is likely to be high, for the income stream at the time of repayment may be expected to exceed the income stream at the time of contract.

At the close of war, after peace is declared and the element of uncertainty introduced by it has disappeared, the rate of interest even on short term loans will, contrary to the common view, be high, for then the country is, as it were, beginning anew, and the same causes operate to make interest high as apply in the case of all new countries.

When the effects of war include the issue of depreciated paper money, the rate of interest is affected in a somewhat more complex manner, being then subject to the influence of depreciation, according to the principles explained in Chapter II and statistically treated in Chapter XIX.

§9. *Examples of Influence of Periodicity of Income*

We have considered supposed examples of the effect on the rate of preference exerted by those changes in the income stream due to the growth or waning of natural resources and to the temporary influence of misfortunes and inventions. There remain to be considered examples of more regular changes in the income stream of a rhythmic or seasonal character. Though most persons are not aware of the fact, it can scarcely be doubted that the annual succession of seasons produces an annual cycle in the income stream of the community. This is especially true of agriculture. Grains, fruits, vegetables, cotton, wool, and almost all the organic products flow from the earth at an uneven rate, and require for their production also an uneven expenditure of labor from man during different seasons of the year. Statistics of consumption show that the income enjoyed conforms in general to a seasonal rhythm. Food products are usually made available in the warm months when crops ripen; logs are hauled out of the woods in the winter, floated to mills in the spring, and made into lumber in the summer.

But the tendency to a seasonal rhythm is modified by the existence of stocks of commodities to tide over the periods of scarcity. The ice of winter is stored for summer, and the fruits of summer are canned and preserved for winter. Only so far as such storage and preservation are difficult and expensive, or impair the quality of the goods thus held over, or are impracticable, because of the perishable nature of the goods, does there remain any seasonal change in enjoyed income. The rhythm is different for different industries and for different classes of the population. The farmer is perhaps the most typical for the country as a whole. For him the lowest ebb is in the fall, when gathering and marketing his crops cause him a sudden expenditure of labor, or of money for the labor of others. To tide him over this period he may need to borrow. A whole group of other industries, particularly

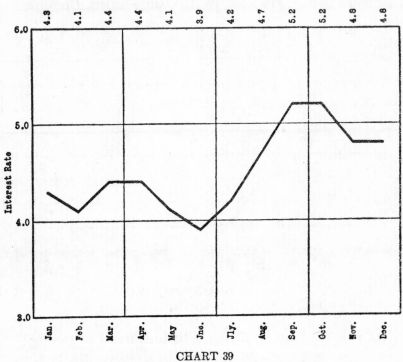

CHART 39

Monthly Average Discount Rates; New York.

those connected with transportation, experience a sympathetic fluctuation in the income stream. In the parlance of Wall Street, money is needed to move the crops. The rate of interest tends upward.

Chart 39 shows, for the period 1869 to 1905, the

monthly average of interest rates on prime, two-name, 60 to 90 day paper.[27]

The theory that interest rates vary with the seasons, rising during the late summer and autumn months and sinking during the winter and early summer months is borne out by Professor W. L. Crum's article, *Cycles of*

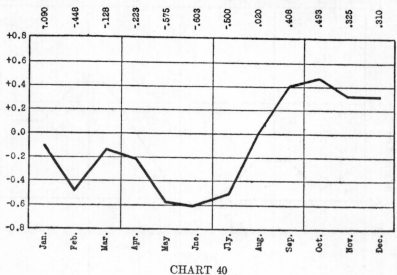

CHART 40

Indexes of Seasonal Variations in Interest Rates.

Rates on Commercial Paper,[28] which treats of monthly fluctuations in commercial paper rates over the period 1874 to 1913.

Chart 40 is a reproduction of Professor Crum's chart showing monthly deviations of interest rates from the annual average of monthly rates over the period 1874 to

[27] The average rates for each month plotted on the chart were compiled from the daily rates published in *The Financial Review.*
[28] The Review of Economic Statistics, January, 1923, pp. 17-27.

1913. It will be noted that the fluctuations shown on Chart 40 are almost identical with those shown on Chart 39. No comparison of *rates* is possible because Chart 40 shows only monthly deviations above and below the average annual rate, while Chart 39 shows the average of actual rates. Both charts show a low for February, a re-

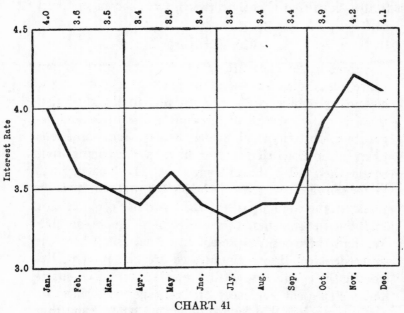

CHART 41

Monthly Averages of Discount Rates, Bank of England.

bound in March and April, a deeper depression in June, then a buoyant advance to the peak in September and October, followed by a slump when the autumn demand for money and credit to handle the crops is past.

In a community dominated by some industry other than farming the cycle would be different. The rates are of course a composite in which the cycles of the manufacturer and of other elements are superimposed upon the cycle of the farmer. The manufacturer's cycle is a little later than the farmer's and shifts the high rates from fall toward winter. Accordingly in England, which is more dominated by the manufacturer, the cycle, though similar to that just observed for the United States, is shifted slightly forward, as is shown in Chart 41.[29]

§10. *Summary*

Although the facts presented in this chapter do not prove the theory presented in previous chapters they are not in conflict with it. According to the theory, if there is a high degree of foresight, self-control, and re-gard for posterity and income streams are large and plentiful in food-element, or have a descending time shape, then, other things being equal, the tendency will be for the rate of interest to be low, capital will be accu-mulated, the community will lend to other communities, and the instruments it creates will be more durable. We find these results present in actual fact where the antecedent conditions enumerated are also present. Re-versing the conditions, we find reversed results. Of course these statistical evidences are very general, since we never can assert that "other things are equal," and thus isolate and measure any one particular factor, as in the more exact inductions of physical science.

[29] See Palgrave, *Bank Rate and the Money Market*, p. 97.

CHAPTER XIX

THE RELATION OF INTEREST TO MONEY AND PRICES

§1. *Price Changes and Interest Rates*

No problem in economics has been more hotly debated than that of the various relations of price levels to interest rates. These problems are of such vital importance that I have gone to much trouble and expense to have such data as could be found compiled, compared, and analyzed. The principal result of these comparisons are given in this chapter.

The general theory of the relationship between the rate of interest and the buying power of money was summarized in Chapter II. The main object of this chapter is to ascertain to what extent, if at all, a change in the general price level actually affects the market rates of interest.

Since the theory of Chapter II presupposes foresight, the question arises at the outset: How is it possible for a borrower or lender to foresee variations in the general price level with the resultant increase or decrease in the buying power of his money? A change in the value of money is hard to determine. Few business men have any clear ideas about it. If we ask a merchant whether or not he takes account of appreciation or depreciation of money values, he will say he never heard of it, that "a dollar is a dollar!" In his mind, other things may change in terms of money, but money itself does not change. Most people are subject to what may be called "the money illusion," and think instinctively of money as constant and incapable of appreciation or depreciation. Yet it may be true that they do take account, to some extent at least, even if unconsciously, of a change in the buying power of money, under guise of a change in the level of prices in general. If the price level falls in such a way that they may expect for themselves a shrinking margin of profit, they will be cautious about borrowing unless interest falls, and this very unwillingness to borrow, lessening the demand in the money market, will tend to bring interest down. On the other hand, if inflation is going on, they will scent rising prices ahead and so rising money profits, and will be stimulated to borrow unless the rate of interest rises enough to discourage them, and their willingness to borrow will itself tend to raise interest.

And today especially, foresight is clearer and more prevalent than ever before. The business man makes a definite effort to look ahead not only as to his own particular business but as to general business conditions, including the trend of prices.

Evidence that an expected change in the price level does have an effect on the money rate of interest may be obtained from several sources. During the free-silver agitation of 1895 and 1896, municipalities could sell gold bonds on better terms than currency bonds. There was a strong desire on the part of lenders to insert a gold clause in their contracts, and to secure it they were willing to yield something in the interest rate.

The same tendency was strikingly shown in California during the inflation period of the Civil War.[1] For a time,

[1] Moses, Bernard, *Legal Tender Notes in California,* Quarterly Journal of Economics, October, 1892, p. 15.

gold contracts could not be enforced, and in consequence interest rates were exceptionally high.

§2. *United States Coin and Currency Bonds*

A more definite test may be made where two standards are simultaneously used. An excellent case of this kind is supplied by comparing two kinds of United States bonds, one payable in coin and the other in currency. From the prices for which these bonds sold in the market it is possible to calculate the interest realized by the investor. The currency bonds were known as currency sixes and matured in 1898 and 1899. The coin bonds selected for comparison were the fours of 1907. The table on page 402 gives the rates of interest realized in the two standards, together with the premium on gold.

Several points in this table deserve notice. In 1870 the investor realized 6.4 per cent in terms of gold but was willing to accept a return of only 5.4 per cent currency. Why should a gold bond be thus inferior to a paper bond? This has become intelligible in the light of the theory which was explained in Chapter II. It meant the hope of resumption. Just because paper was depreciated below gold and there was a chance of bringing it up to par, there was in prospect a great rise in its value, as compared with gold. It was not until 1878, just before resumption, when the prospect of any further rise disappeared, that the relative position of the two rates of interest was reversed. After resumption in 1879, when paper money did reach par with gold, the two bond rates remained very nearly equal for several years, until fears of inflation from Greenbackism and Free-Silverism again produced a divergence. The quotations for 1894, 1895, and 1896 showed a considerably higher rate of interest

TABLE 11

Rates of Interest Realized from Dates Named to Maturity[a]

	Coin	Currency	Price of Gold [a]		Coin	Currency
Jan. 1870....	6.4	5.4	119.9	Jan. 1879....	3.7	4.5
July 1870....	5.8	5.1	112.2	Jan. 1880....	3.8	4.0
Jan. 1871....	6.0	5.3	110.8	Jan. 1881....	3.3	3.4
July 1871....	5.8	5.0	113.2	Jan. 1882....	3.0	3.5
Jan. 1872....	5.3	4.9	109.5	Jan. 1883....	2.9	3.3
July 1872....	5.6	5.0	113.9	Jan. 1884....	2.6	2.9
Jan. 1873....	5.7	5.1	111.9	May 1885....	2.7	2.7
July 1873....	5.4	5.0	115.3	Jan. 1886....	2.6	2.6
Jan. 1874....	5.0	5.0	110.3	Jan. 1887....	2.3	2.6
July 1874....	5.1	4.9	110.7	Mar. 1888....	2.3	2.9
Jan. 1875....	5.0	4.7	112.6	Jan. 1889....	2.2	2.6
July 1875....	5.1	4.4	117.0	May 1890....	2.1	2.6
Jan. 1876....	4.7	4.4	112.9	July 1891....	2.4	3.0
July 1876....	4.5	4.2	112.3	Jan. 1892....	2.6	3.1
Jan. 1877....	4.5	4.4	107.0	Mar. 1893....	2.8	3.1
July 1877....	4.4	4.3	105.4	Nov. 1894....	2.7	3.5
Jan. 1878....	5.0	4.6	102.8	Aug. 1895....	2.8	3.6
July 1878....	3.9	4.4	100.7	Aug. 1896....	3.2	4.3

[a] Specie payments were resumed in 1879 and thenceforward the price of gold was, of course, 100.

in the currency standard than in the coin standard, as well as a higher rate in both standards than in previous years. The contrast is that between 2.7 per cent and 3.5 per cent in 1894, and between 3.2 per cent and 4.3 per cent in 1896. The divergence of the two rates is explain-

[a] This table has been obtained by the aid of the usual brokers' bond tables. In the case of currency bonds, it was only necessary to deduct accrued interest (if any) from the quoted price and look in the table for the interest which corresponds to the price so found and the number of years to maturity. This gives the rate in terms of "currency." In the case of coin bonds, since the quotations are given in currency, it is necessary to divide the quoted price by the price of gold in order to obtain their price in gold (i.e., "coin"), and then proceed as above indicated. We thus get the rate in terms of "coin." The quotations of prices of bonds and gold are the "opening" prices for the months named, and are taken from the Financial Review and its annual summary, The Commercial and Financial Chronicle, 1895, the (New York) Bankers' Magazine and the Bankers' Almanac. After 1884, January quotations were not always available.

[402]

able as the effect of the fear of Bryan's free-silver proposal, incorporated (July, 1896) in the platform of the Democratic party. Had free coinage of silver been restored at the ratio of 16 to 1, since the bondholders had the option of demanding either gold or silver in payment, coin bonds presumably would still have meant gold bonds. Hence investors were ready to accept lower interest on these bonds than on currency bonds.

§3. *Gold and Rupee Bonds*

Having compared the rates of interest of paper and coin bonds, we may next compare those of gold and silver securities. The comparison, to be of value, must be between gold and silver contracts in the same market and with the same security. Fortunately such contracts have been available in the London market of government securities. The loans of India have been made partly in gold and partly in silver, and both forms of securities have been quoted in London.[3] The interest on the silver bonds, or rather rupee bonds, was paid by draft on India. The sums actually received in English money depended on the state of the exchanges. The rate of interest in the silver standard was calculated[4] in the same way as was

[3] The silver bonds or "rupee paper" were issued to raise loans in India, but they were also enfaced for payment in England, and in 1893-1894 some Rx. 25,000,000 were on the London books. Burdett's *Official Intelligencer* (1894), p. 75.

[4] Thus, in 1880 the average price paid in London for "rupee paper" of face value Rx. 1000 yielding 4 per cent, or Rx. 40 per annum, was £79. In order to find the rate of interest realized by the investor, we must translate £79 into silver. The average rate of exchange in 1880 was 20d. per rupee. Hence £79 were equivalent to 948 rupees. That is, speaking in terms of silver (or, more exactly, in terms of exchange on India), the price of a 4 per cent bond was 94.8, which, if the bond be treated as a perpetual annuity, yields the investor 4.3 per cent. In the same year, an India gold bond yielded 3.6 per cent.

shown for coin bonds in §2. The results follow:

TABLE 12

Rates of Interest Realized from Dates Named to Maturity or in Perpetuity [5]

	Rupee [a]	Gold [b]	Difference	Exchange on India
				Pence per Rupee
1865	4.3	4.1	.2	23.2
1868	4.3	4.0	.3	23.0
1870	4.3	4.0	.3	23.6
1871	4.1	3.8	.3	23.2
1872	3.9	3.7	.2	22.6
1873	3.9	3.7	.2	22.4
1874	3.9	3.8	.1	22.2
1875	4.0	3.6	.4	21.9
1876	4.1	3.7	.4	20.5
1877	4.1	3.7	.4	20.9
1878	4.2	3.9	.3	20.2
1879	4.4	3.7	.7	19.7
1880	4.3	3.6	.7	20.0
1881	4.0	3.4	.6	19.9
1882	3.9	3.5	.4	19.5
1883	4.1	3.4	.7	19.5
1884	4.1	3.3	.8	19.5
1885	4.1	3.5	.6	18.5
1886	4.1	3.5	.6	17.5
1887	4.1	3.4	.7	17.2
1888	4.1	3.1	1.0	16.5
1889	4.1	3.0	1.1	16.5
1890 (1st half)	4.0	3.0	1.0	17.6
1890 (2nd half).....	3.9	3.1	.8	19.3
1891	3.8	3.1	.7	17.1
1892	3.9	3.1	.8	15.3
1893	3.9	3.0	.9	15.0
1894	3.9	3.0	.9	13.5
1895	3.4	2.8	.6	13.4
1896	3.3	3.1	.2	14.3
1897	3.5	3.1	.4	15.1
1898	3.7	3.2	.5	16.0
1899	3.6	3.2	.4	16.1
1900	3.7	3.4	.3	16.0
1901	3.7	3.5	.2	16.0
1902	3.6	3.5	.1	16.0
1903	3.5	3.5	.0	16.0
1904	3.6	3.7	—.1	16.1
1905	3.6	3.6	.0	16.1
1906	3.6	3.2	.4	16.0

Footnotes to this table are given on page 405.

From this table it will be seen that the rates realized to investors in bonds of the two standards differed but slightly until 1875, when the fall of Indian exchange began. The average difference from 1875 to 1892 inclusive was 0.7 per cent. Within this period, from 1884, exchange fell much more rapidly than before, and the difference in the two rates of interest rose accordingly, amounting in one year to 1.1 per cent. Inasmuch as the two bonds were issued by the same government, possessed the same degree of security, were quoted side by side in the same market, and were similar in all important respects except in the standard in which they are expressed, the results afford evidence that the fall of exchange (after it once began) was, to some extent, discounted in advance and affected the rates of interest in those standards. Of course investors did not form perfectly definite estimates of the future fall, but the fear

---

ᵃ The quotation from which the interest was computed for 1895 and succeeding years is for 3½ per cent rupee paper. All previous quotations are for 4 per cent's. The 4 per cent's were repayable on three months notice; this notice was given in 1894, and the bonds redeemed or converted into 3¼ per cent's before the close of the year. To obtain the rate of interest realized, the London quotations in pounds sterling are first converted into rupees at the current rates of exchange, and then the bonds are treated as perpetual annuities. The results differ from those given in the Investor's Monthly Manual, because the rupee is there converted at a conventional value, not the market value.

ᵇ From 1865 to 1880 inclusive the figures refer to 4 per cent's, repayable October, 1888, or later; those of 1881 are for 3¼ per cent's maturing in 1931, and those for 1885 to 1906 are for 3 per cent's maturing in 1948.

ᶜ This table is made from averages of (usually ten) quotations distributed through each year, taken from the Economist, the Investor's Monthly Manual, and the (London) Bankers' Magazine. The fourth column is founded on the table in the *Report of the Indian Currency Committee* (1893), p. 27, but is corrected to apply to calendar instead of official years.

of a fall predominated in varying degrees over the hope of a rise.

The year 1890 was one of great disturbance in exchanges, the average for the first six months being 17.6 and for the last six months, 19.3. The gold price of the silver bonds rose from an average for the first six months of 73.8 to 83.5 for the last six months, but the rise in their silver price was only from 100.6 to 103.7, showing that the increase of confidence in the future of silver was not great, and, in fact, only reduced the disparity in the interest from 1.0 to .8 per cent.

This great rise in exchange and the slight revival in silver securities occurred simultaneously with the passage of the Sherman Act of July, 1890, by which the United States was to purchase four and a half million ounces of silver per month. The disturbance was doubtless due in some measure to the operation, or expected operation, of that law.

This is not the only case in which the relative prices of rupee paper and gold bonds were probably affected by political action. One of the smallest differences in the two rates occurs in 1878, which was the year of the Bland Act and of the first International Monetary Conference.

After the closure of the Indian mints to silver on June 26, 1893, exchange rose from 14.7 to 15.9, the gold price of rupee paper from 62 to 70, and consequently its rupee price from 101.2 to 105.7.

From this point the exchange again dropped, much to the mystification of those who had predicted an established parity between gold and silver at the new legal rate of 16d per rupee. There was much discussion as to the reasons for the failure of the legal rate to become operative. The chief reason seems to have been that the

closure of the mints to silver attracted into the circulation
silver from other channels, especially old native hoards.
Within a few years, however, this source of supply was
dried up so that the legal par was reached in 1898 and
was maintained thereafter, subject only to the slight variations of exchange due to the cost of shipping specie.

But until the par was proved actually stable by two
or three years' experience, the public refused to have
confidence that gold and the rupee were once more to
run parallel. Their lack of confidence was shown in the
difference in the rates of interest in gold and rupee securities during the transition period, 1893-1898, and the
two or three succeeding years. From 1893 to 1900 inclusive the two rates averaged .5 per cent apart. From
1901 to 1906 inclusive, the average difference was only
.1 per cent,[6] showing that confidence in the gold value
of the rupee had been established.

§4. *Money Interest and Real Interest*

The foregoing comparisons relate to *simultaneous* rates
of interest in two contrasted monetary standards each
actually used for loan contracts. We now turn to a comparison between money rates and real rates of interest,
mentioned in Chapter II. Unfortunately no contracts in
terms of real or commodity standards are available for
quotation. All we can do is to note the changes in the

[6] The preceding comparisons serve only to establish the influence of
the expected divergence between the two standards on the rates of
interest, but afford no exact measure of that influence. In order to
measure the extent to which the fall of silver was allowed for by investors, it would be necessary to examine the rates realized during
specific periods. Somewhat unsatisfactory attempts to do this (both for
the case above of American gold and "currency" bonds and for the case
below of Indian gold and "rupee bonds") were made in my *Appreciation
and Interest,* but are not reproduced here.

price level, translate the actual rates in terms of money into real rates, and compare *successive* periods. Such comparisons are not very satisfactory, since no two periods, not even successive periods, are so alike industrially that we can say that they differ only as to the state of the monetary standard as reflected in the index numbers of prices. Of course, influences other than changes in money affect interest rates.

Detailed tables showing the average annual rate of change in the commodity price level,[7] the rates of money interest, and the rates of real interest for London, New York, Berlin, Paris, Calcutta, and Tokyo are given in basic tables in the Appendix to this chapter. Wholesale commodity prices were used in computing these rates although cost of living indexes would have been preferable for this purpose and more in harmony with my theory of income. But cost of living indexes do not exist for the period covered.

Chart 42 shows the annual rate of change in the commodity price level (upper part) compared with the market rates of interest (lower part) in the London market over the period 1825 to 1927. The chart also gives the real rate by a dotted line, but this may, for the present, be overlooked.

It will be observed that the entire period is broken up into sub-periods, which conform to rather definite and successively contrasted price movements. These sub-periods were allowed to choose themselves, so to say. That is, they were so chosen that each period should show a rather distinct change in the rate of price change as compared with the preceding and succeeding periods.

[7] The basic tables for computing the rate of price changes and the method of computation are given in the Appendix to this chapter §1.

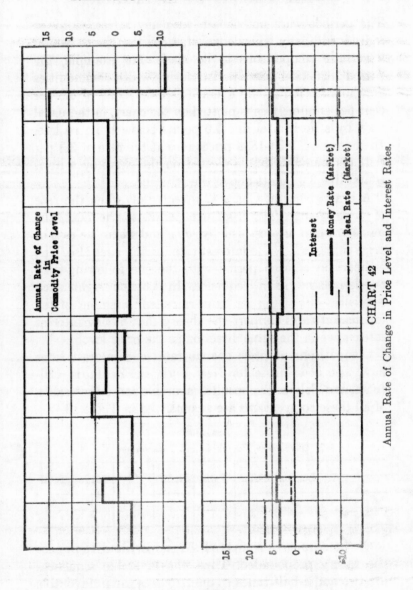

CHART 42

Annual Rate of Change in Price Level and Interest Rates.

The periods were not chosen with any reference to, or indeed with any knowledge of, how the choice would affect the comparisons to be made. For example, the period 1825-1834 was a period during which commodities at wholesale fell at the average (annual) rate of 3.0 per cent per annum; this is plotted on the chart, in the usual way, by a horizontal line 3.0 points below the zero line. In the period 1834-1839 prices rose at the rate of 3.3 per cent per annum; this is plotted on the chart by a horizontal line 3.3 points above the zero line.

A brief glance at Chart 42 reveals that when the rate of price change *falls* from one period to the next, the money rate of interest usually *falls,* and when the rate of price change *rises,* the interest rate usually *rises* also. The comparison of each period with the one following may be designated as a sequence. In London eight such sequences out of ten for bank rates, and nine out of ten for market rates support the theory that money interest rates move in the same direction as the price level.

Comparisons of price change rates and interest rates have also been made for New York, Berlin, Paris, Calcutta, and Tokyo. The results, favorable and unfavorable, of all these comparisons are summarized in Table 13.

TABLE 13
Sequences, Favorable and Unfavorable

	London	Berlin	Paris	N. Y.	Cal-cutta	Tokyo	Total
Favorable ...	17	10	0	4	6	1	38
Unfavorable .	3	2	1	3	3	3	15

Of the sequences compared, 38 support and 15 oppose the theory propounded. Thus, the favorable sequences are two and a half times as numerous as the unfavorable sequences. This is a large preponderance, especially when we consider that there are so many inexactnesses in the statistical data and so many other causes affecting the rate of interest besides changes in the price level.

The same result may be expressed in terms of correlation coefficients. When we correlate interest rates with price changes for the important industrial countries (England, Germany, United States), fairly high coefficients (about $+ 0.7$) are obtained. Correlating the first differences, that is, *changes* in interest rates and rates of price changes, likewise, shows a fairly high relationship in accord with the theory. However, the correlation for the data of all countries combined is insignificant. For all the countries studied we find $+.036$; for the corresponding first differences, $-.165$. It is seen that the well defined movements of prices and interest in the principal countries are largely offset by the movements in the countries of lesser economic importance. To obtain more decisive evidence upon the relationship studied, it is necessary to resort to the more rigorous analysis given in subsequent sections.

The evidence obtained from the comparisons in this section indicate that there is a very apparent, though feeble, tendency for the interest rate to be high when prices are rising, and the reverse. The adjustment is imperfect and rather irregular, but in the great majority of cases the tendency is evident.

§5. *Real Interest Varies More Than Money Interest*

If perfect foresight existed, continuously rising prices would be associated *not* with a continuously rising rate of interest but with a continuing high rate of interest, and falling prices would be associated not with a continuously falling rate of interest but with a continuing low rate of interest, and a constant price level would be associated with a constant rate of interest—assuming, in each case, that other influences than price change remained the same.

This perfect theoretical relationship of interest rates to price levels, assuming perfect foresight, is shown in

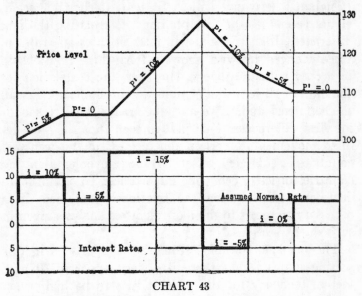

CHART 43

Theoretical Relation of Price Level (P) and Interest Rates (i).

Chart 43, showing high (not rising) interest rates while prices are rising, and low (not falling) interest rates while prices are falling. The real rate would remain constant at, say, 5 per cent under the ideal conditions here assumed.

In this chart, i stands for interest rate and P' for price change, but the upper line indicates the price level. When

in the first period the price level rises, the price change
(P') is assumed to be at the rate of 5 per cent per annum.
In the next period, the price level remains constant so
that price change is zero, and so on as indicated. The
lower curve shows the theoretical effects on the rate of
interest. In the first period, it would be 5 per cent above
normal; in the second period, normal; and so on.

One obvious result of such an ideally prompt and perfect adjustment would undoubtedly be that money interest would be far more variable than it really is and that
when it was translated into real interest this real interest
would be comparatively steady. What we actually find,
however, is the reverse—a great unsteadiness in real interest when compared with money interest.

Real interest, however, as shown by the dotted lines
on Chart 42, changed in the opposite way to money interest, due to the lack of foresight and adjustment.
Attention is called to the period 1852-1857 in London,
during which prices rose very fast (that is, money depreciated) simultaneously with, and mainly because of,
the great gold production. The market rate of interest
averaged 4.7 per cent, which was higher than in any
subsequent or in any previous period. Yet during this
period of apparently highest interest rates, lenders were
receiving, in real interest, less than nothing for their
savings. Also in the inflation period 1914-1920, bank
rates reached their highest peak, 5.2 per cent, while average market rates, at 4.4 per cent, were but little lower
than in 1852-1857. Yet in terms of real commodities those
who saved and deposited or invested at the bank rates or
market rates of interest were mulcted 9 to 10 per cent for
their abstinence and sacrifices. In the following period,
1920-1927, however, the savers and lenders got back more

than all they, or their predecessors, lost in the previous period. The tremendous fall in prices in 1920 and 1921 boosted the real interest rate above 15 per cent. Thus the computed real rate is exceedingly erratic during a serious inflation or deflation.

Chart 44 represents in a different way the same theoretical relationship between price change and the rate of

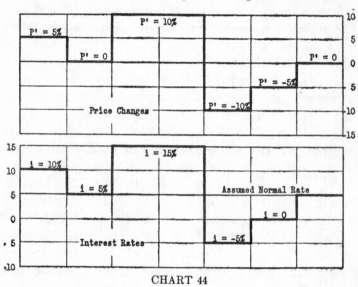

CHART 44

Theoretical Relation of Price Changes (P') and Interest Rates (i).

interest as that depicted on Chart 43. In Chart 44, price change (P') is represented not by the slope of a line, but by distance measured above or below the zero line. Thus when the price level is rising at the rate of 5 per cent per annum, P' is represented by a horizontal line 5 per cent above zero. When prices are stationary, P' drops to zero, and so on. If men had perfect foresight, they would adjust the money interest rate so as exactly to counterbalance

[414]

or offset the effect of changes in the price level, thus causing the real interest rate to remain unchanged at the normal rate.

The following table shows that the standard deviation from the mean is far greater for the computed real rate of interest than for the actual rate of interest.

TABLE 14

Standard Deviations of Money Interest and Real Interest

	Number of Periods	Standard Deviations	
		Market Interest	Computed Real Interest
London	11	.62	6.1
New York	8	1.07	8.5
Berlin	7	.73	5.0
Calcutta	11	.57	7.5
Tokyo	5	.69	7.0

This table shows that the real rate of interest in terms of commodities is from seven to thirteen times as variable as the market rate of interest expressed in terms of money. This means that men are unable or unwilling to adjust at all accurately and promptly the money interest rates to changed price levels. Negative real interest could scarcely occur if contracts were made in a composite commodity standard. The erratic behavior of real interest is evidently a trick played on the money market by the "money illusion" when contracts are made in unstable money. The computed real rate of interest was *minus* 7.4 per cent in New York in the period 1860-1865 and was still lower during 1915-1920. The rate was nearly minus 100 per cent in Germany during the period of most rapid inflation.

Another symptom of the same imperfection of adjustment is the fact that the adjustment is very *slow*. When prices begin to rise, money interest is scarcely affected. It requires the cumulative effect of a long rise, or of a marked rise in prices, to produce a definite advance in the interest rate. If there were no "money illusion" and if adjustments of interest were perfect, unhindered by any failure to foresee future changes in the purchasing power of money or by custom or law or any other impediment, we should have found a very different set of facts.

§6. *Interest Rates and Rates of Price Change*

The roughness of the comparisons between interest rates and price levels thus far made impels to further study of this important problem. For these more rigorous comparisons, the statistics of prices and of bond yields in Great Britain and the United States have been taken, being the only reliable statistics ready at hand which permit of long trend comparisons.

Since the theory being investigated is that interest rates move in the opposite direction to changes in the value of money, that is, in the same direction as price changes, the first analysis made is the same as that already made by rougher methods, the comparison of *price changes* with interest rates.

For the rate of change of prices, the customary link relative expression was at first used in a preliminary study of quarterly United States data for the period 1890-1904. But to ensure full comparability with my related studies of several years ago on price changes and trade variations, the symmetrical expression P' (rate of price change per annum) is used throughout. The precise derivation of P' is given in my paper, *Our Unstable Dollar and the So-Called Business Cycle.*[8] The upper part of Chart 45 gives the correlation coefficient (r) obtained by correlating the long term interest rates as reflected in the yield of British consols with percentage changes in prices computed from the British wholesale index numbers of Sauerbeck and The Statist.[9] The lower part of this chart gives the r's for bond yields and percentage price changes in the United States.[10]

In Great Britain, the price changes from 1820 to 1924 fall into three clearly defined periods, namely, 1820 to 1864, a period of fluctuating prices with no marked upward or downward trend in prices; 1865 to 1897, a period of declining prices; 1898 to 1924, a period chiefly of rising prices, including a big boom from 1915 to 1920, followed by a crash and more stable prices since 1922.

A very brief examination of the charts below indicates that there is little or no *apparent* relationship between *price changes* and interest rates in any of the periods studied in either country except for 1898-1924 in Great Britain. For the period 1820-1864 in Great Britain we obtain a maximum inverse correlation of —0.459, without lagging. For the period 1898-1924, we get as a maximum + 0.623 when i is lagged 4 years and + 0.678 when i is lagged 6 years. Lag means the time interval between a

[8] See Journal of the American Statistical Association. June, 1925, p. 81, footnote 3.

[9] The British bond yields here used were taken from an article by A. H. Gibson, *The Future Course of High Class Investment Values,* The Bankers', Insurance Managers' and Agents' Magazine, January, 1923, p. 15. Reprinted in revised form in The Spectator, March 7, 1925.

[10] The United States bond yields here used were taken from the Statistical Bulletin, 1928-1929, of the Standard Statistics Company. Percentage price changes were computed from the Wholesale Commodity Price Indexes of the United States Bureau of Labor Statistics.

price change and the associated change in the interest rate. Chart 45 shows the results of lagging interest rates behind price changes on the one hand and lagging price changes behind interest rates on the other. For the United States, without lagging, $r = -0.289$, while the highest

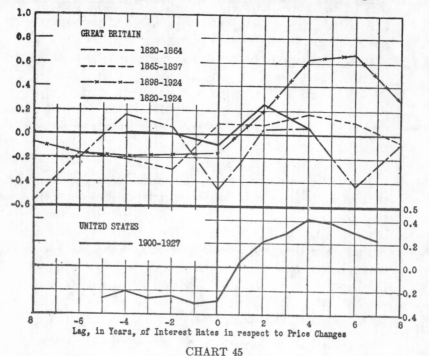

CHART 45

Correlation Coefficients Between P' and i for Various Lags. Yearly Data, Great Britain, 1820-1924; United States, 1890-1927.

correlation is $+0.406$ when i is lagged 4 years. These results suggest that no direct and consistent connection of any real significance exists between P' and i.

The variations in r for different lags may be due to the zigzag cycles in the data correlated. The maximum value

[418]

of r establishes definitely that, characteristically, movements in i lag behind corresponding movements in P'. The small numerical value of r suggests that the relation can be revealed only faintly by P' and i directly. But a little consideration suggests that the influence of P' or i may be *assumed to be distributed in time*—as, in fact, must evidently be true of any influence. This hypothesis proved quite fruitful in my studies several years ago, in the course of which the theory of *distributed influence* or, if we wish to avoid the implication of cause and effect, of *distributed lag* was developed in considerable detail.[11]

The reader may consult the references cited for details. It must suffice here to point out only the essence of the transformation of P' into the derived quantity $\bar{P}'$, measuring the distributed influence of sundry P'. Arithmetically, $\bar{P}'$ is merely a certain weighted average of sundry successive P''s. (See (a) and (b) referred to in the footnote.) In any specific problem the number of successive P''s that enter into the average $\bar{P}''$s depends on the length of the time interval during which the influence of any P' is *assumed* to be perceptible. The weights used vary in a certain functional form, generally that of a skew probability curve. Thus, in applying the theory at least two parameters are involved: (1) the length of the influence interval (which determines the number of P''s

[11] The theory of distributed influence and lag was developed incidentally in the course of my studies of price-trade relations reported in several papers. See (a) *The Business Cycle Largely a "Dance of the Dollar,"* Journal of the American Statistical Association, December, 1923, p. 5, top paragraph; (b) *Fluctuations in Prive-Levels* in The Problem of Business Forecasting by Warren M. Persons, William T. Foster, Albert Hettinger. Boston, Houghton Mifflin Company, 1924, pp. 50-52; and particularly, (c) *Our Unstable Dollar and the So-Called Business Cycle*, Journal of the American Statistical Association, June, 1925, pp. 179-202.

that enter into the composite $\overline{P}'$), and (2) the form of variation of the weights. As indicated in reference (b) in the above footnote, the form of variation of the weights is exactly—but in reverse order—the form in which the distributed influence of any P' tapers off during successive periods of time.[12]

[12] A price change P'_m pertaining to the month t_m exerts an influence, $F(t_{m+\lambda})$, whose intensity is proportional to 8 during t_{m+3}, to 7 during t_{m+4}, ..., to 1 during t_{m+10}, to 0 during t_{m+11}.

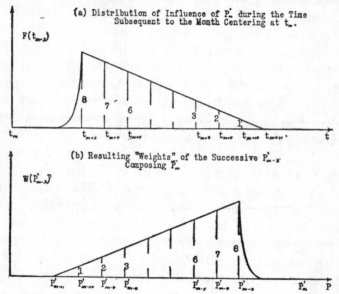

(a) Distribution of Influence of P'_m during the Time Subsequent to the Month Centering at t_m.

(b) Resulting "Weights" of the Successive $P'_{m-\lambda}$ Composing $\overline{P}'_m$

Conversely the aggregate influence on the affected variable during the month t_m consists of the various $P'_{m-\lambda}$ which enter with the following weights tapering off in arithmetical progression; P'_{m-3} with weight 8, P'_{m-4} with weight 7, ..., P'_{m-10} with weight 1, P'_{m-11} with weight 0. The numerical measure of this composite influence is:

$$\overline{P}'_m = \frac{1}{36}[8\,P'_{m-3} + 7\,P'_{m-4} + \dots\. + 1\,P'_{m-10} + 0\,P'_{m-11}],$$

the divisor 36 being the sum of the weights,

$$36 = 8 + 7 + \dots\. + 1 + 0.$$

[420]

In the present study we must limit our investigation to only one type of distribution of influence and variation of weights. The form chosen is the simple straight line function or arithmetical progression which proved most effective and easily calculated in my 1925 study.

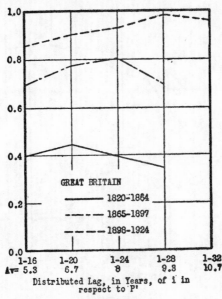

CHART 46

Correlation Coefficients Between $\bar{P}'$ and i for Various Distributions of Lag. $\bar{P}'$ is the Combined Effect at Any Point of Time of the Influence of Preceding P' 's with Lags Distributed. Yearly Data, Great Britain, 1820-1924.

Several periods of influence range, however, were tried. The results for the British and American yearly data are shown in Charts 46 and 47.

The figures at the bottom of Charts 46 and 47 refer to the number of years over which the effect of price changes is taken into account in the correlations between $\bar{P}'$ and i. For example, in Chart 46, the figures 1–16 mean that the

[421]

effect of a price change is assumed to begin the first year after the change and to cease at the end of 16 years. The weighted average of the distributed lag is 5.3 years. The longest distribution shown at the right is from 1 to 32 years, or a weighted average of 10.7 years.

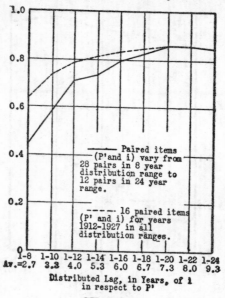

CHART 47

Correlation Coefficients Between $\bar{P}'$ and i for Various Distributions of Lag. $\bar{P}'$ is the Combined Effect at Any Point of Time of the Influence of Preceding P''s with Lags Distributed. Yearly Data, United States, 1900-1927.

The charts picture only the effects of the distributed lag when interest rates follow behind price changes.

Experiment proved that when price changes were lagged behind the distributed influence of changing interest rates, the correlation coefficients were too small to have any significance.

The high and consistent correlations shown in the

above charts are in striking contrast to the results previously obtained from correlating P' directly with i. The assumption that a change in prices occurring during one year exhausts its influence upon interest rates in the same year or in another single year is shown to be quite wrong, as might be expected. Our first correlations seemed to indicate that the relationship between P' and i is either very slight or obscured by other factors. But when we make the much more reasonable supposition that price changes do not exhaust their effects in a single year but manifest their influence with diminishing intensity, over long periods which vary in length with the conditions, we find a very significant relationship, especially in the period which includes the World War, when prices were subject to violent fluctuations.

The British figures for 1820-1864 give the lowest correlations of any included in this study. These low figures are possibly due in part to the less accurate price indexes in those early years. It is noteworthy that the correlation coefficients are distinctly lower for the United States in the period 1900-1927 than they are for Great Britain in the period 1898-1924. It is also interesting that for Great Britain in 1898-1924, the highest value of r ($+ 0.980$) is reached when effects of price changes are assumed to be spread over 28 years or for a weighted average of 9.3 years, while for the United States the highest r ($+ 0.857$) is for a distribution of the influence due to price changes over 20 years or a weighted average of 7.3 years.

Chart 48 shows graphically the smoothing effect of distributing the influence of P' over various periods.

By assuming a distribution of effect of price changes over several years according to the form described above, the relationship between price changes and interest rates

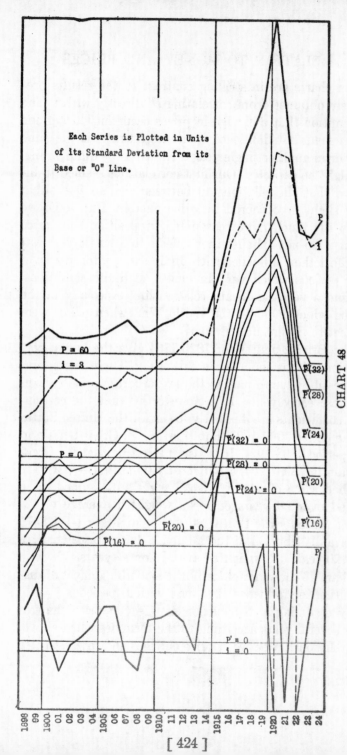

Each Series is Plotted in Units of its Standard Deviation from its Base or "0" Line.

P = 60
i = 3
P = 0

$\bar{P}(32) = 0$
$\bar{P}(28) = 0$
$\bar{P}(24)` = 0$
$\bar{P}(20) = 0$
$\bar{P}(16) = 0$

P' = 0
i = 0

P
i

$\bar{P}(32)$
$\bar{P}(28)$
$\bar{P}(24)$
$\bar{P}(20)$
$\overline{P(16)}$

P'

1898 99 1900 01 02 03 04 1905 06 07 08 09 1910 11 12 13 14 1915 16 17 18 19 1920 21 22 23 24

CHART 48

Curves Showing P, P', $\bar{P}$ and i. Yearly Data, Great Britain, 1898-1924.

which was only faintly revealed by the first direct comparisons is clearly revealed. The high correlation coefficients obtained by means of the method of distributing the influence of P' and i show that the theory tested in this chapter conforms closely to reality, especially during periods of rather marked price movements.

Furthermore the results and other evidence, indicate that, over long periods at least, interest rates *follow* price movements. The reverse, which some writers have asserted, seems to find little support. Experiments, made with United States short term interest rates, to test the alternative hypothesis of distributed influence of interest rate changes instead of price changes, gave results of negligible significance. Our investigations thus corroborate convincingly the theory that a direct relation exists between P' and i, the price changes usually preceding and determining like changes in interest rates.

§7. *Short Term Interest Rates and Prices in the United States*

A study of short term commercial paper rates in relation to short term price movements corroborates the evidence obtained from correlating long term interest rates and price changes. The New York interest rates on short term commercial paper have been correlated with changes in the quarterly wholesale price indexes computed from monthly indexes of the United States Bureau of Labor Statistics for the periods 1890-1914 and 1915-1927.[13]

[13] Interest rates were taken from The Statistical Bulletin, 1928-1929, of The Standard Statistics Co. The price indexes are computed from the United States Bureau of Labor Statistics. See Appendix to this chapter, §2, for these quarterly data.

On Chart 49 are plotted the curves showing the quarterly price indexes and the P' and $\overline{P}'$ derived from them, with the interest rates for the entire period 1890-1927. $\overline{P}'$ is shown for 120 quarters or 30 years.

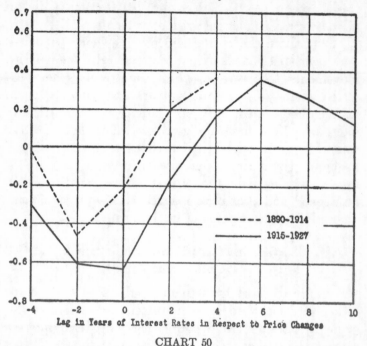

CHART 50

Correlation Coefficients Between P' and i: for Various Lags, Quarterly Data, United States, 1890-1927.

These curves of quarterly data tell much the same story as is told by the curves representing yearly data, shown in Chart 48, for Great Britain. $\overline{P}'$ obviously corresponds much more closely to i than does P'.

Chart 50 shows the rather erratic variation of the r's computed from i and P' directly without distributing the effects of price changes.

[426]

on the farmer of the deflation of 1920 are now, in 1929, sufficiently acute to make farm relief a pressing political problem and that these economic effects may be expected to persist for many years to come. A further probable explanation of the surprising length of time by which the rate of interest lags behind price change is that between price changes and interest rates a third factor intervenes. This is business, as exemplified or measured by the volume of trade. It is influenced by price change and influences in turn the rate of interest.

§8. *Interest Rates and Price Indexes*

Thus far we have considered the relation of *changes* in the price level and interest rates. It remains to study the relations of the *price levels* themselves to interest rates. The same basic data are used as in the preceding sections, but we now correlate the price indexes directly with the interest rates in Great Britain and the United States.

Chart 52 shows the British long term interest rates (bond yields) plotted with the wholesale price index for the years 1820-1924.

It is apparent that the P curve and the i curve, as plotted, conform very closely. Furthermore, lagging interest rates one year gives the highest obtainable degree of correspondence. The corresponding data for the United States, plotted on Chart 57 below without lagging i, shows the same close relationship between P and i.

On Chart 53 are plotted the curves of the correlation coefficients computed for P and i for Great Britain and the United States.

The r's for the whole period 1820-1924 for Great Britain are not shown on Chart 53 since they reveal nothing not shown by the *r*'s for the shorter periods. These highly significant correlations seem to establish definitely that over long periods of time high or low interest rates *follow* high or low prices by about one year.

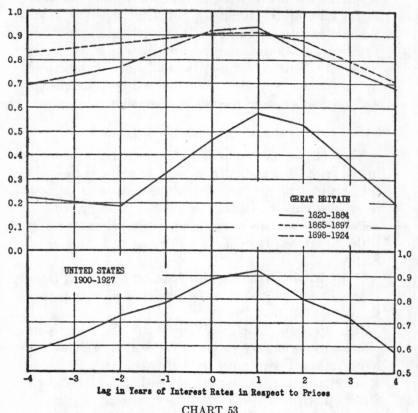

CHART 53

Correlation Coefficients Between *P* and *i* for Various Lags. Yearly Data, Great Britain, 1820-1924; United States, 1900-1927.

Comparison of short term interest rates with quarterly index numbers gives results of no significance for the period 1890-1914. On the contrary, the *r*'s obtained from

[430]

comparing these series over the period 1915-1927 are high; without lagging $r = + 0.709$; lagging one quarter, $r = + 0.829$; two quarters, $r = + 0.891$; four quarters, $r = + 0.838$. In both periods the coefficients of correlation grow smaller as the P's are lagged behind i, while they grow larger when i is lagged behind P. The results from the analysis of the short term data, while differing in some respects, may be said to confirm the results obtained from comparing the long term data.

§9. *Elimination of Trends*

These high correlations do not necessarily mean that the interest rate will always be high when prices are high and low when prices are low, but the tendency toward this is definitely established.

The correlations obtained for all periods and subperiods considered are unusually high. It is necessary to guard against the possibility that these coefficients are of the familiar nonsense type, and are spuriously high because of the presence of *secular trend* forces that affect both P and i. Due consideration was given to the control devices that have wide acceptance in the literature of statistics, such as "elimination of trend" and "seasonal" fluctuations. The general methodology of analysis of time series is still in the process of formulation. The specific problem of trend analysis is still largely unsolved.[15] In the present case, it is rather doubtful that trend forces are involved which should be eliminated. What is desired in

[15] See Pearson and Elderton, *The Variate Difference Method,* Biometrica, Vol. XIV, 1923, pp. 281-309; W. M. Persons, *Statistics and Economic Theory,* Review of Economic Statistics, Vol. VII, No. 13, July, 1925, pp. 179-197; Anderson, *The Decomposition of Statistical Series into Components,* Journal of the Royal Statistical Society, Vol. XC, pt. 3, 1927, pp. 548-570.

all the preceding comparisons of price levels and interest rates is to discover what precise relation obtains between interest rates and prices *in the long run*. It is like giving the play of *Hamlet* without Hamlet to eliminate the secular trends of i and P from a study of long term relationships in which these very secular trends are most important and often dominant influences.

However, to anticipate possible criticisms and errors, the results of eliminating secular trends of prices and interest rates have been studied. These additional studies are also made for another and more important purpose, namely, to discover whether or not the shorter so-called *cyclical movements* of prices influence long-term interest rates in the same way as the long *secular price movements* have been shown to do. For simplicity, least square straight line and parabola trends were used. These will answer sufficiently the present purpose. In addition, a cubic trend was applied to the yearly data for the United States for the period 1900 to 1927 and to the British data for the corresponding period.

Charts 54, 55, and 56 show the curves of price levels and interest rates in Great Britain for the period 1820-1924 with straight line trends and parabolic trends plotted, while Chart 57 shows the corresponding curves for the United States for the period 1900-1927.

The results, after eliminating these secular trends, are interesting and amazing. The correlation coefficients with straight line trends eliminated are naturally smaller than when these trends are included, but they are still significantly high except for the period 1865-1897 in Great Britain. In the majority of cases, the characteristic lag of about a year of interest rates behind prices gives the highest correlation.

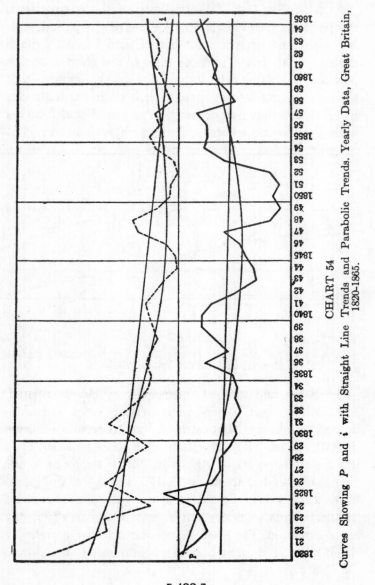

CHART 54

Curves Showing P and i with Straight Line Trends and Parabolic Trends. Yearly Data, Great Britain, 1820-1865.

As a further test of the validity of the comparisons, the parabola trend deviations for the recent period, ending with the high point for both P and i in 1920, have been computed and plotted, though the charts are not here shown. It might be supposed that the elimination of a parabolic trend from these violently fluctuating series would leave only erratic wiggles in the P and i curves with little or no correspondence with each other. That

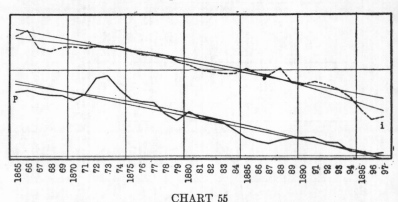

CHART 55

Curves Showing P and i with Straight Line Trends Parabolic Trends. Yearly Data, Great Britain, 1865-1897.

price levels and interest rates are very closely related, even when great secular and cyclical forces are eliminated, is clearly demonstrated by the results of these investigations. The correlation coefficients obtained from the data for the period ending in 1920 with the parabolic trends eliminated are about $+0.70$, which certainly indicates that yearly fluctuations, as well as cyclical and secular trends, of prices and interest are generally in the same direction. The coefficients obtained from correlating P and i with straight line trends eliminated are plotted on Chart 58.

[434]

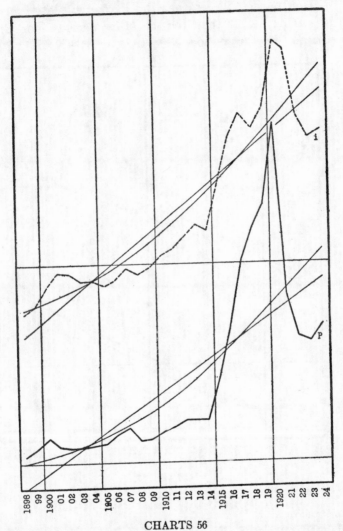

CHARTS 56

Curves Showing *P* and *i* with Straight Line Trends and Parabolic
Trends. Yearly Data, Great Britain, 1898-1924.

[435]

The reader will see that the r's for the latest period are much higher than for the other periods. For Great Britain in the period 1898-1924, $r = +0.851$ with i

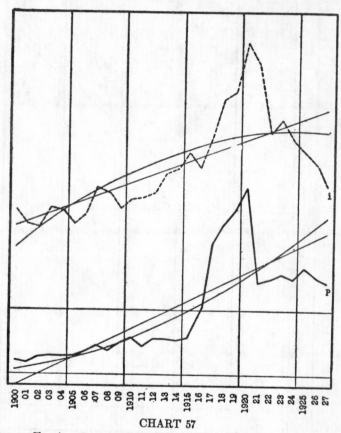

CHART 57

Curves Showing P and i with Straight Line Trends and Parabolic Trends. Yearly Data, United States, 1900-1927.

lagged one year. For the United States for the corresponding period 1900-1927, and with the same lag of i, we get $r = +0.806$. It is not worth while to plot the r's with P lagged behind i, since it is apparent at a glance that r decreases with the lagging of P.

When the parabolic trend is eliminated, the correlation coefficients for the cycles become insignificant ex-

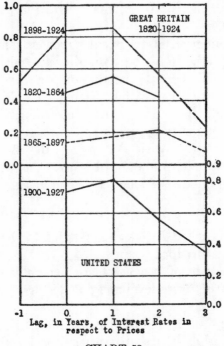

CHART 58

Correlation Coefficients Between P and i with Straight Line Trends Eliminated. Yearly Data, Great Britain, 1820-1865; 1865-1897; 1897-1924: United States, 1900-1927.

cept for the period including the World War. The highest r for the British data for 1820-1864 is $+ 0.319$ when i is lagged one year; for 1865-1897, the highest r is $+ 0.045$ with i lagged two years; for 1898-1924, r is $+ 0.829$ with no lagging, and $+ 0.817$ when i is lagged one year. The

United States data give r's of $+ 0.695$ without lag, and $+ 0.876$ with i lagged one year. Even when a cubic trend is eliminated for 1898-1924 the r's still remain significantly high, namely, without lagging, $r = + 0.794$ and with i lagged one year $r = 0.790$. For the United States without lagging, $r = + 0.525$ and with i lagged one year $r = + 0.769$.

The elimination of the secular trends from the comparisons makes the relationship of i and P depend solely upon the similarity of fluctuations in the shorter or cyclical periods. Even without Hamlet the play proves to be astonishingly informing and interesting. It is quite definitely demonstrated that, in times of marked price changes, as in the World War period, the effects of price movements are felt rather quickly upon the rates of interest, even in the case of long term bond yields.

§10. *Relations of Prices and Interest Interpreted*

The studies of P, P' and $\bar{P}'$ in relation to i have brought out four relationships:

(1) The rate of interest tends generally to be *high* during a *rising* price level and *low* during a *falling* price level;

(2) The rate of interest lags behind P' so that often the relationship is obscured when direct comparison is made;

(3) The rate of interest correlates very markedly with $\bar{P}'$, representing the *distributed* effect of lag. For recent years in Great Britain, the close relationship is indicated by $r = + 0.98$ when i is lagged and the effects of P' are distributed over 28 years;

(4) The rate of interest tends definitely to be *high* with a *high* price level and *low* with a *low* price level.

RELATION TO MONEY AND PRICES

We have also seen that the first three sets of facts fit in with the analysis presented, the first corresponding, although only roughly, with the ideal assumption of perfect foresight and adjustment, the second and third corresponding to the more realistic assumption of imperfect foresight and delayed, but accumulated, adjustment.

Two facts have, I think, now been well established. The first, that price changes influence the volume of trade, has been shown in earlier studies made by me.[16] The second, that the volume of trade influences the rate of interest, has been shown by Carl Snyder,[17] Col. Leonard Ayres,[18] Prof. Waldo F. Mitchell,[19] and others.

The evidence for both relationships is not only empirical but rational. Rising prices increase profits both actual and prospective, and so the profit taker expands his business. His expanding or rising income stream requires financing and increases the demand for loans.

In my study of the so-called business cycle, the lag of volume of trade, T, behind price changes when the influence of P' was distributed over a range of 25 months, was found to have a modal value of 9½ months. The

[16] See especially *Our Unstable Dollar and the So-Called Business Cycle*, Journal of the American Statistical Association, June, 1925, pp. 181-202; *A Statistical Relation Between Unemployment and Price Changes*, International Labour Review, Vol. XIII, No. 6, June, 1926, pp. 785-792.

[17] Snyder, Carl, *The Influence of the Interest Rate on the Business Cycle*, American Economic Review, Vol. XV, No. 4, Dec., 1925, pp. 684-699; *Interest Rates and the Business Cycle*, American Economic Review, Vol. XVI, No. 3, Sept., 1926, pp. 660-663.

[18] Ayres, Cleveland Trust Co., Business Bulletin, June 15, 1928, and Aug. 15, 1928.

[19] Mitchell, *Interest Cost and the Business Cycle*, American Economic Review, Vol. XVI, No. 2, June, 1926, pp. 209-221; *Supplementary Note on Interest Costs*, American Economic Review, Vol. XVI, No. 3, Sept., 1926, pp. 451-452.

lag of i behind T using a simple lag was found by Carl Snyder to be 10 to 15 months, by Leonard Ayres to be about 14 months and by Waldo F. Mitchell about 6½ months.

If we add the lag of T behind P' which I found to be over all about 25 months, and the lag of i behind T of 14 months, found by Snyder and Ayres, we obtain a combined lag of i behind P' of 39 months. This combined lag obtained by simple addition is far shorter than the lags discovered in the calculations presented above, whether for yearly or for quarterly price changes in relation to i. Apparently the double distribution of the lag of T behind P' and again of i behind T may result in a greater lag than would be obtained by simple addition.

The fourth relationship stated above must be, I think, regarded as an accidental consequence of the other three. At any rate, it seems impossible to interpret it as representing an independent relationship with any rational theoretical basis. It certainly stands to reason that *in the long run* a high level of prices due to previous monetary and credit inflation ought not to be associated with any higher rate of interest than the low level before the inflation took place. It is inconceivable that, for instance, the rate of interest in France and Italy should tend to be permanently higher because of the depreciation of the franc and the lira, or that a billion-fold inflation as in Germany or Russia would, after stabilization, permanently elevate interest accordingly. This would be as absurd as it would be to suppose that the rate of interest in the United States would be put on a higher level if we were to call a cent a dollar and thereby raise the price level a hundredfold. The price level as such can evidently have no permanent influence on the rate of interest except as a matter of transition from one level or plateau to another.

The *transition* from one price level to another may and does work havoc as we have seen, and the havoc follows with a lag which is widely distributed. The result is that during a period of inflation the interest rate is raised *cumulatively*, so that at the end of this period when the price level is high, the interest rate is also high. It would doubtless in time revert to normal if the new high level were maintained, but this seldom happens. Usually prices reach a peak and then fall. During this fall the interest rate is subject to a cumulative downward pressure so that it becomes subnormal at or near the end of the fall of prices. Thus, at the peak of prices, interest is high, not because the price level is high, but because it has been rising and, at the valley of prices, interest is low, not because the price level is low, but because it has been falling.

Another consideration seems to complete the explanation of the close association between high and low price levels with high and low interest respectively. This is the necessity for banks to cope with maladjustments following inflation and deflation. Mr. R. G. Hawtrey has emphasized this point in a letter to me, and I have summarized his views almost in his own words:

When credit is expanding, the rising price level and high profits bring about a high rate of interest. When the expansion has reached the limit permitted by the stock of gold, the rate of interest is put *still higher* in order to bring about a *fall* in the price level. When the fall in prices takes effect, a low rate of interest becomes appropriate, and when credit contraction has proceeded so far that a redundant supply of gold has accumulated, the rate of interest is depressed still lower in order to bring about a renewed rise in the price level. Thus a high rate of interest corresponds first with rising, then with falling, prices, and so synchronizes with high prices. A low rate of interest corresponds first with falling, and then with rising, prices, and so synchronizes with low prices.

The process of inflation boosts both prices and interest, until a still further boost of interest is made by the banks in order to stop the overextension, leaving a peak of prices with high interest before, at, and after that peak, while, contrariwise, the process of deflation reduces both prices and interest until a still further reduction of interest is made by the banks in order to stop the depression, leaving a valley of prices with low interest before, at, and after the valley.

Such considerations seem to be sufficient to explain the otherwise puzzling and apparently irrational coincidence which we have so often found to exist between high and low prices and high and low interest rates.

The only alternative interpretation of which I can think is that a high or low price level is not a monetary and nominal affair but a matter of real commodities. Sometimes, as in France and Italy just cited, the high prices may be closely associated with impoverishment. If it were true that a high price level usually signified a real scarcity of goods—a low income stream—while a low price level usually signified relative abundance, we could explain our puzzle by the relation of time preference to the size of the income stream. But the facts in general do not seem to justify such an interpretation,[20] least of all in the United States in the War years when the correlations are the highest. During that period, incomes increased at a tremendous rate, and interest rates advanced *pari passu*.

[20] See the author's *The Money Illusion*. New York, Adelphi Company, 1928, pp. 41-42.

§11. *Relations of Interest to Business and Prices*

As implied by what has just been said regarding banking policy, the relationships of P' and i are mutual. A change in i undoubtedly has an effect upon P' as well as the reverse. Our analyses have demonstrated that, in a decisive majority of instances, price changes precede changes in i. This does not mean that changes in the interest rate can never be used to forecast changes in prices and in business activity.[21] In fact, an arbitrary increase in i at any time does tend to pull down the level of general commodity prices, while a decrease in i tends to increase P. This is a fact which has been quite well established and is made use of by central banks in formulating their banking and credit policies.

The influence of changes in interest rates upon prices and business activity is made use of also by forecasting agencies in making their prognostications of business and price movements for the near future.[22] The fact that i follows P', in most instances over secular and cyclical periods, is not inconsistent with the other fact that every increase or decrease in i exerts an influence upon P in the

[21] Prof. Knut Wicksell was one of the first to recognize the influence of interest rates upon prices. See his book, *Geldzins und Güterpreise;* Prof. Alfred Marshall, Prof. Gustav Cassel, Rt. Hon. Reginald McKenna, Chairman of the Midland Bank of London, Mr. R. G. Hawtrey, of the Treasury of Great Britain, and many other well known economists, bankers, and business men have emphasized that business activity is influenced and may be largely controlled by manipulation of the discount rate.

[22] Mr. and Mrs. K. G. Karsten, for example, in their forecasts, make use of commercial paper rates in computing their forecasts of wholesale prices and business activity. They find an r of -0.98 between (1) the logarithms of P' and (2) the logarithms of the deviations of commercial interest rates from bond yields.

opposite direction. Within limits, a fall in the rate of interest may and often does produce a rise in prices and in business activity almost immediately. This effect may be continued for many months until increased prices again become dominant and pull the interest rate up again.

In so far as the rate of interest is cause and the price movements are effect, the correspondence is *just the opposite* of that which occurs in so far as the price movements are cause and the interest movements effect.

It is outside the scope of this treatise, which has to do only with things which affect the theory of the rate of interest, to attempt to explain fully all the very complicated relations connecting interest and business. The studies completed or in progress in my office show some interesting results which I hope to publish later.

It is unfortunate that many students in this field seem to take it for granted that there is one and only one definite cycle, or that the cycle is controlled by one and only one definite influence. I have been accused of inconsistency for presenting several seemingly incompatible theories concerning the business cycle. As a matter of fact, I have never as yet studied the so-called business cycle as a whole. I have only studied a few of its elements or aspects.[23]

§12. *Interest Rates and Bank Reserves*

That there is a relationship between bank reserves and the rate of bank discount is perhaps self-evident. Every banker and business man is familiar with it. J. P. Nor-

[23] For instance, *Our Unstable Dollar and the So-Called Business Cycle,* Journal of the American Statistical Association, June, 1925, pp. 179-202.

ton [24] found such a correlation and the relationship finds expression in practically every treatment of commercial banking.

This relationship furthermore carries over into the rates fixed on commercial paper. Mr. W. Randolph Burgess [25] has made a study of this relationship which he expresses briefly as follows:

"Banks are the custodians of money in this country. When the bankers have much money to lend, *money rates tend to be easy;* when they have little to lend, money rates tend to be firm. The amount a banker can lend depends upon his reserve position. Therefore, the reserve position of the banks of the country determines short term money rates, and the causes of changes in money rates are to be found in the causes of changes in the reserve position of banks."

Mr. Burgess presents an impressive inductive verification of this theory for the period 1904 to 1909 by comparing the changes in the short term money rate with the changes in the average surplus or deficit in the reserves of New York City Clearing House Association Banks.

The same relationship, Mr. Burgess finds, obtains under the Federal Reserve System between the excess or deficit in reserves of twenty-three New York City Banks and the closing call money rate for intra-week periods between the balancing of the reserves by the Federal Reserve Banks. Over longer periods of time, the relationship is shown by the similarity in the movement of the open

[24] *Statistical Studies in the New York Money Market,* Chapters VII and VIII.

[25] *Factors Affecting Changes in Short Term Interest Rates,* Journal of the American Statistical Association, Vol. XXII, New Series, No. 158, June, 1927, pp. 195-201.

market interest rate for prime 4-6 months commercial paper and the average daily bills discounted for member banks by all Federal Reserve Banks.

The Federal Reserve Act requires the pooling of member banks' reserves with the Federal Reserve Banks. These reserves must average the minimum legal requirements and balancing periods are maintained once a week in large cities and twice a month elsewhere. Surplus and deficit reserves are, therefore, impossible for periods of more than two weeks at the very maximum under this system. But the influence of the banks on the money market rates are now effected through borrowings at the Federal Reserve Banks. Thus a period of member banks borrowing corresponds in its relation to the money market to a period of deficit reserves under the National Banking Act, and a period when member banks are paying off their loans at the Reserve Bank corresponds to a period of excess reserves.

A similar correspondence between commercial paper rates and gold reserves is shown by a recent study by Colonel Leonard Ayres, of the Cleveland Trust Company.[26]

Curiously enough, this well known and sound relationship between bank reserves and interest rates is often confused with the entirely different, generally incorrect, but commonly believed proposition that the rate of interest is high when money in general is scarce, and low when money in general is abundant. The thought seems to be if the rate of interest is called the price of money it is natural to conclude that abundance of money, like abundance of wheat or anything else, makes its price low, while scarcity of money makes its price high.

[26] Cleveland Trust Company, Business Bulletin, June 15, 1928.

But the price of money in the sense of the rate of interest is a very peculiar kind of price. It is, as we know, the deviation from par of the price of present money in terms of future money. It is not very analogous to the price of wheat. The real analogy with the price of wheat is not the rate of interest but the *purchasing power* of money. In that sense it is perfectly true that the price of money is high or low with its scarcity or abundance. But in the other sense it is not true. Moreover, as we have seen, when the price of money, in the sense of the purchasing power of money, is low, that is, when the price level is high, and when, therefore, presumably the quantity of money is large, we do not then find the rate of interest low, as the theory outlined above requires. On the contrary, we find a high price level associated with a high interest rate.

That short term interest rates vary inversely with bank reserves, however, fits in with our theory of interest as related to real income. A low bank reserve is, among other things, a symptom of a prospective general increase in the income of the community. When business is optimistic, which means when future income looms large, there is an impatient desire to discount that big future and to make it even bigger by investing present income, provided the investment can be financed. Evidently the immediate effect is to increase bank loans and consequently to increase deposits. These results tend to lessen the ratio of bank reserves to liabilities. Thus the banker is led to raise his rate. It *seems* that the rise merely reflects his reserve situation. But back of this situation is the demand for loans, and back of that something more fundamental—the rising income stream, a period of increasing prosperity, of invention and progress, or of great financing. From these changes, rather than from a merely technical banking situation, come high rates of interest.

Thus the banker registers the effect of the increasing income stream. The reverse situation of descending income stream, lessened opportunity to invest, lessened loans and deposits, tend toward idle reserves and low interest.

Normally the banking function should do little more in relation to the rate of interest than to transmit the effects of the income stream. This would be substantially the case if we had a scientific adjustment of the ultimate source of bankers' reserves, the world's supply of monetary gold. If this were so adjusted as to maintain a constant purchasing power of that gold and so of money units, the banker could be trusted to adjust properly, even if unconsciously, the rates of interest to the income situation of the country.

Unfortunately, we do not yet have such a scientific currency system, but are still exposed to every wind that blows in the gold bullion market. The consequence is that superimposed on the normal credit operations are abnormal ones by which the rate of interest is perverted through the very banking machinery which should make it normal.

Banking thus becomes, in practice, not simply a register of fundamental economic influences, not merely their facilitator, but a most powerful independent influence. Practically, then, the banking machinery often interferes with, rather than transmits, the normal influence of society's income situation. If the gold mines become depleted, gold reserves become inadequate to support the growing inverted pyramid of credit based upon it and required by the expanding income of society. The banker then has no choice, under the law, but to raise his rates in self-defense. The result is a shrinkage of credit when an expansion is needed, a fall of prices and high bank rates at the very time that low money rates of interest are needed. The real rates are then doubly high—high because the money rates are high and still higher because of the appreciation of money.

These maladjustments are largely responsible for the so-called business cycle. When they are serious, not only are the consequences disastrous but there is little then left in the market figures of interest to register the influence of fundamental income conditions.[27] The interest rate then registers, rather, a choking or stalling of the banking machinery. In an acute panic, scarcity of money itself has made interest high. Money of any kind brought into the market at such times will relieve the stringency and lower the rate of interest. To relieve the money stringency, the United States has, in times past, poured money into the channels of trade by prepaying interest on bonds, and clearing houses have accomplished it by issuing clearing house certificates.

The establishment of the Federal Reserve System has stabilized prices and interest rates in the United States, although the cataclysm of war in 1914-1921 upset the price level and the normal correspondence between real and money rates of interest as they had never been upset before.

At present, the Federal Reserve System exerts a normalizing influence and seems to be groping to apply the

[27] Conditions of this type emphasize the importance of thorough study of the institutional factors influencing market interest rates such as that made by Mr. A. W. Marget in his doctoral dissertation *The Loan Fund* presented to the faculty of Harvard University in 1926-1927.

stabilizing principles which for many years have been suggested by Wicksell, Cassel, and other economists.

Even these efforts, while in the end they save us from price convulsions and real-interest convulsions, nevertheless themselves involve a slight interference with the natural effects of the income situation. The rediscount rate, when raised, restricts credit and stops price inflation; and when lowered, liberates credit and stops price deflation. As the effect, in either case, tends to be cumulative as long as the slight artificial raising or lowering is in force, the interference with the normal course of events need only be slight, almost negligible. It would not be surprising if a difference of one half of 1 per cent from an ideally normal rate should prove usually sufficient. Maintained sufficiently long, this deviation from a normal interest rate may prevent a very abnormal deviation in our monetary standard.

Some slight interferences are inherent in any such banking system, not only as an incident to the supremely important function of preventing inflation and deflation, but also as a necessary price to pay for the very existence of a banking system. In order to maintain a liquid condition and to avoid risk of bankruptcy, each bank must occasionally put its loan policy out of line with the ideal requirements of the income situation.

But, as we gradually perfect our banking technique and policies, we shall get closer and closer to a condition in which the rate of interest as a whole will reflect the income influences discussed in this book. The money rate and the real rate will become substantially the same, and any action of the banker which can be called an interference with, rather than a registering of, fundamental economic conditions will become almost negligible.

[450]

§13. *Summary*

We have found evidence general and specific, from correlating P' with both bond yields and short term interest rates, that price changes do, generally and perceptibly, affect the interest rate in the direction indicated by *a priori* theory. But since forethought is imperfect, the effects are smaller than the theory requires and lag behind price movements, in some periods, very greatly. When the effects of price changes upon interest rates are *distributed* over several years, we have found remarkably high coefficients of correlation, thus indicating that interest rates follow price changes closely in degree, though rather distantly in time.

The final result, partly due to foresight and partly to the lack of it, is that price changes do after several years and with the intermediation of changes in profits and business activity affect interest very profoundly. In fact, while the main object of this book is to show how the rate of interest would behave if the purchasing power of money were stable, there has never been any long period of time during which this condition has been even approximately fulfilled. When it is not fulfilled, the money rate of interest, and still more the real rate of interest, is more affected by the instability of money than by those more fundamental and more normal causes connected with income impatience, and opportunity, to which this book is chiefly devoted.

CHAPTER XX

OBJECTIONS CONSIDERED [1]

§1. *Introduction*

SINCE 1907, when *The Rate of Interest* was published, other students of the problem of interest have published their comments, objections, and criticisms. I have taken the opportunity to answer directly in various publications [2] most of the criticisms. It would serve no useful purpose to reprint these individual replies in this place. Rather, in this chapter, I shall state my understanding of the criticisms of my theory and shall offer replies where reply seems called for. This procedure will serve two purposes. First, it will present to the reader points of view and approaches to the problem of interest other than my own. Secondly, it will provide occasion for the statement of my position on the principal controversial problems in the theory of interest still remaining unsettled among economists. [3]

[1] For historical development and detailed criticisms of interest theories the reader is referred to Böhm-Bawerk, *Capital and Interest*. A brief historical résumé is given in Cassel, *The Nature and Necessity of Interest*, Chap. I, pp. 1-67.

[2] These articles are included in the general bibliography at the end of the book.

[3] References to the authors of the views which I am stating impersonally in the text will be made, where possible, in footnotes. It is hoped that this procedure will prevent the impression that I am attempting any exhaustive critique of the interest theory of others.

OBJECTIONS CONSIDERED

§2. *Income and Capital*

Income, which, as I have stated before, is the most important factor in all economic theory and in interest theory in particular, resolves itself in final analysis into a flow of psychic enjoyments or satisfactions during a period of time. While this concept is the ideal, we can, for purposes of objectivity, approximate this ideal and at the same time impute to the income concept varying degrees of measurability by using in place of psychic income any of the following: real income, cost of living as a measure of real income, or money income.

One objection to the psychic concept of income as a basis for a theory of interest is that it is too narrow and restricted. It is held that the analysis of interest based on this concept "finds the cause of the changes in rates solely in the changed ratio between the stocks of present and of future consumption goods," while the "interest rate market is a funds market, not a machine or raw material or present consumables market." [4]

"Nor is it entirely clear," continues this criticism, "why, in Fisher's view, the consumption perspective should read the law in point of interest rates to all equipment loan contracts, rather than, as Böhm-Bawerk sometimes appears to assert, the other way about. Why should not both sorts of demands be regarded as of equal title in causal effectiveness in the interest adjustment on final loans?" [5]

I reply that I do not exclude "equipment loan contracts" from due consideration, but I do maintain that such intermediate loans are made for the purpose of se-

[4] Davenport, H. J., *Interest Theory and Theories*. American Economic Review, Vol. XVII, No. 4, December, 1927, pp. 636-656.

[5] *Ibid.*, p. 650.

curing larger incomes in the future, and larger incomes mean larger consumption. Production loans then are made only in contemplation of future consumption. Hence, though loans for the acquisition of intermediate goods do greatly preponderate in the loan markets, these loans have power to affect the interest rate only by changing the relative amount of future incomes compared to present incomes.

To the criticism that the consumption concept of income when used as the foundation of interest theory presents but a partial analysis of the supply and demand factors which are operative in determining interest rates, I make this reply: Interest rates are not a resultant of the supply of, and demand for, either capital goods or of capital values—sometimes conceived of as a loanable fund or funds, except as these signify the supply of and demand for income. An investment of capital, so called, is nothing more nor less than the sacrifice of income in anticipation of other, larger, and later income. It is a case of flexing the income stream, reducing it in the present or early future and increasing it in the remoter future. The income stream, so fundamental in the interest problem, includes incomes from all sources. It includes the value of the services of land, machines, buildings, and all other income-producing agents. Upon the value of these services, discounted at the prevailing rate of interest, the valuation of said land, machinery, buildings, and so on depends. What is properly called funds is this valuation of the income stream or portions of it. It should be evident that the approach to the problem of interest through the income stream and the supply of and demand for income gives to the problem the broadest possible basis.

The second indictment of narrowness of my concept

of income denies my contention that *savings are not income*. One writer states this criticism as follows: "As a financial fact, there can be no saving and addition to capital value until there is first a property right to an income calculable in monetary terms (a financial present worth) to be saved. Hence to deny that monetary savings are monetary income is in simple common sense to deny a *fait accompli*; it is to assume the existence of the effect before its cause." [6]

In so far as our disagreement here is a matter of words, it may be that my terminology is at fault. I used the term *earnings* to include capital gain and the term *income* in the sense of the value of services rendered by capital. There is little objection to changing this terminology, *if we are willing to give up saying that capital value is the capitalized value of expected income.* We could *then* maintain that capital gain is income. But if income includes only those elements on the anticipation of which the value of capital depends, then the increase in the value of capital is most emphatically not income. [7]

In my reply to one critic, [8] I pointed out that this criticism seems to overlook, or omit, the mutual relations of

[6] Fetter, Frank A., *Clark's Reformulation of the Capital Concept.* Economic Essays Contributed in Honor of John Bates Clark, pp. 151-152, footnote on p. 153; cf. also Flux, *Irving Fisher on Capital and Interest,* Quarterly Journal of Economics, Vol. XXIII, Feb., 1909, pp 307-323.

[7] See my articles: *Are Savings Income?* Journal of the American Economic Association, Vol. IX, No. 1, April, 1908, pp. 1-27; *Professor Fetter on Capital and Income,* Journal of Political Economy, Vol. XV, No. 7, July, 1907, pp. 421-434; *Comment on Professor Plehn's Address,* American Economic Review, Vol. XIV, No. 1, Mar., 1924, pp. 64-67; and The *Concept of Income in the Light of Experience,* English reprint from Wieser Festschrift, Vol. III.

[8] *A Reply to Critics,* Quarterly Journal of Economics, Vol. XXIII, May, 1909, pp. 536-541.

discount and interest which constitute the *raison d'être* for the concepts which I have called capital and income. It is chiefly because savings do not enter into these discount relations on equal terms with other items of income that savings do not form a part of what I have called the income concept. I do not think there are reasons of terminology alone sufficient to justify the inclusion of savings in income. But, if savings are to be so included, some other term must be applied to take the place of what I have called income. The justification of these statements must rest on my books themselves and on later papers devoted to this subject.

But it is held that even aside from the relation of savings and income, a concept of income as services is quite useless. Services are both heterogeneous and incommensurable.[9] They cannot be summated to constitute a stock of services. They cannot be thrown together as if all were alike.

An examination of my *The Nature Of Capital and Income* (for example p. 121), will show that I do not treat all services as alike and capable of being added together. I have emphasized that miscellaneous services cannot be added together until each is multiplied by its price and all are thus reduced to a common denominator.

This criticism of my theory of income seems to overlook the fact that, while enjoyable services (psychic income) and objective services are themselves incommensurable, their values are not. Moreover, when the summation is completely carried out, the values of the physical elements cancel *among themselves* and leave as the net result only the values of the psychical elements.

[9] Fetter, *Interest Theories, Old and New*, American Economic Review, Vol. IV, No. 1, March, 1914, pp. 68-92.

OBJECTIONS CONSIDERED

It may be objected that, at one stage in this process, income appears to be more closely related to the expenditure of money than to its receipt and, as such, seems out of keeping with the ordinary idea of income. This seeming contradiction between money income and enjoyable income is readily resolved if we consider debits and credits. When money is spent, the expenditure itself is, it is true, outgo to be debited to the commodities bought with it. But these commodities afterward render a return in satisfactions. These satisfactions are certainly not expenditures, but receipts. Whether money spending is associated with outgo or income is entirely dependent on whether we fix attention on the loss of the money or the gain of the goods and services for which the money is spent.

These services, which constitute income, are related to capital in several ways. As income services, they flow from, or are produced by human beings and the physical environment. When I first came to the study of income and capital, I developed the concept of capital as a *stock* of *wealth* existing at an *instant* of time, and of income as a *flow of wealth* during a *period* of time, which concept I advanced in 1896.[9a] I found it necessary in 1897 to modify my concept of income, and so stated.[10] Since then I have found no reason for further modification either of the concept of capital as a *stock of wealth* existing at an *instant* of time, or of the concept of income as a *flow of services* through a *period* of time, while the *values* of these are respectively *capital value*, and *income value*, often abbreviated into capital and income.

[9a] *What is Capital?* The Economic Journal, Vol. VI, Dec., 1896, pp. 509-534.

[10] *The Rôle of Capital in Economic Theory*, The Economic Journal, Vol. VII, Dec., 1897, pp. 511-537.

"It is not possible," it is objected, "to conceive of a literal stock of services at an instant of time; it is possible to conceive of their present worth as a financial fund at an instant of time. Services (taken in the sense of uses either of wealth or of human beings) may conceivably be delayed or hastened, but they are in their very nature a flow; they cannot be heaped up and constitute a stock of services. They can, at most, as they occur be 'incorporated' in durable forms of wealth. If this is so, then why this elaborate contrast between a *flow* of services, and a *fund* of something quite different? It is the vestigial remains of the older conception that Fisher has been obliged to discard." [11]

While, however, I agree that these concepts of capital (as a fund of wealth) and income (as a flow of services) are not commensurate with the theory of interest, it would be a mistake to conclude from the emphasis placed on capital *value*, not capital *goods*, in the *The Nature of Capital and Income*, which was written as an introduction to *the theory of interest*, that the concept of capital goods emphasized by me in 1896 has been shelved as useless.

In the first place, the *goods* concept is itself a step in the formulation of the *value* concept, and secondly, *The Nature of Capital and Income* does not attempt to cover all of the four different relations between capital and income but only that one relation, income value to capital value, which is of importance to the *theory of interest*.

This valuation concept of capital, which in my view is necessary to the solution of the interest problem, does not distinguish between land and "produced means to

[11] Fetter, *Clark's Reformulation of the Capital Concept.* Economic Essays Contributed in Honor of John Bates Clark, p. 152.

further production." Some writers,[12] who hold this latter concept of capital, have contended that my treatment of land as typical of capital in general has led me to erroneous conclusions.

In particular, my criticism of the naïve productivity theories is said to fall down because of this consideration. But, as I have before written,[13] "my strictures on the ordinary productivity theories are not dependent on the putting forward of 'land' as typical of all forms of capital" or the particular definition of capital which I have used, but are, for the most part, merely a résumé of the strictures of Böhm-Bawerk, whose definition of capital excludes land. In other words, these criticisms hold true quite regardless of whether land is included in the capital concept or not.

However, while I recognize certain differences which exist between land and so-called artificial capital, these differences are of degree only, and do not carry the importance in most phases of economic theory which adherents of this concept of capital attribute to them. Professor J. B. Clark has presented [14] the similarities and dissimilarities of land and other durable agents so comprehensively and adequately that I shall not attempt to go over again this question at this point. However, one phase of this comparison is of importance. It is claimed by those [15] who hold land to be non-reproducible and, therefore, to lack a cost of production, that its value is

[12] Seager, *The Impatience Theory of Interest*, American Economic Review, Vol. II, No. 4, December, 1912, pp. 834-851; Brown, *Economic Science and The Common Welfare*.

[13] *The Impatience Theory of Interest*, American Economic Review, Vol. III, No. 3, September, 1912, pp. 610-615.

[14] Clark, *Distribution of Wealth*, pp. 338-344.

[15] For example, Seager and Brown, cited above.

governed by factors quite different from those determining the value of reproducible agents whose production does involve costs of production.

In brief, the contention is that the discount or capitalization principle of valuation upon which my theory rests is applicable only to land, since land value is not affected by cost of production. "If land, the limited gift of nature," one critic writes, "were truly representative of capital, then Fisher's reasoning would be unassailable." [16]

But since land, it is implied, is not representative of capital in that it does not involve a cost of production, the valuation process which applies to land does not apply to those *"produced* means to further production" which do incur costs in their production. To a consideration of the relation of cost of production to capital value, therefore, we now turn.

§3. *Cost of Production as a Determinant of Capital Value*

The criticism that my views as to the relation of cost of production and capital value are invalid because of the use of land as typical of capital has been advanced by several writers.[17] In its most concrete form, it applies to the example which I presented of the case where an orchard was held to be worth $100,000 because this sum represented the discounted value of the expected income from the orchard of $5,000 per annum. But even if we change the orchard to machines, houses, tools, ships (that is, "produced means to further production") the principle that the value of anything is the discounted value of its

[16] Seager, cited above, p. 844.

[17] Seager, Brown, and Flux cited above; also Loria, *Irving Fisher's Rate of Interest,* Journal of Political Economy, Vol. XVI, Oct., 1908, pp. 331-332.

expected income stands unrefuted. This is not to say cost of production does not have an influence. But past costs have no influence on the present value of a capital good, except as those costs affect the value of the future services it renders and the future costs. *Future* costs influence this value more directly by being themselves discounted at the current rate of discount. It is certainly true that if the reproduction cost of the capital goods is lowered, their production will be stimulated, the supply of services they render will be increased, the valuation of these services, i.e., the income from these capital goods per unit will be lowered, and, therefore, quite aside from any effect on the discount rate, the capitalization of this reduced income will tend to be lowered. Furthermore, this fall in the value of the capital goods will be brought down to a point, through the operation of the opportunity principle, where it is brought into conformity with the new cost of production of the capital good plus a margin to represent the amount of interest.

But, although it is true, it is objected, that under the supply and demand analysis, an increase in the supply of a single commodity will lower its value, the same does not follow when applied to all goods. "Exchange values and prices are relations among goods. Increase the supply of one good and the ratio at which it exchanges for others or for money will change to its disadvantage. If, however, you increase at the same time the supplies of all goods, including gold, the standard money material, you affect simultaneously both sides of all ratios of exchange and consequently the ratios should remain substantially as before. It is just such an increase of goods of all sorts and descriptions that is denoted by Böhm-Bawerk's phrase, 'the technical superiority of present over future goods', or by the more familiar phrase 'the productivity of capital'. Admitting the physical-productivity of capital (and Fisher does not question it), the value-productivity of capital or, more accurately, an increase in the total value product as a consequence of the assistance which capital renders to production seems to me to follow as a logically necessary consequence. . . . Since there is nothing in the assumption that the productivity of all instruments is doubled that involves any serious change in the expense of producing the instruments, the productivity theorist certainly *would* claim that under these conditions there must be, if not a doubling, certainly a very substantial increase in the rate of interest." [18]

I can perhaps do no better than to repeat in part the reply which I made to this criticism in 1914.[19] "But the increased productivity of capital will entail a decreased price, or value per unit, of the products of that capital. And in addition there may be an increase in the expense of producing the capital, if, for instance, it is reproducible only under the laws of diminishing returns or increasing costs. Evidently it does not follow that the net return on capital-value will be permanently increased. In short, the expenses of production, on the one hand, and the price of the product of the capital multiplied by the increased product itself, on the other hand, will tend to adjust themselves to each other and to the rate of interest. But this rate of interest, according to my philosophy, instead of being permanently raised, will be ultimately lowered, for to double the productivity of capital will mean ultimately a much larger income to society than before, and

[18] Seager, cited above, pp. 842-3, 847.
[19] *The Impatience Theory of Interest,* American Economic Review, Vol. III, No. 3, September, 1913, pp. 614-615.

this larger income tends to lower the rates of impatience of those who own it. So long as the rate of interest does not fall to correspond with the lower rates of impatience, there will continue to be profit in reproducing the productive capital until adjustment is attained—whether by decrease in the price of the products or by increase in the cost of the capital, or both, does not matter. In any case this adjustment must be by lowering and not by raising the rate of interest, for the rate of interest cannot be raised if the rates of impatience are not raised, and the rates of impatience cannot be raised if, as is assumed, the income stream is increased in size without being altered in other respects."

Very possibly, Professor Seager and I may have been arguing at cross purposes, for, of course, *in the transition period* while productivity is being doubled, the rate of interest may be raised. This is amply provided for in my theory. But even during the transition period something more is required than increased productivity in order that the rate of interest shall rise; the cost of making the change must be reckoned with and deducted from the income stream. Mere physical productivity will not suffice.

Having stated my views, it will serve to present clearly the difference of opinion to quote an illustration which Professor Harry G. Brown has furnished me of his views on the matter.

"Smith is a fisherman. His boat (capital necessary to his business) is wearing out and will last little longer. He catches, in general, 40 halibut a week, which he sells for $1 each, or $40 a week. He is also a good carpenter and can make himself a boat in a week's time. But to do so, he must give up the $40 worth of fish he could catch, or the $40 for which he could sell them. For him the *cost* of building a boat is $40. That is its *cost* in the sense of the *sacrifice* Smith must make in other products (fish) of his labor, if he builds the boat.

"Jones offers to sell him an exactly similar boat already built for $150. Smith refuses to pay over $40. Since other fishermen do the same, the *demand* for boats is such that Jones can't get $150. The fact is that the income Smith could get from his fish, which he expects to catch *this* week ($40) affects the price Jones can charge (value) for a boat (capital good) already built. This $40 worth of fish is not income *from the boat we are about to value*. It certainly is not the value of *that* income or *its discounted value*. And it is not a *future* cost of the *to-be-valued boat*.

"The cost you are thinking of as 'included' in your formulation (discount principle of capital value) is, for example, the expected cost (say 5 years hence) of replacing a worn-out or broken seat, broken oarlocks, etc., and the annual cost of painting. But the $40 which measures the cost to Smith of duplicating Jones' boat will make Smith unwilling to pay $150 even though your formulation, taken by itself, would let him—for he *must* have *some* boat. And Smith would have a curious mind if the $40 cost affected him only *through* first making him think of more plentiful and therefore less valuable future services. It has a *direct* effect on his price offer, not an effect consequent solely on a revaluation of expected future services.

"You can't *make* the psychology of the fisherman, Smith, fit into your formula. It's better to make a formula that *fits* what Smith's mind really does."

I accept all of Professor Brown's reasoning and conclusions except his application to me. His contention that the cost of duplicating existing capital will influence the value of that capital is perfectly correct, but so is the discount formula.

The two are not inconsistent. If they were, by the same logic, the generally accepted formula by which the value of a bond is calculated in every broker's office is contradicted every day whenever a cheaper bond is available. The first axiom in economics is, naturally, to get anything

the cheapest way whether that way is to make it one-
self, buy a substitute or otherwise, for in Professor
Brown's reasoning it is solely the existence of an alternative cheaper way which makes the supposed disturbance.

The reasoning proves too much. Suppose Jones offers
Smith a bond at one price and Smith refuses because he
can get another just like it for less. He would choose the
cheaper and he would have a "curious mind" if the
cheaper cost affected him only through first making him
think elaborately of the discount process. All he needs to
know is that if Jones' bond is worth the price offered the
cheaper one is even more clearly worth while. And Jones
will sit up and take notice, possibly reducing his price.

The cheaper bargain thus has in Professor Brown's
sense a "direct" effect on the price of Jones' bond, not an
effect solely on a revaluation of expected services. But we
cannot here conclude that the usual mathematical formula for the price of a bond was incorrect.

There is no more definite and universally accepted
formula in the whole realm of economics and business
than that referred to. It is used *every day* in brokers'
offices. It gives the price of a bond in terms of the interest
basis, the nominal interest and the time of maturity. It
is the type, par excellence, of the capitalization principle
both in theory and practice. It is not impaired by any
undercutting of the market.

The boat is, economically, a sublimated bond. If Jones
offers it to Smith for $150, while Smith can get it cheaper
the discount principle is not invalidated. There is simply
a readjustment in the boat as in the bond market. Moreover in an individual transaction where there is no marginal point reached by repeating the transaction—only
one boat, not a series—there are wide limits within which

the buyer gets his consumer's surplus and the seller his producer's surplus. Only when there is a series of successive boats or bonds do we have a full fledged example of the margin where consumer's rent disappears and an equality replaces inequalities.

In the isolated case we should be content to say that Smith will not pay more than the capitalized value. In the case of the conventional series of boats, the marginal boat will be such that the capitalization principle and the cost principle will both apply. The seventh boat, let us say, will cost Smith $100 whether to make or to buy. Jones and other boat owners will have reduced their price from $150 and Smith will have found that to make so many boats will have cost $100 instead of $40, to say nothing of the important fact that he would have to wait much more than a week.

All these points are covered in my presentation, for Professor Brown's example is only one of the myriad examples of alternative opportunities. Smith, like everybody else, will use the cheapest way in the sense of choosing the income stream of labor and satisfaction having the maximum present worth at the market rate of interest.

Professor Brown has his eyes on the opportunity part of the picture and no one has stressed that part more than I. But interwoven with it and consistent with it, in the analysis of a perfect market in which the individual is a negligible factor, is the principle that every article of capital is valued at the discounted value of its expected services and costs.

I do not intend to underestimate the importance of the cost concept. The importance it holds in my mind is not to be measured by the number of pages devoted to it in my books, the main purpose of which was to study capitalizations of income. I believe that the position on cost which was taken by Professor Davenport [20] is in general the correct one. What I attempted to point out was that those double-faced events, which I have called interactions, and which always have a double entry, a positive and negative entry, in social bookkeeping, are not ultimately cost any more than they are ultimately income. I also tried to emphasize that cost enters into capitalization on equal terms with income, *when the cost is future*. Past cost does not affect present valuations except indirectly, as it affects future expected income and cost.

No one would maintain that obsolete machinery, even in good condition, could be appraised on the basis of its cost. The only cases in which cost (with interest) is equal to value is where this value is also equal to the estimate of worth on the basis of future expectations; when, in other words, cost is superfluous as a determinant of value. That cost does influence value by limiting supply, thereby affecting the quantity and value of future services, cannot be questioned. It is natural that business men should not follow this roundabout relation, but connect directly cost with value. This, however, is no reason for economists to fail to analyze the relation in all its complications.

§4. *Impatience as Determinant of the Interest Rate*

Certain characteristics of *The Rate of Interest* led to the unfortunate deduction on the part of many readers [21]

---

[20] Davenport, *Value and Distribution.*

[21] Cf. Seager and Flux, cited above, and particularly Fetter, *Interest Theories Old and New,* American Economic Review, Vol. IV, No. 1, March, 1914, pp. 69-72.

of that volume that I regarded *impatience* as the *sole* and *complete* determinant of the rate of interest. While I have tried in this book to forestall similar misinterpretations of my theory, and while it does not seem possible to me that any reader could now charge me with being a pure impatience theorist, it will serve a useful purpose to consider the various factors involved in this question.

We may draw upon Professor Fetter's writings for a clear statement of the issue between the productivity theory and the time preference theory of interest. He states positively that time preference is the sole cause of interest, although he assumes that physical productivity is essential to the emergence of value productivity.[22] He declares that his theory was new in assigning priority to capitalization over contract interest and in giving a "unified psychological explanation of all the phenomena of *the surplus that emerges when undervalued expected incomes approach maturity,* the surplus all being derived from the value of enjoyable (direct) goods, not by two separate theories, for consumption and production goods respectively." [23] [Italics mine.]

I have no criticism to make of this statement of the operation and effect of time preference so far as it goes. It seems to me to coincide sufficiently with the treatment which I have presented under the first approximation. There incomes were *assumed* to exist and to be rigidly fixed in amount and in time without our bothering to ask *how* they were produced. Nature offered no options to substitute one income stream for another. One could modify his income stream only by borrowing or lending.

[22] Fetter, *Interest Theories Old and New,* American Economic Review, March, 1914, pp. 74, 76, 77.
[23] *Ibid.,* p. 77.

Under the hypothetical conditions so assumed, time preference would cause interest without help from any rate of return over cost. But such assumed conditions never do or can exist in the real world.

Of course a constant rigid physical productivity, yielding unchanging physical income streams, is contrary to the observed facts of life, just as unchanging time preference for each individual at all times and under all conditions is an absurdity. In real life men have the *opportunity* of choosing among many optional income streams. When such opportunities exist, time preference alone does not and cannot explain the emergence of interest. As a mathematical problem, the rate of interest would under the conditions of the second or third approximations be indeterminate without introducing the influence of the opportunity or productivity factor.[24]

Productivity, that is, the possibility of increasing the present value of the income stream, introduces new variables which have to be determined as a part of the interest problem and every new variable requires a new equation or condition.

It happens that, for lack of applying this mathematical principle, writers have often thought themselves in greater disagreement on the explanation of interest than they really were. Wordy warfare has been waged among the various productivity theorists and the capitalization

[24] As is always possible in solving simultaneous equations we can, if we wish, express certain of the variables, such as those relating to productivity, or opportunity, namely the rates of return over cost, in terms of the other variables and thus seem to eliminate them. In my first book I tried, for the most part, thus to present the rate of return over cost, or as I then called it, the rate of return on sacrifice as determined through the rate of preference. But we can just as well in like manner eliminate time preference and present it in terms of rate of return.

or time preference theorists. Each combatant seems to think that he and he alone has hit upon the correct and complete explanation and that, therefore, any other explanation is necessarily false. As a matter of fact, both productivists and time valuists are substantially right in their affirmations and wrong in their denials. Thus, theories which have been presented as antagonistic and mutually annihilatory are in reality harmonious and complementary.

§5. *Productivity as a Determinant of Interest Rates*

When the true nature of the income concept is grasped, it will be found that it includes within itself many special cases which have been advanced by various writers in explanation of the rate of interest. The relation of both impatience and opportunity to the rate of interest, in my opinion, can be comprehended accurately only by analyzing rigorously these concepts and determining the effect of each upon the income stream. By this procedure, we arrive at a fundamental explanation of the nature of impatience and of return on income invested and see how, by changes in the income stream, these rates are brought into conformity with the rate of interest.

I have always felt that John Rae came closer than any of the earlier writers to grasping all the elements of the interest problem. According to Rae, all instruments may be arranged in an order depending on the rate of return over cost. This amounts to saying that the formation of any instrument both adds to and subtracts from the preexisting income stream of the producer, its cost being the subtracted item and the return, the added one. The statement of Rae that for a certain cost of production an instrument will yield a certain return, is merely a form of my statement that a certain decrease of present income will be accompanied by a certain increase in future income. The relation between the immediate decrease and future increase will vary within a wide range, wherein the choice will fall at the point corresponding to the ruling rate of interest.

The same relationship was conceived by Adolphe Landry in his *Intérêt du Capital*. He states that one of the conditions determining the rate of interest is the "productivity of capital", in the peculiar sense which he gives to this phrase,[25] which is, in effect, the rate of return over cost.

It has seemed to me that much of the criticism, both favorable and unfavorable, of my book, *The Rate of Interest*, has been based on the erroneous assumption that the so-called productivity element found no place in my theory. Much of the misunderstanding of my theory may have been fostered by the lack, in my first book, of a good term with which to express this productivity factor in interest.

As a consequence, one critic, Professor Seager, writes that I refuse to admit that what Böhm-Bawerk calls the "technical superiority of present over future goods", and what other writers have characterized more briefly as "the productivity of capital" has any influence on the comparison between present gratifications and future gratifications in which, as he believes, the complete and final explanation of interest is to be sought.

"The most striking fact about this method of presenting his factors", this criticism continues, "is that he dissociates his discussion completely from any account of the production of wealth. From a perusal of his *Rate of*

[25] Landry, *L'Intérêt du Capital*, pp. 66-95.

Interest and all but the very last chapters of his *Elementary Principles* (chapters which come *after* his discussion of the interest problem), the reader might easily get the impression that becoming rich is a purely psychological process. It seems to be assumed that income streams, like mountain brooks, gush spontaneously from nature's hillsides and that the determination of the rate of interest depends entirely upon the mental reactions of those who are so fortunate as to receive them. . . . The whole productive process, without which men would have no income streams to manipulate, is ignored, or, as the author would probably say, taken for granted." [26]

My views are quite contrary to those here set forth. As I wrote in 1913: [27]

"What Professor Seager calls the 'productivity' or 'technique' element, so far from being lacking in my theory, is one of its cardinal features and the one the treatment of which I flattered myself was most original! The fact is that my chief reason in writing the *Rate of Interest* at all arose from the belief that Böhm-Bawerk and others had failed to discover the true way in which the 'technique of production' enters into the determination of the rate of interest. Believing the 'technical' link in previous explanations unsound, and realizing as keenly as Professor Seager does the absolute necessity of such a link, I set myself the task of finding it. In the desirability of this I emphatically agree with Böhm-Bawerk."

I do not assume, except temporarily in the first approximation, that "income streams, like mountain brooks, gush spontaneously from nature's hillsides", and this is temporarily assumed, precisely as physicists temporarily assume a vacuum in studying falling bodies, or, to take a

[26] Seager, *The Impatience Theory of Interest*, American Economic Review, Vol. II, No. 4, December, 1912, pp. 835-837.
[27] *The Impatience Theory of Interest*. American Economic Review, Vol. III, No. 3, September, 1913, p. 610.

better but still imperfect analogy, precisely as, in treating supply and demand, we first assume a fixed supply before introducing the supply schedule or supply curve. This assumption gives place in the second approximation and the third approximation to the more complicated conditions of the actual world. My method of exposition is here, as usual, to take one step at a time, which means to introduce one set of variables at a time. All other things, *for the time being,* are assumed to remain equal. I realize that this is not the only method and that it may not be the best one, but it is at least a legitimate method.

On the other hand, it does not seem to me that the theory of interest is called upon to launch itself upon a lengthy discussion of the productive process, division of labor, utilization of land, capital, and scientific management. The problem is confined to discover how production is related to the rate of interest.

It should not, however, be assumed from what has been said that I regard all productivity theories as sound. Mention was made in Chapter III of the "naïve" productivity theories which hold that interest exists simply because nature, land and capital are productive.

§6. *Technical Superiority of Present Goods*

Böhm-Bawerk is among those who sensed the inadequacy of time preference or impatience as the sole determinant of the rate of interest. Yet he calls his theory the *agio* theory of interest, since he finds the essence of the rate of interest in the agio, or premium, on present goods when exchanged for future goods.

Böhm-Bawerk presented the agio theory, or what is here called the impatience or time preference theory, clearly and forcibly, and disentangled it from the crude and incorrect notions with which it had previously been associated. It was only when he attempted to explain the emergence of this agio by means of his special feature of "technical superiority of present over future goods" that, in my opinion, he erred greatly.

Böhm-Bawerk distinguishes two questions: (1) Why does interest exist? and (2) What determines any particular rate of interest?

In answer to the first question, he states virtually that this world is so constituted that most of us prefer present goods to future goods of like kind and number. This preference is due, according to Böhm-Bawerk, to three circumstances: (1) the "perspective underestimate" of the future, by which is meant the fact that future goods are less clearly perceived, and therefore less resolutely striven for, than those more immediately at hand; (2) the relative inadequacy (as a rule) of the provision for present wants as compared with the provision for future wants, or, in other words, the relative scarcity of present goods compared with future goods; (3) the "technical superiority" of present over future goods, or the fact, as Böhm-Bawerk conceives it, that the roundabout or capitalistic processes of production are more remunerative than those which yield immediate returns.

The first two of these three circumstances are undoubtedly pertinent, and are incorporated, under a somewhat different form, in this book. It is the third circumstance—the so-called technical superiority of present over future goods—which, as I shall try to show, contains fundamental errors.

My criticism of this third thesis, however, does not, as some have implied, consist in denying the *existence* or *importance* of the "technical" element in interest but in denying the soundness of the way in which Böhm-Bawerk applies it. It was for the purpose of presenting what in my view constitutes the true character of this element that I have placed so much emphasis on the opportunity principles given in Chapters VII, VIII, XI and XIII of this book.

According to Böhm-Bawerk, labor invested in long processes of production will yield larger returns than labor invested in short processes. In other words, labor invested in roundabout processes confers a technical advantage upon those who have command of that labor. In the reasoning by which Böhm-Bawerk attempts to prove this technical superiority, there are three principal steps. The first consists of postulating an "average production period," representing the length of the productive processes of the community; the second consists of the proposition that the longer this average production period, the greater will be the product; and the third consists in the conclusion that, in consequence of this greater productiveness of lengthy processes, present goods possess a technical superiority over future goods.

Although the first two of these three steps are of secondary importance, the following remarks concerning them are in point. The concept of an average production period is, I believe, far too arbitrary and indefinite to form a basis for the reasoning that Böhm-Bawerk attempts to base upon it. At best, it is a special, and very hypothetical, case not general enough to include the whole technical situation.

Böhm-Bawerk himself, in his reply to my original criticism, asserts his agreement with my contention concerning the second step that, while long processes are in general more productive than short processes, this is not a universal truth. Of the infinite number of possible longer processes only those which are more productive than shorter ones are chosen.[28] This is what was noted in Chapter XI when it was shown that the O curve is concave simply because the reëntrant parts are skipped!

It is the third step which is crucial to the theory of the technical superiority of present goods, namely, that the productiveness of long processes gives a special technical advantage to the possessor of present goods or present labor. This advantage produces, so Böhm-Bawerk asserted, a preference for present over future goods which is entirely apart from, and in addition to, the preference due to the underendowment of the present. Granting, for the moment, the validity of the concept of a production period, and that the longer the period, the greater its product, it may still be shown that no such technical superiority follows. Böhm-Bawerk regards this part of his theory as the most essential of all, and repeatedly states that the theory must stand or fall by the truth or falsity of that part.

Böhm-Bawerk supports his assertion of the existence of a technical superiority [29] by elaborate illustrative tables.[30] Each table is intended to show the investment

---

[28] *Positive Theorie des Kapitales.* "Meine These schränkt vielmehr diese Wirkung ausdrücklich auf 'klug gewählte' Verlängerungen ein und lässt überdies, indem sie ihr Zutreffen nur 'in aller Regel' oder, wie ich in der ersten Auflage sagte, 'im grossen und ganzen' behauptet, das Vorkommen von Ausnahmen offen." *Exkurs* I, p. 3.

"Wenn Fisher hiemit nicht mehr in Abrede stellen wollte, als was ich oben auf S. 3 des *Exkurse* I selbst in Abrede gestellt habe, dass nämlich nicht alle längeren Produktionsumwege nur deshalb, weil sie länger sind, auch produktiver sein müssen, so wären wir in vollem Einklang." *Exkurs* IV, p. 105.

[29] *The Positive Theory of Capital,* p. 266.

[30] In *The Rate of Interest* there is presented an exhaustive analysis of

possibilities of a month's labor available in any particular year. That longer processes are more productive than shorter ones, Böhm-Bawerk indicated by an increasing number of units of product for each successive year. The marginal utility of each year's yield when obtained is illustrated by a decreasing series, since the marginal utility of a stock of goods decreases as the number of units in the stock increases. Since the year 1888 was considered as the time of reference, or the first year in which the investment of labor was to be made, the numerical series representing the marginal utilities of the optional products as of the respective years of their production was reduced, by discounting, to a series of numbers representing the marginal utility of each year's yield as of the year 1888. The subjective value of each year's yield as of the year 1888, Böhm-Bawerk obtained by multiplying the number of units of each year's yield by its reduced marginal utility.

Of course, that investment of the month's labor available as of any particular year would be made which showed the maximum present value. When, however, the table of any one year is compared with that of any succeeding year, the maximum present subjective value selected is the greater the earlier the month's labor is available.

For example, a month's labor available in 1888 was shown to be most advantageously invested in the process which yielded the maximum present subjective value of 840 in 1890. But a month's labor available in 1889 yielded

the validity of the proof presented by these tables of the theory of technical superiority advanced by Böhm-Bawerk. While it does not seem advantageous to repeat here this analysis, since it is available in my previous book to any reader who may be interested, it is pertinent to present the conclusions drawn therefrom.

its maximum present value when invested so as to mature in 1893. In this latter case, however, the maximum was only 720 as compared with the maximum of 840 for a month's labor available in 1888.

Böhm-Bawerk therefore concludes that a month's labor available in 1888 is more productive than one available in 1889, 1890 or any succeeding year. In other words, entirely independent, according to him, of the perspective underestimate, and the under-endowment of the present, there inheres a technical superiority in present over future goods.

"This result", he writes,[31] "is not an accidental one, such as might have made its appearance in consequence of the particular figures used in our hypothesis. On the single assumption that longer methods of production lead generally to a greater output, it is a necessary result; a result which must have occurred, in an exactly similar way, whatever might have been the figures of quantity of product and value of unit in the different years."

But Böhm-Bawerk is mistaken in ascribing any part of this result to the fact that the longer processes are the more productive. In his tables he assumes the existence of one or both of the *other two* factors—the relative under-provision for the present as compared with the future, and the perspective undervaluation of the future, due to lack of intellectual imagination or emotional self-control. It is these elements, and these alone, which produce the advantage of present over future goods which the tables display.

That the result does not at all follow from "the single assumption that longer methods of production lead generally to a greater output" and has nothing whatever to

[31] *The Positive Theory of Capital*, p. 268.

do with that assumption, we can see clearly if we make the opposite assumption from that of Böhm-Bawerk, namely, that the longer the productive process the smaller will be the return. The very same result would still follow. The labor would still be invested at the earliest possible moment. In other words, let the figures representing units of product decrease instead of increase. The only difference would be that the month's labor available in 1888 would now be so invested as to bring returns in that year instead of being invested in a two years' process as before. If calculations are performed for each year and the results are compared, it will appear that the investment in 1888 yields the highest return, just as it did on the previous hypothesis.

Again, the same result would follow if the productivity increased and then decreased in all the tables, or if the productivity should first decrease and then increase. As long as the figure representing reduced marginal utility decreases, the "units of product" may be of *any description whatever*, without in the least affecting the essential result that the earlier the month's labor is available, the higher is its value.

On the other hand, if the conditions are reversed and the reduced marginal utility does *not* decrease, the earlier available labor will *not* have a higher value, whatever may be the character of the "units of product."

Böhm-Bawerk, however, specifically denies this: [32]

"The superiority in value of present means of production, which is based on their technical superiority, is not one borrowed from these circumstances [i.e., the perspective underestimate of the future and the relative underendowment of the present]; it would emerge of its own strength even if these were not active at all. I have intro-

* *The Positive Theory of Capital*, p. 268.

duced the two circumstances into the hypothesis only to make it a little more true to life, or, rather, to keep it from being quite absurd. Take, for instance, the influence of the reduction due to perspective entirely out of the illustration."

In his table it is true that the month's labor available in the present is more highly valued than the same month's labor available at a later date. But Böhm-Bawerk carefully retained in his illustration *one* of the "two circumstances" which he told us could be discarded, namely, the relative overprovision for the future. To leave one of these two circumstances effective instead of both is merely to change slightly the series of "reduced marginal utility". The change in the particular numbers is quite immaterial *so long as the series is still descending,* and it does not matter whether the descent is due to perspective or to the relative underprovision for the present, or to both.

The only fair test of the independence of Böhm-Bawerk's third factor—the alleged technical superiority of present over future goods—would be to strike out *both* the other elements (underestimate and overprovision of the future) so that there should be no progressive decrease in marginal utilities; in other words, to make the numbers representing "reduced marginal utilities" all equal. Böhm-Bawerk, for some reason, hesitates to do this. He says: [33]

"But if we were also to abstract the difference in the circumstances of provision in different periods of time, the situation would receive the stamp of extreme improbability, even of self-contradiction."

Even if this be true, and in my view it is not, it is no reason for refusing to push the inquiry to its limit. When

[33] *Positive Theory of Capital,* p. 269.

this is done, however, the figures of present value of the various yearly products become absolutely alike; hence the maximum of the former, if there be a maximum, must be identical with the maximum of the latter.

Though Böhm-Bawerk did not consider this case in his tables, he speaks of it briefly in his text, but seems to be somewhat puzzled by it. He says: [34]

"If the value of the unit of product were to be the same in all periods of time, however remote, the most abundant product would, naturally, at the same time be the most valuable. But since the most abundant product is obtained by the most lengthy and roundabout methods of production—perhaps extending over decades of years— the economic center of gravity, for all present means of production, would, on this assumption, be found at extremely remote periods of time—which is entirely contrary to all experience."

Böhm-Bawerk's confusion here is probably to be ascribed to his insistence on the *indefinite* increase of product with a lengthening of the production period. Practically we ought to assume that somewhere in the series the product decreases. We would then have a more practical illustration of the fact that the labor available this year and that available next year stand on a perfect equality.

The conclusion is that, if we eliminate the "other two circumstances" (relative underestimate of, and overprovision for, the future), we eliminate entirely the superiority of present over future goods. The supposed third circumstance of technical superiority, in the sense that Böhm-Bawerk gives it, turns out to be non-existent.

The fact is that the only reason any one does prefer the product of a month's labor invested today to the product of a month's labor invested next year is that today's

_____
[34] *Positive Theory of Capital*, p. 269.

investment will mature earlier than next year's invest-ment.[35] If a fruit tree is planted today which will bear fruit in four years, the labor available today for plant-ing it is preferred to the same amount of labor available next year for the reason that if the planting is deferred a year, the fruit will likewise be deferred a year, matur-ing in five instead of four years from the present. It does not alter this essential fact to speak of the possi-bility of a number of different investments. A month's labor today may, it is true, be spent in planting slow-growing or fast-growing trees, but so may a month's labor invested next year. It is from the preference for the early over the late fruition of *any* productive process that the so-called technical superiority of present over future goods, as conceived by Böhm-Bawerk, derives all its force.

Böhm-Bawerk, however, attempts to prove that his third circumstance—the alleged technical superiority of present goods—is really independent of the first two, by the following reasoning: [36]

". . . if every employment of goods for future periods is, not only technically, but economically, more remunerative than the em-ployment of them for the present or near future, of course men would withdraw their stocks of goods, to a great extent, from the service of the present, and direct them to the more remunerative service of the future. But this would immediately cause an ebb-tide in the provision for the present, and a flood in the provision for the future, for the future would then have the double advantage of having a greater amount of productive instruments directed to its service, and those instruments employed in more fruitful method of production. Thus the difference in the circumstances of provision,

[35] This is true under the assumption, implied in Böhm-Bawerk's tables, that the product is the same except as to the time of its availability, namely, that the series of figures called "units of product" are identical as shown in his tables.

[36] *Positive Theory of Capital*, pp. 269 and 270.

which might have disappeared for the moment, would recur of its own accord.

"But it is just at this point that we get the best proof that the superiority in question is independent of differences in the circumstances of provision: so far from being obliged to borrow its strength and activity from any such difference, it is, on the contrary, able, if need be, to call forth this very difference. . . . We have to deal with a third cause of the surplus value, and one which is independent of any of the two already mentioned."

The argument here is that if "the other two circumstances" which produce interest, namely, underestimate of the future and underendowment of the present, are temporarily absent, they will be forced back into existence by the choice of roundabout processes. In other words, the technical superiority of present goods produces interest by restoring the other two circumstances. But this is tantamount to the admission that technical superiority actually depends for its force on the presence of these other two circumstances and is *not* independent. The essential fact is that the presence of technical superiority does not produce interest when the other two are absent.[37]

Although Böhm-Bawerk devoted many pages in the third edition of his book and the Supplements (Exkurse) to answering my criticisms,[38] I can find nothing in his answers which affects the main argument as set forth

[37] See von Bortkiewicz, *Der Kardinalfehler der Böhm-Bawerkschen Zinstheorie.* Jahrbuch für Gesetzgebung, Verwaltung und Volkswirtschaft, 1906, pp. 61-90.

See also von Schaposchnicoff, *Die Böhm-Bawerksche Kapitalzinstheorie.* Jahrbücher für Nationalökonomie und Statistik. Verlag von Gustav Fischer, Jena, Dritte Folge, Bd. XXXIII (LXXXVIII), pp. 433-451.

[38] *Positive Theorie des Kapitales.* Dritte Auflage, and *Exkurse zur Positive Theorie des Kapitales.* See especially Exkurse IV and Exkurse XII.

above.[39] I have omitted certain of the less important of my original criticisms to which Böhm-Bawerk has replied.

Perhaps the most interesting point about Böhm-Bawerk's failure correctly to formulate the "technical" feature which he thus vainly sought is that it is really much simpler than he imagined. It does not require his elaborate tables and comparisons among their many columns. Merely the first column of his tables contains implicitly the true "technical" feature in one of its many forms of choosing from among optional income streams. This shows the successive amounts of product obtainable for a series of production periods of different lengths. This series is exactly analogous to the successive ordinates in Chart 16 showing the lumber to be obtained from a forest at different dates. There comes a point in such a series or such a curve, where a further lengthening of the time by one year will add to the product over the preceding year (i.e., will yield a rate of return over cost

---

[*] Böhm-Bawerk claims that merely to *find out* the factors operative in a given problem is not the same thing as to *explain* those factors. He thinks that my theory of interest would be adequate only if the mathematical solution of the problem by means of simultaneous equations, and what he calls the "causal" solution were the same, or at least somewhat similar.

Of course, these two types of solution are not the same. The causal solution cannot be so simply conceived as to make one factor solely *cause* and *another* solely effect. The advance of all science has required the abandonment of such simplified conceptions of causal relationship for the more realistic conception of equilibrium.

Here, all factors are considered as variables. Any disturbance in one factor reacts on all the others, and the variations in these other factors react upon the factor of original disturbance. The mathematical solution of the problem of interest by means of simultaneous equations recognizes the mutual interdependence of all the factors in the interest problem and, at the same time, yields a determinate solution for the problem.

both reckoned in kind) at a rate harmonizing with the rate of interest. Oddly enough Böhm-Bawerk does not mention this derivative from his table. Another form, more nearly what Böhm-Bawerk apparently was groping for, could have been presented had his table been extended to include not merely one dose of 100 days labor but many such doses and if "labor" and "product" were reduced to a common denominator. Then the product of the marginal labor would be the return while the labor itself would be the cost from which return over cost could be derived. But the comparisons which Böhm-Bawerk actually employed are beside the point.

§7. *Interest as a Cost*

From the foregoing criticisms and discussion it will, I hope, be seen that I have given full recognition, in this book, to the elements of productivity, technique of production, and cost, and that my chief objections to their treatment by many other writers is either that their treatment is inadequate and leaves the problem of interest indeterminate, or simply that they do not reduce the problem to its simplest terms.

In particular, it has been noted that the ultimate economic cost is labor and that all money payments and industrial operations intervening between labor and satisfactions may, in the large view, be dropped out. I have endeavored, in this and in other ways, to articulate the theory of interest with sound accounting principles, even when no great damage would be done to interest theory, as such, if unsound accounting were allowed to enter.

The most flagrant case of unsound accounting injected into this discussion is, in my opinion, when waiting is regarded as a cost.

This grows out of the common tendency to account for all economic values in terms of cost. When we cannot find the cost, we invent it. We feel sure interest must be fully accounted for in terms of cost. When we find inadequate the cost of producing capital or the cost of managing it or of organizing it or of investing it, we fall back on waiting, abstinence, or labor of saving.

It is true that these words are used by some writers to mean nothing more than what I have included in the phrase impatience or time preference. In these cases the question is merely one of terminology. In a large number of instances, however, the abstinence or waiting theory seems to me to differ from the impatience theory not only in words but in essence. In this the assumption is made that abstinence or waiting exists as an independent item in the cost of production, to be added to the other costs and to be treated in all ways like them.

If abstinence or waiting or labor of saving is in any sense a cost, it is certainly a cost in a very different sense from all other items which have previously been considered as costs. An illustration will make clear the difference between true costs and the purely fictitious or invented cost of waiting. According to the theory that waiting is a cost, if planting a sapling costs $1 worth of labor, and in 25 years, without further expenditure of labor, or any other cost whatever (*except* waiting) this sapling becomes worth $3, this $3 is a mere equivalent for the entire cost of producing the tree. The items in this cost are, it is claimed, $1 worth of labor and $2 worth of waiting.

According to the theory of the present book, however, the cost of producing the tree is the $1 worth of labor, and nothing more. The value of the tree, $3, exceeds that cost by a surplus of $2, the existence of which as interest it is our business to explain. Labor cost and waiting are too radically different to be grouped together as though each were a cost in the same sense as the other.

The cost of waiting can neither be located in time, independently of the item waited for, nor can it, like any other item, be discounted, for it is itself the discounting. If we discount the discounting, we would have to discount the discounting of the discounting and repeat the process indefinitely.

If we insist on calling waiting or abstinence a cost we reduce to absurdity all our economic accounting. Among other things, the simplest, purest type of income, a perpetual annuity, will be found, by such accounting, to be no income at all.

An able critic and correspondent, after admitting this fact, says simply, "What of it?"

Well, perhaps nothing vital as to the theory of interest itself. And since that is, after all, the sole subject of this book I shall relegate to the Appendix the discussion of What of it? as to accounting.[40]

§8. *Empirical and Institutional Influences on Interest Rates*

The problem of fully determining any specific market rate of interest is an intricate and baffling problem to solve just as is the problem of fully explaining any historical fact whatsoever. This volume makes no claim to being the monumental work necessary to analyze every possible influence that acts upon such a rate. The purpose of the book is rather to isolate the fundamental or basic forces which are operative in the interest problem.

The approach is theoretical, rational, or philosophic, if

[40] See Appendix to this Chapter, §1.

you like, as contrasted with the statistical, empirical, or quantitative approach. While it is true that in the discussion of the theoretical portions of the book, empirical evidence has been employed, this analysis is supplemental to rather than independent of the principles to be illustrated or tested.

The aim in view has therefore dictated the suppression of the innumerable secondary factors in order to focus the analysis upon the primary factors involved. It is these latter factors with which pure economic theory is con-concerned and this book is intended to be a study in pure theory.

As such, its ultimate objective is to explain how the rate of interest would be determined *in vacuo* or under the ideal operation of the assumptions. Outside this domain, there are literally thousands of forces which would have to be analyzed and allowed for before an adequate explanation of an actual market rate of interest could be made.

Thus, after presenting in Chapter II the theoretical relations of changes in the value of money to the rate of interest, we assume thereafter (until we reach Chapter XIX) a constant value of money and therefore the absence of any influence of a changing value of money. Yet we know that such an assumption is seldom realised in this actual world of incessant inflation and deflation.

Although this methodology of pure theory is at one with that employed in the whole range of scientific investigation, it may seem to some open to the criticism of being unreal and therefore presumably defective, if not useless, so far as practical affairs go.[41] While it is impos-

[41] Veblen, *Fisher's Rate of Interest,* Political Science Quarterly, Vol. XXIV, June, 1909, pp. 296-303. Marget, *The Loan Fund,* a doctoral dis-

sible, because of the divergent approaches, to express succinctly the criticisms which revolve about this point, certain examples may be given to set forth their general content and character.

Professor Thorstein Veblen, for example, asserted that interest did not come into existence until a high state of development had been reached in business and in money economy and credit economy. He argued that credit economy giving rise to interest economy has existed for "only a relatively brief phase of civilization that has been preceded by thousands of years of cultural growth during which the existence of such a thing as interest was never suspected" (p. 299).

"In short", Professor Veblen continued, "interest is a business proposition and is to be explained only in terms of business, not in terms of livelihood as Mr. Fisher aims to do" (p. 299). He admitted that business may be the chief or sole method of getting a livelihood, but asserted that business gains are not convertible with the sensations of consumption, as he thought my theory requires (pp. 299 and 300). Any argument for convertibility, or equivalence, is fallacious because "habitual modes of activity and relations have grown up and have by convention settled into a fabric of institutions" (p. 300).

If, at the start, we grant the postulate that the market rate of interest as set on money loans under a money economy or credit economy is the only interest rate existent, we are confronted with the problem of explaining why such a rate of interest exists. Institutions of them-

sertation at Harvard University, 1926; Schumpeter, *Theorie der Wirtschaftlichen Entwicklung*, p. 363. Criticisms of a similar character have been received in private correspondence from several of those who read this book in manuscript, particularly Professors L. D. Edie, B. H. Beckhart, and C. O. Hardy.

selves do not explain it. Institutions and conventions, like business, have been created by men, not from some inexplicable purpose unconnected with their living and feeling, but in order to add to the gratifications they obtain from living. Institutions cannot make men act or think other than as men. These man-made, man-operated institutions are merely tools devised by man to create for him gratifications more readily and more abundantly.

In my analysis, I find man's impatience to enjoy today and his desire to grasp the opportunities to invest so as to provide future enjoyments the fundamental causes which account for the emergence of incomes and of interest. To start with business institutions and attempt to explain the existence of interest as a phenomenon created by banks is like trying to explain value as something created by produce markets and stock exchanges.

Impatience and opportunity are working themselves out in the activities of business institutions, and men cannot avoid the dominance of these impulses and situations when engaged in any activity that demands a choice between present and future income. Interest, therefore, cannot be restricted to an explicit or contractual phenomenon but must be inherent in all buying and selling, and in all transactions and human activities which involve the present and the future.

While I cannot accept the view which would cast overboard theory because it is theory, I am keenly aware of the fact that theory as such does not tell the whole story about an actual rate of interest. Pure theory is not called upon so to do.

But after pure theory has said its last word, there is a broad field for empirical study of omitted factors. While we assumed that the unstable dollar remained stable and worked no interference with the fundamental forces determining the rate of interest, we know that in actual fact, the interference of a changing money value with these forces is tremendous—because of the "money illusion."

Laws, gold movements, stock exchange speculation, banking customs and policies, governmental finance, corporation practice, investment trusts and many other factors work their influences on the so-called money market where interest rates are determined. Practically, these matters are of equal importance with fundamental theory. While theory, in other words, assumes a waveless sea, actual, practical life represents a choppy one.

§9. *Conclusion*

In the study of such a complex and many-sided problem as that of the rate of interest, it is natural (and in fact, very desirable) that there should be many different approaches, views, and methods. Unfortunately, however, this latitude for individual interpretation and analysis has many times invited misunderstanding, confusion, and magnification of non-essential differences.

I have attempted to set forth and analyze in this chapter those matters contained in the criticisms of *The Rate of Interest* which, to my mind, are of major importance, and concerning which there still exists considerable disagreement among students of the interest problem.

Many of these questions seem to me to be based on misunderstandings of my theory of interest. I have been greatly helped by criticisms of this kind to see the shortcomings of my first attempt to expound that theory. I am hopeful that my present efforts to set forth in sharper relief and with greater clarity one solution of the problem of interest will succeed in subordinating these secondary matters to the more important issues of fundamental theory.

This done, I am confident that economic theorists will find that they are not so far apart on matters of fundamental theory as their writings would seem to indicate. When mutual understanding is achieved, they will undoubtedly find that their differences are often more apparent than real, consisting chiefly in the methods of approach and of analysis.

CHAPTER XXI

SUMMARY

§1. *Interest and Purchasing Power of Money*

We have seen that, theoretically, the rate of interest should be subject to both a nominal and a real variation, the nominal variation being that connected with changes in the standard of value, and the real variation being that connected with the other and deeper economic causes.

As to the nominal variation in the rate of interest, we found that, theoretically, an appreciation of 1 per cent of the standard of value in which the rate of interest is expressed, compared with some other standard, will reduce the rate of interest in the former standard, compared with the latter, by about 1 per cent, and that, contrariwise, a depreciation of 1 per cent will raise the rate by that amount. Such a change in the rate of interest would merely be a change in the number expressing it, and not fundamentally a real change. Yet, in actual practice, for the very lack of this perfect theoretical adjustment, the appreciation or depreciation of the monetary standard does produce a real effect on the rate of interest, and that a most vicious one. This effect, in times of great changes in the purchasing power of money, is by far the greatest of all effects on the real rate of interest. This effect is due to the fact that the money rate of interest, while it does change somewhat according to the theory as described in Chapters II and XIX, does not usually change enough to fully compensate for the appreciation or depreciation. The inadequacy in the adjustment of the rate of interest results in an unforeseen loss to the debtor, and an unforeseen gain to the creditor, or *vice versa* as the case may be. When the price level falls, the interest rate *nominally* falls slightly, but *really* rises greatly and when the price level rises, the rate of interest *nominally* rises slightly, but *really* falls greatly. It is consequently of the utmost importance, in interpreting the rate of interest statistically, to ascertain in each case in which direction the monetary standard is moving and to remember that the direction in which the interest rate apparently moves is generally precisely the opposite of that in which it really moves.

It should also be noted that in so far as there exists any adjustment of the money rate of interest to the changes in the purchasing power of money, it is for the most part (1) lagged and (2) indirect. The lag, distributed, has been shown to extend over several years. The indirectness of the effect of changed purchasing power of money comes largely through the intermediate steps which affect business profits and volume of trade, which in turn affect the demand for loans and the rate of interest. There is very little direct and conscious adjustment through fore-sight. Where such foresight is conspicuous, as in the final period of German inflation, there is less lag in the effects.

§2. *The Six Principles*

But the more fundamental theory of interest presupposes a stable purchasing power of money so that the real and nominal rates coincide. In that case the rate is theoretically determined by six sets of equations or conditions: the two Opportunity Principles; the two Impatience Principles; and the two Market Principles. The last pair may be said to cover *prima facie* supply and demand.

(A) The market must be cleared—and cleared with respect to every interval of time. (B) The debts must be paid.

The other two pairs represent the two sets of forces, one objective and the other subjective, behind supply and demand. The subjective pair expresses the influence of human impatience or time preference.

(A) The rate of time preference depends on the character of the various individuals concerned and on each individual's prospective income, its size, time-shape and risk. (B) Each individual's rate of time preference tends, at the margin of choice, to harmonize with the market rate of interest. Human impatience to spend and enjoy income is crystallized into the market rate.

The objective pair expresses the influence of investment opportunities.

(A) Each individual is encompassed about by opportunities to change the character of his prospective income stream. (B) At the margin of choice, any additions to an individual's future income at the cost of more immediate income constitutes a return over that cost, the rate of which return over said cost is also crystallized into the market rate of interest.

So the rate of interest is the mouthpiece at once of impatience to spend income without delay and of opportunity to increase income by delay.

Thus both from the subjective and the objective field appear prototypes, one of each for every individual, of the market rate of interest.

That rate, i, is equal to every individual's degree of impatience or rate of time preference, f, and also to his investment opportunity rate or rate of return over cost, r.

Yet these equations are not enough to make the problem determinate without those of the other four sets of determining conditions (clearing the market, repaying debts and empirical dependence of impatience and investment opportunity).

Much less is it possible to determine the rate of interest from the subjective side alone, through time preference, or from the objective side alone, through investment opportunity, or "productivity", or "technique of production".

The full explanation requires both (as well as the market principles) in order that there may be as many independent equations as unknown variables in the problem. Moreover there is not merely one rate of interest; there are many, one for each interval of time. And even so the explanation is full only under the theoretical conditions presupposed. If we pass beyond the presuppositions in order to approximate closer to the actual world, we find that, to be determinate, the problem requires more and more equations of a more and more empirical nature. This is especially true as (1) we introduce risk with its innumerable and omnipresent ramifications, involving in particular a multiplicity of rates of interest even for the same period of time; and as (2) we extend our view to admit variations in all other prices besides the rates of interest, involving thereby the whole economic equilibrium, not only of the loan market but of all markets, each interacting on every other; and as (3) we extend our view from one theoretical market to the actual markets of the whole world, involving thereby all the relations of international trade; and as (4) we take account of any other factors which may not be included in the foregoing specifications so as to take account, in particular, of all "institutional" influences, laws, politics, banking practices, government finance and so on to the end.

In the economic universe, as in astronomy, every star reacts on every other. From a practical point of view we cannot ignore the many perturbations. But from the theoretical point of view we gain clearness, simplicity and beauty, if we allow ourselves to assume certain other things equal, and confine our laws to a little part of the whole, such as the solar system.

From such a point of view, the second approximation is the most instructive, rather than the first which rules out the important element of investment opportunity, or than the third which becomes too complicated and vague for any complete theoretical treatment.

§3. *The Nature of Investment Opportunity*

In the second approximation—which, as we have just noted, contains all that is most typical in the theory of the rate of interest—the distinctive factor is the rate of return over cost or the investment opportunity rate. This is also the most difficult factor to picture, isolate, and disentangle from the rate of interest which it helps determine. Therefore, it is a matter of great importance pedagogically to make that distinction clear. The investment opportunity rate is distinct from the market or loan rate of interest because an investment opportunity is distinct from a loan. Investment opportunity, as here used, does not include a mere loan at the market rate of interest nor any other purchase-and-sale transaction made merely on the basis of the market rate. The definition of investment opportunity is specially framed to exclude mere loans. It is any opportunity of an individual to modify his prospective income other than by merely lending or borrowing (or the equivalent, buying or selling) at the market rate of interest.

Under this definition and the assumptions employed in the theory there can never be any doubt as to whether a given proposed transaction is an investment opportunity or a market loan or purchase. In the case of a market loan or purchase the individual cannot vary the rate of interest by any act of his, such as varying the size of his transactions. Under our assumptions of a perfect market his influence on the market rate is not only unconscious but infinitesimal and therefore entirely negligible in our analysis in which his motivity is of the essence. In the case of an investment opportunity, on the other hand, *he can vary the rate of return* by varying the size of his operations.

This contrast between the theoretical constancy of the one and the variability of the other, in relation to individual action, is due to the fact that in the public market the individual is a negligible element, while an investment opportunity is more private and personal to him or his group. The former is typified by the purchase, say, of a Liberty bond, or other standard securities. The latter is typified by building a factory, improving a sales organization, deepening the shaft of a mine—cases where the marginal rate of return is under the control of the individual since he sets the margin.

Of course it is true that, in almost every such operation, there are elements of purchase and sale in which the market rate of interest is an implicit ingredient, but as long as the operation is not exclusively a mere market interest affair and contains other ingredients, the rate is subject to variation with the extent of the operation and so is to be called a rate of return over cost. We are here interested in those other ingredients which produce the variability and thus differentiate such a rate from the market rate of interest. They are the non-commercial or non-trading ingredients; they concern production and technique rather than trade. They deal not with the market place, but with nature, environment, and the refractory conditions which surround and hamper us in our efforts to secure income. They exist even when no market exists, when a Robinson Crusoe, a hermit, or an isolated ranchman battles with soil and the elements for his daily bread.

The rate of return over cost, under the law of diminishing returns, is thus far more elementary and primeval than the rate of interest, and however incrusted that rate of return may become with other elements which grow out of modern market conditions it is still the basic objective condition underlying our problem.

Thus the rate of return over cost is distinguished from the rate of interest (1) by varying with the extent of the individual's investment; (2) by being consciously recognized, as thus variable [1] and controllable, by the individual; (3) by being, therefore, a personal and individual matter and not altogether a public market matter; (4) by being directly related to producing as contrasted with trading.

---

[1] It is true that in the hard-tack case and some other extreme and hypothetical cases considered, it was assumed that for a certain interval the O curve was assumed to be straight. To include such a theoretical case, the statements in the text need a slight modification. But such extreme cases are not typical even in the theory and are probably never exemplified in practice.

THE THEORY OF INTEREST

§4. *Investment Opportunity for Society as a Whole*

In modern society hermits and self-supporting ranches are so rare that we cannot find any important cases where investment opportunities exist in pure primitive form and apart from the alloy of trading. In fact, the most typical investment opportunities are not only full of such alloys but are tied up with market financing operations. Almost every big investment opportunity is married to a productive loan.

The best picture on a big scale of investment opportunity, divested so far as may be of all ancillary market features, is to be found by considering society as a whole instead of the individual.

Society as a whole cannot borrow or lend as an individual can. This world can, for instance, add nothing to this year's income by a loan from elsewhere and subtract this amount with interest from future income. Yet it can and does vary and control the total income stream according to investment opportunity.

This picture, in the large, of society arranging, modifying, adjusting its total income stream as between this year and later years is the most important picture we can draw of investment opportunity not only because it automatically leaves out borrowing and lending, or buying and selling, but also because it automatically reduces the picture of income to its fundamental terms of real or, as I prefer to call it, enjoyment income and its obverse, labor pain. We do not have to think so vividly, as we do in the case of an individual, of money items and intermediate processes. We can without difficulty fix our attention on the final consumption. Society is like Robinson Crusoe picking and eating his berries, however complicated may be the apparatus which intervenes between the labor of picking and the enjoyment of eating.

Society may add to or subtract from its income stream at will at any period, present or future. But beyond a certain point every addition at one period must be at the cost of a subtraction at some other period. If future income is added, the increment so added is a return on and at the cost of a decrement in less remote income. The rate of return over cost is thus a social phenomenon of great significance. There are two and only two ways in which society may effect the present cost and the future return. It may effect the present cost by exerting more present labor or by abstaining more from present consumption; and it may realize the future return over that cost either in the form of more future consumption or of less future toil.

Both the present and the future adjustments are effected by changing the use made of capital instruments including land and human beings. That is, the labor, land, and other capital of society may be used in many optional ways and in particular may be invested for the early or remote future.

If the capital instruments of the community are of such a nature as to offer a *wide* range of choice, we have seen that the rate of interest will tend to be *steady*. If the range of choice is *narrow,* the rate of interest will tend to be *variable*. If the range of choice is relatively rich in *future* income as compared with the more immediate income, the rate of interest will tend to be high. If the range of choice tends to favor *immediate income* as compared with more remote future income, the rate of interest will tend to be *low*.

Thus, for the United States during the last century,

its resources were of such a character as to favor future income. This is true, for a time at least, in every undeveloped country, and, as we have seen, gives the chief explanation of the fact that the rate of interest in such localities is usually high. The same is true of countries recovering from war. Today, for instance, Germany resembles a pioneer country. Her present income is necessarily low, but her prospect of a higher and increasing income in a few years is very great. The range of choice is dominated by "low today and high tomorrow."

The range of choice in any community is subject to many changes as time goes on, due chiefly to one or more of three causes: first, a progressive increase or decrease in resources; second, the discovery of new resources or means of developing old ones; and third, change in political conditions.

Under the first head may be noted the impending exhaustion of the coal supply in England, as noted by Jevons and other writers. This will tend to make the income stream from that island decrease, at least in the remote future, and this in turn will tend to keep the rate of interest there low. Under the second head, the constant stream of new inventions, by making the available income streams rich in the future, at the sacrifice of immediate income, tends to make the rate of interest high. This effect, however, is confined to the period of exploitation of the new invention, and is succeeded later by an opposite tendency. During the last half century the exploitation of Stephenson's invention of the locomotive, by presenting the possibility of a relatively large future income at the cost of comparatively little sacrifice in the present, tended to keep the rate of interest high. As the period of extensive railroad building is drawing to a close, this effect is becoming exhausted, and the tendency of the rate of interest, so far as this particular influence is concerned, is to fall.

On the other hand, the invention of the automobile, and the inventions and discoveries in electricity and chemistry have succeeded the railroads as a field for investment and have required new sacrifices of immediate income for the sake of future income. Thus, as fast as the first effect of any one invention, tending to raise interest, wears off and is succeeded by its secondary effect in lowering interest, this secondary effect is likely to be offset by the oncoming of new inventions.

As to the third head, political conditions which affect the rate of interest, such as the insecurity of property rights which occurs during political upheaval, as in Russia recently, tend to make the pure or riskless rate of interest low. At the same time it adds an element of risk to most loans, thereby diminishing the number of safe and increasing the number of unsafe loans. Hence the commercial rate of interest in ordinary loans during periods of lawlessness is likely to be high. Reversely, during times of peace and security, the riskless rate of interest is comparatively high, while the commercial rate tends to be low.

§5. *Time Preference*

We turn now to the remaining factor, namely, the dependence of time preference of each individual on his selected income stream. We have seen that the rate of preference for immediate as compared with remote income will depend upon the character of the income stream selected, but the manner of this dependence is subject to great variation and change. The manner in which a spendthrift will react to an income stream is very different from the manner in which the shrewd accumulator of capital will react to the same income stream. We have seen that the time preference of an individual will vary with six different factors: (1) his foresight; (2) his self-control; (3) habit; (4) the prospective length and certainty of his life; (5) his love of offspring and regard for posterity; (6) fashion. It is evident that each of these circumstances may change. The causes most likely to effect such changes are: (1) training to foster a realization of the need to provide against the proverbial "rainy day"; (2) education in self-control; (3) formation of habits of frugality, avoiding parsimony on the one hand and extravagance on the other; (4) better hygiene and care of personal health, leading to longer and more healthful life; (5) incentives to provide more generously for offspring and for the future generations; (6) modification of fashion toward less wasteful and harmful expenditures for the purpose of ostentatious display.

These various factors may act and react upon each other, and may affect profoundly the rate of preference for present over future income, and thereby influence greatly the rate of interest. Where, as in Scotland, there are educational tendencies which instill the habit of thrift from childhood, the rate of interest tends to be low. Where, as in ancient Rome, at the time of its decline, there is a tendency toward reckless luxury, competition in ostentation, and a degeneration in the bonds of family life, there is a consequent absence of any desire to prolong income beyond one's own term of life, and the rate of interest tends to be high. Where, as in Russia, under the Czars, wealth tended to be concentrated and social stratification to be rigid, the great majority of the community, on the one hand, through poverty and the recklessness which poverty begets, tends to have a high rate of preference for present over future income, whereas, at the opposite end of the ladder, the inherited habit of luxurious living tends, though in a different way, in the same direction. In such a community, the rate of interest is likely to be unduly high.

§6. *Conclusion*

From the foregoing enumeration, it is clear that the rate of interest is dependent upon very unstable influences many of which have their origin deep down in the social fabric and involve considerations not strictly economic. Any causes tending to affect intelligence, foresight, self-control, habits, the longevity of man, family affection, and fashion will have their influence upon the rate of interest.

§7. *The Future*

From what has been said it is clear that, in order to estimate the possible variation in the rate of interest, we may, broadly speaking, take account of the following three groups of causes: (1) the thrift, foresight, self-control, and love of offspring which exist in a community; (2) the progress of inventions; (3) the changes in the purchasing power of money. The first cause tends to lower the rate of interest; the second, to raise it at first and later to lower it; and the third to affect the nominal rate of interest, in one direction and the real rate of interest in the opposite direction.

Were it possible to estimate the strength of the various forces thus summarized, we might base upon them a prediction as to the rate of interest in the future. Such a prediction, however, to be of value, would require more painstaking study than has ever been given to this subject.

Without such a careful investigation, any prediction is hazardous. We can say, however, that the immediate prospects for a change in the monetary standard seem to be toward its stabilization; that this will tend toward a general prosperity, the main effects of which should be in the direction of lowering the rate of interest; that changes in thrift, foresight, self-control, and benevolence are for the most part likely to intensify these factors and thus to lower the rate of interest; and that the progress of discovery and invention shows now a tendency to increase in speed, the immediate result of which should be to raise the rate of interest but finally to lower it.

APPENDIX TO CHAPTER I

§ 1 (to Ch. I, § 1)

Quotations from Professor Canning's book

THE importance to the accountant of a clear and consistent concept of income and of capital is emphasized by Professor John B. Canning in his book, *The Economics of Accountancy; A Critical Analysis of Accounting Theory.*

It may not be amiss at this point to put forward a comparative appraisal of the accountant's views and those of Fisher. And it may be convenient to make that appraisal upon the basis adopted for comparison, viz., scope of subject matter contemplated, mode of analysis pursued, and point of view taken.

With respect to the first there can be no possible doubt that Fisher's work is immensely superior. How much of his views will ultimately prevail among economists and among accountants no one need consider. Only a guess could be made. What the event will ultimately prove, too, might as readily be a fact about the two professions as a fact about Fisher's theory. But as a general, comprehensive treatment of the theory of income, there is nothing to compare favorably with it in either literature. (p. 172.)

* * * *

In a late article Fisher says: "I believe that the concept of income is, without exception, the most vital central concept in economic science and that on fully grasping its nature and interrelations with other concepts largely depends the full fruition both of economic theory and of its applications to taxation and statistics."[1] If he had written instead that *income is, without exception, the simplest and most fundamental concept of economic science, that only by means of this concept can other economic concepts ever be fully developed and understood, and that upon beginning with this concept depends the full*

[1] American Economic Review, Vol. XIV, p. 64.

APPENDIX

fruition of economic theory in economic statistics, it would 'have been an equally true and a more significant statement. (p. 175.)

* * * *

The present writer believes that had Fisher written *Income and Capital*, beginning with a chapter on the topic of psychic income and ending with a chapter on wealth considered as a kind of embodiment of services directly or indirectly to become income, his work would not only have been more useful to the thoughtful reading public at large, but also and most particularly, to accountants and economists.

There is very real occasion for regret that the professional accountants have found so little occasion to work in the subject of final objective income. It can hardly be doubted that, in their enterprise (income accounts) they, at times, lose sight of the fact that such statistics are wanted primarily for the ordering of the mode of living of the persons interested. For example, it is usually pressure upon shareholders for the wherewithal to meet living expenses that excites the clamor for larger dividends. Full statement of the earning prospects that condition the upbuilding of surplus would, at least, prevent their urging dividend payments contrary to their own best interests. Full statement, too, even though no dividends are forthcoming, may put the shareholders in a favorable position — through selling part of their holdings or borrowing upon them — to maintain their customary scale of living. By keeping more constantly in mind the gap between the enterprise earnings and the mode of life of the persons interested, the usefulness of their income statistics could be greatly enhanced.

From the economist's point of view, and for the good of the public, it is of very great importance that the accountants should make their income statistics as full and as complete as the conditions of their professional practice will permit. (pp. 176 and 177.)

APPENDIX TO CHAPTER X

§ 1 (to Ch. X, § 2)

[Geometric representation of incomes for three years

IF we proceed from the consideration of two years to that of three, we may still represent our problem geometrically by using a model in three dimensions. Let us imagine three

APPENDIX

mutually perpendicular axes from an origin O called respectively OX', OX'', OX''', and represent the income combination or income stream for the particular individual by the point P, whose coördinates c', c'', and c''' are the three years' income installments with which the individual is initially endowed. Then through the point P draw, instead of the straight line in the previous representation, a *plane ABC* cutting the three axes in A, B, and C. This plane has a slope with reference to the two axes OX' and OX'' of $\frac{OB}{OA}$ equal to $1 + i'$ (unity or 100 per cent plus the rate of interest connecting the first and second years), and has a slope with reference to the axes OX'' and OX''' represented by $\frac{OC}{OB}$ equal to $1 + i''$ (unity plus the rate of interest connecting the second and third years). Now suppose the space between the axes to be filled with willingness *surfaces* laminated like the coats of an onion, such that for all points on the same surface, the total desirability or wantability of the triple income combination or income position represented by each of those points will be the same. These surfaces will be such as to approach the three axes and the planes between them, and also such that the attached numbers representing their respective total wantabilities shall increase as they recede from the origin. The plane ABC drawn through P at the slope fixed by the rates of interest just indicated will now be tangent to some one of the willingness surfaces at a point Q, which is the point at which the individual will, under these conditions, fix his income situation, for every point on the plane ABC will have the same present value, and every point on this plane is available to him by borrowing and lending (or buying and selling) at the rates i' and i'', but not all of them will have the same desirability, or wantability. He will select that one which has the maximum wantability, and this will evidently be the point Q, at which the plane is tangent to one of the family of willingness surfaces. This point will be such that the rates of time preference will be equal to the rate of interest.

[509]

APPENDIX

So much for the individual. The market problem determining the rate of interest is here solved by finding such an orientation for the various *planes* through the given points called P's as will bring the center of gravity of the tangential points, the Q's, into coincidence with the fixed center of gravity of the P's.

To proceed beyond three years would take us into the fourth dimension and beyond. Such a representation cannot be fully visualized, and therefore has little meaning except to mathematicians.

APPENDIX TO CHAPTER XII

§ 1 (to Ch. XII, § 1)

Algebraic expression of rate of time preference

If W signifies wantability, or utility, or desirability and this year's income is signified by X' and next year's by X'', then $\Delta W'$ may be taken to signify the present wantability of, or want for, a small increment, $\Delta X'$ of money *this* year and $\frac{\Delta W'}{\Delta X'}$ will be the want-for-one-more unit of money this year. Also $\Delta W''$ is the present want for a small increment, $\Delta X''$, of money available *next year*, and $\frac{\Delta W''}{\Delta X''}$ will be the present want-for-one-more unit of money available next year.

Exact mathematical theory requires that the marginal wants per unit of money are the *limits* of those ratios when the increments approach zero as their limits, or $\lim \frac{\Delta W'}{\Delta X'}$ and $\lim \frac{\Delta W''}{\Delta X''}$ ordinarily written in the differential calculus: $\frac{dW'}{dX'}$ and $\frac{dW''}{dX''}$ which, for short, may be called w' and w''.

The rate of preference, f, for a unit of present money over a unit of next year's may be defined as $f = \frac{w' - w''}{w''}$.

APPENDIX

§ 2 (to Ch. XII, § 3)

Equality of marginal rate of time preference and rate of interest implies that desirability of income stream is made a maximum

ASSUME at first that only two years are considered. The fact that total desirability or wantability of the individual, as reckoned at the beginning, depends on the amount of income this year and next year may be represented by the equation

$$W'' = \mathbf{F}(c' + x', c'' + x''),$$

where W'' represents his total wantability, and the equation represents this W'' as a function of his income stream consisting of $c' + x'$ this year and $c'' + x''$ next year. This W'' is represented in Chapters X and XI by the numbers attached to the several Willingness or Wantability lines, each representing a certain level of wantability of Individual *1*. But as we shall here consider only one individual, we omit the subscript numbers, 1, 2, ..., n. The individual under consideration will attempt to adjust x' and x'' so as to maximize W. We are to prove algebraically that the condition that W shall be a maximum implies also that the rate of interest i shall be equal to the individual's rate of preference f. The condition[1] that W shall be a maximum is that the total differential of W or of its equal $\mathbf{F}(c' + x', c'' + x'')$, called below $\mathbf{F}(\ )$ shall be zero; thus

$$dW = \frac{\partial \mathbf{F}(\ )}{\partial x'}\, dx' + \frac{\partial \mathbf{F}(\ )}{\partial x''}\, dx'' = 0,$$

where the ∂'s represent the partial differentials with respect to x' and x''.

From this equation it follows that

$$-\frac{dx''}{dx'} = \frac{\partial \mathbf{F}(\ )}{\partial x'} \Big/ \frac{\partial \mathbf{F}(\ )}{\partial x''}.$$

The *left*-hand number of this equation is $1 + i$, as may be seen by differentiating the equation of the loan as originally stated, viz.:

[1] See any text book on the calculus, e.g. Wilson, E. B. *Advanced Calculus*. Boston, Ginn & Co., 1912, pp. 118–125.

[511]

$x' + \dfrac{x''}{1+i} = 0$. This differentiation yields $-\dfrac{dx''}{dx'} = 1 + i$.

The *right*-hand member, being the ratio of this year's marginal wantability to next year's marginal wantability, is by definition equal to $1 + f$. Substituting the new value for the right- and left-hand members, we have

$$1 + i = 1 + f,$$

whence it follows that $i = f$, which was to have been proved.

The same reasoning may now be applied to three or more years. The total wantability for any individual is a function of the total future income stream. In other words,

$$W = \mathbf{F}(c' + x', c'' + x'', \ldots\ldots, c^{(m)} + x^{(m)}).$$

The individual tries to make this magnitude a maximum. In terms of the calculus, this is equivalent to making the first total differential equal to zero namely,

$$dW = \frac{\partial \mathbf{F}(\ )}{\partial x'}\, dx' + \frac{\partial \mathbf{F}(\ )}{\partial x''}\, dx'' + \ldots\ldots + \frac{\partial \mathbf{F}(\ )}{\partial x^{(m)}}\, dx^{(m)} = 0.$$

This total differential equation is equivalent, according to well-known principles of the calculus to a number of subsidiary equations obtained by making particular suppositions as to the different variations. Let us, for instance, suppose that only x' and x'' vary in relation to each other and that x''', x^{iv}, $\ldots\ldots$, $x^{(m)}$ do not vary. Then in the above equation all terms after the second disappear and the equation reduces, as before, to

$$-\frac{dx''}{dx'} = \frac{\partial \mathbf{F}(\ )}{\partial x'} \bigg/ \frac{\partial \mathbf{F}(\ )}{\partial x''}.$$

So that, again, $1 + i' = 1 + f'$, and therefore $i' = f'$.

This expresses the relation between the first and second years. If we wish, in like manner, to express the corresponding connection between the second and third years, let us assume that x' as well as x^{iv}, $\ldots\ldots$, $x^{(m)}$ are constant but that x'' and x''' vary. Then the first term of the equation and all after the third disappear, and the equation reduces to

[512]

$$-\frac{dx'''}{dx''} = \frac{\partial \mathbf{F}(\ )}{\partial x''} \Big/ \frac{\partial \mathbf{F}(\ )}{\partial x'''}.$$

In other words, $1 + i'' = 1 + f''$, or $i'' = f''$. Similarly, $i = f$ for every other pair of successive years.

We have here, in mathematical language, the reason that the point of maximum total wantability is also the point at which the marginal rate of time preference for a unit of each year's income over that of next year's income is equal to the rate of interest connecting these two years.[2]

APPENDIX TO CHAPTER XIII

§ 1 (to Ch. XIII, § 9)

Rate of return over cost expressed in the notation of the calculus

In the notation of the calculus, the rate of return over cost, called in the text r_1', is defined in terms of the partial differential quotient with the opposite sign of next year's income with respect to this year's income of Individual 1. That is, by definition $1 + r_1' = -\dfrac{\partial y_1''}{\partial y_1'}$ and $1 + r_1'' = -\dfrac{\partial y_1'''}{\partial y_1''}$. Analogous formulas express the remaining r's for Individuals $1, 2 \ldots \ldots n$.

§ 2 (to Ch. XIII, § 9)

Rate of return over cost derived by differential equations

The magnitudes of $1 + r_1'$, $1 + r_1''$, $\ldots \ldots$, $1 + r_1^{(m)}$, or $-\dfrac{\partial y_1''}{\partial y_1'}$, $-\dfrac{\partial y_1'''}{\partial y_1''}$, $\ldots \ldots$, $-\dfrac{\partial y_1^{(m)}}{\partial y_1^{(m-1)}}$, may be expressed in terms of y_1', y_1'', $\ldots \ldots$, $y_1^{(m)}$ by differentiating the equation for the effective range of choice, $\phi_1 (y_1', y_1'', \ldots \ldots, y_1^{(m)}) = 0$.

[2] The mathematical reader will note that the function $\mathbf{F}$ here representing *total* wantability W is vitally related to the functions $\mathbf{F}$ in Chapters XII and XIII, representing the marginal rate of time preference f, since $1 + f$ is the ratio of the differential quotient of W relatively to this year's income to the corresponding differential quotient for next year's income.

APPENDIX

§ 3 (to Ch. XIII, § 7, also § 9)

Mathematical proof that the principle of maximum present value is identical with the principle that the marginal rate of return over cost is equal to the rate of interest.

THE mathematical proof that the principle of maximum present value of optional income streams is identical with the Investment Opportunity Principle B or that the rate of marginal return over cost is equal to the rate of interest is as follows:

The present value V_1 of any income stream y_1', y_1'', ..., $y_1^{(m)}$, of Individual *1* or their combined discounted value is

$$V_1 = y_1' + \frac{y_1''}{1 + i'} + \ldots\ldots + \frac{y_1^{(m)}}{(1+i')\,(1+i'')\ldots\ldots(1+i^{(m-1)})}.$$

The condition that this expression shall be a maximum is that the first differential quotient shall be zero. That is,

$$dV_1 = dy_1' + \frac{dy_1''}{1+i'} + \ldots\ldots + \frac{dy_1^{(m)}}{(1+i')(1+i'')\ldots\ldots(1+i^{(m-1)})} = 0.$$

This last equation expresses the relations which must exist between dy_1', dy_1'', ..., $dy_1^{(m)}$, in order that the income stream, y_1', y_1'', ..., $y_1^{(m)}$, may have the maximum present value.

This condition contains within itself a number of subsidiary conditions. To derive these, let us consider a slight variation in the income stream, affecting only the income items pertaining to the first two years, y_1', and y_1'' (the remaining items, y_1''', ..., $y_1^{(m)}$, being regarded for the time being as constant) and let us denote the magnitudes of dy_1' and dy_1'', under this assumption of restricted variations, by $\partial y_1'$ and $\partial y_1''$. Then, under the condition assumed of constancy of y_1''', y_1^{iv}, ..., $y_1^{(m)}$, dy_1''', dy_1^{iv}, ..., $dy_1^{(m)}$, are equal to zero, and the equation becomes

$$\partial y_1' + \frac{\partial y_1''}{1 + i'} = 0.$$

[514]

From this, it follows directly that

$$-\frac{\partial y_1{}''}{\partial y_1{}'} = 1 + i'.$$

But the left-hand member of this equation is by definition one plus the marginal rate of return over cost. Since we have designated the rate of return over cost by $r_1{}'$ we may substitute $1 + r_1{}'$ for the expression $-\dfrac{\partial y_1{}''}{\partial y_1{}'}$, and write the above equation thus:

$$1 + r_1{}' = 1 + i',$$

or thus:

$$r_1{}' = i'.$$

In other words, the condition that the marginal rate of return over cost is equal to the rate of interest follows as a consequence of the general condition that the present value of the income stream must be a maximum. This proposition and its proof are analogous to those in regard to desirability or wantability, which have already been discussed in the Appendix to Chapter XII, that the condition of maximum wantability is equivalent in the condition that the marginal rate of preference is equal to the rate of interest.

The same reasoning may be applied to any pair of successive years. Thus, if we assume variations in y'' and y''', without any variations in the other elements of the income stream, y', y^{iv}, $\ldots\ldots$, $y_1{}^m$, the original differential equation becomes

$$\frac{\partial y_1{}''}{1 + i'} + \frac{\partial y_1{}'''}{(1 + i')(1 + i'')} = 0,$$

or

$$-\frac{\partial y_1{}'''}{\partial y_1{}''} = 1 + i'',$$

or

$$1 + r_1{}'' = 1 + i'',$$

or

$$r_1{}'' = i''.$$

All this reasoning implies, in using the differentiation process, that there is continuous variation, and that, at the margin, it is possible to make slight variations in any two successive years' incomes without disturbing the incomes of the other years.

APPENDIX

§ 4 (to Ch. XIII, § 9)

Geometrical explanation of the proposition expounded in § 3 of this Appendix

BUT the foregoing proof by algebra may not appeal to many students as much as the proof by geometry.

We know (see Chapter X, § 3 and Chapter XI, §§ 4 and 5) that the present value of any income position on the Market line is the same as that of any other income position on that line.

It follows that the present value of any point on a given Market line is measured by the intercept of that line on the horizontal axis, for that intercept evidently measures the present market value of one particular point on the Market line (namely its lower end) and, as just stated, this must have the same present value as every other point on the Market line.

It follows that as the Market line is moved further away from the origin (keeping its direction unchanged) the intercept becomes greater, and thus the present value of every one of the points on the Market line becomes greater correspondingly.

When, therefore, the line is thus moved as far as possible, so that it thereby assumes the *position of tangent to the Opportunity line*, the present value of every point on it and, therefore, of that point of tangency must be greater than that of any other point on the Opportunity line, since any other such point will necessarily lie on a Market line nearer the origin.

The same proof applies in three dimensions, substituting Opportunity surface for Opportunity line and Market plane for Market line. By analogy the proof may be extended to n dimensions.

APPENDIX

§ 5 (to Ch. XIII, § 9)

Maximum total desirability is found when rate of time preference is equal to the rate of interest

In the last section was outlined a geometric proof that the income stream possessing the maximum present value is such that the rate of interest (connecting each pair of successive years) is equal to the rate of return over cost (for the same pair of successive years).

The geometric method also supplies a simple proof that the maximum total desirability, or wantability, is to be found in the case of that income stream which satisfies the above mentioned condition and, at the same time, has a rate of time preference equal to the rate of interest. In geometric terms for two dimensions this means that this most desirable income position or point is where the Market line, which is tangent to the Opportunity line, is tangent to a Willingness line.

Consider two parallel Market lines, one tangent to the Opportunity line and the other somewhat nearer the origin; and consider the two points Q and S where these two are respectively tangent to a Willingness line. We are to prove that the total desirability or wantability of Q is greater than that of S. Draw a straight line from the origin through S and produce it until it cuts the first Market line at, say, T.

It is evident, of course, that of all the points on any given Market line the point of tangency with a Willingness line is the most desirable income position. Therefore, Q is more desirable than T. We assume that the Willingness lines are such that the farther we recede along a straight line from the origin the more desirable the income situation. Therefore, T is more desirable than S.

Therefore, Q being more desirable than T, and T than S, Q is more desirable than S, which was to have been proved.

APPENDIX

§ 6 (to Ch. XIII, § 9)

Walras and Pareto

WALRAS and Pareto probably deserve more attention in interest theory, as in general economic theory, than they have received.

Walras' interest theory forms an integral part of his theory of general economic equilibrium.[1] His solution consists of a demonstration that the problem comprises a number of independent equations exactly equal to the number of unknowns, and that the mathematical solution of these simultaneous equations is a counterpart of the economic process by which the unknowns are determined in the market. There is thus no reasoning in a circle in the Walras system. The number of equations is exactly equal to the number of unknowns.

Walras' treatment of the problem of the determination of the rate of interest is very detailed and highly mathematical. For readers who are not familiar with his treatment I venture to attempt a brief summary. Walras assumes a market for capital goods as well as for services. He assumes that the prices of capital goods depend on the prices of their services. Since some capital goods last longer than others and all are subject to risk, he makes allowance for depreciation, amortization, and insurance.

His treatment combines the subjective and objective elements in a simple and direct manner. His cost of production equations correspond, in a general way, to my opportunity principles. His equation for the demand for savings corresponds, likewise, to my impatience principles.

Pareto's analysis of the problem of the rate of interest[2] is along the lines laid down by Walras, although he was evidently not fully satisfied with Walras' treatment. Neither he nor Walras has developed a systematic theory of income but he

[1] Walras, Leon, *Élements d'Économie Politique Pure.*
[2] Pareto, Vilfredo, *Cours d'Economie Politique.*

shows, in effect, that the substitution of one income stream for another or, as he says, the "transformation in time" is only a particular case of a more general transformation which is dealt with in the theory of production. His indifference equations for consumers correspond in a general way to my impatience principles and the analogous equations for the obstacles in his treatment of production correspond likewise to my opportunity principles.

The fundamental differences between the approach of Walras and Pareto on the one hand and mine on the other seem to be four:

(1) Walras and Pareto determine the rate of interest simultaneously with all the other unknowns of the problem — the quantities of the commodities exchanged and the services used in their production and the prices of the commodities and the services, while I try to isolate the interest problem by assuming that most of such unknowns have already been determined and confine my discussion to the special factors directly affecting the rate of interest.

(2) They both treat what I call interactions or intermediate services along with the ultimate factors — our desires or tastes (les gôuts) and the obstacles which must be overcome to satisfy them — while I try at the outset to get the interactions canceled out, leaving only the income stream and (labor) sacrifice.

(3) Neither Walras nor Pareto has elaborated the concept and principles of an income stream.

(4) Neither has elaborated the concept or principles of opportunity as a choice from among a series of income streams, although it is, in part, implied in Pareto's treatment.[3]

[3] *Cours d'Économie Politique*, Vol. I, p. 314.

APPENDIX

APPENDIX TO CHAPTER XIX
§ 1 (to Ch. XIX, § 4)
Tables giving basic data

TABLE I
London Rates of Interest and Wholesale Price Index, 1820-1927

Year	Interest Rates Market	Bank	Wholesale Price Index (1867–1877 =100)	Year	Interest Rates Market	Bank	Wholesale Price Index (1867–1877 =100)	Year	Interest Rates Market	Bank	Wholesale Price Index (1867–1877 =100)
1820			112	1860	4.1	4.2	99	1900	3.7	4.0	75
1821			106	1861	5.5	5.3	98	1901	3.2	3.8	70
1822			101	1862	2.4	2.5	101	1902	3.0	3.3	69
1823			103	1863	4.3	4.4	103	1903	3.4	3.8	69
1824	3.5	4.0	106	1864	7.4	7.4	105	1904	2.7	3.3	70
1825	3.9	4.0	117	1865	4.6	4.8	101	1905	2.6	3.0	72
1826	4.5	5.0	100	1866	6.7	6.9	102	1906	4.0	4.3	77
1827	3.3	4.5	97	1867	2.3	2.6	100	1907	4.5	4.9	80
1828	3.1	4.0	97	1868	1.8	2.1	99	1908	2.3	3.0	73
1829	3.4	4.0	93	1869	3.0	3.2	98	1909	2.3	3.1	74
1830	2.8	4.0	91	1870	3.1	3.1	96	1910	3.2	3.7	78
1831	3.7	4.0	92	1871	2.7	2.9	100	1911	2.9	3.5	80
1832	3.1	4.0	89	1872	3.8	4.1	109	1912	3.6	3.8	85
1833	2.7	4.0	91	1873	4.5	4.8	111	1913	4.4	1.8	85
1834	3.4	4.0	90	1874	3.5	3.7	102	1914	2.9	4.0	85
1835	3.7	4.0	92	1875	3.0	3.2	96	1915	3.7	5.0	108
1836	4.2	4.4	102	1876	2.2	2.6	95	1916	5.2	5.5	136
1837	4.5	5.0	94	1877	2.3	2.9	94	1917	4.8	5.2	175
1838	3.0	4.1	99	1878	3.5	3.8	87	1918	3.6	5.0	192
1839	5.1	5.1	103	1879	1.8	2.5	83	1919	3.9	5.2	206
1840	5.0	5.1	103	1880	2.2	2.8	88	1920	6.4	6.8	251
1841	4.9	5.0	100	1881	2.9	3.5	85	1921	5.2	6.2	155
1842	3.3	4.3	91	1882	3.4	4.1	84	1922	2.7	3.7	131
1843	2.2	4.0	83	1883	3.0	3.6	82	1923	2.7	3.5	129
1844	2.1	2.5	84	1884	2.6	3.0	76	1924	3.5	4.0	139
1845	3.0	2.7	87	1885	2.0	2.9	72	1925	4.1	4.6	136
1846	3.8	3.3	89	1886	2.1	3.0	69	1926	4.5	5.0	126
1847	5.9	5.2	95	1887	2.4	3.3	68	1927	4.3	4.7	122
1848	3.2	3.7	78	1888	2.4	3.3	70				
1849	2.3	2.9	74	1889	2.7	3.6	72				
1850	2.2	2.5	77	1890	3.7	4.5	72				
1851	3.1	3.0	75	1891	2.5	3.3	72				
1852	1.9	2.2	78	1892	1.5	2.5	68				
1853	3.7	2.7	95	1893	2.1	3.1	68				
1854	4.9	2.1	102	1894	1.0	2.1	63				
1855	4.7	2.9	101	1895	.8	2.0	62				
1856	5.9	6.1	101	1896	1.4	2.5	61				
1857	7.1	6.7	105	1897	1.8	2.6	62				
1858	3.1	3.2	91	1898	2.6	3.3	64				
1859	2.5	3.7	94	1899	3.3	3.8	68				

SOURCES:

The market rates of interest:
 The prevailing rate on prime bankers' or merchants' three months bills.
 1824–1858: Evidence of D. B. Chapman before the Committee on the Bank Act, 1857, Sess. 2, X, Pt. I, p. 463. (Also reprinted in Hunt's Merchants' Magazine, Vol. 41, 1859, p. 95.)
 1858–1927: Computed from The Economist, *Commercial History and Review*, Supplement, published annually.
The bank rates of interest:
 The discount rate of the Bank of England.
 1824–1843: *Burdett's Official Intelligencer*, 1894, p. 1771.
 1844–1885: *Report of the Royal Commission on Depression of Trade*, 1886, p. 373.
 1885–1927: Computed from The Economist, *Commercial History and Review*, Supplement, published annually.
Wholesale Price Index (1867–1877 = 100):
 Sauerbeck-Statist, Journal of The Royal Statistical Society, Vol. XCI, Pt. III, 1928, pp. 394–411.

APPENDIX

TABLE II
New York Rates of Interest and Wholesale Price Index, 1866-1927

YEAR	INTEREST RATES MARKET 60–90 day paper	4–6 month paper	WHOLESALE PRICE INDEX (1913 = 100)	YEAR	INTEREST RATES MARKET 60–90 day paper	4–6 month paper	WHOLESALE PRICE INDEX (1913 = 100)
1866	6.8		168	1900	4.4	5.7	81
1867	8.2		151	1901	4.3	5.4	79
1868	7.7		142	1902	4.9	5.8	84
1869	9.6		135	1903	5.5	6.2	86
				1904	4.2	5.1	86
1870	7.0		125	1905	4.4	5.2	86
1871	6.8		119	1906	5.7	6.3	89
1872	8.9		122	1907	6.4	6.7	94
1873	10.1		121	1908	4.3	5.0	90
1874	6.0		117	1909	4.0	4.7	97
1875	5.5		112				
1876	5.2		104	1910	5.0	5.7	101
1877	5.2		97	1911	4.0	4.8	93
1878	4.8		89	1912	4.7	5.4	99
1879	5.1		85	1913	5.6	6.2	100
				1914	4.8	5.5	98
1880	5.2		94	1915	3.5	4.0	101
1881	5.2		93	1916	3.4	3.8	127
1882	5.7		95	1917	4.7	5.1	177
1883	5.6		93	1918	5.9	6.0	194
1884	5.2		87	1919	5.4	5.6	206
1885	4.1		82				
1886	4.8		81	1920	7.4	7.5	226
1887	5.8		81	1921	6.5	6.8	147
1888	4.9		83	1922	4.4	4.7	149
1889	4.9		83	1923		5.0	154
				1924		3.9	150
1890	5.7	6.9	81	1925		4.0	159
1891	5.4	6.5	80	1926		4.2	151
1892	4.1	5.4	75	1927		4.0	147
1893	6.6	7.6	77				
1894	3.0	5.2	69				
1895	3.7	5.8	70				
1896	5.8	7.0	67				
1897	3.5	4.7	67				
1898	3.8	5.3	70				
1899	4.2	5.5	75				

SOURCES:
The market rates of interest:
Prime two-name 60–90 day commercial paper rates;
Review of Economic Statistics, January, 1923, p. 28.
Prime two-name 4–6 month commercial paper rates;
1890–1918: Review of Economic Statistics, January, 1919, p. 95.
1919–1922: Review of Economic Statistics, June, 1923, p. 132.
1923–1927: The Survey of Current Business, February, 1928, p. 127.
Wholesale Price Index (1913 = 100):
United States Bureau of Labor Statistics, Index Numbers of Wholesale Prices on a Pre-War Base, 1890–1927; also Monthly Labor Review, February, 1927, p. 167.

APPENDIX

TABLE III

Berlin Rates of Interest and Wholesale Price Index, 1861–1912

YEAR	INTEREST RATES		WHOLESALE PRICE INDEX	YEAR	INTEREST RATES		WHOLESALE PRICE INDEX
	Market	Bank	(1913 = 100)		Market	Bank	(1913 = 100)
				1890	3.7	4.5	89
1861	3.0	4.0	96	1891	3.0	3.9	95
1862	3.0	4.0	92	1892	1.8	3.2	84
1863	3.5	4.1	90	1893	3.2	4.1	77
1864	5.1	5.3	90	1894	1.7	3.1	72
1865	4.6	5.0	92	1895	2.0	3.1	71
1866	6.2	6.2	97	1896	3.0	3.7	71
1867	2.9	4.0	105	1897	3.1	3.8	77
1868	2.5	4.0	103	1898	3.6	4.3	82
1869	3.2	4.1	98	1899	4.5	5.0	82
1870	4.5	4.8	92	1900	4.4	5.3	87
1871	3.8	4.2	99	1901	3.1	4.1	82
1872	4.0	4.3	110	1902	2.2	3.3	81
1873	4.5	5.0	119	1903	3.0	3.8	80
1874	3.3	4.4	113	1904	3.1	4.2	83
1875	3.7	4.7	104	1905	2.9	3.8	86
1876	3.1	4.1	101	1906	4.0	5.1	88
1877	3.3	4.4	103	1907	5.1	6.0	98
1878	3.4	4.3	93	1908	3.6	4.9	93
1879	2.7	3.7	83	1909	2.8	3.8	93
1880	3.1	4.2	94	1910	3.6	4.6	91
1881	3.4	4.4	90	1911	3.5	4.4	97
1882	3.9	4.5	86	1912	4.1	4.9	108
1883	3.1	4.1	85				
1884	2.9	4.0	78				
1885	2.9	4.1	74				
1886	2.1	3.3	69				
1887	2.3	3.4	70				
1888	2.1	3.3	76				
1889	2.7	3.7	84				

SOURCES:

The market rates of interest:
  Report of the Royal Commission on Depression of Trade, 1886, p. 373; computed from
  The Economist, *Commercial History and Review*, Supplement, published annually.
The bank rates of interest:
  Report of the Royal Commission on Depression of Trade, 1886, p. 373; computed from
  The Economist, *Commercial History and Review*, Supplement, published annually.
Wholesale Price Index (1913 = 100):
  The index number used is that of the Statistisches Reichsamt, published in Wirt-
  schaft und Statistik and converted from the base (1861–1870 = 100) to the base
  (1913 = 100).

APPENDIX

TABLE IV

Paris Rates of Interest and Wholesale Price Index, 1872–1914

Year	Interest Rates		Wholesale Price Index	Year	Interest Rates		Wholesale Price Index
	Market	Bank	(1913 = 100)		Market	Bank	(1913 = 100)
				1900	3.2	3.3	86
				1901	2.5	3.0	82
1872	4.2	5.1	125	1902	2.4	3.0	81
1873	5.0	5.2	125	1903	2.8	3.0	83
1874	4.0	4.3	114	1904	2.2	3.0	81
1875	3.2	4.0	112	1905	2.1	3.0	85
1876	2.3	3.4	112	1906	2.7	3.0	90
1877	1.8	2.3	113	1907	3.4	3.5	94
1878	2.0	2.2	104	1908	2.1	3.1	87
1879	2.2	2.6	101	1909	1.7	3.0	87
1880	2.5	2.8	104	1910	3.0	3.0	93
1881	3.7	3.9	101	1911	2.4	3.1	98
1882	3.4	3.8	99	1912	3.1	3.3	102
1883	2.6	3.1	87	1913	3.9	4.0	100
1884	2.4	3.0	87	1914	3.0	4.1	102
1885	2.5	3.0	86				
1886	2.2	3.0	82				
1887	2.4	3.0	80				
1888	2.8	3.3	83				
1889	2.6	3.1	86				
1890	2.6	3.0	86				
1891	2.6	3.0	85				
1892	1.8	2.7	82				
1893	2.2	2.5	81				
1894	1.8	2.5	75				
1895	1.6	2.1	74				
1896	1.8	2.0	71				
1897	1.8	2.0	72				
1898	2.1	2.2	74				
1899	3.0	3.1	80				

Sources:

The market rates of interest:
Report of the Royal Commission on Depression of Trade, 1886, p. 373; computed from The Economist, *Commercial History and Review*, Supplement, published annually.

The bank rates of interest:
Report of the Royal Commission on Depression of Trade, 1886, p 373; computed from The Economist, *Commercial History and Review*, Supplement, published annually.

Wholesale Price Index (1913 = 100):
Statistique Générale de la France on base (1901–1910 = 100) converted to base (1913 = 100).

[523]

APPENDIX

TABLE V

Calcutta Rates of Interest and Wholesale Price Index, 1861–1926

YEAR	INTEREST RATES Bank	WHOLESALE PRICE INDEX (July 1914 = 100)	YEAR	INTEREST RATES Bank	WHOLESALE PRICE INDEX (July 1914 = 100)	YEAR	INTEREST RATES Bank	WHOLESALE PRICE INDEX (July 1914 = 100)
			1890	5.8	63	1920	6.1	201
1861	4.2	50	1891	3.1	64	1921	5.6	178
1862	5.1	50	1892	3.5	71	1922	5.8	176
1863	5.5	52	1893	4.9	69	1923	6.0	172
1864	8.7	56	1894	5.4	66	1924	6.7	173
1865	6.9	59	1895	4.3	64	1925	5.6	159
1866	9.1	67	1896	5.7	70	1926	5.2	148
1867	5.1	63	1897	7.9	82			
1868	5.8	57	1898	8.1	67			
1869	6.0	63	1899	5.9	65			
1870	5.7	58	1900	5.3	77			
1871	4.7	50	1901	5.5	75			
1872	5.0	53	1902	4.9	69			
1873	3.9	54	1903	4.9	66			
1874	6.2	58	1904	4.9	65			
1875	5.7	52	1905	5.1	72			
1876	6.8	54	1906	6.4	85			
1877	8.4	69	1907	6.1	90			
1878	5.3	74	1908	5.8	96			
1879	6.3	68	1909	5.2	86			
1880	4.7	59	1910	5.3	81			
1881	5.3	53	1911	5.5	83			
1882	6.6	53	1912	5.4	93			
1883	6.8	53	1913	6.0	98			
1884	6.4	57	1914	5.5	100			
1885	5.4	57	1915	5.7	112			
1886	6.0	55	1916	6.9	128			
1887	5.6	56	1917	6.0	145			
1888	5.5	60	1918	5.5	178			
1889	7.0	63	1919	5.6	196			

SOURCES:

The bank rates of interest:

The annual average bank rate at the Bank of Bengal and the Imperial Bank of India.
1861–1869: Furnished by Messrs. Place, Siddons, and Gough, Brokers, of Calcutta.
1870–1920: India, Department of Statistics, *Statistical Tables Relating to Banks in India*, 7th issue, 1920, p. 9.
1921–1926: *Ibid*, 13th issue, 1926, p. 9. These data are for the Imperial Bank of India.

Wholesale Price Index (End of July 1914 = 100):

1861–1913: Atkinson's *Wholesale Price Index, 1861–1908*. From 1909 to 1918 compiled by the Department of Statistics of India on same line of construction as employed by Atkinson. Converted to the base of end of July 1914 = 100. Published in the Journal of the Royal Statistical Society, March, 1897, June, 1898, March, 1903, September, 1909.
1914–1926: Wholesale Price Index of the Indian Commercial Intelligence Department (Statistical Branch). Published in *Prices and Wages in India*, July, 1914–December, 1918, and in the Indian Trade Journal, 1921–1926.

APPENDIX

TABLE VI
Tokyo Rates of Interest and Wholesale Price Index, 1887–1926

YEAR	INTEREST RATES	WHOLESALE PRICE INDEX	YEAR	INTEREST RATES	WHOLESALE PRICE INDEX
	Market	(1913 = 100)		Market	(1913 = 100)
			1910	5.7	89
			1911	5.3	93
			1912	6.8	99
			1913	7.3	100
			1914	7.7	95
			1915	8.1	97
			1916	6.6	117
1887	5.4	49	1917	5.5	147
1888	6.3	50	1918	5.8	193
1889	6.6	52	1919	7.3	236
1890	6.8	56	1920	8.0	259
1891	7.0	55	1921	8.0	200
1892	6.2	56	1922	8.0	196
1893	5.5	58	1923	8.0	199
1894	7.1	59	1924	8.0	206
1895	7.7	65	1925	7.7	202
1896	7.5	60	1926	6.9	180
1897	8.4	78			
1898	9.1	71			
1899	7.5	78			
1900	8.9	74			
1901	9.9	72			
1902	8.4	72			
1903	6.6	75			
1904	6.9	80			
1905	8.0	86			
1906	6.4	84			
1907	7.3	90			
1908	7.7	90			
1909	6.9	87			

SOURCES:

The market rates of interest:
The rate of discount of the Bank of Japan for Commercial Loans, taken from *The Financial and Economic Annual* of Japan, issued by The Department of Finance. The figures given in the table are computed where necessary by taking the arithmetic mean of the Highest and Lowest discount rate on Commercial Bills at the Bank of Japan. Where the quotation is given in "sen," which represents the daily interest on a loan of 100 yen, the source quotation has been converted to an annual basis by multiplying by 3.65.

Wholesale Price Index (1913 = 100):
The index number is taken from Franklin L. Ho, *Prices and Price Indexes in China*, Chinese Economic Journal, June, 1927, p. 26, and was computed by him from the index numbers of the following compilers:
1873–1902: Japanese Commission for the Investigation of Monetary Systems.
1902–1913: Department of Agriculture and Commerce.
1913–1926: Bank of Japan.

APPENDIX

In Chapter XIV of *The Rate of Interest* "virtual," or "real," rates of interest were computed from "nominal," or "money," rates of interest by making adjustments for appreciation in the value of money calculated from index numbers of prices. In this book, the money rates of interest are adjusted directly to the rates of change in the general price level. These two methods, of course, yield identical results, since the one is the obverse of the other.

The average annual percentage changes in the general price level, given in the Tables VII to XI inclusive, are computed from the wholesale price indexes of the several countries. The index numbers for two dates, as 1825 and 1834, give us a measure of the price level at those two dates, and from these it is easy to calculate the average annual percentage change. The method is the same as that employed for finding the rate of interest by which $1, by compounding, will amount to a given sum in a given time. Theoretically, since the loans here included run usually perhaps thirty to ninety days, the quotations of rates of interest averaged should begin at the first of the two dates, and cease, say, sixty days before the second. But the index numbers are not always for definite points of time, nor can the interest quotations be subjected to such minute corrections without an immense expenditure of labor. Hence, the method adopted has been to average the rates for all the years of a period, e.g., for the ten years, 1824–1834. The annual percentage change in the price level is reckoned between those dates. If the index numbers present the price levels at the middle of 1825 and 1834, then the average interest rates ought in theory to include only the last six months of 1825 and the first four months of 1834. But it seems better to include too much at both ends than to omit the averages for 1825 and 1834 altogether, for the reason that an average is the more valuable the greater the number of terms included.

The real interest rates are obtained by subtracting from the money rate for any period the rate of annual change in the price level for the same period.

[526]

APPENDIX

TABLE VII

Rates of Interest in Relation to Annual Rates of Change in the Price Level, London, 1825–1927

	BANK RATE	MARKET RATE	ANNUAL RATES OF CHANGE IN THE PRICE LEVEL	REAL INTEREST IN COMMODITIES (BANK)	REAL INTEREST IN COMMODITIES (MARKET)
1825–1834	4.2	3.4	−3.0	+7.2	+6.4
1834–1839	4.4	4.0	+3.3	+1.1	+0.7
1839–1852	3.7	3.4	−2.7	+6.4	+6.1
1852–1857	3.8	4.7	+5.8	−2.0	−1.1
1858–1864	4.4	4.2	+2.4	+2.0	+1.8
1864–1870	4.3	4.1	−1.6	+5.9	+5.7
1870–1873	3.7	3.5	+4.8	−1.1	−1.3
1873–1896	3.2	2.5	−2.6	+5.8	+5.1
1896–1913	3.6	3.1	+1.9	+1.7	+1.2
1914–1920	5.2	4.4	+14.5	−9.3	−10.1
1920–1927	4.8	4.2	−10.9	+15.7	+15.1

TABLE VIII

Rates of Interest in Relation to Annual Rates of Change in the Price Level, New York, 1860–1927

	PRIME TWO NAME 60–90 DAY COMMERCIAL PAPER RATES	ANNUAL RATES OF CHANGE IN THE PRICE LEVEL	REAL RATE OF INTEREST IN COMMODITIES (MARKET)
1860–1865	6.9	−14.3	−7.4
1865–1871	7.8	+8.1	+15.9
1871–1879	6.4	−4.3	+10.7
1879–1889	5.1	−0.2	+5.3
1889–1896	4.9	−3.1	+8.0
1896–1915	4.7	+2.1	+2.6
1915–1920	5.1	+14.9	−9.8
1920–1927	5.0	−6.3	+11.3

APPENDIX

TABLE IX

Rates of Interest in Relation to Annual Rates of Change in the Price Level, Berlin, 1864–1912

	BANK	MARKET	ANNUAL RATES OF CHANGE IN THE PRICE LEVEL	REAL INTEREST IN COMMODITIES (BANK)	REAL INTEREST IN COMMODITIES (MARKET)
1864–1867	5.1	4.7	+5.0	+0.1	−0.3
1867–1870	4.2	3.3	−4.5	+8.7	+7.8
1870–1873	4.6	4.2	+8.2	−3.6	−4.0
1873–1886	4.2	3.2	−4.3	+8.5	+7.5
1886–1891	3.7	2.7	+6.2	−2.5	−3.5
1891–1896	3.5	2.5	−5.9	+9.4	+8.4
1896–1912	4.4	3.5	+2.6	+1.8	+0.9

TABLE X

Rates of Interest in Relation to Annual Rates of Change in the Price Level, Paris, 1872–1914

	BANK	MARKET	ANNUAL RATES OF CHANGE IN THE PRICE LEVEL	REAL RATE OF INTEREST IN COMMODITIES (BANK)	REAL RATE OF INTEREST IN COMMODITIES (MARKET)
1872–1896	3.2	2.6	+2.4	+0.8	+0.2
1896–1914	3.0	2.6	−2.0	+5.0	+4.6

APPENDIX

TABLE XI

Rates of Interest in Relation to Annual Rates of Change in the Price Level,
Calcutta, 1861–1926, Tokyo, 1887–1926

		BANK	ANNUAL RATES OF CHANGES IN THE PRICE LEVEL	REAL RATE OF INTEREST IN COMMODITIES (BANK)
Calcutta,	1861–1866	6.6	+5.7	+0.9
	1866–1871	6.1	−6.0	+12.1
	1871–1875	5.8	+5.4	+0.4
	1878–1881	5.4	−11.2	+16.6
	1883–1897	5.5	+3.1	+2.5
	1897–1899	7.3	−11.2	+18.5
	1899–1901	5.6	+6.9	−1.3
	1901–1904	5.1	−4.8	+9.9
	1904–1913	5.6	+4.4	+1.2
	1913–1920	5.9	+11.2	−5.3
	1920–1926	5.9	−5.2	+11.1
Tokyo,	1887–1899	7.0	+3.8	+3.2
	1899–1902	8.7	−2.6	+11.3
	1902–1913	6.9	+2.9	+4.0
	1913–1920	7.0	+12.7	−5.7
	1920–1926	7.8	−6.4	+14.2

APPENDIX

§ 2 (to Ch. XIX, § 6)

Tables of interest rates

TABLE XII

Interest Yield on British Consols, 1820–1924
(Given in pence per 100-pound investment)

YEAR	INTEREST	YEAR	INTEREST	YEAR	INTEREST
1820 . .	1059	1855 . .	796	1890 . .	685
1821 . .	976	1856 . .	773	1891 . .	689
1822 . .	908	1857 . .	784	1892 . .	683
1823 . .	913	1858 . .	743	1893 . .	670
1824 . .	793	1859 . .	757	1894 . .	653
1825 . .	851			1895 . .	622
1826 . .	909	1860 . .	766	1896 . .	596
1827 . .	866	1861 . .	787	1897 . .	587
1828 . .	851	1862 . .	774	1898 . .	595
1829 . .	800	1863 . .	777	1899 . .	618
		1864 . .	799		
1830 . .	838	1865 . .	805	1900 . .	662
1831 . .	903	1866 . .	818	1901 . .	700
1832 . .	860	1867 . .	774	1902 . .	699
1833 . .	820	1868 . .	767	1903 . .	678
1834 . .	798	1869 . .	775	1904 . .	680
1835 . .	791			1905 . .	668
1836 . .	805	1870 . .	778	1906 . .	679
1837 . .	792	1871 . .	776	1907 . .	713
1838 . .	774	1872 . .	778	1908 . .	697
1839 . .	787	1873 . .	778	1909 . .	713
		1874 . .	778		
1840 . .	798	1875 . .	768	1910 . .	740
1841 . .	806	1876 . .	758	1911 . .	756
1842 . .	783	1877 . .	755	1912 . .	788
1843 . .	756	1878 . .	757	1913 . .	815
1844 . .	725	1879 . .	739	1914 . .	801
1845 . .	730			1915 . .	916
1846 . .	752	1880 . .	732	1916 . .	1034
1847 . .	825	1881 . .	720	1917 . .	1097
1848 . .	842	1882 . .	716	1918 . .	1055
1849 . .	778	1883 . .	712	1919 . .	1110
		1884 . .	713		
1850 . .	746	1885 . .	725	1920 . .	1277
1851 . .	741	1886 . .	714	1921 . .	1258
1852 . .	725	1887 . .	707	1922 . .	1091
1853 . .	737	1888 . .	724	1923 . .	1034
1854 . .	784	1889 . .	689	1924 . .	1051

SOURCE: Gibson, A. H. *The Future Course of High-Class Investment Values.* Bankers', Insurance Managers' and Agents' Magazine, January, 1923, pp. 15–34.
The Wholesale Price Indexes used in making correlations are the Sauerbeck-Statist Indexes given in Table I.

APPENDIX

TABLE XIII

Interest Rates on 15 Railroad Bonds, United States, 1900–1927

YEAR	AVERAGE PER CENT	YEAR	AVERAGE PER CENT	YEAR	AVERAGE PER CENT
1900 . . .	4.05	1910 . . .	4.16	1920 . . .	5.79
1901 . . .	3.90	1911 . . .	4.17	1921 . . .	5.57
1902 . . .	3.86	1912 . . .	4.21	1922 . . .	4.85
1903 . . .	4.07	1913 . . .	4.42	1923 . . .	4.98
1904 . . .	4.03	1914 . . .	4.46	1924 . . .	4.78
1905 . . .	3.89	1915 . . .	4.64	1925 . . .	4.67
1906 . . .	3.99	1916 . . .	4.49	1926 . . .	4.51
1907 . . .	4.27	1917 . . .	4.79	1927 . . .	4.31
1908 . . .	4.22	1918 . . .	5.20		
1909 . . .	4.06	1919 . . .	5.29		

SOURCE: *The Statistical Bulletin* of The Standard Statistics Company, Inc., 1929–1930, page 58.
The Wholesale Price Indexes used in making correlations are the indexes of the United States Bureau of Labor Statistics given in Table II.

APPENDIX

TABLE XIV

Interest Rates on 4–6 Months' Commercial Paper, United States, by Quarters, 1890–1927

Computed from Monthly Average Rates Published in the Statistical Bulletin of The Standard Statistics Company, Inc., 1929–1930, page 19

YEAR	INTEREST PER CENT	YEAR	INTEREST PER CENT	YEAR	INTEREST PER CENT	YEAR	INTEREST PER CENT
1890	5.31 5.06 5.46 7.16	1900	4.70 3.89 4.22 4.73	1910	4.56 4.77 5.45 5.24	1920	6.36 7.23 7.95 7.94
1891	5.36 5.30 5.72 5.18	1901	3.84 3.95 4.56 4.75	1911	3.98 3.66 4.17 4.30	1921	7.74 7.02 6.06 5.30
1892	3.94 3.19 4.06 5.24	1902	4.31 4.49 5.01 5.87	1912	3.95 4.11 5.03 5.88	1922	4.85 4.30 4.03 4.55
1893	5.61 7.05 9.26 4.70	1903	5.22 5.03 5.79 5.84	1913	5.20 5.59 5.95 5.64	1923	4.77 5.05 5.04 5.07
1894	3.25 2.98 3.12 2.80	1904	4.78 3.88 3.89 4.27	1914	4.08 3.82 5.81 5.43	1924	4.75 4.26 3.30 3.32
1895	3.51 3.11 3.50 4.48	1905	3.91 3.91 4.35 5.41	1915	3.66 3.68 3.34 3.11	1925	3.74 3.90 4.06 4.40
1896	5.62 4.69 7.10 5.85	1906	5.13 5.34 6.01 6.27	1916	3.13 3.30 3.69 3.60	1926	4.26 4.02 4.22 4.44
1897	3.23 3.41 3.76 3.70	1907	6.09 5.61 6.26 7.50	1917	3.92 4.70 4.89 5.45	1927	4.00 4.12 3.96 3.96
1898	3.72 4.53 3.80 3.25	1908	5.76 4.00 3.75 4.00	1918	5.72 5.89 5.94 5.94		
1899	3.20 3.53 4.28 5.44	1909	3.57 3.40 3.89 5.07	1919	5.25 5.43 5.39 5.59		

APPENDIX

TABLE XV

Wholesale Price Indexes of the United States, by Quarters, 1890–1927

Computed from the Monthly Wholesale Price Indexes of The United States Bureau
of Labor Statistics

(1913 = 100)

YEAR	INDEX NUMBER	YEAR	INDEX NUMBER	YEAR	INDEX NUMBER	YEAR	INDEX NUMBER
1890 . .	78.7 79.4 82.2 82.2	1900 . .	82.0 80.6 80.1 79.3	1910 . .	103.0 103.4 101.2 96.0	1920 . .	233.3 244.9 232.8 195.4
1891 . .	81.5 82.0 79.2 77.7	1901 . .	78.5 77.7 79.3 81.4	1911 . .	93.3 90.5 93.5 94.2	1921 . .	161.8 144.8 141.3 140.7
1892 . .	74.9 72.7 75.0 77.4	1902 . .	81.2 83.4 84.0 88.6	1912 . .	95.6 99.7 99.9 100.9	1922 . .	140.6 146.6 154.4 155.3
1893 . .	81.3 78.3 73.7 73.8	1903 . .	88.4 85.1 84.5 83.8	1913 . .	100.1 99.3 100.6 99.9	1923 . .	156.9 156.1 151.5 152.1
1894 . .	69.6 67.6 69.5 68.7	1904 . .	86.4 84.2 84.8 86.8	1914 . .	98.5 97.1 99.8 97.0	1924 . .	150.9 146.6 148.4 153.9
1895 . .	67.5 71.7 71.0 70.1	1905 . .	86.8 85.5 85.5 86.4	1915 . .	98.9 99.4 99.9 104.8	1925 . .	160.5 156.3 160.0 157.2
1896 . .	68.1 66.1 64.8 68.0	1906 . .	87.1 87.8 87.3 91.2	1916 . .	115.5 122.0 126.4 143.3	1926 . .	154.2 151.5 150.1 148.3
1897 . .	66.5 65.2 67.4 68.8	1907 . .	92.4 93.8 95.0 93.1	1917 . .	157.4 180.3 188.0 182.7	1927 . .	146.2 144.0 146.8 149.6
1898 . .	69.5 71.2 68.7 68.8	1908 . .	88.7 89.4 90.5 91.9	1918 . .	188.9 190.5 199.9 202.3		
1899 . .	71.0 72.9 76.2 80.2	1909 . .	93.1 96.2 98.0 101.7	1919 . .	196.0 201.2 212.7 217.3		

APPENDIX

APPENDIX TO CHAPTER XX

§ 1 (to Ch. XX, § 17)

Waiting as a Cost

IF waiting were a cost like other costs, it would be subject to the law of discount, according to which the capital-value of any article of wealth is equal to the discounted value of its expected income less the discounted value of its expected outgo. The value of the tree which has been mentioned, taken, say, at the end of 14 years, will actually be about $2, and this is the discounted value of the $3 of income which the tree will yield at the end of eleven more years. According to what I believe to be the correct theory, this $3 is the only future item involved in this example. But according to the theory here criticised, this is not the case. Besides this positive item of income, $3 due in eleven years, we have to deal with a series of eleven negative items called "waiting" distributed through these eleven years, and amounting to the interest — about 10 cents for the first year and gradually increasing to 15 cents for the last year. If the waiting-items were *bona fide* annual costs — like, for instance, actual labor-costs of pruning the trees — the process of discount would properly be applied to them. That is, if these waiting costs really exist, they ought to be discounted and their discounted value ought to be deducted from the discounted value of the $3 of expected income. But we should then have to assign as the value of the tree not the correct figure of $2 but an incorrect figure of much less. The fact that we cannot thus discount so-called "waiting" costs as we discount all true costs is a proof that the "cost of waiting" even if we insist on calling it such differs radically from true costs.[1]

If we are to have any logical, usable self-consistent theory of income and capital, all items of income, positive or negative — the negative ones being "costs" — must be discountable.

[1] See Böhm-Bawerk, *Recent Literature on Interest* (1884–1899), p. 35.

APPENDIX

But, as an answer to this objection, it might be argued by the abstinence theorists (if I may ascribe to them the best argument I can think of) that while waiting-cost is certainly not a *discountable* cost, nevertheless its inclusion in the list of costs obviates the necessity of discounting the other items of cost or of income. If all income and all cost items, including waiting, are counted at full value — not discounted at all — the capital may be valued simply by taking their net sum. Thus, to count "waiting" as a cost appears as an alternative and plausible method of keeping accounts. By this system we could apparently get rid of discounting and merely add and subtract items regardless of their situation in time. While this procedure obviates the objection to the abstinence theory of cost, so far as its application to *capital* value is concerned, it leaves objections equally great to its application to *income*. If waiting is a genuine economic cost, it must certainly be included on the outgo side of the income account. To show how this would apply to the cost of the tree, the following table is presented.

Income Account of Tree if Waiting is Cost

	TRUE INCOME	ALLEGED OUTGO		ALLEGED NET INCOME	TRUE CAPITAL VALUE AT END OF YEAR
1st year	$0.00	Labor	$1.00		
		Waiting	.05		$1.05
2d year	0.00	"	.05		1.10
3d year	0.00	"	.05		1.15
* * *	* * * *	* * * * *		* *	* * *
14th year	0.00	"	.10		2.00
* * *	* * * *	* * * * *		* *	* * *
25th year	3.00	"	.15		3.00
Total	$3.00		$3.00	00.0	

According to this method of accounting, we see that, during the year in which the sapling is planted, its cost consists of labor to the extent of $1, expended, let us say, at the beginning of the year, and 5 cents' worth of waiting suffered during the course of that first year. During the second year a waiting cost of about the same amount is incurred, and so on for each succeeding year, the cost of waiting gradually increasing, as the tables of compound interest would indicate, until in the fourteenth year it amounts to 10 cents, and in the twenty-fifth year to 15 cents. The total cost for the 25 years will then be $3, and the return to the planter at the end, from the sale of the tree, will also be $3. Consequently, if we take the whole period from the first application of labor to the final sale of the tree, the net income will be zero. This result is, to say the least, somewhat surprising, but not so much so as some other results of the same species of bookkeeping, as the following additional examples will show.

Suppose a person owns an annuity amounting to $100 a year for 10 years. According to the ordinary method of keeping accounts, his income consists of this $100 a year each year. But if we count the waiting as a cost, we shall find that the income for each year is less than $100. The owner of such an annuity will, during the first year, have to suffer "waiting" to the extent of $39, supposing interest is at 5 per cent; for this is the increase in value of his annuity during that year, due to his waiting for the future installments of income of which his annuity consists.[2] His net income during that year, therefore, according to such accounting, is not $100, but $100 − $39, or $61. During the second year his income in this second year is somewhat greater, for the cost of "waiting" is only $35. His net income is, therefore, $100 − $35, or $65. Similar computations carried out for succeeding years are shown in the table on the following page.

Is it good bookkeeping to introduce a new and anomalous element of cost which results in making the net income of the annuitant not the $100 which he actually receives and which common sense recognizes as the income from the annuity but

[2] This is evident, since the value of his annuity, capitalized at 5 per cent, reckoned at the beginning, is $772, whereas, reckoned at the end of the first year, before his $100 is paid, it is $811.

APPENDIX

Income Account of Annuity if Waiting is Cost

	TRUE INCOME	ALLEGED OUTGO		ALLEGED NET INCOME	TRUE CAPITAL VALUE AT BEGINNING OF YEAR
1st year . .	$100	Waiting	$39	$61	$772
2d year . .	100	"	35	65	711
3d year . .	100	"	32	68	646
4th year . .	100	"	29	71	578
5th year . .	100	"	25	75	507
6th year . .	100	"	22	78	432
7th year . .	100	"	18	82	354
8th year . .	100	"	14	86	272
9th year . .	100	"	9	91	186
10th year . .	100	"	5	95	95
	$1000		$228	$772	

the queer sums given in the table, namely, $61, $65, $68, and so forth?[3]

To push this criticism to the limit, let us finally consider a perpetual annuity of $100 a year. In this case we shall find that the "cost of waiting" each year is the full $100, for the value of such an annuity, reckoned at 5 per cent, is $2000 reckoned at the beginning of each year, and $2100 reckoned at the end.

[3] It may be of interest to note that this error is the inverse of, or complementary to, the more common one by which the net income is the $100 less the "depreciation." In the first year this would be $772 less $711, or $61, so that the "income" is $39. This sort of accounting, when, instead of depreciation, there is appreciation or savings, would make savings appear as income instead of capital. This savings, or depreciation, fallacy is especially discussed in *Are Savings Income?* American Economic Association Journal, April, 1908, and *The Income Concept in the Light of Experience*. It has been the subject of much controversy. Some economists who fall into this savings-are-income, depreciation-is-outgo fallacy in some parts of their system fall into the waiting-is-cost fallacy in other parts. Both cannot be right. Each exhibits the evil consequences which ensue from playing fast and loose with the concepts of capital and income. If we wish to indulge in such a metaphor as "I got it at the 'cost' of waiting," we can do so but only at the "cost" of inaccuracy. Neither of these so-called "costs" is more than a metaphor.

APPENDIX

If this annual $100 cost of waiting is to be regarded as a negative item of income and, like other costs, is to be subtracted from the positive income, we are forced to conclude that the owner of such a perpetual annuity receives each year no income whatever! For, if we deduct from the $100 of positive income the $100 cost of waiting, the remainder each year is zero! Yet a perpetual annuity is the simplest, purest case of income.

It should now be obvious that the theory which calls "waiting" a cost has worked out its own absurdity. If taken seriously and introduced into an accounting system it either interferes with the discount or capitalization principle or else distorts and even obliterates the income reckoning in its simplest, or most typical form, that of a perpetual annuity. It falsely simplifies the formula for valuing capital.

The idea that the value or price of an article should equal its cost seems to possess a certain fascination for many students of economics. That it is false has been sufficiently shown by Böhm-Bawerk through reasoning somewhat similar to the foregoing. That it is *absurd* when carried to its logical conclusion will be evident if we consider what happens if the same method of bookkeeping is carried out with respect to the future as well as the past. It is a poor rule which will not work both ways. This rule, applied to future expected income and outgo, yields the strange result that the capital value of any article instead of being less than its expected income is equal to it. Thus, to revert to the case of the tree, let us take its value at the end of 14 years. It is then worth $2, which, in the parlance of the abstinence theorists, is equal to its previous costs of production, consisting of $1 worth of labor plus $1 worth of waiting during the 14 years. It is also, in like manner, equal to the future income to be derived from it, which consists of $3 worth of actual receipts from the sale of the tree, due at the end of eleven more years, less the cost of waiting for those $3, which amounts to $1.

In the same way, the ten-year annuitant just considered has, at the beginning, property worth $772. This, according to

[538]

APPENDIX

proper bookkeeping, is the discounted value of the future income of $100 a year for 10 years, the total amount of which income is $1000. But, according to the abstinence theory, logically carried out, the income which the annuitant receives for the whole period is, as has been shown, not this $1000, but $772, which is just equal to the value of the property.[4] Pursuing the method of limits, we find that, for the owner of a perpetual annuity, the same proposition would hold good. According to the true and ordinary method of reckoning, the total income from such an annuity is infinity, although its present capital value is only $2000. But according to the abstinence theorists the income itself is not infinite, but only $2000.

Those who are enamored of the alluring simplicity and neatness of the formula of the abstinence theorists, by which the capital value is not greater than *past* cost of production, but exactly equal to it, can scarcely be attracted by the exaggerated simplicity of the inverse theorem which is also involved, namely, that the capital value of any *future* expected income is not less than that income, but exactly equal to it also.

The fallacy of the abstinence theorists lies in the simple fact that waiting has no independent existence as a "cost." We can never locate it in time, nor estimate its amount, without first knowing some *other* more real and tangible costs. Waiting means nothing unless there is something to be waited for, and the cost of waiting can only be estimated in proportion to the magnitude of that which is so waited for. What is waited for is some payment or other event constituting income or outgo. But waiting for income or outgo is not itself income or outgo.

[4]Lest the non-mathematical reader should be puzzled by this result, which seems to contradict the fact already brought out, that, under the pseudo-reckoning of the abstinence theorists, the net income is zero every year, it must be remembered that this zero income is repeated an infinite number of times, and that when we deal with infinity we can get reliable results only by the method of limits. The mathematical reader will find no difficulty in showing, by the method of limits, that there is a "remainder term" which will, in the supposed accounting, make the total income distributed through all eternity simply equal to the capital value, $2000.

APPENDIX

The mere accrual of value as we draw nearer the items constituting true income is neither income nor outgo but capital gain. The typical picture we should carry in our mind is of a saw-tooth curve consisting alternately of a gradual ascent along a discount curve, and a sudden drop as an income coupon is detached. The only income in this picture is the series of sudden drops, on which all the rest hangs. The gradual ascent in each saw tooth is not income; otherwise it would (largely) duplicate the true income. Nor is it outgo; otherwise it would (largely) negative the true income.

In the case of a bond *selling at par* these alternate ascents and drops are equal, and we carelessly speak of both as interest or as income. But the instant the bond sells above or below par we recognize the difference. If we follow this out we can scarcely go astray.

Even to those who do not formally accept any cost theory of interest, the interest itself will seem in some sense to be a cost, and in most books on economics, interest, however explained, is regarded as one of the costs of production. It is true that for a debtor who pays interest, the interest is, to *him*, a real cost, and is debited on his books. But we need only to be reminded of the debit and credit bookkeeping of the first chapter to see that this item is counterbalanced on the books of the creditor, to whom this interest is by no means a cost, but, on the contrary, an item of income. For society as a whole, therefore, even in the case of interest which is explicitly paid, it cannot be said that it constitutes a cost of production. In the case of a person who works with his own capital, the truth of this statement is even more evident. Economists who state that the independent capitalist must charge off interest as one of his costs of production seem to forget that such self-paid interest must be charged back again as income also. Labor sacrifice is quite different. It is a real cost and in no time bookkeeping can it be cancelled out. The fallacy of assuming that interest is a cost is doubtless due to the habit of regarding production from the point of view of the "enter-

[540]

priser." Since he usually *pays* interest, he comes to think of it purely as a cost.

I have devoted considerable space to the refutation of the abstinence theory so far as it is more than verbal, and collides with any workable theory of income, because its errors are so subtle and insidious as to beguile many of the best and most wary of economists.

BIBLIOGRAPHY

I. WORKS ON INTEREST THEORY.

1. *Books:*

BÖHM-BAWERK, EUGEN VON. *Capital and Interest.* London, Macmillan and Co., 1890. xlv, 431 pp.

BÖHM-BAWERK, EUGEN VON. *The Positive Theory of Capital.* Translated by William Smart, London, Macmillan and Co., 1891. xl, 428 pp.

BÖHM-BAWERK, EUGEN VON. *Recent Literature on Interest (1884-1889).* New York, The Macmillan Co., 1903. xlii, 151 pp.

BÖHM-BAWERK, EUGEN VON. *Positive Theorie des Kapitales.* Dritte. Auflage, Innsbrück, Wagner'schen Universitäts-Buchhandlung, 1912. xxiii, 652 pp. Also *Exkurse,* 477 pp.

BÖHM-BAWERK, EUGEN VON. *Kleinere Abhandlungen über Kapital und Zins.* Wien und Leipzig, Hölder-Pichler-Tempsky A. G., 1926. viii, 585 pp.

BROWN, HARRY GUNNISON. *Economic Science and the Common Welfare.* Columbia, Missouri. Lucas Brothers, 1926. xiii, 273 pp. Especially Part II, Chapters III and IV, pp. 76-170.

CARVER, THOMAS NIXON. *The Distribution of Wealth.* New York, The Macmillan Co., 1904. xvi, 290 pp.

CASSEL, GUSTAV. *The Nature and Necessity of Interest.* London, Macmillan and Co., 1903. xii, 188 pp.

CASSEL, GUSTAV. *The Theory of Social Economy.* New York, Harcourt, Brace and Co., 1924. xiv, 654 pp.

CLARK, JOHN BATES. *Distribution of Wealth.* New York, The Macmillan Co., 1899. xxviii, 445 pp.

DAVENPORT, H. J. *Value and Distribution.* University of Chicago Press, 1908. xi, 582 pp.

FETTER, FRANK A. *Economic Principles.* New York, The Century Company, 1915. x, 523 pp.

FISHER, IRVING. *The Rate of Interest.* New York, The Macmillan Co., 1907. xxii, 442 pp.

BIBLIOGRAPHY

GONNER, E. C. K. *Interest and Savings*. London, Macmillan and Co., 1906. xv, 172 pp.

HEINZE, GERHARD. *Statische oder Dynamische Zinstheorie?* Leipzig, Dr. Werner Scholl, 1928. viii, 165 pp.

HOAG, CLARENCE GILBERT. *A Theory of Interest*. New York, The Macmillan Co., 1914. x, 228 pp.

JEVONS, W. STANLEY. *Theory of Political Economy*. 3rd edition, London, Macmillan and Co., 1888. lvi, 296 pp.

LANDRY, ADOLPHE. *L'Intérêt du Capital*. Paris, V. Biard and E. Brière, 1904. 367 pp.

PARETO, VILFREDO. *Cours d'Économie Politique*. Lausanne, F. Rouge, 1896 and 1897. Tome Premier, viii, 430 pp. Tome Second, 426 pp.

PARETO, VILFREDO. *Manuel d'Économie Politique*. Paris, V. Giard and E. Brière, 1909. 695 pp.

RAE, JOHN. *The Sociological Theory of Capital*. New York, The Macmillan Co., 1905. lii, 485 pp.

SAX, EMIL. *Der Kapitalzins*. Berlin, Julius Springer, 1916. viii, 249 pp.

WALRAS, LÉON. *Éléments d'Économie Politique Pure*. Lausanne, F. Rouge, 1900. xx, 491 pp.

2. *Articles:*

ANSIAUX, M. *Le Phénomène de L'Intérêt et son Explication*. Revue de L'Institut de Sociologie. Deuxième Année, Tome I, Bruxelles, 1921-1922, pp. 47-57.

BILGRIM, H. *Analysis of the Nature of Capital and Interest*. Journal of Political Economy. Vol. XVI, March, 1908, pp. 129-151.

BÖHM-BAWERK, EUGEN VON. *Capital and Interest*. Quarterly Journal of Economics. Vol. xxi, November, 1906, pp. 1-21; February, 1907, pp. 247-282.

BORTKIEWICZ, L. VON. *Der Kardinalfehler der Boehm-Bawerkschen Zinstheorie*. Jahrbuch fuer gesetzgebung, Band 30, 1906, pp. 61-90, Leipzig, Duncker und Humblot, 1906.

CARVER, T. N. *The Place of Abstinence in the Theory of Interest*. Quarterly Journal of Economics, October, 1893, pp. 40-61.

CHAPMAN, S. J. *Must Inventions Reduce the Rate of Interest?* Economic Journal, Vol. XX, September, 1910, pp. 465-469.

BIBLIOGRAPHY

DAVENPORT, H. J. *Interest Theory and Theories.* American Economic Review, Vol. XVII, No. 4, December, 1927, pp. 636-656.

DAVIES, G. R. *Factors Determining the Interest Rate.* Quarterly Journal of Economics, Vol. XXXIV, May, 1920, pp. 445-461.

FETTER, FRANK A. *Interest Theories Old and New.* American Economic Review, Vol. IV, No. 1, March, 1914, pp. 68-92.

FETTER, FRANK A. *Clark's Reformulation of the Capital Concept,* in Economics Essays Contributed in Honor of John Bates Clark, pp. 136-156, New York, The Macmillan Co., 1927.

FISHER, IRVING. *Professor Fetter on Capital and Income.* Journal of Political Economy, Vol. XV, July, 1907, pp. 421-434.

FISHER, IRVING. *Are Savings Income?* Journal of the American Economic Association, Vol. IX, No. 1, April, 1908, pp. 1-27.

FISHER, IRVING. *A Reply to Critics.* Quarterly Journal of Economics, Vol. XXIII, May, 1909, pp. 536-541.

FISHER, IRVING. *Capital and Interest.* Political Science Quarterly, Vol. XXIV, No. 3, 1909, pp. 504-516.

FISHER, IRVING. *Capital and Interest: Reply to Professor Veblen.* Political Science Quarterly, Vol. XXIV, September, 1909, pp. 504-516.

FISHER, IRVING. *The Impatience Theory of Interest.* Scientia, Vol. IX, April 1, 1911, pp. 380-401.

FISHER, IRVING. *The Impatience Theory of Interest.* American Economic Review, Vol. III, No. 3, September, 1913, pp. 610-615.

FLUX, A. W. *Irving Fisher on Capital and Interest.* Quarterly Journal of Economics, Vol. XXIII, February, 1909, pp. 307-323.

GONNER, E. C. K. *Considerations about Interest.* Economic Journal, Vol. XVIII, March, 1908, pp. 42-51.

GRAZIANI, AUGUSTO. *Capitale e Interesse.* Società Real di Napoli, 1925, pp. 33-92.

LANDRY, ADOLPHE. *Irving Fisher: The Rate of Interest.* Revue d'Économie Politique, 23 Année, 1909, Bulletin Bibliographique, pp. 156-159. Paris, L. Larose and L. Tenin, 1909.

LORIA, A. *Irving Fisher's Rate of Interest.* Journal of Political Economy, Vol. XVI, October, 1908, pp. 331-332. *Reply* by Irving Fisher, same issue, pp. 532-534.

LOWRY, DWIGHT M. *The Basis of Interest.* American Academy of Political and Social Science, March, 1892, pp. 53-76.

BIBLIOGRAPHY

SCHUMPETER, JOSEPH. *Eine "Dynamische" Theorie des Kapitalzinses.* Zeitschrift für Volkswirtschaft, Sozialpolitik und Verwaltung, 1913, pp. 599-639. Vienna, Manzche, K. U. K. Haf-Verlags und Universitätsbuchhandlung, 1913.

SHAPOSCHNICOFF, N. von. *Die Böhm-Bawerksche Kapitalzinstheorie.* Jahrbüchern für Nationalökonomie und Statistik, Dritte Folge, Bd. XXXIII (LXXXVIII), Jena, Gustav Fischer, pp. 433-451.

TAUSSIG, F. W. *Capital, Interest and Diminishing Returns.* Quarterly Journal of Economics, Vol. XXII, May, 1908, pp. 333-363.

VEBLEN, T. *Fisher's Rate of Interest.* Political Science Quarterly, Vol. XXIV, June, 1909, pp. 296-303.

II. OTHER WORKS DEALING WITH INTEREST.

1. *Books:*

ADLER, KARL. *Kapitalzins und Preisbewegung.* Leipzig, Duncker und Humblot, 1913. 48 pp.

BECKHART, BENJAMIN H. *The Discount Policy of the Federal Reserve System.* New York, Henry Holt and Co., 1924. xii, 604 pp.

BOUCHER, PIERRE B. *Histoire de L'Usure.* Paris, Chaigneau, 1806. 215 pp.

BROWN, MARY W. *The Development of Thrift.* New York, The Macmillan Co., 1900. x, 222 pp.

CANNING, JOHN B. *The Economics of Accountancy.* New York, The Ronald Press Company, 1929. viii, 367 pp.

DICK, ERNST. *The Relation Between the Rate of Interest and the Level of Prices.* Distributed by H. R. Scott, Kodaikanal, S. India, March, 1928. 83 pp.

EDIE, LIONEL D. *Economics: Principles and Problems.* New York, Thomas Y. Crowell Co., 1926. xx, 799 pp.

EDIE, LIONEL D. *Money, Bank Credit, and Prices.* New York, Harper & Brothers, 1928. xiv, 500 pp.

FETTER, FRANK A. *Modern Economic Problems.* New York, The Century Company, 1917. xi, 498 pp.

FISHER, IRVING. *The Income Concept in the Light of Experience.* English translation of article in *Die Wirtschaftstheorie der Gegenwart*, Vol. III of the *Wieser Festschrift*, Vienna, 1927. 29 pp., in translation.

FISHER, IRVING. *The Nature of Capital and Income.* New York, The Macmillan Co., 1927. xxi, 427 pp.

BIBLIOGRAPHY

GIFFEN, ROBERT. *The Growth of Capital.* London, George Bell and Sons, 1889. 169 pp.

GRIMES, JOHN ALDEN and CRAIGUE, WILLIAM HORACE. *Principles of Valuation.* New York, Prentice Hall Inc., 1928. xvii, 274 pp.

KOCK, KARIN. *A Study of Interest Rates.* London, P. S. King, 1929. 264 pp.

MONTAGNE, JEAN. *Le Capital.* Paris, Albin Michel, 1919. 253 pp.

NORTON, JOHN P. *Statistical Studies in the New York Money-Market.* New York, The Macmillan Co., 1902. vi, 180 pp.

PALGRAVE, R. H. INGLIS. *Bank Rate and the Money Market.* New York, E. P. Dutton and Co., 1903. xxiii, 237 pp.

RABY, R. C. *The Regulation of Pawnbroking.* New York, Russell Sage Foundation, 1924. 63 pp.

RYAN, FRANKLIN W. *Usury and Usury Laws.* Boston, Houghton Mifflin Company, 1924. xxix, 249 pp.

WICKSELL, KNUT. *Über Wert, Kapital und Rente.* Jena, Gustav Fischer, 1893. xvi, 143 pp.

WICKSELL, KNUT. *Geldzins und Güterpreise.* Jena, Gustav Fischer, 1898. xi, 189 pp.

2. *Articles:*

BIRCK, L. V. *Moderne Scholastik. Eine Kritische Darstellung der Böhm-Bawerkschen Theorie.* Weltwirtschaftliches Archiv., 24 Bd., October, 1926, Heft 2, pp. 198-227.

BONN, H. *Geld und Kapitalmarkte im Jahre 1924.* Wirtschaftsdienst, Vol. X, Feb. 6, 1925, pp. 247-248.

BURGESS, W. RANDOLPH. *Factors Affecting Changes in Short Term Interest Rates.* Journal of the American Statistical Association, Vol. XXII, New Series, No. 158, June, 1927, pp. 195-201.

CASSEL, GUSTAV. *The Future of the Rate of Interest.* Skandinaviska Kreditaktiebolaget, January, 1926. Stockholm, P. A. Norstedt & Söner, 1926, pp. 1-4.

CASSEL, GUSTAV. *The Rate of Interest, the Bank Rate, and the Stabilization of Prices.* Quarterly Journal of Economics, Vol. XLII, August, 1928, pp. 511-529.

CASSEL, GUSTAV. *Discount Policy and Stock Exchange Speculation.* Skandinaviska Kreditaktiebolaget, October, 1928. Stockholm, P. A. Norstedt & Söner, 1928, pp. 57-60.

BIBLIOGRAPHY

CLEVELAND TRUST COMPANY. *Business Bulletin*, June 15, 1928, and August 15, 1928.

CONRAD, OTTO. *Der Kapitalzins*. Jena, Jahrbücher für Nationalökonomie und Statistik, 3 Folge, Band 35, 1908, pp. 325-359.

CRUM, W. L. *Cycles of Rates on Commercial Paper*. Review of Economic Statistics. Prel. Vol. V, No. 1, January, 1923, pp. 17-29.

FETTER, FRANK A. *Recent Discussion of the Capital Concept*. Quarterly Journal of Economics, Vol. XV, November, 1900, pp. 1-45.

FISHER, IRVING. *Appreciation and Interest*. Publications of the American Economic Association, Vol. IX, No. 4, August, 1896, pp. 331-442.

FISHER, IRVING. *What Is Capital?* Economic Journal, Vol. VI, December, 1896, pp. 509-534.

FISHER, IRVING. *The Rôle of Capital in Economic Theory*. Economic Journal, Vol. VII, December, 1897, pp. 511-537.

FISHER, IRVING. *The Rate of Interest after the War*. Annals of the American Academy of Political and Social Science, Vol. LXVIII, November, 1916, pp. 244-251.

FISHER, IRVING. *Comment on President Plehn's Address*. American Economic Review, Vol. XIV, No. 1, March, 1924, pp. 64-67.

FRIDAY, DAVID. *Factors which Determine the Future of the Rate of Interest: Economic Principles of Supply and Demand*. Trust Companies, Vol. XXIII, July, 1921, pp. 9-12.

GIBSON, A. H. *The Future Course of High-Class Investment Values*. Bankers', Insurance Managers', and Agents' Magazine, January, 1923, pp. 15-34.

GIFFEN, SIR ROBERT. *Accumulations of Capital in the United Kingdom in 1875-85*. The Journal of the Royal Statistical Association, Vol. LIII, 1890, pp. 1-35.

HARGER, C. M. *Problems of Interest Rates*. Financial World, Vol. XXXII, June 23, 1919, p. 19.

INOSTRANIETZ, M. *L'Usure en Russie*. Journal des Économistes, 1893, Ser. 5, Vol. XVI, pp. 233-243. Paris, Administration et Redaction, Librairie Guillaumin et C., 1893.

JAY, PIERRE. *Call Money Market in New York City and the Interest Rates Charged Therein*. Economic World, Vol. XIX, April 10, 1920, pp. 511-513.

KEMMERER, E. W. *War and the Interest Rate*. Economic World, Vol. XVI, November 2, 1918, pp. 616-619.

BIBLIOGRAPHY

KEMMERER, E. W. *Rediscounting and the Federal Reserve Discount Rate.* American Bankers' Association Journal, Vol. XII, April, 1920, pp. 582-584.

LEVY, R. G. *Du Taux Actuel de L'Intérêt et de ses Rapports avec la Production des Métaux Précieux et les Autres Phénomènes Économiques.* Journal des Économistes, March, 1899, p. 334; April, 1899, p. 28.

MAGEE, JAMES D. *Call Rates and the Federal Reserve Board.* American Economic Review, Vol. X, March, 1920, pp. 59-65.

MITCHELL, W. F. *Interest Cost and the Business Cycle.* American Economic Review, Vol. XVI, No. 2, June, 1926, pp. 209-221.

MITCHELL, W. F. *Supplementary Note on Interest Cost.* American Economic Review, Vol. XVI, No. 4, December, 1926, pp. 660-663.

MITCHELL, W. F. *Interest Rates as Factors in the Business Cycle; with a Reply by J. E. McDonough.* American Economic Review, Vol. XVIII, March, 1928, pp. 217-233.

MOURRE, BARON. *Les Causes des Variations du Taux de L'Intérêt.* Revue d'Economie Politique, 1924, pp. 45-64. Paris, Librairie de la Société du Recueil Sirey, Léon Tenin, Directeur, 1924.

PERSONS, WARREN M., and FRICKEY, EDWIN. *Money Rates and Security Prices.* Review of Economic Statistics, Vol. VIII, No. 1, January, 1926, pp. 29-46.

PERSONS, WARREN M. *Money Rates, Bond Yields and Security Prices.* Review of Economic Statistics, Vol. IX, No. 2, April, 1927, pp. 93-102.

PINSCHOF, C. L. *The World's Return to Gold: the Ultimate Effect on Rates of Interest.* Acceptance Bulletin of the American Acceptance Council, November 30, 1925, pp. 4-5.

PLEHN, CARL C. *Notes Concerning the Rates of Interest in California.* Quarterly Publication of the American Statistical Association, September, 1899, pp. 351-352.

PRICE, T. H. *Do High Interest Rates Presage Deflation?* Commerce and Finance, Vol. VIII, November 12, 1919, pp. 1511-1512.

REEVE, S. A. *Interest and Dividends; Other Features of Interest; Irrevocability of Interest.* Modern Economic Tendencies, 1921, pp. 204-231, 254-342.

RIST, CHARLES. *La Hausse du Taux de L'Intérêt et la Hausse des Pris.* Revue Économique Internationale, X Année, Vol. I, pp. 462-493. Bruxelles, Goemaere, 1913.

BIBLIOGRAPHY

SCHMIDT, F. *Die Abhaengigkeit der Wechselkurse von Zinsgeschaeften und die Marktzinsdifferenz.* Schmollers Jahrbuch, 1919, pp. 339-365. München, Leipzig, Duncker und Humblot, 1919.

SEAGER, HENRY R. *The Impatience Theory of Interest.* American Economic Review, Vol. II, No. 4, December, 1912, pp. 834-851.

SMITH, J. G. *Measurement of Time Valuation.* American Economic Review, Vol. XVIII, June, 1928, pp. 227-247.

SNYDER, CARL. *The Influence of the Interest Rate on the Business Cycle.* American Economic Review, Vol. XV, No. 4, December, 1925, pp. 684-699.

SNYDER, CARL. *Interest Rates and the Business Cycle.* American Economic Review, Vol. XVI, No. 3, September, 1926, pp. 451-452.

Tables Showing: Rates on United States Treasury Certificates Issued During 1920-21; Rates of Discount Charged by the Bank of England and by the Open Market in London; Bank Rates of Discount Charged in Selected Money Markets; Changes in Central Bank Rates in World Monetary Centers. Review of Economic Statistics, March, 1921, pp. 70, 73.

WESTERFIELD, RAY B. *Effect of Falling Prices and Interest on Foreign Loans and on War Debts.* The Annalist, January 4, 1929, pp. 5-7.

WICKSELL, KNUT. *Influence of the Rate of Interest on Prices.* Economic Journal, Vol. XVII, June, 1907, pp. 213-220.

YOUNG, ALLYN A. *An Analysis of Bank Statistics for the United States; III Regional Differences: 1901-1914.* Review of Economic Statistics, Vol. VII, No. 2, 1905, pp. 86-104.

INDEX

A

Abstinence, a cost, 178-179, 486-487; interest taking justified by, 180; not discountable, 534-539; (waiting), by capitalist, 180; (waiting) not a cost, 534-541; (waiting) theory of interest, 180, 178-179, 486-487, 534-541.

Adjustment, individual, of impatience (Willingness), interest rate (Market), and investment (Opportunity), 272-275; by investment without loans, 266*ff*.; by loans and investment, 269*ff*.

Agio theory, of interest, 473.

Allied debt settlements, 314*n*.

Alternative uses of wealth (capital), 125-149, 150-177, 178-205.

Agriculture, seasonal changes in, affect interest rates, 394-398.

Annuities and the waiting theory of interest, 536-539.

Appreciation and depreciation, effect of, on interest rates, x, 36-44, 493-497; foresight offsets, 37-39; measures to offset, 38-39.

Assumptions of first approximation stated, 101-102.

Auspitz und Lieben, cited, 252.

Australia, interest rates in, 390.

Average, yearly, rates of interest, 520-525.

Ayres, L. P., cited, 439; relation between gold reserves and interest rates, 446.

B

Bank reserves and interest rates, 444-450.

Betterments, repairs and renewals, options of making, 194-200.

Bloch, Ivan, cited, 375.

Böhm-Bawerk, E. von, x; agio theory, 473*ff*.; cited, 313, 452*n*; discussed, 473-485; excludes land from capital, 459; explanation of technical superiority, 475-476; quoted, 476*n*, 478, 479-480, 481, 482-483; shows fallacy in socialists' condemnation of interest, 51; technical superiority of present goods, 471-485.

Bonds, coin and currency, interest rates on, 401-403; gold and rupee, interest on, 403-407; value of, determined by (1) expected benefits, (2) interest rate, 17.

Bond yields and price changes (Great Britain) correlated, 416-442; (United States) correlated, 417-442.

Borrower, a seller, 113.

Borrowers, not represented by poor, 112; types of, 108-111.

Borrowing and lending, changes shape of income stream, 113; determined by personal qualities, income stream and interest rate, 250*ff*.; equivalent to selling and buying, 112; income (not capital) transferred by, 94; limits of, for individual

INDEX

Commodity interest, 164-165, 179-182, 190-192.

Comparative advantage principle, 175.

Comparative advantages, method of, gives maximum present worth, 152-177.

Computation of real rate from money rate of interest, 526.

Conditions determining interest rate, summary of, 226 *ff.*; tabular scheme, 228.

Consumption, the end of production, 454.

Consumption goods, relation of, to interest rate, 453-454.

Consumption loan. *See* Personal loan.

Continuous reckoning of interest, 25-26.

Contractual interest. *See* Explicit interest.

Correlation coefficients, bond yields and price changes, 417-420; interest rates and price changes, 411; obtained by lagging price changes, 418; with price lag distributed, 419-429.

Cost, defined, 157; *future*, alone enters into valuation, 15; capitalized, 467; a negative income item, 15; *past*, affects value through supply, 16; through income, 467; relation of to interest, 485-487; return over, 150-188. *See also* Return over cost.

Costs, as disadvantages, 154 *ff.*

Cost of living, 6; ever present in interest, 180-181; the money measure of real income, 6-7; a negative item, 7.

Cost of production, less than value of product, 49-52; past and future, contrasted, 461-462; relation of, to value and interest, 460-467.

Cost theory of interest, 57.

Cost of the use of a good, 8-9.

Cost of waiting. *See* Waiting, *also* Abstinence.

Crum, W. L., on seasonal variations in interest rates, 396.

Currency, depreciation of. *See* Appreciation and depreciation, *also* Price level.

Currency bonds, 401-402.

D

Day, Clive, cited, 336; on interest rates in Java, 375.

Davenport, H. J., cited, 34, 467; criticism by, considered, 453-454.

Del Mar, Alexander, theory of interest of, 165.

Depreciation, appreciation and interest rates, 493-497; (and appreciation) of money, effect on interest rates, 36-44, 47; foresight offsets, 37-39; measures to offset, 38-39.

Discoveries, effects of, similar to inventions, 347. *See also* Invention.

Distributed lag, definition of, 419-420, 420*n*; applied to interest rates and price changes, 416-429.

Distribution, effect on, of thrift, 333-338; functional, misconceived by classical economists, 332-333; functional, relation to interest, 331-333; personal, of first importance, 333-338; personal, relation of, to interest, 333-338; personal, treatment of, by Pareto, King, Stamp, Mitchell, Rae and others, 334; theory of, in relation to interest theory, 325-340; of wealth, effect of, on interest rates, 378-381, 384-391.

INDEX

est rate, 120; determines spending or saving, 335-338; differs for each individual and each income, 96-97; preference for present over future income, 99; individual, adjusted to interest rate and opportunity, 272-275; individual, depends on income stream, 249*ff.*; individual, depends on personal qualities, 249*ff.*; measured, 62; relative to income stream, equations for, 290; relative to interest rate, equations for, 291; represented by a Willingness line, 238-240, shown on chart, 239.

Impatience, rates of, equalized through borrowing and lending, 104-106, 117-119; high degree (rate) of, accompanied by high interest, borrowing, spending, and flimsy instruments, 373; identical with interest rate, 104-106; low rate of, accompanied by interest, lending, saving, durable instruments, 373.

Impatience and Investment opportunity, 280-282.

Impatience and opportunity, combined in my theory, ix; contrasted, 183; determines institutions and interest rate, 489-491.

Implicit interest, 8, 61, 117, 209, 382.

Improvidence, loans to offset, 357.

Increments in value are not income, 26-28.

Ingo, a substitute for *outgo,* 19*n.*

Interactions, described, 20-21.

Income, annuity, assuming waiting a cost, 536-539; from tree, assuming waiting a cost, 535-

536; all, produced from capital wealth, 332; all, is (1) rent, (2) interest, 32-34; all, subject to capitalization, 58; assumed to flow spontaneously, 102; basis of capital concept, 3; and capital separated by bookkeeping principles, 25; derived from capital goods, capital value derived from income, 14-15; early enjoyment, preferred to deferred enjoyment, 63-65; excludes capital gain, 332; not a flow of wealth, 457; from land is (1) rent, (2) interest, 33; human enjoyment, 5; in economics, 13; identical with interest, 332; and capital gain, 332; increased by invention, 354-355; individual, adjusted to interest rate, 253*ff.*; the most fundamental economic concept, 3, 42; net, equals enjoyment less labor pain, 22-23; net, of a corporation is zero, 23; the important factor, 91-94; objective or real, 5; opportunity to increase future, 103; and *outcome,* 19*n*; produced by capital goods and men, 19; psychic, measured, 453, 456-457; real, consists of *outer* events, which give *inner* enjoyments, 5-6; real, measured by cost of goods consumed, 9-10; as a rate per cent on its capitalized value, 58; relations of, to capital, 3-35; a series of events, 3; subjective or psychic, 3, 4, 5; supply and demand of, explains interest rate, 454; total, equals enjoyment income, 23-24; variations in, cause loan classification, 360-365.

Income concept, basic, ix; epitomized, 3-12; restated, 453.

tivity, not *physical* productivity, 54-57; determined by marginal rather than average growth, 165; early laws and practices concerning, 48; exploitation theory of, 48-52; as a fine, 52-53; futility of prohibitions of, 52-53, 116-117; high rates of, in China, due to poverty, 378; implicit in sale contract, 117; includes all income, 331-332; ineradicable, 116-117; loan, involves risk, 207-208; many different rates of, 206-210, 299; market rate of, adjusts impatience rate, through borrowing, 250-251 (charted); market rate of, adjusts impatience rate, through lending, 251 (charted); market rate of, affects borrowing and lending, 250; market rate of, brought to equilibrium, 256-258; market rate of, influenced by each individual, 256*ff.*; market rate of, represented by a line, 235-238; shown on chart, 237; money and real, 36-44, 407-416, 416-442; money and real, divergence due to lack of foresight, 43-44; naïve productivity theories of, 53-57; not a part but the whole of income, 58; as a price, illustrated, 69; in primitive codes, 48-49; productivity an element but not the only one, 53-54; pure rate of, on loans devoid of risk, 34-35; the ratio of rent to value of the rent bearer, 32; real, computed from money rate, 526; real, more variable, because of "money illusion," 411-416; real, negative, 415-416; relation of, to rent, 331-332; rent, profits and wages, not mutually exclusive, 32-34;

steady, variable, high, and low rates of, 501; theoretical rate of, fixed by six principles, 494*ff.*; views of, by socialists, 49-52; zero or negative rates of, discussed, 40-41, 67, 183, 185-192, 282-286, 311, 415-416.

Interest, rate of, 3; adjusted to clear the market, 121; affected by productivity, 182; affected by regard for posterity, 376; affected by risk, 381-383; affected by scarcity of food, 381; affected by time shape of income stream, 383-387; affected by uncertainty of life, 216-217; affects repairs and investments, 202-204; affects wages, 328-330; on Allied debts, method of computing, 314n; as an average of individual degrees of time preference, 99; on business loans based on enjoyment income, 359-360; cannot be determined by impatience (time preference) rates alone, 124; a change in, shifts maximum present value of option, 141*ff.*; changes choice of income stream (options), 142*ff.*; changes in, change capital value, 91-93; compared with changes in price level, 408-451; contrasted with return over cost, 499; defined, 13; depends on individual impatience rates, 144*ff.*; depends *in part* on interest rate, 144; depends on supply and demand of this year's real income relative to next year's income, 46; determination of, 119-124; by four principles, 122-124; by impatience and opportunity, 372; by investment opportunity, impatience, and exchange, 149; in loan market, 98; by society's choice of income streams, 143*ff.*; determines choice of income stream, 143*ff.*; degree of impatience, 120; range of choice of options, 170-174; due to "average rate of growth of animals and plants," 165; during decline of Rome, 376-377; examples of wide fluctuations, 44; expressed in basic standard, 43; fixed for the individual, 119; high on small loans, 213-215; individual, adjusted to impatience and opportunity, 272-275; influence on prices of services, 326-328; link between income and capital, 13; maximum present value, marginal return over cost, in formulas, 514-515; maximum present value, marginal return over cost, by geometric method, 516; may be zero or negative, 40-41, 67, 183, 185-192, 282-286, 311, 415-416; measured in goods and money, 36-44, 45-46; measured in two diverging standards, 39; the most pervasive price, 33; must clear the market, 122, 149; not explained as price of money, 46-47; not involved in enjoyment income or labor pain, 326-328; not reasoning in circle, 144-147; paradox of, 144-149; on personal loans, accounted for, 359; premium on present over future goods, 36; the price between present and future goods, 61; and price level, 399-451, 493-497; the price of money, 13; problem of, in geometric terms, 231-287; problem merely stated not solved by supply and demand, 46; in relation to impatience rate, equations for, 291; relation of, to prices, 399-451, 493-497; relation of, to supply and demand depicted, 260*ff.*; relative to standard of measurement, 41; and saving, 286-287; on short loans, 360-363; steadied by stable income stream, 300; in terms of goods, 42; varies with income, 299-301, 302-315; varies with seasonal changes in income, 394-398.

Interest, rates of, affected by invention, 342-347; affected by risk, 207-227; correlated with price changes, 429-438; dispersed by invention, 342-347; fluctuations in, self-corrective, 202-205; France, 523, 528; Germany, 522, 528; on gold (coin) and paper and silver bonds, 401-407; Great Britain, 520, 527; India, 524, 529; influenced by Federal Reserve System, 449-450; Japan, 525, 530; money and real, normally identical, 43; and price changes, 399-451, 520-533; and price indexes correlated, 429-438; and price level, theoretical relation of, 412-414; raised by catastrophes, 391; relation of, to bank reserves, 444-450; relation of, to business and prices, 443-444; relation of, to income, 454; to invention, 342-347; short term, correlated with price changes, 423-429; United States, 521, 527; yearly average, 520-525.

Interest problem, stated in mathematical formulas, 288-301, 302-315.

Interest theory, complete, includes price theory and all other economic theories, 131*n*; must include wage theory, 331; of Walras and Pareto, con-

Land and artificial capital contrasted, 459-460; as capital, 458-459.

Landry, Adolphe, cited, 73, 471.

Lawrence, J. S., cited, 375.

Laws, relating to interest, 214.

Lender, a buyer, 113.

Lenders, not represented by rich, 112; types of, 108-111.

Lending. *See* Borrowing and lending.

Life expectancy, effect on impatience, 84-85.

Loans, change shape of income stream, 106-112; long, reasons for, 363-369; a means of equalizing impatience rates, 104-106; money, represent income transfers, 108; present worth of, equal repayments, 123, 149; productive, present opportunities to vary income, 112; public, both consumption and productive, 369-371; reasons for and effects of, 371; relation of, to impatience rate, 231.

Loanable capital. *See* Capital, loanable.

Loan contract, a sale, 112-113.

Loan interest. *See* Interest, loan.

Loan market, evolves a common interest rate, 98, 99, 104-112.

Luxury, habit of. *See* Habit.

M

Marginal desirability, determines choice of income stream, 130*ff.*; relation of, to interest, 61-62.

Marginal return over cost, maximum present value, and interest rates in formulas, 514-515; shown by geometric method, 516; must equal marginal time preference, 182.

Marginal rate of return over cost equal to interest rate, 169.

Marginal time preference must equal marginal return over cost, 182.

Marginal utility, 62, 62*n*. *See* Marginal desirability.

Market equilibrium, 255-262, 275-287.

Market line, adjusted to opportunity line, 266*ff.*; compared to willingness line, 240-246.

Market principles, cover supply and demand of incomes, 495; generalized form of, in equations, 296-297; shown by equations, 291-292.

Marshall, Alfred, cited, 252.

Mathematics, use of, in text, ix, 231-322.

Mathematical method, application of, to interest problem, 231-262, 263-287, 288-301, 302-315, 316-322; value of in economics, ix. *See also* Formula method and Geometric method.

Maximum desirability, principle of, 148; influence on interest rate, 118, 122; shown by geometric method, 517.

Maximum present value, marginal return over cost, interest rate, in formulas, 514-515; by geometric method, 516; principle, 175.

Maximum present worth principle, restatement of, 152-155, 159.

Menger, Karl, cited, 216.

Michigan, interest rates in, 389.

Mining, type of income stream from, 130-139; communities, interest rates in, 387-388.

Misfortune, loans to offset, 356.

Mitchell, Wesley C., cited, 322, 439.

Mohlberg, Dr. W., money fluctuations and accounting, 44.

INDEX

Russell Sage Foundation, studies of small loans by, 214.

Russia, rate of interest in, 375.

Russians, characteristics of, make for high interest rates, 376.

S

Savings, not income, 455; relation of, to interest, 286-287.

Schmalenbach, E., money fluctuations and accounting, 44.

Schmidt, Dr. F., money fluctuations and accounting, 44.

Schumpeter, Joseph, cited, 489.

Scotch, characteristics of, lower interest rates, 374, 377.

Scotland, interest rates in, 374.

Seager, H. R., cited, 467; criticisms by, 459, 471-472; views of, on increased productivity and interest rate, 462; on land as capital, 460; on physical and value productivity, 461-462.

Seasons, changes in, change income streams and interest rates, 394-398.

Second approximation, stated, 125-129.

Secular trends, elimination of, from correlations, 431-438.

Self-control, effect of, on impatience, 83.

Seligman, E. R. A., on interest in early Rome, 377.

Selling. *See* Buying and selling; Borrowing and lending.

Services, criticism of, as income, 456; enjoyable, measurability of, 456-457; as tree income, 8.

Short loans, essence of, 363.

Slavery and forced labor result from poverty, 335-337.

Smith, Edgar L., cited, 220.

Snyder, Carl, cited, 439.

Socialists, views of, on interest, 49-52.

Speculation reduces risks, 221*ff*.

Spending, buying present income, 113-115; compared with investing, 113-115; depletes future income, 114; a form of investment, 114.

Spending and investing, differ only in degree, 9; the problem of interest, 29-30.

Stamp, Sir Josiah, on distribution, 334.

Standard deviations, of money interest and real interest, 415.

Statistical study of prices and interest, x, 399-451, 520-533.

Stocks, yield more than bonds, 220.

Stockholders, function of, as risk takers, 218*ff*.

Stock prices, affected by inventions, 352-353.

Subjective income. *See* Income, subjective; and Income, psychic.

Supply and demand of capital, not the cause of interest, 32; and income, relation of, to interest, 454; to interest rates, depicted, 260*ff*.; discussed, 260-262, 286-287.

Sweeney, H. W., money fluctuations and accounting, 44.

T

Technical superiority of present goods, Böhn-Bawerk's theory of, 471-485.

Third approximation, stated, 206-208.

Thrift, relation of, to interest rate, 333-335; to saving, 333-338.

Thomas, L., money fluctuations and accounting, 44.

Time preference, marginal rates of, equalized by loans, 117-119;